Recruitment and Selection in Canada

Victor M. Catano · Steven F. Cronshaw

Willi H. Wiesner · Rick D. Hackett

Laura L. Methot

Monica Belcourt, Series Editor

I(T)P® Nelson

an International Thomson Publishing company

Toronto • Albany • Bonn • Boston • Cincinnati • Detroit • London • Madrid • Melbourne
Mexico City • New York • Pacific Grove • Paris • San Francisco • Singapore • Tokyo • Washington

I(T)P® International Thomson Publishing

The ITP logo is a trademark under licence

Published in 1997 by

I(T)P® Nelson

A division of Thomson Canada Limited
1120 Birchmount Road
Scarborough, Ontario M1K 5G4

Visit our Web site at **http://www.nelson.com/nelson.html**

Canadian Cataloguing in Publication Data
Main entry under title:
   Recruitment and selection in Canada

(ITP Nelson series in human resources management)
Includes bibliographical references.
ISBN 0-17-604827-8

1. Employees – Canada – Recruiting.   2. Employee
selection – Canada.   I. Catano, Victor M.
(Victor Michael), 1944-   II. Series.

HF5549.5.R44R417 1997   658.3'11'0971   C96-990075-9

Publisher	Jacqueline Wood
Acquisitions Editor	Sarah Clarke
Production Editor	Lynda Chiotti
Project Editors	Anita Miecznikowski, Edward Ikeda, Jenny Anttila
Senior Production Coordinator	Carol Tong
Art Director	Sylvia Vander Schee
Interior Design	Holly Fisher
Lead Composition Analyst	Zenaida Diores

Printed and bound in Canada

1 2 3 4 (BBM) 99 98 97 96

Recruitment and Selection in Canada

Brief Contents

Contents

About the Series

There is one asset within organizations that provides the competitive advantage for many organizations: human resources. While the purchase of facilities and the adoption of technology are considered major long-term decisions, and accorded the appropriate time and money, senior executives do not give the same consideration to the investment in human resources. Yet, many studies in human capital suggest that investments in human resources do provide a good return, and unlike other resources, are renewable. Because knowledge about the effective management of an organization's employees is critical, ITP Nelson is publishing a series of texts dedicated to those managers and human resources professionals who are responsible for the productivity and satisfaction of employees.

The texts in the ITP Nelson Series in Human Resources Management include *Managing Performance Through Training and Development*, *Occupational Health and Safety, Human Resources Management Systems, Recruitment and Selection in Canada, Compensation Management in Canada* (1998), and *Human Resources Planning* (1998).

The ITP Nelson Series in Human Resources Management represents a significant development in the field of HR for many reasons. Each book in the series (except for *Compensation Management in Canada*) is the first Canadian text in the functional area. Human resources practitioners in Canada must work with Canadian laws, Canadian statistics, Canadian policies, and, Canadian values. This series serves their needs. It also represents the first time that students and practitioners have access to a standardized guide to the management of many HR functional areas. This one-stop resource will prove useful to anyone involved with the effective management of people.

The publication of this series signals that the HR field has advanced to the stage where theory and applied research guide practice. Because the field is still emerging, and new tools and methods are being invented, theory and research are discussed along with common practices used by Canadian HR professionals. The books in the series present the best and most current research in the functional areas of HR. This research is supplemented with examples of successful practices used by Canadian companies who are leaders in the HR area. Each text identifies the process of managing and implementing effective strategies, thus serving as an introduction to the functional area for the new student of HR and as a validation manual for the more experienced HR practitioner. Cases, exercises, discussion questions, and references contained at the end of each chapter provide opportunities for further discussion and analysis.

As you read these texts, I hope you share my excitement at being involved in the development of an important profession, one that affects daily interactions with our own employees as well as those in organizations with whom we conduct business.

Monica Belcourt
SERIES EDITOR
AUGUST 1996

About the Authors

VICTOR M. CATANO

Dr. Catano is Professor and Chair of Psychology at Saint Mary's University, Halifax, N.S. He obtained a B.Sc. in electrical engineering from Drexel University in Philadelphia and went on to complete both a master's and a Ph.D. in psychology at Lehigh University, Bethlehem, PA. He is a registered psychologist in Nova Scotia. Dr. Catano joined the Saint Mary's faculty following the completion of his doctoral degree and was instrumental in establishing Saint Mary's master's program in industrial/organizational psychology. He has also served as a Special Lecturer at the Technical University of Nova Scotia and as a Visiting Research Fellow at the Canadian Forces Personnel Applied Research Unit in Toronto. He is currently an Honorary Adjunct Professor in the graduate faculty at Dalhousie University. Dr. Catano has served as President of the Association of Psychologists of Nova Scotia, a member of the Nova Scotia Board of Examiners in Psychology (the body responsible for regulating the profession within Nova Scotia), and President of the Canadian Society of Industrial/Organizational Psychology. He is currently the editor of Canadian Psychology, the flagship journal of the Canadian Psychological Association, is a member of the editorial board for Advances in Organizational Behavior, and has acted as a reviewer for numerous scholarly journals and granting agencies.

Dr. Catano has extensive consulting experience in personnel selection and assessment, job analysis, utility analysis, occupational families, attitude surveys, leadership, productivity issues, and industrial relations. His clients have included the Department of National Defence, Asea Brown Bovari, Nova Scotia Government Employees Union, and Manufacturing Research Corporation of Ontario, among others. He has published over 150 scholarly articles, conference papers, and technical reports. His current research interests include the psychology of labour relations, organizational and environmental constraints on productivity, and the impact of psychological environments on the health, safety, and productivity of workers. In recognition of his contributions to the science and practice of psychology in Canada, Dr. Catano was elected a Fellow by the Canadian Psychological Association, and an Honorary Member by the Canadian Forces Personnel Selection Officers Association.

STEVEN F. CRONSHAW

Dr. Cronshaw is Associate Professor of Psychology at the University of Guelph, Ontario. He earned his B.A. and B. Comm. degrees at the University of Saskatchewan in Saskatoon and his M.A. and Ph.D. degrees in industrial/organizational psychology at the University of Akron, Ohio. He is a registered psychologist in the province of Ontario. He joined the faculty at the University of Guelph in 1986. Since then, he has been heavily involved in the development of M.A. and Ph.D. programs in industrial/organizational psychology at that university, with much of his teaching activity centred on graduate courses and supervision of graduate students. Dr. Cronshaw also founded and was the first Executive Director of the Guelph Centre for Occupational Research Inc. (GCORI), which is a research consulting company devoted to transferring human resources management concepts and practical solutions between university environments and external organizations. Largely under the aegis of GCORI, he has consulted widely to Canadian organizations on human rights, selection systems, job analysis, attitude surveying, leadership programs, and other issues related to human resources management. His research activities, spanning numerous journal articles, book chapters, and conference papers, cover a range of topics, including leadership, personnel selection, human rights, utility analysis, and job analysis. He is the author of *Industrial Psychology in Canada*, published in 1991. A biographical entry containing Dr. Cronshaw's personal and work history is published in Marquis' *Who's Who in the World*, 14th edition (1997).

WILLI H. WIESNER

Dr. Willi H. Wiesner received his Ph.D. in industrial/organizational psychology from the University of Waterloo, where he specialized in personnel psychology. He has taught in the Faculty of Commerce at Concordia University in Montreal and is currently Associate Professor of Human Resource Management and Ph.D. Program Coordinator in the School of Business at McMaster University. Dr. Wiesner is a member of the Canadian Psychological Association, the American Psychological Association, the Canadian Society for Industrial and Organizational Psychology, the Society for Industrial and Organizational Psychology (U.S.), the Administrative Sciences Association of Canada, and the Academy of Management. He has served as Institute Coordinator and President of the Canadian Society of Industrial and Organizational Psychology.

Dr. Wiesner has extensive consulting experience in the areas of employee selection, performance appraisal, and other personnel issues. His recent clients include Drake Personnel, the Bartlett Group, the McQuaig Institute, St. Peter's Hospital, Grand River Hospital Corporation, Halton Regional Police Services, Tires Only, AFG Glass, Canada Post (as an associate of Hackett and Associates in Dundas), the Department of National Defence, and the Public Service Commission of Canada (as an associate of EER Technologies in Ottawa). Dr. Wiesner has also presented workshops on employee selection, performance appraisal, training and development, and on team building through the executive development office in the School of Business at McMaster University. His recent research and publication activities have focused on employment interviewing and selection, group decision making, and the use of realistic job previews in recruitment.

RICK D. HACKETT

Dr. Hackett received his Ph.D. in industrial/organizational psychology from Bowling Green State University (Ohio) and is Associate Professor and Chair of the Human Resources/Labour Relations Area of McMaster's Michael D. Degroote School of Business and President of Hackett and Associates Human Resources Consultants Inc. He is also past-president of the Canadian Society for Industrial/Organizational Psychology (CSIOP), a section of the Canadian Psychological Association. Additionally, Dr. Hackett is an ad hoc reviewer for several scholarly journals in management and a member of the editorial board for the Canadian Journal of Administrative Sciences (Human Resources Division).

Dr. Hackett's primary research and consulting interests lie in the area of recruitment, personnel assessment, selection, work attitudes, employee commitment, absenteeism, and performance appraisal.

LAURA L. METHOT

Dr. Methot is an Assistant Professor of Psychology at Saint Mary's University in Halifax. She completed her B.A. in psychology at Saint Mary's University, followed by a master's degree in industrial/organizational psychology and a Ph.D. in applied psychology from Western Michigan University. Her applied work has focused on organizational systems analysis and performance measurement in private and public sector organizations. She co-authored *Fundamentals of Behavior Analytic Research* with Alan Poling and Mark Lesage, and is active in researching sustained attention in human monitors.

Preface

Recruitment and Selection in Canada is designed to meet the needs of undergraduate students and human resources practitioners. It provides an up-to-date review of the current issues and methodologies that are used in recruiting and selecting employees for Canadian organizations. Over the years the field of personnel selection has become more quantitative and subject to both federal and provincial human rights legislation. This book provides an introduction to these technical areas in an easy-to-read style. Each chapter includes many examples, which illustrate how the practices discussed in the text are carried out in both private and public sector organizations. The text offers an introduction to scientifically sound procedures in recruitment and selection that meet technical, professional, and Canadian legal standards. It presents recruitment and selection as essential components of strategic human resources planning and emphasizes their role in enhancing productivity. Starting with a solid scientific foundation, the text introduces organizational and job analyses as the key to developing a recruitment and selection system and to understanding the relationship between improved selection systems and increased organizational productivity. Contemporary developments in interviewing, cognitive ability testing, personality testing, and drug and honesty testing are also included in the text. Recognizing the constraints under which organizations operate, the book includes material on "selecting out" as well as "selecting in." Finally, recruitment and selection are discussed in the context of national and international competition and free-trade agreements.

Recruitment and Selection in Canada offers students and practitioners several advantages. First, it provides an up-to-date introduction to the current developments in recruiting and selecting employees within a Canadian context. It incorporates Canadian material organically into the development of the text rather than "Canadianizing" a popular American one. This approach has allowed us to focus in greater detail on issues of concern to Canadian organizations and to Canadian human resources practitioners.

We have attempted to provide coverage as complete as possible on current issues in recruitment and selection. We do this by integrating the role of recruitment and selection into a context of strategic human resources planning. At all stages of the recruitment and selection process, the text emphasizes the necessity of satisfying both professional and legal requirements and offers guidelines on how this can be accomplished. Increasingly, both students and practitioners must understand the scientific, technical, and legal aspects that form the basis of current recruitment and selection practices. Often, texts on recruitment and selection make little attempt to explain the statistical and technical underpinnings of these topics, or do so in a way that those new to the material cannot comprehend. Unlike these other texts, we have provided complete and thorough introduction to this essential material in a readable, non-technical style that minimizes scientific jargon and emphasizes understanding of the basic concepts in a context of application. To assist understanding, we have also included learning points at the start of each chapter and case or exercise material at the end to illustrate the important principles and concepts contained in each chapter.

This text is written for introductory level, one-semester courses in Human Resources Management, Personnel Psychology, and Personnel Selection. It is also an ideal text for short courses that form part of diploma or professional upgrading programs. One of the strengths of the text is the systematic integration of the different aspects of recruitment and selection with current legal and technical practices. However, the needs of students and instructors may differ across the settings in which this text may be used. Some students may already have had a substantial introduction to the scientific method and measurement issues in other courses that form part of their program. In those cases, Chapter 3, or parts of it, can be omitted. Later chapters in the text, however, do refer to material contained in Chapter 3 or to concepts introduced in it. If these have been omitted, the student can easily read the relevant sections of Chapter 3 in conjunction with the later reference. We have not placed Chapter 3 in an appendix because it is our firm belief that any human resources practitioner must be familiar with the content of Chapter 3 in order to practice recruitment and selection in a professionally acceptable manner.

Similarly, Chapter 5 includes a discussion of issues related to the measurement of performance. It is our firm belief that students must be conversant with all aspects of the recruitment and selection system. Measurement of performance is essential to evaluating the effectiveness of any selection system. Often the problem with poor selection systems is not the selection instruments used, but how performance is measured. Performance is the bottom line and we have integrated that into the text. Again, if performance measurement and evaluation have been covered elsewhere in a student's program, Chapter 5 can serve as a brief, useful review.

In developing both Chapters 3 and 5, we have tried to strike a balance by presenting only the information that any human resources practitioner is likely to need to know. A guiding rule has been, "Is this information essential for human resources practitioners to meet both legal and professional standards in the conduct of their practice?" We feel we have met this standard.

Acknowledgments

The production of any book is a collaborative effort. Many people, other than the authors whose names appear on the cover, play an important role. We would like to acknowledge their assistance and to thank them for their valuable contributions to this process. We have tried to present in this book the latest scientific foundation for human resources management. We could not have done that without the research compiled by our academic colleagues throughout North America and the experience of human resources practitioners in adapting that research to the workplace. This book would not exist if it were not for their work.

We are also indebted to our past and present students who have challenged our ideas and made us be clear in the exposition of our arguments. In particular, we owe a debt to the students in Psychology 428 and Psychology 605 at Saint Mary's University; their feedback on early drafts of this text was invaluable. Likewise, the book benefited immensely from the feedback of reviewers at various colleges and universities across Canada. For taking the time to read the early drafts and share with us their extensive and detailed comments, we thank Eli Levanoni, Brock University, Herman Schwind, Saint Mary's University, Diane White, Seneca College, Robert McManus, Algonquin College, Rick Goffin, University of Western Ontario, Bob Russell, Assiniboine Community College, Dan Scarlicki, University of Calgary, Alan Saks, Concordia University, Edward Rowney, University of Calgary, and Barbara Marshall, Sheridan College.

Monica Belcourt, the editor for this series, deserves special praise. She was the glue that held everything together and kept the project on track. It is truly the case that without her efforts, this book would not have materialized. We must also acknowledge the patience and professionalism of the team at ITP Nelson; first, John Horne and Edward Ikeda, who handled the early development of the book, and then Jenny Anttila, Anita

Miecznikowski, Jackie Wood, and Lynda Chiotti, who shepherded this project to completion.

Finally, we are most grateful to our families and friends who provided us with support and understanding throughout the long nights. They inspired us to think and write clearly.

Victor M. Catano
SAINT MARY'S UNIVERSITY

Steven F. Cronshaw
UNIVERSITY OF GUELPH

Willi H. Wiesner
MCMASTER UNIVERSITY

Rick D. Hackett
MCMASTER UNIVERSITY

Laura L. Methot
SAINT MARY'S UNIVERSITY

Introduction

◆ ◆ ◆
CHAPTER GOALS

This chapter introduces the topics of recruitment and selection in Canadian organizations. After reading this chapter you should

◆ appreciate the importance and relevance of recruitment and selection to Canadian management;

◆ understand the terms recruitment and selection;

◆ understand in a historical perspective where recruitment and selection practices in Canadian organizations come from;

◆ know where recruitment and selection fit into the organization as a whole and the human resources management system in particular;

◆ know which professional associations and groups in Canada have a stake in recruitment and selection;

◆ become familiar with basic ethical issues in recruitment and selection; and

◆ understand how the rest of the chapters in this book work together to present a detailed picture of both the practice and theory of recruitment and selection in Canada.

◆ ◆ ◆
WHY RECRUITMENT AND SELECTION MATTER

Consider the following scenario:

> *Polaris Space Systems, a growing company in southern Quebec, required a design engineer to help in the construction of a communications satellite for launch by the space shuttle Atlantis in spring of 1999. Polaris contacted an international*

recruitment firm to locate suitable candidates for the job. A search across North America, Europe, and Asia yielded three job candidates. With the assistance of the recruitment firm, Polaris interviewed the three candidates and made a job offer to Mr. H, an engineer with 15 years experience in the American space program. Mr. H worked for Polaris over the next four years to supervise the design of communications hardware for the satellite. The satellite was launched on schedule in June 1999, but experienced a major breakdown shortly after being deployed in orbit around the earth. A subsequent investigation by Polaris showed that Mr. H had made serious mistakes in the design specifications for the satellite, resulting in the breakdown of the entire system once the satellite became operational. Communications service providers switched to other satellite companies and the Polaris satellite was abandoned as space junk. Polaris estimated that the cost of the lost satellite would eventually total $100 million, including lost revenues from telecommunications customers and the cost of launching a new satellite.

The above scenario shows that recruitment and selection matter because people make a difference to the success of any project or business. Recruitment and selection are the means by which people, for better or for worse, find their way into the organization. Although not every recruitment and selection mistake is as costly as that of our space engineer, poor practices in recruitment and selection are costly regardless of whether the job is that of janitor on the shop floor or company vice-president in the executive suite. And, indeed, research shows that there are substantial differences in skills among the people in any applicant pool that will translate into large performance differences on the job. These performance differences express themselves in real consequences for the organization and for the manager who does not use effective recruitment and selection practices.

The above example showed how recruiting and selecting the wrong person can result in disaster for an organization. Happily, recruitment and selection can be a source of strength as well as weakness, and can produce decisions that benefit both the organization and the human resources manager's progress within the company. To illustrate this, consider the following example where recruitment and selection worked well:

A management consulting firm, Alpha Inc., was looking for a new senior partner. Alpha placed an advertisement in The Globe and Mail and received 47 résumés. In order to select the best candidate, they asked each to fill out an Alpha application form, and screened the best 10 applicants. These 10 were then asked to come to Alpha headquarters to undergo testing. Those with the best scores were then interviewed, using a behaviourally based interviewing technique. The top three candidates were asked for references, which were checked. Ms. S was identified, on the basis of all these selection techniques, as the best candidate for the job. Right from the beginning, it became apparent that Ms. S was an outstanding choice as a senior partner. She worked tirelessly to increase business in the Toronto office, with the result that she brought in $20 million of new business in her first year alone. Employees at all levels of Alpha Inc. soon recognized that Ms. S was a highly skilled and ethical consultant who was greatly trusted and respected by her clients. The most promising junior staff sought her out as a mentor because of her great range of expertise and her respectful, caring treatment of staff. Two years after being hired, Ms. S was awarded a national prize for consulting excellence by an internationally recognized professional association. The Toronto office has continued to expand, largely due to Ms. S's efforts, and the firm is now planning to start up offices in Hamilton and Ottawa as well.

The two preceding vignettes illustrate the difference between very ineffective and very effective performance by key people recruited and selected into their respective organizations. The point to be made is that recruitment and selection can spell the difference between the success and failure of an enterprise, especially when all firms in an industry are constantly searching for, and taking advantage of, every possible competitive advantage. In short, effective recruitment and selection confer a competitive advantage on those organizations willing and able to invest in these practices. This book describes principles and methods of recruitment and selection that are effective for many jobs and organizations. As a starting point for this effort, we will offer more precise definitions for recruitment and selection on which we can build in later chapters.

◆ ◆ ◆

RECRUITMENT AND SELECTION DEFINED

For the purposes of this book, which focuses on recruitment and selection practices in Canadian organizations, we adopt the following definitions of recruitment and selection.

Recruitment is the generation of an applicant pool for a position or job in order to provide the required number of candidates for a subsequent selection or promotion program. This is done to meet management goals and objectives for the organization as well as current legal requirements (human rights, employment equity, labour law, and other legislation). Recruitment also may involve elements of self-selection, such as when job applicants are given realistic previews of the job followed by an opportunity to choose whether they wish to be moved into a subsequent selection process.

BOX 1.1 RECRUITMENT AND SELECTION OF TRANSIT OPERATORS

One highly visible job in Canadian cities from Victoria to St. John's is that of transit operator. Transit companies and commissions from coast to coast (and as far north as Yellowknife), some large and some small, have the responsibility of providing public transportation to their urban populations. To do this, they must recruit and hire workers of many different skills into positions throughout the organization: senior- and middle-level managers, street supervisors and superintendents, mechanics, cleaners, and many others. Transit experts generally agree that the most critical job is that of transit operator, that is, the person who delivers the front-line service by driving the bus and conveying passengers from place to place. Transit operators also make up the largest employee group in any transit company.

BOX 1.1 (continued)

Where does recruitment and selection come in and why are these important to the operation of transit companies? To begin with, the financial health of the transit company depends on attracting and keeping a loyal ridership. These are the management goals of many such companies. Because there are viable alternatives to public transportation, such as private automobiles and cabs, the company must strive to provide the safest and most comfortable ride at a reasonable cost or risk losing riders to other forms of transportation.

What are the major factors that you would consider when deciding whether to take a city bus to a concert or to take a private vehicle? Which of the following have you identified? A clean and tidy bus? A pleasant, helpful operator? A smooth ride without too much bumping and jostling? A safe, trouble-free trip with no sudden stops or running over curbs? Getting picked up on time? Arriving at your stop on schedule? Many people list these factors when they are asked why they use, or do not use, transit services, and all of these factors are at least to some extent under the control of the operator driving the bus. Furthermore, anyone who takes public transit regularly will know that there are big differences between operators in how well they provide these things. Done well, these services will help meet management goals of attracting and holding the ridership that the company needs to stay in business; done poorly, these services will drive away riders to other forms of transportation.

Now the importance of properly recruiting and selecting transit operators becomes clear. The transit company should choose as new operators those people who have the potential to do the right things and to do them well. So what types of people might the company be looking for? Probably conscientious people who get along well with the general public, people who are safety conscious and do not get stressed when they are stuck in heavy traffic and are running behind schedule. The purpose of recruitment is to advertise the job so that people with high potential for it will be encouraged to apply, as well as to make sure that various groups not traditionally associated with transit operation (e.g., women) will apply for work with the company so that they can be put into the selection system. The purpose of the selection process is to identify and choose the "right" people from the pool of qualified job applicants that has been provided through recruitment. These "right" people will then help the transit company by meeting the goals and objectives set by management (e.g., for customer service and traffic safety) as well as current legal requirements (e.g., women must be given a fair chance at the job). The selection process is done by various means, including testing and interviewing, as described in later chapters of this book.

Selection is the choice of candidates from the previously generated applicant pool in a way that will meet management goals and objectives as well as current legal requirements. For our purposes, selection can involve any of the following: hiring at the entry level from applicants external to the organization, promotion or lateral transfer of people within the organization, and movement of current employees into training and development programs.

◆ ◆ ◆
THE ORIGINS OF RECRUITMENT AND SELECTION

ANCIENT HISTORY

At first glance, our example of recruitment and selection for transit operators looks like a 20th century solution for a 20th century problem. However, even a brief look into history shows that advanced societies with extensive transportation systems existed thousands of years ago. For example, the ancient Romans built a vast network of roads to connect all the parts of their far-flung empire from Britain to Asia. A considerable degree of task specialization and organization was required to accomplish this feat, as is true for a transit company or any other organization of size today. Even if modern societies have switched their source of locomotive power from the muscles of horses and people to machines driven by internal combustion engines, many of the challenges of building and maintaining transportation networks remain the same. Except for the slaves who were an involuntary source of labour, the Romans certainly experienced many of the same challenges and problems that we have today in attracting and selecting the right people to undertake, complete, and manage vast projects such as aqueducts or road systems.

Without doubt, organizations and societies have relied on recruitment and selection, as they have on other employment systems (Begin, 1991), for thousands of years. For example, Wang (1994) reports that China has relied for over 1300 years on a complex system of imperial examinations for selecting candidates into the civil service. To better understand the role of recruitment and selection in modern organizations, it is helpful to look at how societies may have handled these issues in the past and at how our thinking about recruitment and selection compares to these earlier notions. (In fact, when we look at this question more closely, it seems that not much has changed over the millennia.)

To begin with, as shown in the example of Roman road builders, recruitment and selection in any formal sense only makes sense in societies of some size and complexity where large groups of people doing various tasks must work together toward a common goal. These conditions probably first appeared in some parts of the world about 10 000 years ago, at the time when relatively large social groups congregated into agricultural settlements and then later into cities. In these more complex societies, some people became artisans, others labourers, others soldiers, and still others priests and rulers. With this greater specialization, individual differences in aptitude and skill must have become apparent to those in power and it is likely that these ancient societies responded with practices meant to capitalize on these differences. In other words, these societies must have devised ways to recruit and select people who would be the best soldiers, clerks, or skilled labourers so that the society could be properly defended, administered, and maintained.

Writings still exist from ancient times showing those peoples who did make the necessary distinctions called for in recruitment and selection. In one of the earliest written sources, the Greek philosopher Plato from the 4th century B.C. paints a vivid picture of his society in *The Republic*. He explains that societies come together for the purpose of meeting needs (food, shelter, clothing) that individuals alone cannot satisfy. In doing so, the state achieves greater efficiency of production, because workers can specialize in jobs for which they have the most natural aptitude. Plato even recommends for the most vital job, that of soldier or guardian of the state, that individuals chosen should possess "suitable natural aptitudes," including psychological characteristics of keen perception and courage combined with physical characteristics of speed and strength. He is clearly advocating some form of recruitment and selection, although he does not discuss in detail a specific mechanism for accomplishing this.

A number of societies from around the time of Plato, and even earlier, reached a level of social organization that made some form of recruitment and selection likely. In many cases, we must speculate about the existence of these practices because either no written record is left or written records are fragmentary. However, the internal organization and defence of the state have always been considered so important that few societies of any size or complexity would leave to chance the recruitment and selection for key positions within their government and military institutions. The same is true today. For example, Cronshaw (1991), when discussing selection practices in his book *Industrial Psychology in Canada*, gives most of his attention to recruitment and selection practices in the Canadian federal government and military because these are the most advanced, and well funded, existing in this country. In both cases, very large amounts of time and money have been invested to ensure that the core functions of the government and military are adequately provided for through qualified and experienced people. To do otherwise, either today or in Plato's time, would be to court disaster by compromising the most fundamental economic, social, and political institutions that hold society together.

MEDIEVAL EUROPE

Our discussion of the historical roots of recruitment and selection now looks at the medieval period in Europe. The mainstay of economic wealth in feudal Europe was the agricultural system, with a subservient peasant class working for and serving the aristocracy. During the same period, however, a class of artisans arose in the towns and cities to supply handmade goods (including metal and wood items and foodstuffs). With the rise of the artisans came the guild system as the beginnings of our modern labour movement, and with the guilds arose an apprenticeship system to provide for the training of skilled artisans. Feudal European society was based on a class system and fathers recruited their sons into the guilds. With the coming of the Industrial Revolution, workers moved from the countryside into the cities and mass production replaced individual craft work. During the social and economic turmoil of the Industrial Revolution, there is little evidence that recruitment and selection played a significant part in the functioning of large factories. Sources such as Gregg (1971) report that whole families were hired and worked from dawn until dusk in dingy and unsafe mines and factories at starvation wages. There was no obvious attempt to manage human resources in the modern sense during this period in history.

TWENTIETH CENTURY SCIENTIFIC MANAGEMENT

At the beginning of the 1900s, an intellectual movement began, which changed the face of industry and set the stage for human resources management throughout the remainder of this century. Frederick Winslow Taylor and others developed their principles of scientific management whereby workers would be "scientifically" selected, trained, organized, and managed in order to greatly increase their efficiency (Taylor, 1911). These ideas represented a dramatic break with management practices existing from the beginning of the Industrial Revolution, whereby workers were viewed as a cheap and virtually inexhaustible labour resource to be brought in and worked en masse without the benefit of any activities we would recognize as human resources management. For example, as the first of his four elements of scientific management, Taylor described the use of a scientific apparatus to measure the perceptual speed of workers who were inspecting ball bearings in a large bicycle factory. He reports laying off workers with poorer perceptual skills as one means to improve efficiency and productivity in the factory. The testing apparatus used by Taylor is similar to measures of reaction time used by psychologists today for assessing perceptual and cognitive skills. With this and other discoveries, a turning point was reached, which would result in the rapid growth and development of human resources management throughout the remainder of this century. Recruitment and selection in turn moved into a prominent position in this rapidly growing field.

The impact of scientific management on recruitment and selection in the 20th century cannot be overemphasized. In fact, many of the concepts and methods discussed in subsequent chapters of this book (beginning with Chapter 3 on scientific methods) have their origins in the scientific management movement. These concepts and methods—for example, the use of job analysis described in Chapter 4 and structured interviewing in Chapter 9— are 20th century inventions. However, recruitment and selection have been with us off and on, in one form or another, for thousands of years. Begin (1991) points to this fact and adds that there is also considerable variation in how recruitment and selection are carried out today, depending on the specific organization or industry. For example, the space engineer in the first example of this chapter (of whom there might be a few hundred in the world) would be recruited and selected in a very different way than would semi-skilled workers for an industrial plant in rural Saskatchewan. In other words, the scientific concepts of recruitment and selection described in this book, which find a great deal of professional acceptance in our post-industrial society, must still be applied within a larger community where the work gets done and larger purposes are achieved. It is to this subject that we

BOX 1.2 WHAT IS THERE IN A NAME?

Recruitment and selection should contribute through the human resources system to the efficiency, effectiveness, and productivity of the larger organization. But to get the most out of their efforts, human resources specialists must determine what it is that recruitment and selection can contribute to the organization. This naming game is complicated by the fact that some people are able to contribute more than others to the organization and to the larger society, thus making it desirable to discriminate between people and put people to work doing the things they are best at. For example, according to Plato, the best soldiers in ancient Greece were those who possessed keen perception, courage, speed, and strength. In any group of people selected at random, there will be some who possess these qualities in good measure and others who do not. Today, human resources managers would refer to these characteristics as worker specifications and would seek to recruit and select people with worker specifications that are best suited to the job.

The first step in recruitment and selection is to name what workers bring to a job that will help the organization the most. This naming of what the employer wants in a new worker can be done in various ways. One approach commonly used is to identify the knowledge, skills, abilities, and other attributes, or KSAOs, the best workers bring to the job (with the idea that these KSAOs will be later assessed in job applicants). Another approach is to define the *competencies* workers must have to perform to a level of excellence on the job. A third approach is to identify *critical incidents,* which are examples of especially effective and ineffective behaviour on the job. A fourth approach is to point out the *performance standards* that workers must meet on the job. All of these approaches can be used to describe either worker potential to do the job or the actual contribution a worker is expected to make once in the job. These approaches are not mutually exclusive and two or more of them may be combined into a single methodology (e.g., a competency model may draw on critical incidents and performance standards). Job analysis methodologies are discussed again in Chapter 4, which describes ways that industrial psychologists and others can label person and job variables in the recruitment and selection process.

So, what is there in a name? As it turns out, a name means a great deal. The proper naming of the person and job variables in the recruitment and selection system is of fundamental importance. The kinds of methods used and results achieved in the recruitment and selection process will depend greatly on the labels used when analyzing the job, regardless of whether those labels are KSAOs, job competencies, critical incidents, performance standards, or all of the above.

now turn—the role and contribution of recruitment and selection within the organizations and institutions that make up contemporary Canadian society.

◆ ◆ ◆
HOW RECRUITMENT AND SELECTION CONTRIBUTE TO THE HR MANAGEMENT PROCESS AND THE ORGANIZATION

Recruitment and selection is just one part, albeit an important one, of the larger process of human resources management within Canadian organizations. In turn, effective human resources management is just one contributor toward organizational survival, success, and renewal. This is as true today as it was in Plato's day. But readers will better appreciate the importance and role of recruitment and selection in today's organization if they understand the function of human resources management within the organization as a whole. It is to this task that we now turn.

We will start from the perspective of the larger organization by proposing the general model diagrammed in Figure 1.1. This model has several advantages for the human resources management practitioner.

- *Advantage 1.* It is a systems model. Systems models are meant to be broad and comprehensive, taking in the full scope of whatever process or system is represented. This allows the practitioner to see the larger organizational picture within which human resources management must operate. Systems models also reflect the relationships between the various components of the system, thus giving the practitioner an overview of how the parts of the organizational system work together to achieve desired outcomes.

- *Advantage 2.* The model in Figure 1.1 represents the typical organization in the private sector of the economy. That is, a system is set up to produce and sell a product or service on the open market.* Because many students of human resources management will eventually find jobs in these organizations, it is helpful, if not essential, to understand the functioning of

---

*Figure 1.1 presents a general model for profit-making businesses. Organizations in the public sector (e.g., the transit companies described at the beginning of this chapter) work in somewhat the same way, except that they receive their money input from public sources such as income and property tax revenues. Money surpluses that are realized are retained in the organization or are returned to a centralized government office, rather than being distributed to individuals as dividends.

this larger enterprise. Many other students will find work in the public sector, where the model is still useful in understanding the role of human resources management in transforming labour inputs to outputs. The outputs in the public sector would include factors such as the number of citizens served, complaints resolved, or the number of files processed.

♦ *Advantage 3*. The model contains typical measures that are embedded within every organizational system (e.g., for purposes of financial reporting, cost and inventory control, and human resources management planning). Human resources practitioners must know something of these measurement systems to be effective in their work. It is important to recognize that managers and workers in the various departments must have timely and accurate measurement information for planning, process control, coordination of materials and people, and evaluation of financial success. A sampling of measurements taken in the organization system are given in the right-hand side of Figure 1.1 beside their corresponding stages in the systems model. At least some of these measures come out of the human resources function, including performance appraisals, individual production records, and attitude surveys.*

♦ *Advantage 4*. The systems model in Figure 1.1 is a practical and intuitive representation of what organizations are about, rather than being overly academic. The components in it are given the everyday names used by owners, managers, and workers. We hope that this realism built into the model contributes to your practical understanding of where and how human resources management, including recruitment and selection, fits into the larger organizational picture.

♦ *Advantage 5*. The model captures what is important to organizations in the real world. For example, money is a key concern for any manager because, without it, the system ceases to exist (the company goes bankrupt). Money therefore has a prominent place in the model. In most companies, the practical importance of money can be seen in the preoccupation by many managers with their budget.

Why are the final outputs at the bottom of Figure 1.1 money, rather than the product or service sold to the buyer in the marketplace? Again, the

---

*A large part of the information that flows through any organizational system comes out of the production, service-delivery, and accounting functions.

FIGURE 1.1 A General Model for Organization Functioning

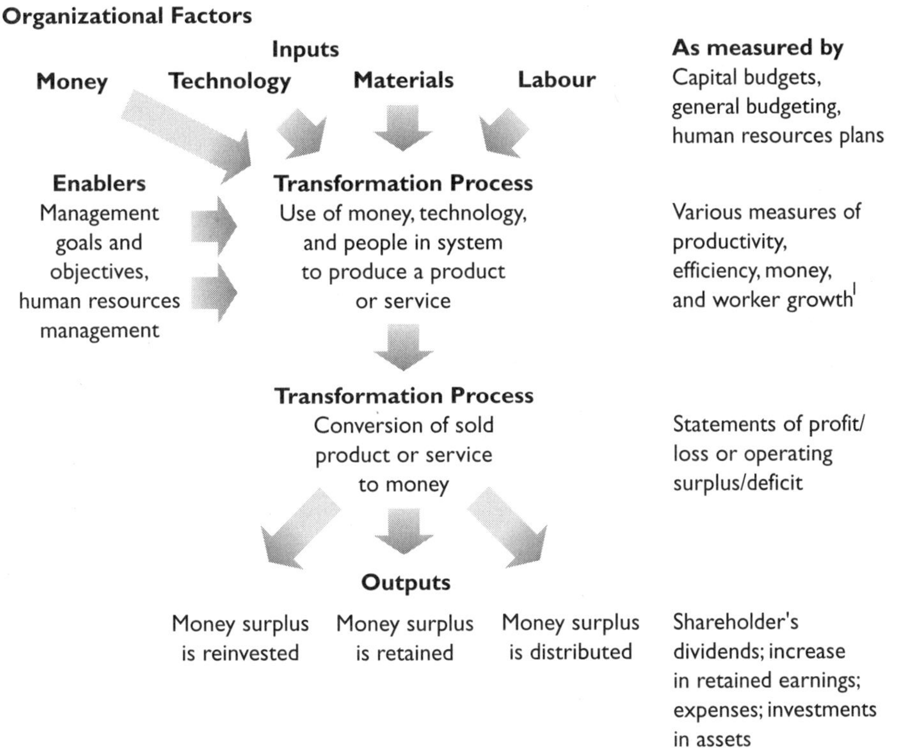

Organizational Factors

		Inputs			**As measured by**
Money	**Technology**	**Materials**		**Labour**	Capital budgets, general budgeting, human resources plans

Enablers
Management goals and objectives, human resources management

Transformation Process
Use of money, technology, and people in system to produce a product or service

Various measures of productivity, efficiency, money, and worker growth[1]

Transformation Process
Conversion of sold product or service to money

Statements of profit/loss or operating surplus/deficit

Outputs

Money surplus is reinvested	Money surplus is retained	Money surplus is distributed	Shareholder's dividends; increase in retained earnings; expenses; investments in assets

[1] Includes HR measures such as individual performance ratings, absence, work attitudes, and so on.

model was designed with realism in mind. Even if the intermediate output of the organization (i.e., products or services) may be of great value to the larger society (e.g., a serum for curing cancer or services to clean up the environment), the organization does not realize its "payoff" in the practical sense until the output is sold and money appears in its bank accounts. Concerns about money have a pervasive influence throughout the organization, including human resources. Many managers discover this basic but sometimes unpleasant truth when their department is restructured and downsized to achieve cost savings.

Now that we have seen some of the advantages of the systems model, we will discuss it in more detail and examine the role of human resources management (including recruitment and selection) within the larger organizational system. There are four basic components in the systems model: inputs, transformation processes, outputs and enablers. *Inputs* are those things that go into a system to be acted on and combined within the transformation process. For example, car parts purchased from supplier companies are an input to an automotive assembly plant (the assembly plant being the organization system for the purpose of this example). Labour is another input because the assembly plant requires skilled and trained people to operate equipment and maintain the plant. Technology comprises the machines and procedures used in production. Money simply represents the financial contribution that stakeholders (e.g., owner, shareholders) have made to start the business and keep it going. In the first *transformation process* the inputs are taken into the system, then are converted and combined to generate a product or service. In our auto plant example, the transformation process is an assembly line whereby materials (car parts, frames, engines) are put together by workers into a completed automobile using the available technology. The automobile rolls off the end of the assembly line as the *output* of the production system, which is in turn converted by a second transformation process to money at the point of sale. This money is placed in the bank, then tracked by the organizational accounting system. In the case of the car manufacturer, the conversion of the product to money occurs when the cars are sold from the factory to retail car dealers.

If the organizational system as a whole is efficient, effective, and productive enough, then the manufacturer's financial statements will show a profit or surplus, which will move as a money surplus to the bottom level of Figure 1.1. This money surplus can be reinvested in the company to acquire new technology, people inputs, or raw materials for the production process, retained by the company as money in the bank, or distributed back to shareholders as dividends. Money distributed back to the business owner or shareholders may be invested in other businesses, which in turn recruit and hire workers through their human resources systems.

Summarized in a simplified version of Figure 1.1, the components are related to each other as shown on page 17.

Because the enablers are most relevant of the four systems components to human resources management, and to the topic of recruitment and selection in this book, we have left our discussion of them for last so that they can be dealt with in depth. As our simplified model shows, enablers are closely connected to the transformation process. Enablers contribute to the organi-

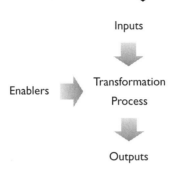

zational system by assisting the transformation process to efficiently and effectively combine the inputs in generating outputs. The two enablers in Figure 1.1 are management goals and objectives (to give the necessary direction and coordination to the productive effort); and human resources management practices and policies (to support and enable the integration of the labour input into the productive process). One might also point out three additional enablers not on Figure 1.1: the engineering function (to support the introduction of technology); the inventory function (to acquire materials and feed them into the production process), and the accounting function (to track money through the system). Of course, it is the human resources enabler to which we will give the most attention because recruitment and selection are the central focus of this book.

We will now point out an aspect of the systems model in Figure 1.1 that should have special significance for the aspiring human resources manager. The basic principle is as follows: Human resources management must carefully coordinate its activities with the other enablers and with the transformation processes as a whole if the larger organization system is to function properly. Furthermore, at least some share of this responsibility for coordination falls on human resources. This leads to our second principle for human resources success: Human resources managers must think in systems terms and have the welfare of the whole organization in mind. If managers become ghettoized within their own specialty (fail to see the organizational forest for the trees), stop recognizing the contributions of the other enablers, and fail to coordinate their efforts with these other enablers, they will soon find senior management questioning human resources' "value added" to the firm. Take for example the value being added by the selection process at the Diamond Star plant of Chrysler-Mitsubishi. They used a five-step selection procedure that included job previews, panel interviews, and assessment centres to screen 20 000 applicants. The corporation qualified 6700, and ulti-mately hired 300, at a cost of about (U.S.) $13 000 a hire. This expense is relatively minor when the cost of a $25 000-a-year employee, staying 30 years, is $4 million (representing a million dollar investment, on a net present value basis). Organizations that use these sophisticated selection techniques report higher employee productivity than those who do not. They capture the best part of the labour market, leaving the rest for less careful competi-tors. In today's highly competitive and cost-conscious world, that ability to prove value added will decrease the possibility of restructuring, downsizing, and outsourcing of human resources functions (including outplacement of the human resources managers themselves).

Ghettoization can also occur within human resources subspecialties, including recruitment and selection. We have heard of specialists who only conduct job analyses or spend the bulk of their time only doing selection interviews within their little corner of the human resources department. Although these activities may well be necessary, these people run the risk of their jobs becoming static and routinized and getting increasingly discon-nected from the other enablers and the transformation processes. Again, human resources must be in full touch with the needs of the larger organi-zation—a staff unit's (enabler's) reason for existing is to support line units pursuing the central mission of the organization. More than ever, human resources professionals at all levels must have an understanding and appreci-ation of their interdependencies with, and reliance on, other stakeholders throughout the organization. To carry out recruitment and selection in a closed box somewhere in the human resource department is not a viable option in today's world.

The human resources enabler in Figure 1.1 can be better understood by breaking it down further into its component parts and examining the trajec-tory of the individual worker within the organizational system. This more detailed perspective on the human resources management process is summa-rized in Figure 1.2. As shown at the far left-hand side of the figure, the employee engages for the first time with the organization system through the processes of recruitment and selection. After arriving in the organization, the newcomer usually undergoes an orientation, then he or she is ready to make a long-term productive contribution within the transformation process. To make this contribution as productive as possible and to ensure that the person is properly meshed with the other inputs and enablers in the system,

FIGURE 1.2 Stages in Employee Transition and Involvement in the HR Management Process

Entry	Transition	Contribution	Exit
◆ Recruitment ◆ Selection	◆ Newcomer orientation	◆ Training and development ◆ Performance evaluation and management ◆ Compensation ◆ Motivational programs	◆ Voluntary separation ◆ Outplacement ◆ Retirement

the human resources department will usually undertake other interventions, such as training and development, performance evaluation, compensation, and motivation. Finally, as the worker's time with the organization draws to a close, the department may assist in exit from the organization through outplacement and other means. As Figure 1.2 shows, recruitment and selection sets the stage for other human resources interventions—if recruitment and selection are done properly, the subsequent movement of the worker through the organizational system is made easier and the individual makes a long-term positive contribution to organizational survival and success. When this happens, human resources management becomes more of an enabler within the organizational system as a whole. Conversely, if the worker enters the organization on a flat trajectory because of poor recruitment and selection, then the entire system is adversely affected and human resources becomes less of an enabler. But, as we have already seen, in today's competitive and unforgiving business environment human resources must be able to enable or else face a grim (but deserved) fate at the hands of results-oriented senior managers.

◆ ◆ ◆

CANADIAN PROFESSIONAL ASSOCIATIONS WITH A STAKE IN RECRUITMENT AND SELECTION

Recruitment and selection activities within human resources management are frequently carried out by in-house human resources staff, sometimes assisted by consultants from management consulting firms. These in-house

BOX 1.3 USING HUMAN RESOURCES INFORMATION SYSTEMS TO MAKE HR A BETTER ENABLER

Organizations have developed human resources information systems (HRIS) as one way to make the human resources function a better enabler. Cascio and Awad (1981), in their book on the subject, point to three elements that are basic to modern HRIS: (1) the systems concept (already dealt with in this chapter); (2) computer hardware and software; and (3) a human resources measurement and reporting system installed on the computer. They suggest that the HRIS must perform four interrelated activities to be useful as a human resources enabler: (1) HRIS must provide an inventory of current human resources; (2) It must forecast supply and demand; (3) It must assist in planning that increases the number of qualified workers in the organization through recruitment and selection; and (4) It must provide control and evaluation procedures, giving feedback to the rest of the organization on the contribution of human resources to organizational goals and objectives. Human resources information systems are difficult and expensive to design and develop but, once in place, the value to human resources managers is obvious: HRIS allows them to think in systems terms and make the necessary decisions while avoiding mental overload. Decision making is made manageable because detailed human resources information on thousands of workers can be handled quickly and efficiently with the assistance of computers. HRIS is a tool that can make the human resources manager more effective and efficient as a contributor to organizational success. It increases the accountability of human resources management to senior management and at the same time it demonstrates the value that HRM adds to the productive process. Rampton, Turnbull, and Doran's (1996) *Human Resources Management Systems* provides a complete discussion of the role of management systems in recruitment and selection for those who are interested in this topic.

staff and consultants come to human resources management from various educational backgrounds, which are augmented by practical experience in managing human resources (see Box 1.4).

Many practitioners and consultants involved in human resources management hold membership in one or more professional associations and may be certified or registered with an association or professional licensing body in their area of specialization. Box 1.5 gives some basic information on three important associations having an interest in recruitment and selection practices in Canada. These associations have professional involvements well beyond, and in addition to, recruitment and selection. With membership in these associations come certain rights and obligations, including adherence to ethical codes or standards, as discussed in the next section.

BOX 1.4 SEVERAL CAREER PATHS INTO RECRUITMENT AND SELECTION

Ms. L became interested in human resources management when taking a business program at a community college. After obtaining her college degree in 1993, she took three additional courses in order to earn her Certificate in Human Resources Management from the Human Resources Professionals Association of Ontario (HRPAO). Since then, Ms. L has worked as a human resources specialist in a large manufacturing plant in southern Ontario. Among the projects she has worked on is the running of an assessment centre used by her employer to hire new workers into the plant. Ms. L hopes to eventually move into a senior human resources management position with her present employer or with a similar company in the manufacturing sector.

Mr. R moved into the field after completing his degree in sociology at a Quebec university in 1985. He started work in the human resources department of an aircraft parts manufacturer located in Montreal and over the following year earned his Human Resources Certificate with the Association des professionnels en ressources humaines du Quebec. In 1990, he accepted work with a new employer in a more senior HR position and has been promoted again since then. Much of his time is spent in recruitment and selection activities, especially in monitoring the results of an employment equity program put in place by his current employer.

Mr. D graduated from a four-year business program in the early 1960s with a major in human resources management and a minor in finance. He then entered the consulting field by taking a job with a large management consulting firm. After that, he joined the provincial Institute of Certified Management Consultants (see Box 1.5), earning his designation as a Certified Management Consultant three years later. He has made two career moves since that time, devoting most of his time to human resources work, including design of selection systems for major clients. He is currently a senior associate with a national consulting firm based in Vancouver.

Ms. S obtained a bachelor's degree in psychology at a major Canadian university in the early 1980s. During her undergraduate program, she had taken a course in industrial and organizational psychology and became interested in pursuing a career in personnel work. She then completed a two-year graduate program in industrial and organizational psychology and graduated with a master's degree in that discipline. Since that time, Ms. S has worked in the human resources department of a major urban hospital. Over her career with the hospital, much of her time has been spent testing and interviewing job applicants to various positions throughout the organization, although she works part time in compensation and benefits as well.

Ms. M also decided to pursue graduate studies in industrial and organizational psychology, but after graduating with her master's degree, she continued to get a Ph.D. in the late 1970s. Shortly after graduation, she got a job with an internationally based consulting firm, where a large part of her work was to design and implement

BOX 1.4 (continued)

large-scale recruitment and selection systems for banks, insurance companies, and other financial institutions. Soon after graduation, Ms. M became registered as a psychologist with the provincial licensing body and became active in a volunteer capacity with the Canadian Psychological Association. She is now a partner with the consulting firm and takes regular overseas assignments to assist clients in Europe and Asia with installation and maintenance of their selection systems.

BOX·1.5 SOME PROFESSIONAL ASSOCIATIONS INVOLVED IN RECRUITMENT AND SELECTION

Human Resources Professionals Association of Ontario (HRPAO)

2 Bloor Street West, Suite 1902, Toronto, Ontario M4W 3E2. Phone: 416-923-2324.

Scope of Professional Activities: Leadership, assistance, and education to people working and studying in the field of human resources

Membership Qualifications: Completion of education and training as described under professional certification offered; student status is available for those taking at least three HRPAO approved courses in a post-secondary or degree program

Professional Certification Offered: Certified Human Resources Professional (CHRP); must complete the Certificate in Human Resources Management (CHRM) through accredited courses at Ontario colleges or universities; three years full-time professional supervisory experience in HR; sponsorship by a CHRP member in good standing

Ethical Guidelines or Standards: HRPAO Code of Ethics

Institute of Certified Management Consultants of Ontario

BCE Place, 181 Bay Street, P.O. Box 835, Toronto, Ontario M5J 2T3. Phone: 416-860-1515.

Scope of Professional Activities: Management consulting, including change management

Membership Qualifications: University degree or five years equivalent experience; active in management consulting in Canada; must be sponsored by two CMC's (see below)

Professional Certification Offered: Certified Management Consultant (CMC); must write competency examinations and have at least three years of consulting experience

Ethical Guidelines or Standards: Uniform Code of Professional Conduct

Canadian Psychological Association (including The Canadian Society for Industrial and Organizational Psychology)

151 Slater Street, Suite 205, Ottawa, Ontario M1P 5H3. Phone: 613-237-2144.

Scope of Professional Activities: Delivery of psychological services, including testing and assessment

Membership Qualifications: Master's or Ph.D. degree in psychology

Professional Certification Offered: None; professional licensing is regulated by colleges of psychology in each of the provinces

Ethical Guidelines or Standards: Canadian Code of Ethics for Psychologists

♦ ♦ ♦
AN INTRODUCTION TO ETHICAL ISSUES

Ethics are the means by which we distinguish what is right from what is wrong, what is moral from what is immoral, what may be done from what may not be done. Of course, the laws of our country also tell us what is permissible and what isn't by imposing penalties, such as fines or imprisonment, on violators. Ethics is a difficult subject because it deals with the large grey area between those behaviours that society punishes as illegal and those rare behaviours that everyone readily agrees are scrupulously noble and upright. A careful consideration of ethics is important because human resources management requires the balancing of the rights of management with those of workers, as well as the rights of the human resources professional with those of the larger society.

Two examples of ethical dilemmas in recruitment and selection will help to illustrate why ethics are so important. For the first, put yourself in the position of a management consultant who is asked by a large employer to design and implement a system to select workers for a manufacturing plant. The plant is unionized and there is a history of poor union/management relations. Management informs you that they intend to break the union and, as a part of this effort, you are to come up with a selection system that will screen out all new job applicants having pro-union attitudes. The idea is to skew the workforce towards management so that the union can be broken in a future decertification vote. What's more, you are to keep the purpose of the selection system a secret and are asked by management to sign a contract in which you promise not to reveal their intentions to the union, the labour board, or any other outsiders. Where do your loyalties lie? Whose interests should you serve? Is it wrong for you, as the management consultant, to accept a fee to do what management is asking?

For the second ethical dilemma, imagine that you are a human resources manager who is considering the use of a selection system that you know will do a good job at selecting the best workers, but that also screens out members of visible minorities at a rate much greater than for the white majority. Should you use this system or try to find another that does not screen out so many members of visible minority groups? What if the new system does not do as good a job at selecting the best workers? Should you favour societal goals of increasing visible minority representation in the workforce or the interests of your company?

These two ethical dilemmas raise difficult questions that cut to the very core of ethics. But such questions are unavoidable because ethics are central to any group representing itself as a professional association. Fortunately, professional human resources associations in Canada have written codes and standards to provide guidance on ethical matters to their members (see Box 1.6). Naturally, these codes factor heavily into the recruitment and selection work done by human resources professionals and described in this book.

BOX 1.6 LOOKING FOR COMMON GROUND: ETHICAL CODES

The three professional associations described in Box 1.5 have ethical codes that apply to their members. In all codes, members are required to obey the laws of the country, avoid conflicts of interest, and to remain current in their fields of expertise. In addition, these ethics codes outline other obligations that their members have to management and workers, as well as the larger society. One of the principles from the *Code of Ethics* for the Human Resources Professionals Association of Ontario (HRPAO) states that their members shall "demonstrate commitment to such values as respect for human dignity and human rights and promote human development in the workplace, within the profession and society as a whole." The *Uniform Code of Professional Conduct* of the Institute of Certified Management Consultants of Canada (CMC) describes responsibilities that their members have to the public, the profession, other members, and to the client. Under the section titled Responsibilities to the Public, CMC members are liable for suspension or expulsion if they "behave in a manner unbecoming to the profession." Finally, the *Canadian Code of Ethics for Psychologists* written by the Canadian Psychological

Association (CPA) presents the following four ethical principles, which provide a guide for individual ethical decision making: respect for the dignity of persons, responsible caring, integrity in relationships, and responsibility to society.

All of these ethical codes place constraints on what their members may, and may not, do when practising recruitment and selection. However, ethical decision-making is not always clear-cut; often decisions must be made in the grey areas of morality where reasonable people differ in what they consider to be right and wrong. To complicate matters even more, an action that is considered ethical under one code might be deemed unethical under another. These inconsistencies can and do occur because the HRPAO, CMC, and CPA ethical codes differ in content, scope, and emphasis. The bottom line to this discussion is that ethics are a complex matter and they have the potential to be the Achilles's heel of many a promising human resources career. Professionals practising in recruitment and selection should read carefully, then discuss with colleagues, the ethical codes that apply to them and their work.

◆ ◆ ◆
A PREVIEW OF THE REMAINING CHAPTERS IN THIS BOOK

The remaining chapters of this book present a detailed treatment of the science and practice of recruitment and selection in Canada. In Chapter 2, we look at the legal and legislative context for recruitment and selection in Canada. Recruitment and selection practices have been seriously affected by human rights and employment equity over the past 20 years and this second chapter discusses important implications of these trends for the present and future practice of recruitment and selection. Chapter 3 lays down a conceptual platform for a later discussion of the techniques and methods of recruitment and selection in Canada by describing how the scientific method has been adapted to recruitment and selection. This third chapter becomes crucial, because as we have already seen, human resources management as a whole adheres to the principles set down by the scientific management movement early in this century. As a consequence, a basic understanding of the scientific method is necessary for any informed discussion of recruitment and selection. Chapter 4 discusses job analysis, which is the means by which job and person variables are identified for the purpose of recruitment and selection. In fact, job analysis provides the essential information for all of the recruitment and selection activities described in Chapters 5 through 9 of the book. Taken together, then, the material in Chapters 2, 3, and 4 provides a basic framework of legal and scientific principles, as well as detailed job information, on which recruitment and selection systems are built.

The next five chapters of the book (5 through 9) discuss how recruitment and selection are done. Chapter 5 deals with the job performance end of the recruitment and selection problem. That is, we show how performance of individual workers can be measured as a criterion against which to evaluate the success of recruitment and selection efforts. Chapter 6 discusses recruitment strategies that can be used to attract a qualified applicant pool in preparation for selection. Chapters 7 and 8 examine different selection methods that can be used in screening the applicant pool to find the most qualified workers, including work samples, assessment centres, and psychological tests. In Chapter 9, the subject of employment interviews is discussed, with an emphasis on structured interviews, which have been found to be highly effective selection tools. Chapter 10 reviews strategies that are used to combine information from different selection methods as part of making selection decisions. Finally, in the last chapter of the book (Chapter 11), we look at trends that will have an impact on recruitment and selection practices in future.

◆ ◆ ◆
SUMMARY

This chapter describes the larger context for recruitment and selection in Canada. Essentially, effective recruitment and selection are important because they contribute to organizational productivity and worker growth. Recruitment and selection practices, which have found a place in organization practices for thousands of years, still have an essential role to play in contemporary organizations. In recognition of this, professional associations and groups have staked their claims in recruitment and selection, developing ethical codes to regulate the activities of their members. You should keep this chapter in mind as you read through the remainder of the book. You will better understand the relevance of that material if you appreciate the historical, societal, and organizational reasons for recruitment and selection.

EXERCISES

1. Briefly sketch out two profiles. The first profile is that of your "most preferred co-worker"; that is, the person that you have worked with at some time in the past and you would most like to work with again. What was that person like? What skills and abilities did he or she have? Then sketch out a second profile of your "least preferred co-worker"—the person whom you would least like to work with again. Compare the profiles and discuss how use of recruitment and selection might be helpful in matching you with your most preferred co-worker in future.

2. Contact a human resources manager in a local company and set up an appointment. Show him or her Figure 1.2 (Stages in Employee Transition and Involvement in the Human Resources Management Process). Ask how the company handles each of the stages of entry, transition, contribution, and exit. Ask what they think of the value and benefit of recruitment and selection in stage one. Bring back your observations for discussion with the class.

3. As a class or in small groups, discuss the two scenarios raised in the ethics section of this chapter. Decide what the human resources professional

should do in each instance and provide an ethical justification for your decision.

4. Sketch out your preferred career track in human resources management. What professional associations would you join and what activities would you engage in? Where does recruitment and selection fit in to the mix of activities that you have planned for yourself?

References

Begin, J.P. 1991. *Strategic Employment Policy: An Organizational Systems Perspective*. Englewood Cliffs, NJ: Prentice-Hall.

Cascio, W.F., and E.M. Awad. 1981. *Human Resources Management: An Information Systems Approach*. Reston, VA: Reston Publishing.

Cronshaw, S.F. 1991. *Industrial Psychology in Canada*. Waterloo, Ontario: North Waterloo Academic Press.

Gregg, P. 1971. *A Social and Economic History of Britain: 1760-1970*. Toronto: Harrap and Co.

Plato. 1953. *The Republic*. Penguin Classics.

Rampton, G., I. Turnbull, and A. Doran. 1996. *Human Resources Management Systems*. Scarborough, Ontario: Nelson Canada.

Taylor, F.W. 1911. *The Principles of Scientific Management*. New York: W.W. Norton and Company.

Wang, Z.M. 1994. "Culture, Economic Reform, and the Role of Industrial and Organizational Psychology in China" (Chapter 14). In H.C. Triandis, M.D. Dunnette, and L.M. Hough, ed., *Handbook of Industrial and Organizational Psychology*, Vol. 4. 2nd ed. Palo Alto, CA: Consulting Psychologists Press.

2

Legal Issues

◆ ◆ ◆
CHAPTER GOALS

This chapter presents an overview of the legal issues in Canada affecting the practice of recruitment and selection. After reading this chapter you should

- understand the major legal issues affecting employment practices of recruitment and selection used in Canadian organizations;

- understand the importance of historical origins and stakeholder interests in shaping the content and direction of legislation impacting on recruitment and selection;

- know the relevant human rights and employment equity legislation and policy, as well as employment standards and labour law, affecting recruitment and selection (direct quotes from the legislation and policy are presented in this chapter to familiarize readers with the wording of the original sources);

- understand how legal concerns translate into recruitment and selection practices used in Canadian organizations;

- know the key legal concepts that have an impact on recruitment and selection in this country (e.g., direct discrimination, bona fide occupational requirements); and

- be able to use the basic concepts and principles discussed in the chapter in the development of non-discriminatory recruitment and selection systems.

This chapter is organized into three parts. In Part I, we will describe the key legislation and legal means in Canada affecting recruitment and selection practices. In this first part of the chapter, the following questions are addressed: What legislation exists? How is that legislation enforced? In Part II, we discuss a number of important legal concepts that have come out of legislation described in Part I. If these legal concepts are well understood, a more informed effort can be made to develop non-discriminatory recruitment and selection programs. In Part III, we provide some practical guidance on what to do, and what not to do, in recruitment and selection, based on the material covered in the previous two parts of the chapter.

Most extracts and examples in this chapter are taken from human rights, employment equity, employment standards, or labour law in the federal jurisdiction. Although many other examples are available from the provincial and territorial jurisdictions (for human rights, employment standards, and labour law) and from the provincial, territorial, and municipal jurisdictions (for employment equity), we will draw mainly from the federal scene for two reasons. First, other jurisdictions often draw on federal legislation as a model when drafting their own legislation and programs, hence a close examination of federal legislation and programs will tell us something about what other jurisdictions in the country are doing. Second, the use of examples from the federal jurisdiction avoid the problem of restricting coverage to any particular province or area of the country.

◆ ◆ ◆
PART I: A BASIC BACKGROUND IN LEGAL MEANS FOR NON-DISCRIMINATORY RECRUITMENT AND SELECTION

In this first part, we will look at four legal means that affect employment practices in recruitment and selection: (1) constitutional law; (2) human rights law; (3) employment equity; and (4) labour law, employment standards, and related legislation. *Constitutional law* is the supreme law of Canada and has a pervasive impact on employment practices, as it does in all spheres of Canadian society, including economics and social life. *Human rights* legislation across Canada prohibits discrimination in both employment and the provision of goods and services (e.g., rental housing, service in restaurants), with many of the complaints dealt with by human rights commissions involving employment discrimination. *Employment equity* programs are administrative mechanisms set up in many Canadian organizations, frequently as a response to employment equity legislation by federal, provincial, or municipal governments, which produce widespread changes in employment systems, including recruitment and selection. Employment equity programs are intended to promote the entry and retention of people

◆

from designated groups (including women, visible minorities, and aboriginal, and disabled people), so recruitment and selection practices assume much importance in these systems. *Labour law, employment standards, and related legislation* grant certain employment rights to both employers and employees in Canada, but also impose a wide range of employment responsibilities and obligations as well. Some of this legislation has direct effects on recruitment and selection, but these effects vary by the specific legislation and where it is in force. As you can see, even at this early point in the chapter, not all legal means are the same—a fact that is illustrated by Box 2.1.

MEANS ONE: CONSTITUTIONAL LAW

The Constitution of Canada consists of a series of acts and orders passed since 1867 by the British and Canadian Parliaments (Simon, 1988). These separate acts and orders begin with the British North America Act of 1867 and end with the Constitution Act of 1982. Sections 1 to 34 of Part 1 of the Constitution Act of 1982 are called the Canadian Charter of Rights and Freedoms. The Constitution, taken as a whole, serves as the supreme law of Canada, as the Subsection 52(1) from the Constitution Act of 1982 states:

> *52. (1) The Constitution of Canada is the supreme law of Canada and any law that is inconsistent with the provisions of the Constitution is, to the extent of the inconsistency, of no force or effect.*

All laws in Canada that come into force in a dispute between a private person and a branch of government (whether legislative, executive, or administrative) fall under the Constitution (Simon, 1988). In fact, the Constitution has precedence over all the other means discussed in this chapter.

A section of the Constitution often cited in employment law is Section 15 of the Canadian Charter of Rights and Freedoms. Section 15 lays out the principle of equality rights as follows:

> *15. (1) Every individual is equal before and under the law and has the right to the equal protection and equal benefit of the law without discrimination and, in particular, without*

BOX 2.1 NOT ALL LEGAL MEANS ARE THE SAME

The four legal means discussed in this chapter have varied historical roots and they address needs of different stakeholder groups in society. *Constitutional law*, which has its origins in the British North America Act of 1867, spells out the division of powers between the federal and provincial governments, as well as the rights and freedoms that Canadians enjoy under governments at all levels. All citizens are stakeholders under constitutional law and all of us are directly or indirectly affected by its provisions. *Human rights legislation* (federal and provincial) exists in Canada partly in response to international conventions declared by the United Nations and partly due to domestic pressure to reduce the severity of discrimination in the workplace and in other areas such as housing and provision of services. Human rights acts prohibit discrimination on protected grounds such as race or sex and the legislation is restrictive in that its provisions have no force beyond the protected groups. *Employment equity* legislation and programs have evolved in Canada both as a response to affirmative action programs in the United States and to pressures within our own country to increase workforce diversity. Employment equity addresses the concerns of designated groups (visible minorities, women, aboriginal people, and disabled people) and has no force or effect beyond these stakeholder groups. *Labour laws* in the federal and provincial jurisdictions across Canada are a response to a long history of labour union activity undertaken to improve worker job security,

wages, hours, working conditions, and benefits (Dessler and Duffy, 1978). These laws provide mechanisms for collective bargaining and union certification, and rules for a "fair fight" between management and union as well as protecting the public interest (Dessler and Duffy, 1978). Of course, the stakeholders under this legislation are unionized workers covered by collective agreements and managers in unionized workplaces. *Employment standards*, both federal and provincial, trace their origins back to the British North America Act and reflect societal norms about the respective rights and responsibilities of employers and their employees, whether these employees are unionized or not. Employment standards covered in legislation across Canada include statutory school-leaving age, minimum age for employment, minimum wages, vacations and leave, holidays with pay, and termination of employment. All workers in Canada, and their managers, are stakeholders in this legislation. *Other legislation*, including regulation of workers in the federal government, results from unique conditions in those specific sectors and is restricted to addressing the needs of those stakeholders. As a general rule, human rights and employment equity address the problem of discrimination, whereas the remainder of the legal means (labour law, employment standards, and related legislation) provide mechanisms to resolve procedural or contractual disagreements between specific stakeholders named in the legislation. (Examples of the latter would be promotion based on the merit

◆

BOX 2.1 (continued)

principle for federal government employees, seniority rights in collective agreements for employees of Crown corporations, or other types of contractual and legal obligations between employer and employee in either the private or public sectors.) However, even this basic distinction between anti-discrimination legislation and procedural/contract enforcement legislation can blur in practice. For example, equal pay between men and women for work of equal value, which is a discrimination issue, comes under human rights acts in some provinces and employment standards legislation in others (Stone and Meltz, 1988).

In this chapter, we can only hint at the complexity of the issues involved in the legality of recruitment and selection practices. As a starting point, human resources professionals should understand the origins, purpose, and stakeholders of each legal means if they are going to professionally manage recruitment and selection activities. Then they will have to keep up with legislative changes on a continuing basis.

---

discrimination based on race, national or ethnic origin, colour, religion, sex, age or mental or physical disability.

(2) Subsection (1) does not preclude any law, program or activity that has as its object the amelioration of conditions of disadvantaged individuals or groups including those that are disadvantaged because of race, national or ethnic origin, colour, religion, sex, age or mental or physical disability.

The discrimination provision in Subsection (1) of the Charter resembles provisions in human rights legislation across Canada (see the next section on human rights). Subsection (2) was undoubtedly written with employment equity in mind (see the section following).

As a practical matter, constitutional law will have an indirect impact on the everyday activities of practitioners of recruitment and selection. Its direct effect will only be seen after a recruitment or selection practice has been challenged in a human rights tribunal or court. At this time, lawyers may argue vigorously over jurisdictional or procedural issues that fall under constitutional law. Nevertheless, the practical effect of constitutional law on employment practices, including recruitment and selection, is pervasive because constitutional law sets limits and conditions on what the various levels of government (federal, provincial, and municipal) can legally do to influence or alter employment policies and practices through legislation or jurisprudence. Eventually, these influences will be felt wherever employment policies and practices are applied—in the human resources manager's office or during an employment interview, for example. Therefore, the importance of constitutional law for human resources practice should not be underestimated, even if its effects are transmitted throughout the legislative and judicial systems and may be difficult to trace to any specific employment decision.

MEANS TWO: HUMAN RIGHTS

All of the provinces and territories, as well as the federal government, have passed human rights acts or codes within their respective jurisdictions. These acts and codes prohibit discrimination in employment or in the provision of goods and services. For example, the Canadian Human Rights Act contains the following section (Canadian Human Rights Commission, 1989):

> 8. *It is a discriminatory practice, directly or indirectly, (a) to refuse to employ or continue to employ any individual, or (b) in the course of employment, to differentiate adversely in relation to an employee, on a prohibited ground of discrimination.*

The Canadian Human Rights Act applies to federal government departments, Crown corporations and agencies, and businesses under federal jurisdiction including banks, airlines, railways, the CBC, and Canada Post (Canadian Human Rights Commission, 1994).

Section 8 of the Canadian Human Rights Act refers to "prohibited grounds of discrimination." Under this act, the following are grounds on which discrimination is prohibited (Canadian Human Rights Commission, 1994):

◆ race

◆ national or ethnic origin

◆ colour

- religion

- age

- sex (including pregnancy and childbirth)

- marital status

- family status

- mental or physical disability (including previous or present drug or alcohol dependence)

- pardoned conviction

- sexual orientation

The prohibited grounds of discrimination vary somewhat between jurisdictions; this is shown by Table 2.1, which compares prohibited grounds of discrimination across federal, provincial, and territorial jurisdictions. Note that all jurisdictions prohibit discrimination on the first six prohibited grounds listed in Table 2.1.

Human rights legislation in all jurisdictions provides for the establishment of human rights commissions to enforce that legislation. For example, the Canadian Human Rights Act empowers the Canadian Human Rights Commission to investigate complaints, develop and deliver public information programs, undertake or sponsor research programs, liaise with other human rights commissions, and review federal legislation for conformity with the Canadian Human Rights Act. The commission has a full-time, paid staff to carry out its mandate.

The Canadian Human Rights Commission spends much of its time investigating human rights complaints. It is important to recognize at the outset that human rights protection is predicated on the idea that anyone who believes he or she has been discriminated against, and cannot resolve the problem with the employer, bears the responsibility to file a complaint with the commission. The commission has an established procedure for investigating the complaint, as shown in steps 4–8 in Box 2.2, p. 39. An applicant believing that he or she has been discriminated against in recruitment or selection can lodge a complaint against the employer through this type of mechanism but only in the relevant human rights jurisdiction.

TABLE 2.1 PROHIBITED GROUNDS OF EMPLOYMENT DISCRIMINATION IN JURISDICTIONS ACROSS CANADA

Prohibited Grounds	Federal	British Columbia	Alberta	Saskatchewan	Manitoba	Ontario	Quebec	New Brunswick	Prince Edward Island	Nova Scotia	Newfoundland	Northwest Territories	Yukon
Race or colour	◆	◆	◆	◆	◆	◆	◆	◆	◆	◆	◆	◆	◆
Religion or creed	◆	◆	◆	◆	◆	◆	◆	◆	◆	◆	◆	◆	◆
Age	◆	◆	◆	◆	◆	◆	◆	◆	◆	◆	◆	◆	◆
Sex (incl. pregnancy or childbirth)	◆	◆	◆	◆	◆	◆	◆	◆	◆	◆	◆	◆	◆
Marital status	◆	◆	◆	◆	◆	◆	◆	◆	◆	◆	◆	◆	◆
Physical/Mental handicap or disability	◆	◆	◆	◆	◆	◆	◆	◆	◆	◆	◆	◆	◆
Sexual orientation	◆	◆			◆	◆	◆	◆		◆	◆		◆
National or ethnic origin (incl. linguistic background)	◆			◆	◆	◆	◆	◆	◆	◆	◆	◆	◆
Family status	◆	◆	◆	◆	◆	◆	◆			◆		◆	◆
Dependence on alcohol or drug	◆	◆	◆	◆	◆	◆		◆	◆	◆			
Ancestry or place of origin		◆	◆	◆	◆	◆	◆					◆	◆
Political belief		◆		◆			◆	◆	◆	◆			◆
Based on association					◆	◆		◆	◆	◆			◆
Pardoned conviction	◆					◆	◆				◆		
Record of criminal conviction		◆					◆						◆
Source of income			◆	◆	◆					◆			
Assignment, attachment or seizure of pay											◆		
Social condition/origin							◆				◆		
Language						◆	◆						

Source: Canadian Human Rights Commission. Reproduced with permission of the Minister of Supply and Services Canada, 1993. (Adapted to include 1996 information.)

MEANS THREE: EMPLOYMENT EQUITY

Employment equity legislation has been passed in various jurisdictions across Canada, including the federal government, provinces, municipalities, and cities. This legislation requires organizations to set up and operate employ-

BOX 2.2 FILING A COMPLAINT UNDER THE CANADIAN HUMAN RIGHTS ACT

1. First, the individual who believes he or she has been discriminated against should tell the people involved and attempt to resolve the problem on the spot.
2. If Step 1 does not succeed, seek assistance from someone named under the organization's human rights policy.
3. File a company or union grievance against the practice believed discriminatory.
4. If steps 1–3 do not work, the individual may file a complaint with the Canadian Human Rights Commission.
5. If the complaint fulfils certain conditions (e.g., it is not trivial, frivolous, vexatious, or made in bad faith), the commission may assign an investigator to examine the complaint.
6. After the report from the investigator is filed, the commission may appoint a conciliator who will attempt to bring about the settlement of the complaint.

The commission must then either approve or reject the settlement.

7. After the complaint is filed, the commission may refer the complaint to a Human Rights Tribunal composed of not more than three members. The tribunal then investigates the complaint in a quasi-legal hearing. Both the complainant and the employer are permitted representation by legal counsel in this hearing. The tribunal will either dismiss the complaint or, if the employer is found to have discriminated, levy penalties (e.g., rehiring, financial compensation).
8. A review tribunal may be set up to hear an appeal if one of the parties is not satisfied with the decision under Step 7.
9. If either party is dissatisfied with the decision of the review tribunal, the complaint may go to the federal court system, in some instances ending at the Supreme Court of Canada.

ment equity programs, which Weiner (1993) defines as activities introduced into the human resources system of the organization to ensure equality for all employees in all aspects of employment, including recruiting, hiring, compensation, and training. Some organizations have also voluntarily adopted employment equity programs in the absence of employment equity legislation.

The tenor and purpose of employment equity legislation is best communicated by the wording of the legislation itself. One piece of legislation that had an impact on employment equity programs across Canada is the Employment Equity Act passed by the Canadian Parliament in 1986, which has the following to say:

2. The purpose of this Act is to achieve equality in the work place so that no person shall be denied employment opportunities or benefits for reasons unrelated to ability and, in the fulfilment of that goal, to correct the conditions of disadvantage in employment experienced by women, aboriginal peoples, persons with disabilities and persons who are, because of their race or colour, in a visible minority in Canada by giving effect to the principle that employment equity means more than treating persons in the same way but also requires special measures and the accommodation of differences.

The idea is to address systemic discrimination in employment systems that has disadvantaged members of these designated groups in the past. The means by which this is done is to review employment practices that may present systemic barriers to these groups and undertake measures to eliminate these barriers. This process is described as follows in the federal Employment Equity Act of 1986:

Employer's duty

4. An employer shall, in consultation with such persons as have been designated by the employees to act as their representatives or, where a bargaining agent represents the employees, in consultation with the bargaining agent, implement employment equity by

(a) identifying and eliminating each of the employer's employment practices, not otherwise authorized by a law, that results in employment barriers against persons in designated groups; and

(b) instituting such positive policies and practices and making such reasonable accommodation as will ensure that persons in designated groups achieve a degree of representation in the various positions of employment with the employer that is at least proportionate to their representation

(i)   in the work force, or

(ii) in those segments of the work force that are identified by qualification, eligibility or geography and from which the employer may reasonably be expected to draw or promote employees.

The development and implementation of an employment equity (EE) plan typically involves at least the following steps:

1. Obtain support of senior management for the EE effort.
2. Conduct a survey to determine the present representation of designated groups in the organization's internal workforce.
3. Set future representation targets for designated groups based on availability of qualified workers in the labour market.
4. Remove systemic employment barriers to increase representation for designated groups in the internal workforce.
5. Monitor the changing composition of the internal workforce over time.
6. Make necessary changes to the EE intervention to bring designated group representation up to future targets.

EE programs often require an extensive overhaul of an organization's recruitment and selection system; therefore, the requirements on the employer are generally more stringent than those of human rights, which only require the employer to respond to a specific complaint. Nevertheless, human rights and employment equity have the same ultimate aim: to eliminate discrimination in the workplace against disadvantaged groups and improve their positions in employment systems.

Organizations can choose to voluntarily adopt an employment equity program. However, in many jurisdictions organizations are required to adopt employment equity under municipal, provincial, or federal legislation. Of course, this legislation is delivered through the political process (as is all legislation), which means that, as times change, employment equity may be delivered through different mechanisms, may be strengthened or weakened, or may even be discontinued altogether. For example, in 1995 the Ontario government repealed the Employment Equity Act passed by the previous NDP government and said that it would implement an "equal-opportunity plan" together with business, labour, and community groups to replace the repealed legislation. The government claimed that the plan would better promote hiring and promotion policies based on merit (Scotland, 1995).

MEANS FOUR: LABOUR LAW, EMPLOYMENT STANDARDS, AND RELATED LEGISLATION

All jurisdictions in Canada, federal and provincial, have labour laws passed by their respective legislatures, which stipulate the rights of employees to organize trade unions and bargain collective agreements with employers. In the private sector, all the provinces have passed labour relations acts and, in the federal jurisdiction (e.g., banking, airlines, railroads), the Canadian Parliament has passed the Canada Labour Code. A labour relations board is established under each of the acts and codes to oversee union certifications and handle complaints about unfair labour practices (Milkovich, Glueck, Barth, and McShane, 1988).

As Stone and Meltz (1988) point out, the major impact of labour laws and unionization on recruitment and selection is on the "internal movement" of workers (i.e., promotion, lateral transfer, and demotion). As well, because "closed shop" agreements are legal in Canada (Dessler and Duffy, 1984), some unions have considerable control over external recruiting, even running their own hiring halls from which the employer must hire workers.

Canada also has 13 sets of employment standards legislation across the country and territories. These laws regulate minimum age of employment, hours of work, minimum wages, statutory holidays, vacations, work leaves, and termination of employment (Human Resources Development Canada, 1995-96). They have little impact on recruitment and selection practices, with the possible exception of termination, which might be considered "deselection" of people already in the organization's workforce.

To this point, we have discussed labour law and employment standards in the private sector. The federal and provincial governments have their own labour and employment legislation affecting recruitment and selection. The federal government is a good example of how this legislation works. Two pieces of legislation, the Public Service Employment Act and the Parliamentary Employment and Staff Relations Act, have an impact on recruitment and selection in the Canadian public service. The Public Service Employment Act designates the Public Service Commission of Canada as the central staffing agency for the federal government (Doerr, 1981). Under this Act, candidates from the general public recruited into federal public service hiring competitions (as well as some public service employees) can request an investigation if they believe their qualifications were not properly assessed (Public Service Commission of Canada, undated). Complaints are resolved through mediation and conciliation, or through direct intervention of the Public Service Commission or a deputy head (Public Service Commission of Canada, 1994–95, undated). Appeals may also be lodged against personnel selection processes used by the Public Service Commission. (An important appeal involving the use of psychological testing in the federal public service is summarized in Box 2.3.) The Parliamentary Employment and Staff Relations Act provides the mechanism of collective bargaining between the federal government as employer and the various unions certified to represent federal workers (Doerr, 1981). The legislation is administered by the Public Service Staff Relations Board (PSSRB), which is empowered to hear complaints under the Act and arbitrate collective bargaining disputes (Public Service Staff Relations Board, 1994-95). Some of the PSSRB decisions address promotion practices covered in collective agreements between the federal government and public sector unions, thereby affecting recruitment and selection practices in the public sector.

The four legal means discussed in this chapter influence recruitment and selection through different mechanisms and for different reasons. Table 2.2 summarizes Part I of the chapter by showing impacts of the legal means on three aspects of recruitment and selection. As you can see, the effects of legislation are pervasive and so should be kept in mind when developing recruitment and selection systems.

◆ ◆ ◆
PART II: KEY LEGAL CONCEPTS IN RECRUITMENT AND SELECTION

At this point in the chapter, we introduce several legal concepts that are crucial to non-discriminatory recruitment and selection practices in Canadian organizations. These concepts have become well known in both human rights and employment equity contexts, and find some application in labour law as well. Along with each concept, we will briefly explain its relevance to recruitment and selection.

BOX 2.3 PSYCHOLOGICAL TESTING IN THE FEDERAL GOVERNMENT

In 1986, an appeal board of the Public Service Commission (PSC) heard the complaints of job applicants for the job of collections enforcement clerk with the federal taxation department *(Maloley et al. v. Department of National Revenue (Taxation), 1986)*. Four individuals, who were not hired, alleged that the GIT 320 (a paper and pencil test of cognitive ability) in use at the time for screening job applicants was (1) not properly validated; (2) had an unjustifiably high cutoff score; and (3) was gender biased. Expert witnesses, including several top industrial psychologists, testified on the technical merits of the test at the invitation of either the complainants or the commission. Based on this evidence, the appeal board concluded that the GIT 320 had been validated (using a method called validity generalization, which is discussed later in this book). The two other allegations were dismissed because (1) the PSC had demonstrated the test cutoff score was reasonable and not exces-

sively high under the circumstances and (2) the test was neither biased nor unfair to women. All three allegations about the test were dismissed and the PSC continued to use the GIT 320 in its selection work.

The *Maloley* decision is especially informative because it involves allegations of two distinct types: (1) the first two allegations claimed that the GIT 320 violated procedural rules in the PSC selection system based on the merit principle; and (2) the third allegation claimed the test was discriminatory against women. Here we see an internal appeal board, which normally would deal with procedural and technical matters only, ruling on discrimination issues customarily the prerogative of human rights commissions. This suggests that, in at least some instances, there is a blurring of the divisions separating the four legal means discussed in this chapter. Legal issues in recruitment and selection are made even more complicated as a result.

DIRECT DISCRIMINATION

A widely recognized definition of direct discrimination was used by Justice McIntyre in the 1985 decision by the Supreme Court of Canada in the matter of *O'Malley* v. *Simpsons-Sears* as follows (CHRR, D/3106, 24772):

> *Direct discrimination occurs in this connection where an employer adopts a practice or rule which on its face discriminates on a prohibited ground. For example, "No Catholics or no women or no blacks employed here." There is, of course, no*

TABLE 2.2 JURISDICTIONAL COVERAGE OF ASPECTS OF RECRUITMENT AND SELECTION IN CANADA

	Does the jurisdiction cover ...		
Legal means	Entry-level job applicants?	Incumbent employees in promotion and transfer?	Incumbent employees in training and development?
Constitutional law	YES	YES	YES
Human rights legislation	YES	YES	YES
Employment equity legislation and programs	YES	YES	YES
Labour law, employment standards, and related legislation	OCCASIONALLY	SOMETIMES	SOMETIMES

disagreement in the case at bar that direct discrimination of that nature would contravene the Act.

The application of this definition to human resources practice is quite simple. If direct discrimination occurs, then the burden is on the employer to show that the rule is valid in application to all the members of the affected group. Let us take the example of an employer who is hiring steelworkers for heavy work in a foundry. Based on the stereotyped belief that foundry work (involving heavy lifting and a dirty environment) is unsuited to women, the employer specifies that no women will be hired into the job. This is a clear instance of direct discrimination according to the McIntyre definition given above. When challenged on this employment practice (and a complaint seems likely, given the blatant nature of the discrimination involved), the employer will have to show to a human rights investigator that all women lack the ability to do the work. Or, stated another way, the employer will have to show that there are no women who could perform the work successfully. If even one woman is found who can do the job, the employer's use of the "no women allowed" rule will be struck down by a human rights tribunal or court. In all but rare circumstances, the employer will find it impossible to justify direct discrimination.

The implications of direct discrimination for recruitment and selection are obvious enough. No statement may be made in advertising a job that would prohibit or restrict members of a protected group from seeking that job. For example, a statement in any job advertisement or posting that the employer is seeking "single males" constitutes direct discrimination and is illegal. During the selection process itself, human rights authorities have directed much attention and concern to application forms and interviews as sources of direct discrimination. As a result, some human rights commissions have published guidelines for questions asked by employers on employment application forms and at employment interviews. An excerpt from these guidelines published by the Canadian Human Rights Commission is given in Table 2.3. These guidelines provide practical and detailed advice on how to avoid direct discrimination in many common selection situations and should be carefully heeded by employers.

TABLE 2.3 GUIDELINES TO SCREENING AND SELECTION IN EMPLOYMENT		
SUBJECT	**AVOID ASKING**	**PREFERRED**
NAME	about name change; whether it was changed by court order, marriage, or other reason maiden name	
ADDRESS	for addresses outside Canada	ask place and duration of current or recent address
AGE	for birth certificates, baptismal records, or about age in general	ask applicants if they are eligible to work under Canadian laws regarding age restrictions
SEX	males or females to fill in different applications about pregnancy, child bearing plans, or child care arrangements	can ask applicant if the attendance requirements can be met

TABLE 2.3 (continued)

SUBJECT	AVOID ASKING	PREFERRED
MARITAL STATUS	whether applicant is single, married, divorced, engaged, separated, widowed, or living common-law	if transfer or travel is part of the job, the applicant can be asked if he or she can meet these requirements
FAMILY STATUS	number of children or dependents about child care arrangements	if the applicant would be able to work the required hours and, where applicable, overtime
NATIONAL OR ETHNIC ORIGIN	about birthplace, nationality of ancestors, spouse, or other relatives whether born in Canada for proof citizenship	since those who are entitled to work in Canada must be citizens, permanent residents, or holders of valid work permits, applicants can be asked if they are legally entitled to work in Canada
MILITARY SERVICE	about military service in other countries	inquiry about Canadian military service where employment preference is given to veterans by law
LANGUAGE	mother tongue where language skills obtained	ask if applicant understands, reads, writes, or speaks languages required for the job
RACE OR COLOUR	any question about race or colour, including colour of eyes, skin, or hair	
PHOTO-GRAPHS	for photo to be attached to applications or sent to interviewer before interview	
RELIGION	about religious affiliation, church membership, frequency of church attendance, if applicant will work a specific religious holiday, or for references from clergy or religious leader	explain the required work shift, asking if such a schedule poses problems for the applicant

TABLE 2.3 (continued)

SUBJECT	AVOID ASKING	PREFERRED
DISABILITY	for listing of all disabilities, limitations, or health problems whether applicant drinks or uses drugs whether applicant has ever received psychiatric care or been hospitalized for emotional problems whether applicant has received worker's compensation	ask if applicant has any condition that could affect ability to do the job ask if the applicant has any condition that should be considered in selection
MEDICAL INFORMATION	if currently under physician's care name of family doctor if receiving counselling or therapy	
PARDONED CONVICTION	whether an applicant has ever been convicted if an applicant has ever been arrested whether an applicant has a criminal record	if bonding is a job requirement ask if applicant is eligible
SEXUAL ORIENTATION	about the applicant's sexual orientation	

Source: Excerpted from *Canadian Human Rights Commission.* Reproduced with permission of the Minister of Supply and Services Canada, 1993.

Direct discrimination is much less frequent in Canadian workplaces than it once was. For example, discriminatory job advertising is now quite rare, at least as would be revealed by a survey of job advertisements in major daily newspapers. However, it does persist enough in selection practices to make continued vigilance necessary. One example where direct discrimination still occurs is eligibility for the priesthood in the Catholic Church, which is now, and has always been, closed to women. Human rights commissions are understandably hesitant to violate the historic separation between church and state by pursuing civil action against the Catholic Church, but this example serves to demonstrate how gender-based occupational stereo-typing persists in at least some sectors of our society. Direct discrimination is one manifestation of this stereotyping that will presumably still happen in the future, but much less often than in the past.

ADVERSE EFFECT DISCRIMINATION

Justice McIntyre in the previously discussed decision by the Supreme Court of Canada (*O'Malley* v. *Simpsons-Sears*, 1985) also defined adverse effect discrimination—sometimes also referred to as indirect discrimination—as arising where (CHRR, D/3106, 24772):

> *...an employer for genuine business reasons adopts a rule or standard which is on its face neutral, and which will apply equally to all employees, but which has a discriminatory effect upon a prohibited ground on one employee or group of employees in that it imposes, because of some special characteristic of the employee or group, obligations, penalties, or restrictive conditions not imposed on other members of the work group....*
>
> *An employment rule honestly made for sound economic or business reasons, equally applicable to all to whom it is intended to apply, may yet be discriminatory if it affects a person or group of persons differently from others to whom it may apply.*

The application of this definition to human resources practice is not obvious on first reading, so we will clarify it now by relating it to examples in recruitment and selection.

An example of a recruitment practice that would be open to a charge of adverse effect discrimination would occur when a human resources manager has decided to recruit for the position of welder's apprentice by asking current employees in the shop for the names of suitable friends and relatives. Let us further assume that all of the shop-floor employees are white males. The likely result of this recruitment strategy is that all, or almost all, of the candidates identified by existing employees for the welder's apprentice position will be white males, an outcome that is totally or largely exclusive of women and visible minorities. How does this recruiting strategy lead to adverse effect discrimination? Let us begin by assuming that this recruitment strategy is on its face neutral—the manager does not intend to exclude blacks or women—and that the manager has some reason to believe that the strategy might be a sound and effective business practice for identifying suitable candidates for the position. Let us also assume that the recruitment strategy is equally applicable to all the existing employees and, by extension, to all potential job candidates known to these employees. Nevertheless, this recruitment strategy creates adverse effect discrimination because it imposes on women and visible minorities the penalties or restrictive conditions not imposed on white males, because they are less likely to be nominated for the job. In other words, two groups protected under human rights legislation (i.e., women and visible minorities) have been differently (i.e., negatively) affected by this supposedly neutral recruiting practice and adverse effect discrimination is the result.

Another example of a selection practice involving adverse effect discrimination would be the use of a mechanical comprehension test to select applicants as welder's apprentices. Such tests of mechanical comprehension have been shown to have adverse impact against women, in that the average test scores of women are lower than that of men. If the same test cutoff score was used for men and women or if applicants were offered jobs in order of their test scores (from highest to lowest), proportionately fewer women than men would be hired for the job. In other words, the use of the mechanical comprehension test would impose upon women, as a group protected under human rights legislation, a penalty not imposed upon men. This happens for mechanical comprehension tests even if the test is applied equally to women and men—the crux of the problem is that the test affects women differently than men in the negative sense. Even if the human resources department of the company has reason to believe that the test is predictive of performance for welder's apprentices and does not intend that the test discriminate, a human rights complaint may be launched against the test on the basis of adverse effect discrimination.

The meaning of adverse effect now becomes clear. An employment rule, practice, or policy (e.g., certain recruitment practices or employment tests) having a negative effect on a group protected under human rights legislation, no matter how well intentioned by the employer, comprises adverse effect discrimination.

ADVERSE IMPACT

The concept of adverse impact is closely related to that of adverse affect discrimination. Although at least one noted writer on human rights and employment issues has defined the terms *adverse impact* and *adverse effect* synonymously (Weiner, 1993), we will use a narrower definition that has gained some acceptance in Canada and the United States when recruitment and selection matters are discussed. We will define adverse impact as follows:

> *Adverse impact occurs when the selection rate for a protected group is lower than that for the relevant comparison group (which usually has the highest selection rate).*

As one example, we have discussed a situation where a mechanical comprehension test has adverse impact against women, in that proportionately fewer women than men would be selected into the job.

The usual means of demonstrating adverse impact is to present statistical evidence showing that proportionately fewer of the protected group are selected using the selection device (such as an employment test or interview) or that fewer pass through the selection system taken as a whole. Vining, McPhillips, and Boardman (1986) demonstrate that establishing adverse impact in selection can be a very complex business, but one rough-and-ready rule often applied by employers and human rights authorities for establishing adverse impact in selection is called the *four-fifths* rule. According to this rule, adverse impact is established where the selection rate for the protected group is less than four-fifths that of the comparison group. Table 2.4 demonstrates a situation where a mechanical comprehension test had adverse impact against women according to the four-fifths rule. Despite the widespread adoption of the four-fifths rule in Canada, readers are cautioned that this rule has serious limitations on rational and statistical grounds (Vining, McPhillips, and Boardman, 1986).

BONA FIDE OCCUPATIONAL REQUIREMENT

Most human rights acts in Canada allow the employer to defend a discriminatory policy or practice as a bona fide occupational requirement (BFOR) if there is a good reason for it based on the need of the employer to "engage and retain efficient employees" (Canadian Human Rights Commission,

TABLE 2.4 EXAMPLE OF THE FOUR-FIFTHS RULE IN DETERMINING ADVERSE IMPACT ON WOMEN

Selection Based on Mechanical Comprehension Test

	Total applicant pool (A)	Number of people made job offers (B)	Selection rate (ratio of B/A)
Women	10	1	.10
Men	100	15	.15
Minimum selection rate of women according to the four-fifths rule must be 4/5 × .15			.12

Because the selection rate of women (.10) is less than the minimum selection rate under the four-fifths rule (.12), we conclude that the mechanical comprehension test had adverse impact.

1988, i). The Canadian Human Rights Act has this to say about the use of policies and practices that produce direct or adverse effect discrimination in the workplace (Canadian Human Rights Commission, 1989):

> 15. It is not a discriminatory practice if
> (a) any refusal, exclusion, suspension, limitation, specification or preference in relation to any employment is established by an employer to be based on a bona fide occupational requirement;

For example, an employment test that has adverse impact against a protected group, such as the mechanical comprehension test mentioned earlier, might be defensible under human rights legislation if the test had been previously validated as predictive of job performance (Cronshaw, 1986).

Justice McIntyre clarified the definition of the BFOR in the 1982 Supreme Court of Canada decision of *Ontario Human Rights Commission et al. v. the Borough of Etobicoke* as follows (CHRR, D/783, 6894):

> To be a bona fide occupational qualification and requirement,
> a limitation, such as a mandatory retirement at a fixed age,

must be imposed honestly, in good faith, and in the sincerely held belief that such limitation is imposed in the interests of adequate performance of the work involved with all reasonable dispatch, safety and economy, and not for ulterior or extraneous reasons aimed at objectives which could defeat the purpose of the Code. In addition, it must be related in an objective sense to the performance of the employment concerned, in that it is reasonably necessary to assure the efficient and economical performance of the job without endangering the employee, his fellow employees and the general public.

Justice McIntyre went on to point out that the above definition of the BFOR contains both a subjective and an objective element. The subjective element refers to the employer's state of mind when setting the rule or policy. That is, the limitation levelled on a protected group through a restrictive rule or policy must be imposed in good faith (i.e., without discriminatory intent). The objective element refers to scientific and other evidence that the employer can present to support the use of the restrictive rule or policy. For example, when an employment test has adverse impact on a protected group, such objective evidence would include validation studies demonstrating that the scores on the employment test are predictive of subsequent job performance for those hired (a good example of validation evidence used successfully to defend an employment test is found in the Ontario Board of Inquiry decision of *Persad* v. *Sudbury Regional Police Force*, 1993).

REASONABLE ACCOMMODATION

The concept of reasonable accommodation is closely tied to that of a bona fide occupational requirement. At least two key Supreme Court of Canada decisions *(O'Malley* v. *Simpsons-Sears*, 1985; *Bhinder* v. *CN Rail*, 1985) have affirmed that, where adverse effect discrimination has occurred, the employer is under a duty to accommodate the complainant, short of undue hardship. For example, an employer who administers a standardized employment test in selection may have to demonstrate that administration instructions were appropriately modified in order to allow persons with mental or physical disabilities a fair chance to demonstrate their ability. In the *O'Malley* decision, the employer was placed under a burden to have taken reasonable steps to accommodate the complainant, with hardship occurring at the point where a policy or practice (such as modifying a selection procedure) causes undue interference in the operation of the business or unsupportable expense to the employer. The Supreme Court of Canada went further in the decision of *Central Alberta Dairy Pool* v. *Alberta (Human Rights Commission)* (1990) to elaborate some factors that are relevant to assessing whether an employer has reasonably accommodated for an individual or group protected under human rights legislation. Included among these factors that place the employer under a greater or lesser burden of accommodation are the following:

- ◆ The financial cost to the employer as a result of making the accommodation
- ◆ Disruption of an existing collective agreement
- ◆ The impact of lowered morale on other employees
- ◆ Flexibility of workforce and facilities
- ◆ The magnitude of risk for workers and the general public when safety is compromised.

INDIVIDUAL ACCOMMODATION

The concept of individual accommodation follows that of reasonable accommodation. In the *Bhinder* decision, the Supreme Court of Canada found that, once an employment policy or practice has been established as a BFOR, there is no need for the employer to accommodate to the special circumstances of the individual. For example, let us suppose that an individual with arthritis has asked for reasonable accommodation to this disability and wants to complete a realistic work sample in place of the usual standardized manual dexterity test required of job applicants. Under the *Bhinder* decision, the employer would not be under a burden to grant her request. As stated in that decision, the BFOR refers:

> *...to a requirement for the occupation, not a requirement limited to an individual. It must apply to all members of the*

employee group concerned because it is a requirement of general application concerning the safety of employees. The employee must meet the requirement in order to hold the employment. It is, by its nature, not susceptible to individual application.

However, the *Central Alberta Dairy Pool* decision changed that basis of accommodation to an individual one. In the aftermath of the *Pool* decision, it is likely that the employer using the manual dexterity test will be required to accommodate the arthritic job candidate, even if that person is the only candidate with that disability applying for the job. The employer might accommodate such a candidate by using a realistic work sample or job tryout in place of the standardized test.

The decision of the Canadian Human Rights Tribunal in *Canada (Attorney General)* v. *Thwaites* (1993) clarified the application of the principles in the *Central Alberta Dairy Pool* case as follows (26–27):

In respect of the BFOR defence provided for in Section 15(a) of the CHRA, the Supreme Court of Canada initially held in Bhinder v. C.N. in 1985 that consideration of a BFOR was to be without regard to the particular circumstances or abilities of the individual in question. In the short span of five years, the majority of the Court in Alberta Human Rights Commission v. Central Alberta Dairy Pool, [1990] 2 S.C.R. 489 reversed its position and held that in cases of adverse effect discrimination, the employer cannot resort to the BFOR defence at all. In such cases, there is now a positive duty on employers to accommodate the needs of employees disparately affected by a neutral rule unless to do so would create undue hardship for the employer. Put another way, the employer must establish that the application of the neutral rule or practice to the individual was reasonably necessary in that allowing for individual accommodation within the general application of the rule or practice would result in undue hardship. No longer,

*in such cases, can an employer justify its practice as a BFOR
in relation to safety of employees in a general way and maintain that its discriminatory effect on certain groups of individuals is totally irrelevant.*

Clearly, employers can no longer apply a BFOR as a general practice or policy
and by so doing disproportionately exclude members of a protected group,
especially in the case of mental or physical disability, unless they can successfully argue that accommodating the needs of the adversely affected individual would produce undue economic or administrative hardship for the
organization.

REASONABLE ALTERNATIVE

The concept of reasonable alternative is also closely related to the BFOR.
Under the burden of reasonable alternative, the employer must show that no
reasonable or practical substitute exists for the discriminatory practice. For
example, where the employer uses a cognitive ability test that has adverse
impact on members of visible minorities, a tribunal may require that
employer to show that no other valid selection predictor (e.g., a different
employment test or a structured interview) is available that has less adverse
impact. The concept of reasonable alternative can involve important
elements of individual accommodation as well. As stated in the Canadian
Human Rights Tribunal decision of *Andrews* v. *Department of Transport*
(1994, 92):

*As one component to the BFOR defence, an employer must
usually explain why, as a practical alternative to a blanket
rule, it was not possible to assess individually the risk
presented by the individual employee.*

For example, an employer who administers a manual dexterity test to all job
applicants may have to show a tribunal why it was not possible to provide a
practical work sample test as a reasonable alternative to assess the ability of
one particular disabled applicant to do the job.

SUFFICIENT RISK

The notion of risk is important to the concepts of BFOR, reasonable and individual accommodation, and reasonable alternative. That is, the employer is obliged to accommodate workers, including job applicants, and provide reasonable alternatives up to, but not beyond, a certain level of risk. Tribunals and courts have restricted the application of the risk criterion to those situations where workplace safety is at issue. For example, an airline company may set a visual acuity standard for pilots, requiring that all candidates have uncorrected 20/20 full-colour vision, and defend this standard on the grounds that public safety would be compromised without it. One of the key questions that tribunals and courts have dealt with lately is whether the criterion of risk should be defined as "acceptable risk," "significant risk," "sufficient risk," or some other level. Although the issue is still being debated, one recent Federal Appeal Court decision, *Canada (Human Rights Commission) and Husband* v. *Canada (Armed Forces)* in 1994 established that the appropriate risk criterion applying to a BFOR is whether accommodating an employee with a particular characteristic would create "sufficient risk" to justify rejecting that individual for employment. Sufficient risk was a criterion first suggested in the 1982 Supreme Court decision of the *Ontario Human Rights Commission et al.* v. *The Borough of Etobicoke* (1982) and was reaffirmed by the Court in the *Husband* v. *Canada* decision as follows (CHRR, D/301, 68):

> A BFOR *will be established if there is a "sufficient risk of employee failure" to warrant the retention of an otherwise discriminatory employment qualification (Etobicoke at p. 210 [D/784, para. 6896]). Thus, whether or not an occupational requirement is "reasonably necessary" is dependent, at least in part, on whether members of the group alleging discrimination pose a sufficient risk of harm to themselves or others in the event of employee failure.*

Justice Robertson, in this same decision, further defined sufficient risk as follows (CHRR, D/304, 77):

In my opinion,the proper standard, outlined in Dairy Pool, *supra, embraces a "substantial" increase in safety risk within tolerable limits.*

Justice Robertson goes on to describe some of the following factors that impact on risk assessment for BFORs:

♦ The nature of the employment (e.g., teacher versus airline pilot in the case of visual impairment);

♦ The likelihood of employee failure, stated in empirical, rather than speculative, terms;

♦ Whether risk of employee failure is restricted to health and safety considerations;

♦ The seriousness of the harm arising from employee failure.

The sufficient risk criterion is well above a minimal or nominal risk. A minimal or nominal risk criterion would, for example, suggest that a person with muscular dystrophy should not be hired because that person might be injured in a fall (an organizational policy that many human rights authorities would argue reinforces a stereotype about the physically disabled, rather than being supportable by fact). On the other hand, a severe vision disability in an airline pilot would be well above minimal or nominal risk, because a plane crash caused or contributed to by that disability could kill hundreds of people. In that instance, risk resulting from the disability might well be sufficient to justify the otherwise discriminatory action of refusing to offer the disabled person a job.

LEGAL CONCEPTS APPLIED TO RECRUITMENT AND SELECTION

We will now present two human rights decisions that illustrate the application of the above principles to employers' recruitment or selection systems (see Table 2.5). In both decisions, the employer's system was found wanting and the court or tribunal awarded damages or remedies to the complainant.

The first decision is that of *Action Travail des Femmes* v. *Canadian National* (1984). Here a women's group in Quebec lodged a complaint with the Canadian Human Rights Commission aimed at CN's recruitment and

TABLE 2.5 LEGAL PRINCIPLES IN TWO KEY LEGAL DECISIONS

	Legal Decision	
	---	---
Legal Concept	Action Travail des Femmes v. Canadian National (1984)	Andrews v. Department of Transport
1. Direct discrimination		X
2. Adverse effect discrimination	X	X
3. Adverse impact	X	X
4. Bona fide occupational requirement	X	X
5. Reasonable accommodation		X
6. Individual accommodation		X
7. Reasonable alternative		X
8. Sufficient risk		X

selection practices in the St. Lawrence region. Action Travail des Femmes alleged that CN's practices disproportionately excluded women from non-traditional jobs, including those of trade apprentice, brakeman, and coach cleaner, all of which were male dominated. Furthermore, it was alleged that the employment practices in question were not bona fide occupational requirements. One selection predictor that came under scrutiny by the tribunal was the Bennett Mechanical Comprehension Test, which was used to select people for entry-level positions. The Bennett is known to have adverse impact against women and, in addition, CN had not validated it for the jobs in question. As a result, the tribunal ordered CN to stop using the test. In addition, the tribunal ordered CN to cease a number of other discriminatory recruitment and selection practices. The tribunal also ordered CN to begin a special hiring program with the goal of increasing the representation of women in non-traditional jobs in that company. This decision was widely noted at the time and has influenced recruitment and hiring practices in Canada since then.

The second decision that we will examine is that of *Andrews* v. *Department of Transport* (1994). In that decision, a Canadian Human Rights tribunal criticized a practical hearing test developed to assess a hearing impaired applicant to the Canadian Coast Guard College. The test, which was administered in place of a maximum hearing loss standard for Canadian Coast Guard officers, was designed at a cost of over $100 000 and consisted of fourteen different subtests administered to the applicant on the bridge of an operating Coast Guard ship. The subtest scenarios were administered by Coast Guard staff, who in turn supervised crew members of the ship serving as role players. The applicant's responses to the subtest scenarios were recorded and then compared against predetermined test standards. Andrews subsequently failed the test, was declined admission to the college, and filed a complaint with the Canadian Human Rights Commission. When testifying about the test during the tribunal hearings, expert witnesses criticized it on various grounds, including incomplete technical development, lack of reliability and validity, administration under insufficiently standardized conditions, and absence of norm data against which to compare and interpret the applicant's scores. The tribunal concluded that the practical hearing test was discriminatory and granted monetary compensation to the complainant Andrews.

In the *Andrews* v. *Department of Transport* decision, the tribunal cited all the legal principles previously discussed in this chapter (see Table 2.5). The complainant Andrews lodged his complaint against the Coast Guard on the grounds of physical disability (hearing impairment) and also alleged both direct discrimination and adverse effect discrimination. The application of the hearing loss standard had the effect of producing adverse impact against hearing disabled persons. The tribunal found that the Coast Guard had discriminated against Andrews by refusing him entry to the Coast Guard College and then considered whether the Coast Guard had successfully argued a BFOR defence. The tribunal accepted the subjective element of the BFOR (that the Coast Guard had set the limitation honestly, in good faith and in sincerity that the limitation was necessary), but rejected the Coast Guard argument that they had established the objective element of the BFOR. Importantly, the tribunal found that the Coast Guard had not established the practical hearing test as a BFOR because of the numerous technical problems associated with it. What is more, the tribunal found that Andrews could have been reasonably and individually accommodated by use of a less expensive and simpler test, which would have been a reasonable alternative to the practical hearing test. Finally, the nature of Andrews's disability did not pose sufficient risk to the safe performance of a Coast Guard navigational officer to justify denying him the job.

BOX 2.4 CULTURAL BIAS IN SELECTION TESTING

Much of the legislation and policy discussed in this chapter draws heavily on other countries, especially the United States. Nowhere is this more true than for human rights and employment equity, which are called "equal employment opportunity" and "affirmative action" in the United States. In fact, many Canadian tribunals and courts cite American cases as precedents when making their human rights decisions. In addition, many of the same issues and concerns about recruitment and selection in this country are mirrored in the United States. For example, an article in the *U.S. News & World Report* describes the political upheaval in Chicago over results of a promotional examination for city police officers (Glastris, 1994). Despite a cost of over $5 million paid to consultants to develop a bias-free promotional system, the multiple choice tests used in the promotion competition still had adverse impact against African-Americans and Hispanics. As a result, fewer members of these groups were promoted than were whites, and city politicians were quick to line up on both sides of the controversy. Chicago is a microcosm reflecting wider societal concerns in the United States and Canada over employment testing. The debate over adverse impact and cultural bias in selection testing continues to rage intensely on both sides of the border and is likely to do so for years to come.

Again, Table 2.5 provides a summary of the legal concepts that apply to the two human rights decisions. A comparison between the decisions, which were made 10 years apart, illustrates that at least four important legal concepts (those of reasonable accommodation, individual accommodation, reasonable alternative, and sufficient risk) have assumed greater importance in the 1990s than in the 1980s. It also demonstrates the rapidly evolving character of legal issues in Canadian human resources management—a fact that requires practitioners to continually upgrade their knowledge and skills in this area.

◆ ◆ ◆

PART III: SOME PRACTICAL GUIDELINES IN NON-DISCRIMINATORY RECRUITMENT AND SELECTION

The first two parts of this chapter provided a historical and conceptual back-drop for legal issues in recruitment and selection in Canada. In this third and final part, we present some practical guidelines on how to develop new recruitment and selection practices and on how human resources practitioners can review and improve those practices already in place. The guidelines presented here are exactly that—they are meant to take the reader in the right direction on recruitment and selection matters. They are not meant to be applied in a mechanical fashion; rather, they point to typical problem areas in recruitment and selection, then stimulate critical discussion and appraisal of those systems with an eye to improvement. We wish to emphasize that the issues discussed in this chapter are too complex to offer easy answers to human resources practitioners and expert help (including legal counsel and professional consultation) should be sought when there is insufficient time or expertise to adequately address these legal concerns in-house.

KEY PRACTICAL CONSIDERATIONS IN NON-DISCRIMINATORY RECRUITMENT

Recruitment is a complex human resources activity. This can make it difficult to develop non-discriminatory recruitment practices for protected group members (in the case of human rights legislation) or designated group members (in the case of employment equity). The scope of practices that must be considered is more manageable if the success or failure of recruitment is traced back to two main causes: (1) effectiveness or ineffectiveness of the organization in coming into contact and communication with target group members; and (2) positive or negative perceptions of the organization held by those target group members contacted, whether those perceptions exist before contact or are created by the contact. The first cause simply expresses the fact that people will not apply for a job if they are unaware that the job or organization exists or that the organization is recruiting. The second cause recognizes that getting the word out is not enough—job seekers must have a positive perception of the organization, as well as of their chances of getting the job, before they will apply. That perception is formed in at least two ways: (1) at the time the organization makes the initial contact through its recruiting outreach; or (2) through knowledge gained about the organization and its practices via third parties (e.g., friends, family, or news media).

To be more specific, we present a summary of both effective and ineffective recruiting practices in Boxes 2.5 and 2.6. The information here is meant to give some practical guidance in what to do and what not to do

BOX 2.5 PRACTICES FOR NON-DISCRIMINATORY RECRUITING

EFFECTIVE	INEFFECTIVE
◆ In employment offices, post in a conspicuous spot complete, objective, and specific information on all available jobs	◆ Permit receptionists and recruiters in employment offices to "pre-screen" applicants on the basis of informal criteria (e.g., appearance, dress)
◆ Advertise job openings in media read, viewed or listened to by protected or designated group members	◆ Rely on word-of-mouth advertising
◆ Train employment clerical staff and recruitment officers in outreach recruiting	◆ Post job advertisements only in-house
◆ Use opportunities to visually present protected or designated group members in positive employment roles (e.g., brochures and posters in employment office waiting area)	◆ Rely solely on seniority when promoting employees
	◆ Allow each recruiter to use and communicate idiosyncratic criteria for selecting among job applicants
◆ Establish networks with community groups from which protected or designated group members are drawn	◆ Categorize and stream job applicants based on stereotyped assumptions about protected or designated group membership (e.g., that women are not physically strong enough for certain work)
◆ Set and advertise objectively determined selection criteria for the job	
◆ Base selection criteria on bona fide occupational requirements	

when setting up and running recruitment programs, if the legality of the system is of primary concern. A more in-depth treatment of recruitment practices from a non-legal perspective is given later in this book.

A LEGAL REQUIREMENTS MODEL

The legal concepts discussed earlier in this chapter are summarized and related to each other in the Legal Requirements Model for Selection presented in Figure 2.1. This model is intended as a general guide to help the reader see how the legal concepts defined in the previous section can be applied to deciding whether a selection predictor is legally defensible. Note that the Legal Requirements Model is meant to clarify the application of *legal* concepts in recruitment and selection. Although much contained in the table is consistent with good professional practice in selection, this model is

BOX 2.6 RECRUITING PERCEPTIONS

PRACTICES THAT PROMOTE POSITIVE RECRUITING PERCEPTIONS

- Include role models from protected or designated groups in job advertising
- Implement management practices and policies that recognize and deal with special challenges or difficulties faced by protected or designated groups (e.g., wheelchair ramps for the physically disabled)
- Communicate and demonstrate commitment of senior management to outreach recruiting
- Actively challenge negative myths and stereotypes about protected or designated group members (e.g., through training programs)
- Bring organizational policies and procedures into line with human rights and employment equity legislation
- reward supervisors and managers with the pay and promotion system for success in advancing human rights and employment equity goals
- Build outreach recruiting into departmental and organizational business plans
- Set specific and measurable recruiting targets against which managers can work
- Present protected and designated group members in positive roles within organization newspapers and magazines
- Offer training and development programs to protected and designated group members to address their specific needs in adapting and progressing within the organization
- Modify working conditions as needed to accommodate protected and designated group members

PRACTICES THAT PROMOTE NEGATIVE RECRUITING PERCEPTIONS

- Permit sexual, racial or other forms of harassment in the organization
- Show lack of interest by senior management in improving recruitment practices
- Allow negative myths and stereotypes to persist regarding the capabilities of protected and designated group members
- Leave outreach recruiting unrewarded by the pay and promotion system
- Leave outreach recruiting outside of departmental and organizational business plans
- Tell managers to "do your best" in recruiting protected and designated group members rather than providing them with specific numerical targets

not designed to address professional practice *per se*. Professional principles in selection are emphasized throughout much of the remainder of this book.

The model in Figure 2.1 is set up in a series of steps that the human resources practitioner can follow in reviewing a selection process before it is implemented in an organization. He or she starts at Step 1, "Review use of selection predictor" and moves through a series of ovals in order. In each of these ovals, the practitioner must answer a question either YES or NO, then move along to the next step of the model based on the answer to the preceding question. For example, if the answer to the question in Step 2 "Evidence of direct discrimination" is NO, then the reader moves immediately to Step 6. If the answer is YES, then the reader moves to Step 3. The ovals in the figure all represent points at which the practitioner must make a decision; the boxes on the other hand represent actions that the practitioner should take.

Earlier in this chapter, we emphasized the differences between direct and adverse effect discrimination. Figure 2.1 is divided into two halves to represent this distinction: Steps 2–5 address the possibility of direct discrimination in a selection predictor, Steps 6–12 address the possibility of adverse effect discrimination. It should be noted that the distinction between direct and adverse effect has blurred somewhat recently. For example, the following distinction was made in the *Canada* v. *Thwaites* (1993) decision (31):

> *In the case of direct discrimination, the employer must justify its rule or practice by demonstrating that there are no reasonable alternatives and that the rule or practice is proportional to the end being sought. In the case of adverse effect discrimination, the neutral rule is not attacked but the employer must still show that it could not otherwise reasonably accommodate the individual disparately affected by that rule.*

The tribunal in the *Thwaites* decision states that this difference between direct and adverse effect discrimination "may be semantic" and that, in both cases, "the employer must have regard to the particular individual in question" (31). However, for our purposes of personnel selection, the distinction between direct and adverse effect discrimination does have meaning and is retained in the Legal Requirements Model.

FIGURE 2.1 A Legal Requirements Model for Selection

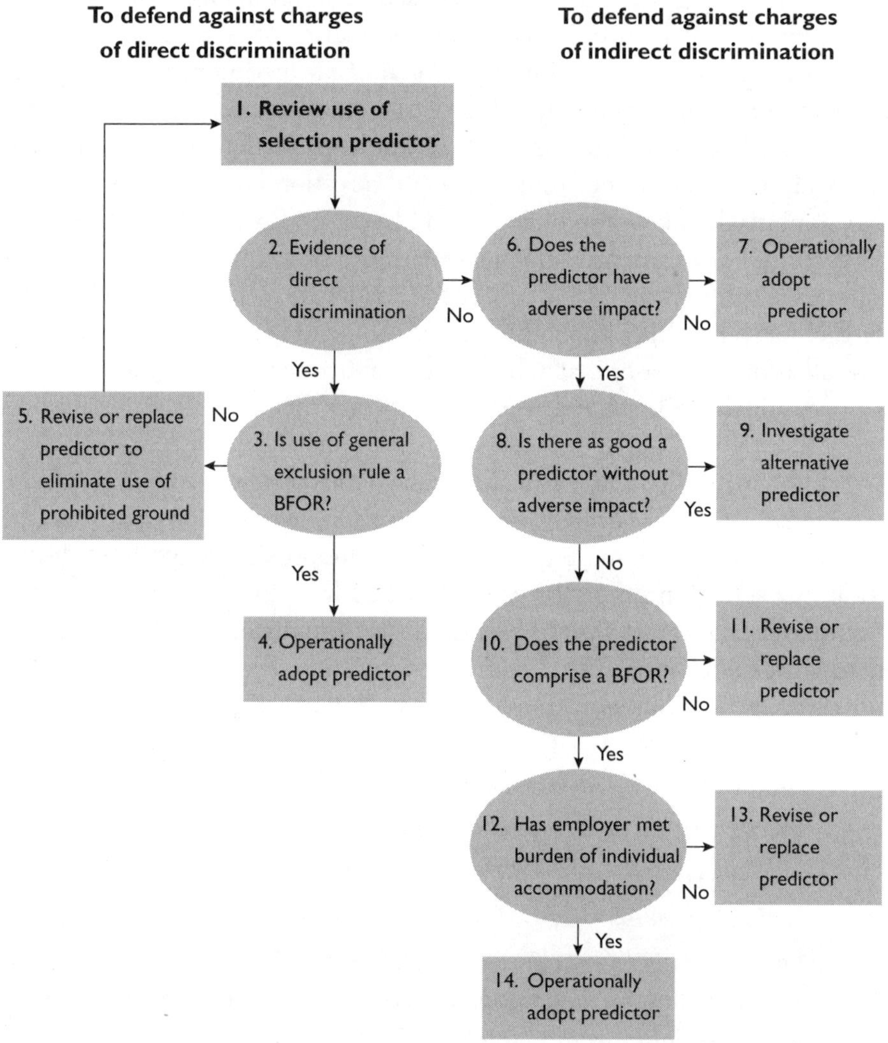

To defend against charges
of direct discrimination

To defend against charges
of indirect discrimination

1. Review use of
selection predictor

2. Evidence of
direct
discrimination

No

6. Does the
predictor have
adverse impact?

No

7. Operationally
adopt
predictor

Yes

Yes

5. Revise or replace
predictor to
eliminate use of
prohibited ground

No

3. Is use of general
exclusion rule a
BFOR?

8. Is there as good a
predictor without
adverse impact?

Yes

9. Investigate
alternative
predictor

Yes

No

4. Operationally
adopt predictor

10. Does the predictor
comprise a BFOR?

No

11. Revise or
replace
predictor

Yes

12. Has employer met
burden of individual
accommodation?

No

13. Revise or
replace
predictor

Yes

14. Operationally
adopt predictor

Source: Cronshaw, 1995.

It is important to note that direct discrimination is less likely to occur (as compared to adverse effect discrimination) when professional human resources managers, test developers, and psychologists are involved in developing selection systems. For example, the human resources professional would probably not trigger a direct discrimination complaint by setting an age standard for a job such as airline pilot (e.g., age 50). Rather, he or she would develop a test or other assessment, such as a work sample, that measures job-related skills of visual acuity or colour vision in place of the age standard. However, the test may well result in adverse impact against the protected group, so triggering an adverse effect complaint. In short, human resources professionals will not need to justify direct discrimination in most cases, but will move directly from Step 2 to Step 6 in the model.

To give you a better idea of how the Legal Requirements Model works, we will discuss each of the steps in more detail and relate it to concepts discussed earlier in the chapter.

Step 1. Review use of selection predictor. This review will normally involve first obtaining a copy of the predictor (e.g., structured interview pattern or psychological test) and related research documents such as research manuals, articles from the scientific literature, and in-house studies. These materials should contain information in such areas as adverse impact, reliability, validity, and utility. This information is referred to later in the model to answer such questions as Does the predictor have adverse impact? Is there an equally good alternate predictor without adverse impact?

Step 2. Evidence of direct discrimination? This first question in the model refers to our definition of direct discrimination earlier in the chapter.

Step 3. Is use of general exclusion rule a BFOR? By its definition, direct discrimination involves the general exclusion of a group or class of people protected under human rights legislation. As pointed out earlier, this scenario is getting rarer in selection, although employers should still be sensitive to the possibility of it happening. If evidence of direct discrimination is found, Pentney (1986) presents two preconditions that the employer must meet to justify the general exclusion rule as a BFOR:

1. *Show that the bona fide occupational requirement which it seeks to invoke is reasonably necessary to the essence of its business; and*
2. *Show a factual basis for believing that all or substantially all persons within the class would be unable to perform the job safely and efficiently, or that it is impossible or impractical to test persons individually.*

In selection terms, these preconditions would translate into

1. *The need to show that the exclusion is related to job performance or safety;*
2. *A burden to demonstrate that all, or substantially all, of those people in the class excluded by the selection standard are incapable of performing the job or present a sufficient safety risk; and*
3. *A burden to show that individual testing of class members affected by the rule is impossible or impractical.*

One area where direct discrimination might still happen with some regularity is in the area of physical or mental disability. For example, a hospital employer might screen out from the hiring process all people with the HIV virus or with AIDS. The concern of the employer would probably centre around the safety of patients during use of invasive techniques (such as injections by syringe). If the hospital did intentionally exclude all persons with HIV/AIDS during selection, then the employer would have to show through the use of objective data that (1) people with HIV/AIDS are a sufficient safety risk; (2) all (or substantially all) persons with HIV/AIDS present a safety risk; and (3) individual testing of applicants with HIV/AIDS is impossible or impractical.

Step 4. Operationally adopt predictor. If the above conditions are met under Step 3, then the selection predictor may be legally defensible. However, the employer should be ready to produce objective data in support of its exclusionary policy.

Step 5. Revise predictor to eliminate prohibited ground. This is the action that is recommended if the general exclusion rule is not supportable as a BFOR. This action might be relatively limited in scope (e.g., if interviewers drop a single question from their interview pattern that asks applicants about family responsibilities) or might be broad (e.g., drop the selection standard that requires all applicants to test negative for HIV/AIDS). Sometimes, where standards of age, height, or weight are dropped, performance tests may be developed to replace them. After the selection predictor is revised, it is a good idea to review it again for evidence of direct discrimination (see the arrow connecting Box 5 to Box 1 in Figure 2.1, page 66).

Step 6. Does the predictor have adverse impact? Let us assume that an age requirement is dropped in favour of a performance test of physical agility for a given job; thus the concern shifts from one of direct discrimination to that of potential indirect discrimination. At this juncture, the possibility of adverse impact should be investigated (see the discussion in Part II of this chapter on evaluating a selection predictor for adverse impact).

Step 7. Operationally adopt predictor. If the selection predictor has no adverse impact, then it might be adopted. If there is adverse impact, then the evaluation of the selection predictor should be continued by moving to Step 8.

Step 8. Is there as good a predictor without adverse impact? This step captures the legal idea that, under the burden of reasonable accommodation, the employer must show that no reasonable or practical alternative exists to the discriminatory practice (see Part II of this chapter).

Step 9. Investigate alternative predictor. If such a predictor exists, then it should be investigated for its feasibility in place of the one having adverse impact. Note that this investigation should consider various factors, including whether the alternative has adequate reliability and validity to justify its use in place of the predictor with adverse impact.

Step 10. Does the predictor comprise a BFOR? If the predictor has adverse impact, and no alternative is reasonably available that does not have adverse impact, then the employee must try to establish that it is a bona fide occupational requirement (again, Part II of this chapter describes in more detail what is needed to establish a BFOR). Steps 8 and 9 taken together put the employer under a "shifting burden of proof" (Cronshaw, 1986). That is, if a selection predictor is found to have adverse impact against a protected group, the burden shifts to the employer to show that the use of this predictor is a BFOR.

Step 11. Revise or replace predictor. If it cannot be established as a BFOR, then it must be revised or replaced to either eliminate the adverse impact or to establish a BFOR.

Step 12. Has the employer met the burden of individual accommodation? As pointed out in Part II of this chapter, the BFOR now also places the employer under the burden of individual accommodation during recruitment and selection of those protected group members who have special needs. Further, the employer must accommodate to the point of undue hardship or sufficient risk.

Step 13. Revise or replace predictor. Again, if this criterion is not met, the employer will have to revise or replace the selection predictor.

Step 14. Operationally adopt predictor. If this final criterion is met, then the employer can adopt the selection predictor with some assurance that it is legally defensible.

The Legal Requirements Model illustrates that selection practitioners must make many complex decisions and tradeoffs if they wish to make their selection systems as legally defensible as possible. Much technical data must be collected and interpreted— a task that many human resources generalists have limited time and knowledge to undertake. The model is best used when these data are available and in an open discussion format where managers can question and challenge each other's assumptions about what constitutes a legally defensible selection predictor. Even then, the legal issues are complex enough that managers may hold differing opinions about whether a predictor is legally defensible and legal consultation might be sought. Nevertheless, application of conceptual models like this one to practical selection problems should provide more defensible selection systems over the long run.

◆ ◆ ◆

SUMMARY

The Canadian workforce has always been ethnically heterogeneous, and now it is becoming increasingly diverse with regard to race, gender, and disabilities. Given that recruitment and selection are crucially important human resources activities for achieving diversity, human rights and employment equity are here to stay. As well, a large segment of the Canadian workforce is unionized, which means that labour codes and related legislation will affect recruitment and selection practices in many Canadian organizations. However, as this chapter shows, legal issues in recruitment and selection are complex and take a great deal of time, study, and experience to master. What is more, the legal scene changes constantly and rapidly as new legislation, legislative amendments, human rights policies, and tribunal or court decisions are introduced. This requires practitioners in recruitment and selection to regularly update their knowledge and skills in legal issues. We can expect the legal scene to continue growing and developing in the foreseeable future as members of disadvantaged groups continue to seek fuller participation in the Canadian labour market and as employers and employees (unionized and non-unionized) continually renegotiate their relationship through labour law and employment standards.

E X E R C I S E S

1. Go to a local business and ask for a copy of their application form. Ask the nearest office of the provincial or federal human rights commission for their guidelines on questions permitted on application forms. How well does the employer do? Are there any improvements to their application form that you could recommend?

2. Locate the Canadian Human Rights Reporter (CHRR) in your college or university library. Find a recent decision published in the CHRR that involves recruitment or selection. Which of the principles discussed in this chapter come into play in the decision? What are the implications when human resources professionals design recruitment or selection systems in Canada?

3. Divide the class into small groups. Each group uses the Legal Requirements Model to evaluate a selection predictor as described in a human resources trade magazine or discussed in the later chapters of this book. The groups then report their findings back to the class. What conclusions did the groups draw about the legal defensibility of the predictor? If the groups disagreed in their conclusions, why did this happen? Can the class reach consensus about whether the predictor is legally defensible? If not, what are the implications for human resources practice?

References

Canadian Human Rights Commission. 1988. *Bona Fide Requirement Policy*. Ottawa: Canadian Human Rights Commission.

Canadian Human Rights Commission. 1989. *Office Consolidation: Canadian Human Rights Act*. Ottawa: Minister of Supply and Services Canada.

Canadian Human Rights Commission. 1994. *Filing a Complaint with the Canadian Human Rights Commission*. Ottawa: Minister of Supply and Services Canada.

Canadian Human Rights Commission. Undated. *A Guide to Screening and Selection in Employment*. Ottawa.

Cronshaw, S.F. 1986. "The Status of Employment Testing in Canada: A Review and Evaluation of Theory and Professional Practice." *Canadian Psychology* 27, 183–95.

Cronshaw, S.F. 1991. *Industrial Psychology in Canada*. Waterloo, Ontario: North Waterloo Academic Press.

Cronshaw, S.F. 1995. "Human Rights and Employment Testing." Presented at the annual conference of the Canadian Psychological Association in Charlottetown, PEI.

Dessler, G., and J.F. Duffy. 1984. *Personnel Management*, 2nd ed. Scarborough, Ontario: Prentice-Hall.

Doerr, A.D. 1981. *The Machinery of Government in Canada*. Toronto: Methuen.

Glastris, P. 1994. "The Thin White Line: City Agencies Struggle to Mix Standardized Testing and Racial Balance." *U.S. News & World Report*, August 15: 53–54.

Human Resources Development Canada. 1995-96. *Employment Standards Legislation in Canada*. Ottawa.

Milkovich, G.T., W.F. Glueck, R.T. Barth, and S.L. McShane. 1988. *Canadian Personnel/Human Resource Management: A Diagnostic Approach*. Plano, Texas: Business Publications Inc.

Pentney W. 1986. "The BFOQ Defence since Etobicoke." *Canadian Human Rights Reporter*, Vol. 7, C/86-1.

Public Service Commission of Canada. 1994-95. *Annual Report*. Ottawa.

Public Service Commission of Canada. Undated. *Investigations: An Overview.* Ottawa: Public Service Commission of Canada, Appeals and Investigations Branch.

Public Service Staff Relations Board. 1994–1995. *Parliamentary Employment and Staff Relations Act: Ninth Annual Report of the Public Service Staff Relations Board.* Ottawa.

Scotland R. 1995. "Ontario Introduces Bill to Repeal 'Quotas': Aims to Restore 'Merit Principle'." *The Financial Post,* October 12: 4.

Simon, P.L.S. 1988. *Employment Law: The New Basics.* Don Mills, Ontario: CCH Canadian Limited.

Stone, T.H., and N.M. Meltz. 1988. *Human Resource Management in Canada,* 2nd ed. Toronto: Holt, Rinehart and Winston.

Vining, A.R., D.C. McPhillips, and A.E. Boardman. 1986. "Use of Statistical Evidence in Employment Discrimination Litigation." *The Canadian Bar Review* 64: 660–702.

Weiner, N. 1993. *Employment Equity: Making It Work.* Toronto: Butterworths.

3

Scientific Methods

◆ ◆ ◆
CHAPTER GOALS

This chapter develops the idea that personnel recruitment and selection strategies based on information obtained through scientific methods are more likely to benefit an organization than decisions based on impressions or intuition. The chapter starts with an introduction to scientific methodology and goes on to examine basic measurement concepts that underlie contemporary recruitment and selection practices; it ends with a discussion of cost-benefit techniques that are appropriate for human resources management. This chapter is an excellent review for those who have had previous courses on research methods and psychological measurement. For others, it is an overview of research terms and methods. After reading this chapter you should

- appreciate the difference between information discovered through scientific and non-scientific ways of knowing;

- understand the scientific method and several different types of research strategies;

- understand the important role that measurement plays in the scientific process and in describing differences between individuals;

- know what a correlation coefficient is, along with a few other basic statistical concepts used in personnel selection;

- recognize the importance and necessity of establishing the reliability and validity of measures used in personnel selection; and

- be familiar with utility analysis as one way to evaluate personnel selection systems.

◆ ◆ ◆
THE RECRUITMENT AND SELECTION PROCESS

In most employment situations, there are many applicants for each available job. The employer's goal is to hire an applicant who possesses the knowledge, skills, abilities, or other attributes required to successfully perform the job being filled. The employer makes a guess about which applicant will perform the job most effectively. This basic decision, which is made hundreds of times each day throughout Canada, is the end result of a complex process. Correct guesses by the employer have positive benefits for the organization and the employee; bad guesses not only affect the productivity and profitability of the company but may also have negative emotional consequences for the poorly performing employee.

As part of making this decision, the employer must have a good idea of both the duties that will be performed as part of the job and the level of performance required for job success. The employer must identify the knowledge, skills, abilities, or other attributes (KSAOs) that are required for job success and measure or assess KSAOs within individual job applicants. Hiring someone through an assessment of job-related attributes is based on an inference: higher levels of attributes are linked to higher levels of job performance.

THE HIRING PROCESS Every employer who makes a hiring decision follows a hiring process, even though the managers may not realize they are doing so. When a position becomes vacant, or is newly created, the employer has a general idea of the duties to be performed as part of the job. These duties are included in an advertisement used to recruit candidates for the position. This job advertisement may also state broad educational or experiential requirements expected from the candidates. Applicants submit résumés and, after a preliminary screening, a few may be interviewed. Based on review of the applicant's file, work references, and impressions formed during the interview, the employer makes a decision to hire one of the candidates. This decision may reflect the employer's experience, a gut feeling or intuition about a certain candidate, or simply personal preference. The employer has an *idea* of the type of person who will do well in the job or in the organization and looks for an applicant that matches this idealized employee. In any event, the employer is making a guess about which applicant will do well in the job based on information collected from the job applicant. Unfortunately, all too often the employer's guess reveals more about the biases of the employer than it does about either the requirements for the job or the qualifications and abilities of the applicants. Bad guesses lead not only to lower productivity but also to legal difficulties. This brief overview of how things are too often done in Canadian organizations should not be mistaken for how they ought to be done. The information presented in this book illustrates acceptable recruitment and selection practices.

BUILDING A FOUNDATION The chapters in this book explore in depth the topics that make up the typical recruitment and selection process. To move beyond a guess, a selection system must be built upon a sound scientific foundation. In buying a house, you may not need to know how to lay a foundation, but you must be able to tell whether the house's foundation is solid. Often, human resources managers are asked to adopt selection systems; this chapter provides the tools needed to determine if a selection system or procedure rests upon solid footings. The concepts and procedures developed in this *tools* chapter are applied throughout this book.

◆ ◆ ◆
DIFFERENT WAYS OF KNOWING

There are several ways in which we can acquire information about people, places, things, or events. These different methods fall into four broad categories. While the three non-scientific methods of tenacity, authority, and rationalization provide us with information, the scientific method produces the most accurate information. This is due to the fundamental difference between scientific and non-scientific methods: science is self-correcting. Information that is acquired through a scientific process can be "falsified"; that is, the information can be disproved through objective, empirical means. The following sections provide greater detail on these different ways of knowing.

NON-SCIENTIFIC METHODS

METHOD OF TENACITY Often we accept as fact statements that have been made repeatedly over an extended period of time. By continuing to believe that something is true, it becomes true. For example, believing that "women are not suited to be police officers" may lead to selection policies that exclude women from that occupation. This belief may have more to do with stereotypes or traditional roles assigned to women than with their actual ability or skill to do the job. A few years ago, Al Campanis, who was an executive with the Los Angeles Dodgers baseball team, demonstrated how knowledge based on tenacity influenced personnel decisions. He had been invited to the TV show "Nightline" to discuss the employment of blacks and other minorities in front office positions. Campanis expressed the view that blacks did not have the "necessities" for appointment to executive positions in professional baseball. The statement not only led to Campanis' resignation but had a negative impact on a multi-million dollar industry. More recently in Canada, two Reform Party Members of Parliament expressed the views that an employer should have the right to move homosexual and black employees "to the back of the shop" or even to fire them to accommodate clients' prejudices. Both members were suspended from their party for making those remarks (The Reform Party's Days, 1996). Tenacity produces the poorest quality information. As we discussed in Chapter 2, personnel and other staffing decisions based on this type of information may well have serious legal and financial consequences for an organization.

METHOD OF AUTHORITY We often accept as true statements made by people in positions of authority or sources we consider infallible. These may include our own or others' experience, values, and norms derived from a culture or religious system, or statements made by "experts" such as editorial writers for *Report on Business* or *The Financial Post*. People in organizations frequently seek out authorities for insight into how to manage. Autobiographies of the latest corporate hero are examined for guidance; thousands of dollars are spent sending staff to training seminars conducted by the latest corporate guru. If you accepted Al Campanis as a leading authority on staffing baseball organizations, you probably would not hire many blacks to fill non-playing positions. Corporate cultures define truth, as well. If you worked for IBM, you might believe that wearing a white shirt and tie each day improves creativity and productivity; if you worked for Apple Computers, you might believe just the opposite. The problem here is that truth based on authority is not absolute; it depends on both the authority and the acceptance of the authority by the believer. Not all people accept or recognize the same authority; one person's management expert may be another person's fool.

METHOD OF RATIONALIZATION This method refers to knowledge developed through the process of reasoning, independent from observation. An individual begins with an initial set of assumptions (which are accepted as true) and uses these to derive new statements or truths. Mathematicians and philosophers develop *a priori* assumptions and apply logic to deduce new knowledge. Of course, the derived knowledge is only true within the context of the *a priori* assumptions. Different starting assumptions lead to different conclusions. If you believed that (a) blacks do not have the "necessities" to be baseball executives and (b) good executives are critical to an organization's success, you could easily reason that blacks should not be hired as baseball executives. If you started with the assumptions that (a) race is irrelevant to performance as a baseball executive and (b) good executives are critical to an organization's success, you would come to the conclusion that the best executive should be hired, regardless of race. Each of these conclusions is correct within the context of its assumptions. The starting assumptions serve as the authority for the new knowledge.

INTUITION Often human resources decisions are made through intuition; a manager hires someone because of a *good feeling* about the applicant. Intuition is a form of rationalization based on vague or fuzzy, unstated assumptions and a deductive process that may not always be logical. As with other forms of rationalization, once the initial source of knowledge is accepted, so must be the derived information. There is no means to challenge the correctness of decisions based on intuition.

SCIENTIFIC KNOWLEDGE

Human resources decisions affect the lives of individuals and organizations. Those decisions must be as accurate as possible. Science produces the highest quality information; it accepts as true only the information that can withstand continued challenges to its accuracy. Science is self-correcting. Information is checked for accuracy with methods that are objective; this means that scientific methods can be examined, critiqued, and used by others. Scientific knowledge is constantly undergoing revision. Even in the space of a few years, previously accepted truths may become outmoded through new discoveries.

CHARACTERISTICS OF SCIENCE The quality of scientific knowledge reflects the nature of the scientific process. Science is characterized by several essential features (Whitehead, 1967):

- *Science is concerned with reality*—objects and events exist apart from an observer.

- *Science accepts causality*—the universe, including human behaviour, is based on a set of orderly relations, which can be described, predicted, and explained.

- *Science is empirical*—reliable knowledge about the universe is obtained through observation of objects and events. While reasoning is required as part of the scientific process, it alone does not produce new knowledge; it is used to organize the observed objects and events.

- *Science is public*—observations are subject to error; therefore, scientific knowledge must be made available to others for criticism and review. Approaching all knowledge with a degree of skepticism helps to establish its truthfulness or falsity.

- *Science provides method*—science employs specific rules and procedures in the quest for new knowledge. A hallmark is the inclusion of controls built into the procedure, which serve to check or verify the truthfulness of the newly discovered knowledge.

◆ ◆ ◆
THE SCIENTIFIC APPROACH

The scientific approach includes a number of methods that can be used to generate knowledge. Regardless of any special features, a scientific method follows a common strategy. Kerlinger (1986) outlined four general steps in this process.

STATEMENT OF THE PROBLEM

This is often the most difficult, yet the most important, part of the process. This step involves taking a generally vague idea or feeling and transforming it into a statement that captures the issues at hand. For example, people may have very strong feelings about the appropriateness of selecting women for police SWAT teams. The reason for their beliefs may be captured by the statement, "Women are not suited for roles on police SWAT teams." Once the idea is expressed, it can be pursued to the next stage. Simply expressing the idea does not make it true, as may be the case with non-scientific methods. The statement must be tested.

HYPOTHESIS

A hypothesis is a proposition about the relation between two or more events, objects, people, or phenomena. It is an attempt to redefine the problem in terms that are amenable to objective investigation. It is a prediction about relations that can be tested. Many hypotheses are presented as "If X happens, then Y results" type of statements. Believing that women are not suited for police SWAT teams might lead you to propose that the aggressiveness required to subdue criminals is related to gender. This belief is expressed in the following hypothesis:

H_1: There is a relationship between gender and aggression.

REASONING AND DEDUCTION

While hypothesis H_1 can be examined empirically, more precision is achieved by deducing the consequences of the hypothesis. Based on experience, previous knowledge, or empirical work, we may expect to find higher levels of aggression in males. This reasoning leads to a change in the initial hypothesis:

H_2: Males are more aggressive than females.

The reasoning/deductive process may lead to examination of new or different problems. If aggressiveness is needed for success in SWAT team roles and women are less aggressive than men, placing women in SWAT units should lead to lower levels of success. This prediction is expressed in a new hypothesis:

H_3: If women are placed in SWAT units, the level of success will decrease.

Of course, all these hypotheses remain conjecture subject to verification.

OBSERVATION/TEST/EXPERIMENT

Up to this point, the scientific approach is similar to the non-scientific methods of knowing in that all the activity, so far, has emphasized reasoning. Reasoning is only part of the scientific process; it is not the final step. The relationship specified in the hypothesis must be tested empirically. The most critical step is to gather empirical evidence that is relevant to the hypothetical relationship.

OPERATIONAL DEFINITIONS In science, *empirical* means that an event is capable of being experienced; that it can be observed or measured, either directly or indirectly. Many hypotheses involve relationships between abstract events. While it is fairly easy to categorize humans into groups of males and females, it is more problematic to define *success*. Before any testing can take place, abstract constructs, like success, must be defined in a manner that allows observation and measurement. This is done through use of *operational definitions*, which define an abstract construct in terms of specific procedures and measures. Operational definitions are very specific to the study in which they are used and may differ between studies. SWAT team success could be defined as the rating assigned by a supervisor to a SWAT unit after its participation in a training exercise, or the number of medals or awards given to members of the unit over a period of time; it could also be defined in many other ways. Operational definitions may differ in their *construct validity*, that is, the degree to which they represent, or capture the essence of, the abstract construct. Medals and awards made to members of a SWAT team may have little relevance to success in subduing criminals (e.g., members may be given awards to mark the number of years of service in the unit). Construct validity is an important concern in any scientific investigation.

VARIABLES The events, objects, people, or phenomena referenced in hypothetical propositions must vary in amount, degree, or kind. Such *variables* must have at least one defined characteristic that has at least two values. The variable of gender has two values—male and female. There must be at least two values associated with the variable of SWAT team success; the exact number of values depends on how it is operationally defined. In terms of a rating definition for success, a two value pass/fail system could be used, as could a five point letter grade system of A, B, C, D, or F, a 100-point system, or one of many others.

RESEARCH PLAN Once the variables relevant to the hypothesis are defined, a *research plan* is developed. A research plan, or research design, lays out the framework for making measurements or observations on the variables. The research plan specifies the strategy used in collecting data; it identifies the subjects or participants, the environment in which they will be measured, the frequency with which they will be measured, and any interventions or manipulations that the investigator will introduce into the environment. One way in which research designs vary is the degree of control given to the investigator.

OBSERVATIONAL STUDIES In *observational studies*, the researcher exercises very little control or manipulation of variables; the investigator records naturally occurring behaviours and establishes patterns of relationships between different aspects of the observed behaviour. A police force assigns women to SWAT teams; but there are still SWAT units to which women have not been assigned. Comparing the performance ratings given to these two types of SWAT teams provides a test of H_3. If units with mixed teams had lower performance ratings, we might conclude that the hypothesis is correct. Unfortunately, the lack of control allows alternative conclusions to be drawn. The performance of the SWAT team may have more to do with the ability of the teams' leaders and senior officers than with the gender composition of the team. The ability and experience of the mixed team's officers may have been less than those commanding the all-male unit. Although there is a relationship between the presence of women and team performance, the lack of control over other variables makes it very difficult to attribute the lower performance rating to the presence of women in the SWAT team or to the leadership of the units.

EXPERIMENTAL DESIGNS In *experimentation*, the researcher actively manipulates variables and controls different aspects of the environment to exclude alternative explanations for the observed events. To test H_3, an investigator finds two SWAT teams that are similar in terms of performance capability; the investigator then assigns members and officers to each of the teams in a way that equates the ability and experience within each unit. One team is assigned only males while the second is assigned males and females. This is the only difference between the two units. Each team is rated under identical training conditions. If the mixed team receives lower ratings, there is more justification for attributing the cause of the poor performance to the composition of the unit. The control procedures lead to greater confidence in making cause and effect statements.

QUASI-EXPERIMENTAL DESIGNS Unfortunately, many situations do not lend themselves to experimentation either on the grounds of practicality or ethical considerations. In these instances, investigators fall back on less obtrusive strategies. In practice, applied research falls somewhere between the two extremes of pure observation and pure experimentation. In most studies, it is possible to implement some control and to manipulate variables to reduce the number of alternative explanations. In *quasi-experimental* research, we do not have the ability to randomly assign people to the different conditions, or groups. We can, however, manipulate variables that may have an effect on outcomes. It is highly unlikely that any police force would allow a researcher to randomly assign police officers to SWAT teams. The researcher works with teams that are already in place, similar to those in an observational study. The inability to randomly assign members to teams allows for the possibility that the units differ on a number of factors, in addition to gender, which might produce differences on the outcome measure. As in experimentation, the researcher manipulates, controls, and measures these conditions as part of comparing the performance of both teams. Both units might undergo a set of standardized exercises, (e.g., a simulated attack or a hostage rescue operation). While differences between the performance of the two teams could be due to factors other than the teams' gender composition, the quasi-experimental design reduces the number of alternative explanations. Quasi-experimental research strategies are often used to evaluate the results of personnel selection and recruitment efforts.

THE NULL HYPOTHESIS Testing hypotheses is somewhat more involved than described above. Would any decrease in performance of the mixed team, no matter how small, be accepted as proof of H_3? Could the difference in performance ratings be due to chance or to errors in measurement, rather than to actual differences in performance? To assess this possibility, researchers actually test a *null hypothesis*, H_0, which proposes that there will be no difference or no relationship in the data collected across different conditions. The null hypothesis that corresponds to H_3 would be:

H_0: If women are placed in SWAT units, the level of success will not decrease.

In other words, the performance of the mixed gender crew will be the same as the all male crew, with the exception of slight variation due to chance factors such as measurement error.

STATISTICAL SIGNIFICANCE If the null hypothesis is rejected, the alternative hypothesis, in this case H_3, is assumed to be true. Statistical procedures are used to evaluate the likelihood that a difference across groups occurs by chance. In general, the larger a difference between two groups on some measurement, the less likely that difference is attributable to chance. As part of the research plan, the investigator specifies the size of an empirical difference that is used to reject the null hypothesis and to accept the alternative. If there is only one chance in 20 (a probability of .05) that a difference of such size could have occurred by chance, the difference is said to be *statistically significant*; that is, the difference is probably NOT due to chance. A statistically significant result does not automatically mean that the research hypothesis is accepted. The researcher must also show that alternative explanations for the results are unlikely, a task that is more easily accomplished with a well-designed experiment.

DRAWING CONCLUSIONS The results of a study, whether positive or negative with respect to the research hypothesis, have implications for both theory and application. In either case, we draw conclusions, based on the empirical evidence, about the initial problem. While there is an end to any one study, the research process is ongoing. The results and conclusions from one study are integrated into a larger body of knowledge. There is always a probability that a research hypothesis should NOT have been accepted. With repeated research over time, evidence accumulates on the appropriateness of the findings from any one study. Similarly, theories and proposed solutions to problems evolve with the knowledge obtained from new studies.

◆ ◆ ◆
THE NATURE OF MEASUREMENT

Measurement plays an important role in the scientific process. Hypothesizing that higher levels of cognitive ability are related to higher levels of job performance implies that both cognitive ability and job performance can be measured. *Measurement* is the assignment of numbers to *aspects* of objects or events according to a set of rules or conventions. The act of measuring an abstract construct such as cognitive ability does not differ from measuring more concrete ones such as job performance. The starting point in measurement is to define the construct that is to be measured. What do cognitive ability and job performance mean? Defining *cognitive ability* as "knowing how to use words and numbers" might produce a different set of measurements than defining it as "knowing how to get things done." Both of these definitions are legitimate ways of defining cognitive ability; yet, each emphasizes different *aspects* of the cognitive ability concept. Similarly, *job performance* could be defined to emphasize either quality or quantity aspects. The next step is to select or to develop a set of operations or measurement procedures that will assign numbers to the different objects to reflect the degree of the aspect inherent in the object. The fundamental assumption in measurement is that relations among numbers assigned to the aspects convey information about relations among the objects themselves.

SCALES OF MEASUREMENT

Most people agree that there are four basic sets of rules by which numbers may be assigned to aspects of objects. Each set of rules constitutes a measurement scale, or level of measurement. From the lowest to highest level, these four measurements scales are *nominal, ordinal, interval,* and *ratio.*

NOMINAL SCALES A nominal scale simply uses numbers to assign labels to aspects of objects; for example, categorizing people on the basis of sex by assigning 1 to males and 2 to females. The numbers do not convey any information about the people or objects, or relations between them, except to identify the class or group to which the person or object belongs. The values of the assigned numbers are arbitrary. The number 2 could have been assigned to males and 1 to females, or 16 and 27, or any other two numbers. The higher valued numbers do not imply that members of a group have more of the aspect being measured. The numbers simply denote that the groups, not the objects or people within the groups, are different from one another. Although classification schemes can be quite complex, the only requirement for a nominal scale is that all members of the same class or group are given the same number, that all members or objects are assigned to a group, and that no two different groups are given the same number.

ORDINAL SCALES An ordinal scale uses numbers to rank order people or objects in terms of a selected aspect. A human resources manager might interview four job applicants, Ms. A, Mr. B, Ms. C, and Mr. D, and decide that in terms of knowing how to get things done, Ms. A is the best candidate followed, in order, by Ms. C, Mr. D, and Mr. B. This order is maintained by assigning the numbers 4, 3, 2, and 1 to Ms. A, Ms. C, Mr. D, and Mr. B, respectively. In this case, a higher number reflects a higher rank order. This initial number assignment is arbitrary; rank 1 could just as easily have been assigned to the best candidate, as long as the remaining numbers were assigned in a consistent fashion to reflect the applicant's degree of know-how. The rank ordering implies that Ms. A has more know-how than any of the other three applicants, that Ms. C has more than Mr. D or Mr. B, and that Mr. D has more know-how than Mr. B. More specifically, if Ms. A is superior to Ms. C and Ms. C is superior to Mr. D, then Ms. A must also be superior to Mr. D. Ordinal numbers convey information about order relationships, and nothing more.

Using an ordinal measure is much like using a measuring stick made out of elastic; rank 1 is assigned to the person or object having the highest property and then the stick is pulled as much as needed until rank 2 coincides with the second highest. No matter how much or how little the stick is pulled, the order of the numbers is maintained. Because of this elasticity, ordinal rankings do not convey any information on the magnitude of the difference between the people or objects being measured. The difference in know-how between Ms. C and Mr. D may be very large or very small; the ranking simply means that Ms. C has more of it. Differences between the rank numbers are also meaningless; for example, the difference between Ms. C's and Mr. D's ranks (3–2=1) may represent a very large difference in know-how, while the same difference between Mr. D's and Mr. B's ranks (2–1=1) may represent only a very slight difference. Similarly, comparisons cannot be made between rank orders obtained from different groups. The human resources manager's assistant might have interviewed and rated, from top down, three other job candidates, Mr. X, Ms. Y, and Mr. Z. It is quite possible that Mr. B, the lowest rated candidate in the first group, is far superior to Mr. X, the top rated candidate in the second group. Rank orders apply only within the group on which they were made.

INTERVAL SCALES An interval scale assigns numbers to reflect not only rank order but also the degree of the property being measured. Differences between interval scale values reflect differences in magnitude of the property. An interval scale requires equal distances or units between measured values. Here, the measuring stick is made out of a rigid substance with constant units between each measurement division; the distance between numbers cannot be stretched to give the second-most property the rank of 2 or the third-most, 3. Instead, the property of one person or object being measured is assigned a number from the measuring stick, which reflects the number of constant units between it and the same property of a different person or object. While there is much discussion over how to construct an interval scale, assume that the human resources manager had one available and used it properly to assign numbers to reflect each applicant's degree of know-how. Each applicant received a rating from a 10-point scale where a value of 10 means that a candidate is perfect and 1 that the candidate is unsuited for the job. The manager assigned Ms. A, Ms. C, Mr. D, and Mr. B scores of 8, 4, 3, and 2, respectively. The differences between assigned numbers represent differences in each candidate's degree of know-how. Ms. A has four more units of know how than Ms. C (8–4=4), while Ms. C has one more unit than Mr. D (4–3=1) and two more than Mr. B (4–2=2). The assigned numbers do not tell anything about the actual amount or magnitude of each applicant's know-how, only that each has so many units as measured by the specific interval scale. The numbers on the scale are arbitrary; another scale, starting at 11 and ending at 38, might have produced values of 32, 20, 17, and 14, respectively, for the four candidates. Nonetheless, the differences in assigned values still represent the same differences in candidates' degree of know-how. However, in terms of the scale values, Ms. A now has 12 more units of know-how than Ms. C (32–20=12). All that's happened here is to take the rigid measuring stick and divide it into smaller units with the starting point called 11 rather than 1. Three units on the new measuring stick equal one on the old. This is the same situation as using either a Fahrenheit or Celsius scale to measure temperature; on one the freezing point for water is called 32, on the other it is labelled 0, but they both report the *same* degree of temperature.

Interval scales allow comparisons across groups. If the assistant manager had assigned values of 9, 3, and 1 from the 10-point scale to Mr. X, Ms. Y, and Mr. Z, those applicants could be compared with the other four (assuming that the assistant manager assigned values the same way as did the manager). Likewise, temperatures in Halifax, Montreal, Toronto, Calgary, and Vancouver could be represented by Celsius scale values and compared to those for London, Paris, Amsterdam, and Rome.

The comparisons made with interval measures are limited to assessing differences between the interval scale values. Because interval scales have arbitrary starting points, ratios formed between interval measures are meaningless. Forming a ratio of Ms. A's to Ms. C's scores on the 10-point scale (8 to 4) suggests that Ms. A has twice as much know-how; comparing them on the other scale (32 to 20) shows a different relation. In both cases, the comparison is inappropriate. This is similar to arguing that a temperature of 30° C is twice as hot as one of 15° C, or that one of 80° F is twice as hot as 40° F.

RATIO SCALES Ratio scales require that the measurement scale used to assign values to properties has equal units and that the starting or zero point on the measurement scale represents the total absence of the property being measured. In other words, regardless of the number of divisions on the rigid measuring stick, the values on the stick must be assigned in a way that a zero on the measuring stick represents the condition where no degree of the measured property is present. In this way, all ratio scales have the same starting value and all scale values are referenced to the true absence of the property. If the human resources manager had a scale with a true zero point, a value that could be assigned to a candidate with absolutely no cognitive ability, then ratios formed between values assigned to different candidates would take on meaning. Additionally, the ratio would not be affected by the number of divisions on the scale. With a true zero point, the first scale might assign values of 6 and 3 to Ms. A and Ms. C, respectively; on the other, their assigned values might be 18 and 9. Each scale suggests that Ms. A has twice as much know-how as Ms. C; the relationship holds regardless of the size of the intervals on each scale. A ratio of the scale values gives a direct estimate of the ratio of the magnitude of the property.

◆ ◆ ◆

MEASURING INDIVIDUAL DIFFERENCES FOR SELECTION

For personnel selection, the purpose of measurement is to describe differences among individuals with respect to those constructs that are important to the task at hand. Defining cognitive ability as knowing how to get things done implies that some people have more know-how than others and that numbers can be systematically assigned to represent each person's degree of know-how. Measurement quantifies characteristics of individuals who belong to a specific group or population. Personnel selection generally focuses on quantifying differences between individual job applicants on the basis of their job-related knowledge, skill level, intellectual abilities, personality attributes, and their likelihood to maximize organizational desires or goals. These characteristics remain, for the most part, relatively stable (Ackerman and Humphreys, 1990).

METHODS OF MEASUREMENT

In the above examples, the human resources manager assigned a number to indicate a person's degree of know-how. The manager is assigning a value to a self-report or self-disclosure made by the applicant. There are other methods that the manager could have used to measure know-how (after Sackett and Larson, 1990):

Behavioural observation occurs when someone measures behaviours that are produced by someone else. Behavioural observation may be either direct or indirect. In the first case, an individual is observed and the quality, frequency, or intensity of some aspect of overt behaviour is recorded. For example, the human resources manager might count the number of times a job applicant pauses in mid-sentence during a job interview. Indirect observation focuses on the products of the behaviour rather than on the behaviour itself. A human resources manager might ask applicants for a secretarial position to type a sample document; the number of errors made or the number of words typed per minute by each applicant is an indirect measure of one aspect of their behaviour.

Self-report measures involve individuals responding to a series of questions, or items, which require them to report on their own characteristics. Interviews and questionnaires constitute self-report measures. Self-reports may serve as (1) substitutes for factual information that can be verified (e.g., asking an individual to report their age); (2) a means to assess constructs that may not be easily observed (e.g., having an individual answer a series of questions related to attitudes, values, intentions, and beliefs); or (3) ways in which to measure an individual's perception of events or other people (e.g., asking an employee to rate the abilities required to perform a given task). Self-reports may consist of responses to single items or to a series of related items, in which case an individual's score is derived from the set of items.

Reports about others involve an individual describing the characteristics of another person. For example, employees may complete a survey that asks them to rate how well a series of items describe their supervisor. In another instance, the human resources manager might draw up a report on a job applicant based on an individual's performance during a job interview.

Unobtrusive measures involve the analysis of archives, records, documents, or other physical evidence to make inferences about characteristics of interest. These physical traces are used as proxies for actual behaviour or for internal states of individuals. For example, increase in employee absenteeism following the hiring of a new supervisor might indicate that problems exist between the supervisor and employees.

Each of these different types of measures has strengths and weaknesses. There is no such thing as a perfect measure. However, it is important that the measure being used captures the essence of the characteristic or aspect under consideration. The measure must also assign values to the different characteristics in a fairly consistent manner.

THE NATURE OF OBSERVED SCORES

Many human characteristics that play an important role in personnel selection remain stable over time. Therefore, the same human resources manager should assign the same score to an applicant on two different occasions, or two different managers should assign the same score to the applicant at the same time. However, this does not generally happen because the assigned scores reflect not only the characteristic being measured but also error. The difference in the two scores is attributed to error that varies randomly over time. For example, the second interview with some applicants may have taken place in a noisy environment, causing the manager to miss vital information needed to assign *degree of know-how* scores. Hardly any human characteristic is measured without error. Measurement models deal with errors in different ways. The classical measurement model (Nunnally and Bernstein, 1994), which has had a major impact on personnel research, assumes that any observed score, X, is a combination of a true score, T, and an error score, e, such that:

$$X = T + e$$

This model assumes that the characteristic being measured is stable and that the only reason an observed score changes from one measurement to another is due to random error. Error scores are independent of the characteristic being measured; errors are attributable to the measurement process, not the individual. That is, the magnitude of error scores is unrelated to the magnitude of the characteristic being measured. The error score for an applicant with a very high level of know-how could be very large, or very small; that same situation would hold for any level of know-how. The model also assumes that true scores and error scores combine in a simple additive manner. We will return to this point a bit later after a brief introduction to some statistical concepts that will aid that discussion. If you are familiar with basic statistical concepts you may want to skip ahead to the section on Reliability.

CORRELATION AND REGRESSION

BASIC STATISTICS If a human resources manager interviewed only a few job applicants, it is possible to directly compare the applicants on the basis of their assigned scores. What if there were a very large number of applicants? How would the manager keep track of all the scores? One way is to use statistical procedures to describe important information contained in the set of applicant scores (Kerlinger, 1986). The manager could compute the *mean* or average score. The mean represents the most typical or "average" score that might be expected within a group of scores; it is the one score that best represents the set of scores. Not every applicant has a score that is similar to the mean score. It is also useful to know how different, on average, any one score is from the mean score and from any other score. The *variance* gives this information. The more the observed scores differ from each other and from the mean, the higher the variance; scores that are tightly clustered around a mean score will have a smaller variance. Often in reporting scores the *standard deviation* is used rather than the variance. The standard deviation is the square root of the variance; it is more convenient to use since it presents information in terms of the actual measurement scale. Knowing both the mean and the variance allows the manager to know the score that an average applicant should attain, and how much variability to expect in applicant scores. If most applicant scores fall within one standard deviation from the mean, then someone with a score that exceeds three standard deviations might be considered an exceptional applicant. For example, if the mean were 50 and the size of the standard deviation were 10, most applicant scores normally would fall between 40 and 60. Scores greater than 80 would be exceptional and indicate that an applicant received a very high rating compared to the average applicant; on the other hand, scores less than 20 would indicate that the applicant fared poorly.

CORRELATION Measures of central tendency and variability are quite useful in summarizing a large set of observations. However, in many areas of personnel selection, the relationship between two variables is of considerable interest. The human resources manager is interested in the relationship between cognitive ability and job performance; that is, the degree to which the variation in cognitive ability is associated with the variation in job performance, or the degree to which the variation in job performance can be predicted from the variation in cognitive ability. A *correlation coefficient* is a statistic that presents information on the extent of the relationship between two variables. To establish this correlation, the manager must have two scores for each applicant, one for cognitive ability and the other for job performance. In the case of job applicants, the manager could establish a know-how score based on the interview or through some other test that was administered to each applicant. But the manager would not have a job performance score since this can only be obtained once the applicants are hired. The manager has two options: (1) The applicants are hired and their job performance is evaluated after a period of time; the performance score of each new employee is then paired with the know-how score obtained at the time of application; or (2) A group of existing employees with known job performance scores could be put through the interview process to determine their degree of know-how with both scores paired for each employee. These two approaches are known as *predictive validity* and *concurrent validity*, respectively, and are reviewed later in this chapter as part of the discussion on criterion-related validity.

Table 3.1 presents hypothetical data obtained from existing workers. Each pair of scores for each employee is graphed on a scatterplot where each axis represents a variable. In Figure 3.1 these data points are enclosed with an ellipse to show the relationship between the two variables. In this case the ellipse tends to tilt upward as both cognitive ability and job performance scores increase. This orientation of the ellipse suggests a linear, positive relationship between cognitive ability scores and job performance scores. High cognitive ability scores are associated with high job performance scores. If the ellipse had tilted downward at the high end of the job performance axis and upward at the low end, it would have suggested a linear, negative

			Predicted Job
Employee	Cognitive Ability, X	Job Performance, Y	Performance, Y'
Mr. E	10	7	6.91
Ms. F	4	5	5.11
Mr. G	5	4	5.41
Mr. H	8	6	6.31
Mr. I	2	4	4.51
Ms. J	6	5	5.71
Mr. K	7	5	6.01
Mr. L	3	6	4.81
Ms. M	8	7	6.31
Mr. N	6	8	5.71

TABLE 3.1 MEASURING A RELATIONSHIP BETWEEN COGNITIVE ABILITY AND JOB PERFORMANCE

For the above data:

$r = .56$

$r^2 = .31$

$Y' = .30\,X + 3.91$

relationship, that high cognitive ability scores are associated with low job performance scores.

CORRELATION COEFFICIENTS While the scatterplot gives a good visual indication of the relationship between the two variables, its usefulness becomes limited as the size of the data set increases. The information in a scatterplot is summarized through an index, r, the correlation coefficient. A correlation coefficient indicates both the *size* and *direction* of a linear relationship between two variables. For the data in Table 3.1, $r = 0.56$. Direction indicates the nature of the linear relationship between the two variables. A positive or direct relationship of the type presented in Table 3.1 is signified by a plus sign. Negative or indirect relationships are indicated by minus signs; for example, $r = -.56$ indicates a situation where high cognitive ability scores predicted low job performance scores. The strength or size of the relationship is indicated by the value of the correlation coefficient. A correlation of $r = 1.00$ indicates a perfect positive, linear relationship between two variables, while $r = -1.00$ indicates a perfect negative, linear relationship.

FIGURE 3.1 Cognitive Ability and Job Performance — I

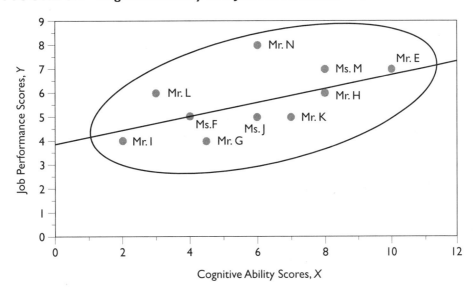

Correlations of $r = 0.00$ signify that there is no linear relationship between the two variables under study. With correlations approaching $r = 0.00$, one variable cannot be used to predict the score on the second variable; knowing the status of the first variable or characteristic does not help you to know anything about the status of the second. The more closely the correlation coefficient approaches a value of either plus or minus 1.00, the more accurately one variable predicts the other.

COEFFICIENT OF DETERMINATION Another index that gives an indication of the strength of a relationship between two variables is r^2, the *coefficient of determination*. This value represents the proportion of variability in one variable that is associated with variability in another. It is the proportion of variability that can be accounted for in one variable by knowing something about a different variable. For Table 3.1, about 31 percent (i.e., $r^2 = .56 \times .56 = .31$) of the variance in job performance ratings can be accounted for by knowing the applicants' cognitive ability scores. Looking at this from a different direction, about 69 percent of the variability in job performance ratings is not related to cognitive ability scores. Both r and r^2 give an indication of the size of a relationship.

SIMPLE REGRESSION The relationship between two variables can also be expressed in terms of a straight line. Remember that a correlation expresses the degree and direction of a linear relationship between two variables. The correlation coefficient is used to derive an equation for a straight line that best fits the data points contained in the scatterplot. This is a *regression line.* The diagonal line in Figure 3.1's scatterplot is the regression line that provides the best fit to the data contained in the ellipse. In regression, one variable is used to predict another. The independent or *predictor variable* is plotted along the X-axis of the scatterplot with the dependent or *criterion variable* plotted along the Y-axis. The equation used to generate the straight line is:

$$Y' = bX + c$$

This equation states that a predicted job performance score, Y', is equal to an individual's cognitive ability score, X, multiplied by b, the regression coefficient, plus c, a constant. The regression coefficient, b, represents the slope of the straight line and the constant, c, represents the intercept, where the line crosses the Y-axis. For the hypothetical data in Table 3.1, $b = .30$, and $c = 3.91$; these values are used to generate a predicted job performance score, Y', for each applicant. These Y' values are also presented in Table 3.1. Notice that the predicted values differ from the actual values; for Mr. E, the difference is relatively small (6.91 v. 7.00) but relatively large for Mr. N (5.71 v. 8.00). The regression line produces the smallest error between predicted and actual values of the criterion variable.

MULTIPLE REGRESSION Many practical situations involve more than two variables. The human resources manager may have not only information about cognitive ability and job performance but also other information obtained from letters of reference and the application form. Each one of these sources of information, on its own, may predict job performance scores to some degree. The set of predictors can be combined into one equation to indicate the extent to which the set, taken as a whole, is related to the criterion variable. The mathematical procedure to compute this equation, while more complicated than the case of two variables, follows the same logic as that for simple regression. Both simple and multiple regression techniques are used to combine information to make human resources decisions.

RELIABILITY

Hardly any human characteristic is measured in an error-free manner. The act of measuring produces a score that measures both the true score and an error component. Reliability is the degree to which observed scores are free from random measurement errors. Reliability is an indication of the stability or dependability of a set of measurements (Kerlinger, 1986). Think of an employer who requires each employee to punch a time clock upon arrival at work. Mr. X, Ms. Y, and Mr. Z, without fail, arrive at work each morning at 8:55 a.m., 8:56 a.m., and 8:57 a.m., respectively. If, on each day, the time clock stamped these same times, exactly, on each employee's time card, the time clock would be considered extremely reliable. The observed score, the time stamped on the time card, is the same as the true score, the time the employees arrived at work; no degree of error has been added to the measurement. On the other hand, if the clock stamped times of 9:03 a.m., 9:00 a.m., and 9:00 a.m. for Mr. X, Ms. Y, and Mr. Z, the measurement would include an error component. Mr. X's time is off by eight minutes, Ms. Y's by four minutes, and Mr. Z's by three minutes. The time clock is not accurate, or reliable, in reporting the time people arrived for work. In this case, the error appears to be unsystematic; the occurrence or degree of the error does not appear to be predictable. Errors may also be systematic; that is, the errors may be made in a consistent, or predictable, fashion. If the time clock were five minutes fast, it would report the three arrival times as 9:00 a.m., 9:01 a.m., and 9:02 a.m. The clock is still reliable in reporting the arrival times of the three employees; but, it is systematically adding five minutes to each worker's time. The observed scores are reliable, but they do not represent the true arrival times. In other words, while the observed scores are accurate, they are not a valid indication of whether the employees started work on time. Systematic errors do not affect the accuracy of the measurements but rather the meaning, or interpretation, of those measurements.

INTERPRETING RELIABILITY COEFFICIENTS

Another way to think of reliability is in terms of the variability of a set of scores. If the measuring instrument is not very accurate, that is, if it adds large random error components to true scores, then the variance of the measured scores should be much larger than the variance of the true scores. Reliability can be thought of as the ratio of true score variance, Var (T), to observed score variance, Var (X); this can be expressed as the following equation:

$$r_{xx} = \frac{\text{Var } (T)}{\text{Var } (X)}$$

where r_{xx} is the reliability coefficient, the degree to which observed scores, which are made on the same stable characteristic, correlate with one another. In this case, r^2 represents the proportion of variance in the observed scores that is attributed to true differences on the measured characteristic. For the arrival times in our example, Var$(T) = 1.0$; for the reported times, Var$(X) = 3.0$, with $r_{xx} = 0.33$. Only 10 percent of the variability in the reported arrival times, $(r_{xx})^2$, is attributable to the true arrival time; the remaining 90 percent of the variability is attributable to the inaccuracy of the time clock. When the time clock is systematically fast by five minutes, Var$(X) = 1.0$, giving an $r_{xx} = 1.00$, the systematic error did not affect the reliability coefficient; the scores are very reliable, but they do not tell anything about the time people actually arrived at work.

FACTORS AFFECTING RELIABILITY

The factors which introduce error into any set of measurements can be organized into three broad categories.

TEMPORARY INDIVIDUAL CHARACTERISTICS Following his interview with the human resources manager, Mr. B is assigned a relatively low score for know-how, which is assumed to be stable over time. If Mr. B were sick on the day of the interview, or extremely anxious or tired, his know-how score might reflect a larger than normal error component. On another occasion when Mr. B is in better shape, he is interviewed again and given a higher know-how score. The difference in the two scores is attributed to the difference in Mr. B's state of well-being, rather than to a change in know-how. Mr. B's ill health negatively affected his performance during the initial interview, leading to a lower score. Factors such as health, motivation, fatigue, and emotional state introduce temporary, unsystematic errors into the measurement process.

LACK OF STANDARDIZATION Changing the conditions under which measurements are made introduces error into the measurement process. Ms. A, Mr. B, Ms. C, and Mr. D are asked different questions during their interviews. Ms. A is interviewed over lunch in a very comfortable restaurant while the other candidates are interviewed in a very austere conference room. Mr. B is given a few minutes to answer each question, but others are given as long as they need. The manager displays a lack of interest in Mr. B during the interview, but reacts very positively to Ms. A. These are just a few of the ways that lack of standardization can enter into the measurement process.

CHANCE Factors unique to a specific procedure introduce error into the set of measurements. Luck of the draw may have done in Mr. B during his interview. His know-how score is based on how he answered a specific set of questions. Mr. B did poorly on the questions he was asked, but he might have done extremely well on any others. Mr. D had no prior experience with interviews while Ms. A knew what to expect from previous experience. Ms. C was distracted and did not understand a critical question.

METHODS OF ESTIMATING RELIABILITY

To measure reliability, we have to estimate the degree of variability in a set of scores that is caused by measurement error. We can obtain this estimate by using two different, but parallel, measures of the characteristic or attribute. Over the same set of people, both measures should report the same score for each individual. This score will represent the true score plus measurement error. Both measures reflect the same true score; discrepancies between the two sets of scores suggest the presence of measurement error. The correlation coefficient based on the scores from both measures gives an estimate of r_{xx}, the reliability coefficient. It is extremely difficult, if not impossible, to obtain two parallel measures of the same characteristic; therefore, several strategies have been developed as approximations of parallel measures.

TEST AND RETEST The identical measurement procedure is used to assess the same characteristic over the same group of people on two different occasions. The human resources manager invites the job applicants back for a second interview. They are asked the same questions in the same order. The correlation of their first and second interview scores estimates the reliability of the know-how scores. High correlations suggest high levels of reliability.

ALTERNATE FORMS Having a person take the same interview twice may lead to a false estimate of the reliability of the interview process. The candidates may recall their original answers to the interview questions; they may also have thought of better answers after the first interview and give the improved answers on the second opportunity. To prevent the intrusion of effects from the first interview, the manager asks the applicants alternate questions during the second interview. The correlation between both know-how scores again estimates reliability, with high correlations once more indicating strong reliability.

INTERNAL CONSISTENCY Both test-retest and alternate forms procedures require two sets of measurements made on different occasions. In the case of interviews, it is quite costly in time and money to put all the candidates through a second interview procedure. Besides, isn't each question in the interview directed at measuring know-how? Why not consider any two questions in the interview to be an example of a test-retest situation, and determine the correlation between scores given to each item in that pair? This is the logic behind establishing reliability through internal consistency. Rather than select any particular pair of items, the correlations between the scores of all possible pairs of items are calculated and then averaged. This average estimates the internal consistency, the degree to which all the questions in the set are measuring the same thing. These estimates are sometimes called *alpha* coefficients, or *Cronbach's alpha*, after the formula used to produce the estimate. *Split-half reliability* is a special case of internal consistency where all the items are first divided into two, arbitrary groups. For example, all the even-numbered items may form one group with the odd-numbered items placed into the second. The correlation over each person's average scores in the two groups is used as the reliability estimate.

INTER-RATER RELIABILITY Measurement in personnel selection is often based on the subjective assessment, or rating, of one individual by another. The human resources manager's assessment of know-how based on the interview is a subjective measurement. How likely would the rating assigned by one judge be assigned by other judges? The correlation between these two judgments estimates the reliability of their assessments. The manager and the assistant manager independently rate each applicant's interview; a high correlation between their two scores suggests that their scores are reliable measures of know-how.

VALIDITY

It is important and necessary to demonstrate that a measure is reliable; it is also necessary to show that the measure captures the essence of the characteristic or attribute. Often, validity is incorrectly thought of as indicating the worth or goodness of a test or other measurement procedure. Validity simply refers to the legitimacy or correctness of the inferences that are drawn from a set of measurements or other specified procedures (Cronbach, 1971). During an employment interview, a human resources manager measures the height of each applicant with a metal measuring tape. These height measurements are likely to be very reliable. What if the manager assumes that taller applicants have more job know-how and hires the tallest people? Are the inferences drawn from the physical height measures valid statements of job know-how? In other words, can the manager make a legitimate inference about know-how from the height data? Could Al Campanis make a legitimate inference about baseball know-how from skin colour?

Before using any set of measurements, it is essential to demonstrate that the measurements lead to valid inferences about the characteristic under study. It is relatively easy to demonstrate that the metal tape provides valid measures of physical height. The metal tape measure can be scaled to an actual physical standard that is used to define a unit of length. The standard exists apart from the measurement process. In the case of length, the standard is a bar of plutonium maintained under specific atmospheric conditions in government laboratories. It is more difficult to demonstrate the validity of inferences made from many psychological measurements because they deal more with abstract constructs, such as cognitive ability or know-how. In most of these cases, independent physical standards for the construct do not exist, making validation more difficult, but not impossible.

VALIDATION STRATEGIES

There are three different, but interrelated, strategies that are commonly used to assess validity. These three different strategies do not mean that there are three different types of validity; validity is a unitary concept (Binning and Barrett, 1989). Figure 3.2 illustrates these three related validation strategies using the know-how data collected by the human resources manager. The manager initially hypothesized that higher levels of cognitive ability were related to higher levels of job performance; this relationship is represented

FIGURE 3.2 **Validation Strategies**

Construct Level

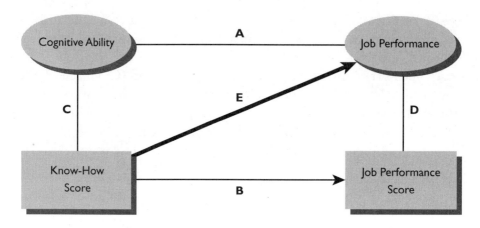

Measurement Level

by Line A. Both cognitive ability and job performance are abstract constructs, which we operationally defined, respectively, as know-how scores based on the employment interview and a job performance score derived from an assessment of an employee's work. Figure 3.2 also presents the relationships between these two constructs and their two measurements; these different relationships help to distinguish between the different validation strategies.

CONSTRUCT VALIDITY Construct validity is the degree to which a set of measures or a measurement procedure captures the essence of an abstract construct. It is the extent to which inferences can be made about an unobserved, abstract construct based on a set of observed measurements. In Figure 3.2, the relationship represented by Line C illustrates construct validity. The issue here is the extent to which inferences based on know-how scores apply to the construct of cognitive ability. If Ms. C has a higher know-how score than Mr. B, can we make the inference that Ms. C has more cognitive ability than Mr. B? Line D also represents a case of construct validation: the degree to which valid inferences can be made about the job performance construct from the measured job performance scores. In other words, do the two measures, know-how and job performance scores, measure the two constructs, cognitive ability and job performance, that they purport to measure? Establishing the construct validity of a measure is often a very difficult procedure. The first step is to clearly define the construct and to identify observable behaviours or events that are related to the construct. The next is to identify the relationships between the construct and other constructs that may be related to it. An analysis of the pattern of relationships is used to establish whether a measure validly represents the construct.

CONTENT VALIDITY Content validity is a special case of construct validity. Each construct has a set of associated behaviours or events; in any measurement situation, only a relatively small handful of these behaviours are measured. For example, 10 questions are used to test your knowledge of the content of this chapter. Based on the number of correct answers, your professor makes an inference about your *knowledge of scientific methods.* Is the inference justified; that is, do the 10 questions measure knowledge of scientific methods? Content validity is based on the consensus of a group of experts that the behaviours being measured do, in fact, fairly represent the behaviours associated with the construct. It is a judgmental process. The content validity of the 10 questions used to measure knowledge of scientific methods could be established by a review of those questions by several experts on scientific methods. Their agreement that the questions fairly represented the information contained in this chapter constitutes content validity.

In Figure 3.2, the same relationships that were examined through construct validation strategies, Line C and Line D, may also be examined through content validation, although this may be easier to do in the case of job performance than cognitive ability. Content validation is more useful when dealing with a construct whose associated behaviours and events are well-defined and clearly understood. The behaviours related to job performance are likely to be fewer and more specific than those related to cognitive ability. A group of experts may find it easier to agree that the measured job behaviours fairly represent job performance than the know-how questions represent the full extent of cognitive ability.

FACE VALIDITY Sometimes content validity is confused with face validity. Face validity is not a recognized validation strategy. It is used to indicate that someone, on the basis of a superficial examination of a test's contents, believes that the test is measuring what it purports to measure. The 10 questions used to measure knowledge of scientific methods may use terms and words found in this chapter and may appear to a non-expert to be valid; however, after detailed examination, a group of subject matter experts may disagree. Face validity raises an interesting issue. On occasion, highly valid tests or measures are not used because "on their face" they do not appear, to non-experts, to be measuring what they are supposed to measure.

CRITERION-RELATED VALIDITY A criterion is an outcome measure; it assesses the degree of success or failure associated with some decision. Job applicants are selected for employment; over time, some of the applicants perform at a higher level than others. Measures of job performance are criterion measures. In selecting job applicants, one goal is to hire only those applicants who will perform at very high levels. But, the applicants have to be hired before job performance can be measured. Is there another variable, which is correlated with job performance that can be measured prior to hiring the applicant? Can we use information from this pre-employment measure to make valid inferences about how an individual will perform once in the job? This is the goal of criterion-related validation.

In Figure 3.2, Line B expresses criterion-related validity. Know-how scores, based on the pre-employment interview, are used to predict job performance scores. The arrow on the line indicates that a prediction is being made from one measure to the other. Criterion-related validation involves establishing a correlation between two measures. However, both those measures must validly represent their underlying constructs. While criterion-related validity focuses on the observable measures, the relationship that is of primary interest is represented in Figure 3.2 by Line E. What the human resources manager really wants to do is predict, or make an inference about, the job performance construct from the know-how scores. As before, Line E represents construct validation; unlike previous cases, the behaviours (know-how scores) associated with one construct (cognitive ability) are measured and associated with a second construct (job performance), which is assumed to be related to the first. Before the manager can conclude that know-how scores predict the job performance construct, the manager must show that both the predictor, know-how scores, and criterion, job performance scores, are valid measures of their respective constructs *and* that a strong relationship exists between the predictor and criterion measures. Unfortunately, many criterion-related validity studies suffer from a failure to demonstrate that the criterion measure is a valid measure of the job performance construct.

PREDICTIVE VALIDITY As mentioned earlier in this chapter, *predictive validation* and *concurrent validation* strategies are types of criterion-related validity. They are the most popular strategy used to validate selection systems. Predictive validation is based on establishing a correlation between predictor scores obtained before an applicant is hired with criteria (performance scores) obtained after an applicant is employed. If all those who apply are hired, both variables can be measured, but at a substantial cost. Many applicants will be hired with the knowledge that they will likely fail on the job. This is not only expensive for the organization but causes a great deal of emotional distress for those applicants who fail. This procedure also raises serious legal and ethical considerations about the rights of job applicants and the obligations of people who make hiring decisions. To circumvent these problems, a variation on this procedure requires that hiring decisions are made without using information from the predictor measure; the hiring decisions are made according to existing procedures while the new predictor is validated. The human resources manager places all the applicants through the interview and collects know-how scores, but the hiring decision is based solely on information contained in the applicants' résumés and references. Job performance information is then collected from the group of hired applicants and correlated with their know-how scores. If the correlation is high, the know-how score is used to select future job applicants. But, there is a problem with this procedure as well. Validity concerns the correctness of inferences made from a set of measurements. Does the validity coefficient, which is based on only those applicants who were hired, apply to all applicants? This will only be the case if the hired applicants fairly represent the total pool of applicants; the only way this can happen is if those hired were randomly selected from the larger pool. Therefore, those who are hired on the basis of the existing selection system will likely differ from those not hired on at least one characteristic, whether or not that characteristic is related to job success.

CONCURRENT VALIDITY Concurrent validation strategies collect predictor and criterion information at the same time from a specific group of workers. The human resources manager interviews all current employees and assigns each a know-how score; at the same time each worker is also assigned a job performance score. While concurrent validation approaches may be easier to carry out, they, too, are problematic. The group of existing workers used to develop the concurrent validity coefficient are likely to be older, more experienced, and certainly more successful than those who apply for jobs. Unsuccessful or unproductive workers most likely are not part of the validation study as they probably were let go or transferred to other positions. The primary concern here is whether a validity coefficient based on only successful applicants can be used to validate decisions based on predictor scores from a pool of both successful and unsuccessful applicants. An additional concern is the same one expressed with predictive validation; does the validity coefficient computed on one group of workers apply to the pool of applicants? Statistically, concurrent validity coefficients will likely underestimate the true validity of using the predictor to make decisions within the pool of applicants.

VALIDITY GENERALIZATION Suppose in attempting to establish the validity of the know-how interview as a predictor of job performance, the human resources manager discovered that there were many other studies which also investigated measures of cognitive ability as predictors of job performance. Could the manager somehow combine all the information provided by these other correlation coefficients to obtain an estimate of the true validity of cognitive ability as a predictor of job performance? These other validity coefficients were obtained under vastly different measurement conditions and from employees who differ dramatically across these studies on a number of characteristics. In other words, can the manager estimate the validity of know-how scores as a predictor of job performance from the validity of inferences based on other measures of cognitive ability found in other work settings with other groups of workers?

Starting in the mid-1970s, Schmidt and Hunter (1977), in conjunction with several colleagues, challenged the idea that a validity coefficient was specific to the context or environment in which it was measured. They used a procedure known as *meta-analysis* to combine validity coefficients for similar predictor and criterion measures reported by different validity studies. In combining the data, meta-analysis weights the results according to the size of the study (i.e., the number of people in the study). On the whole, the smaller the study size, the less accurate the results. Validity studies usually involve relatively small study sizes since most organizations do not hire large numbers of people. Schmidt and Hunter demonstrated that, once the effects associated with study size were removed, the validity between a predictor and a criterion remained relatively stable within similar occupations. For example, the human resources manager could use the know-how interview scores to make predictions about job performance if other validity studies had linked cognitive ability to job performance for similar jobs and if the know-how scores were a valid measure of cognitive ability.

FACTORS AFFECTING VALIDITY COEFFICIENTS

RANGE RESTRICTION When measurements are made on a subgroup which is more homogeneous than the larger group from which it is selected, validity coefficients obtained on the subgroup are likely to be smaller than those obtained from the larger group. This reduction in the size of the validity coefficient due to the selection process is called range restriction. Selection results in a more homogeneous group. The applicant pool reviewed by the human resources manager contains a broad range of know-how. The people selected for employment are more likely to fall in the upper range of know-how; the existing workers are also more likely to have levels of know-how more similar to one another than to the applicant pool. The range of know-how scores for the hired workers is narrower or more restricted than the scores of all the applicants. Statistically, the magnitude of correlation coefficients, including validity coefficients, decreases as the similarity or homogeneity of characteristics being measured increases. There are several statistical procedures that correct for range restriction and provide an estimate of what the validity coefficient is likely to be in the larger group.

MEASUREMENT ERROR The reliability of a measure places an upper limit on validity. Mathematically, the size of a validity coefficient cannot exceed the reliability of the measures used to obtain the data. Validity coefficients obtained from perfectly reliable measures of the predictor and criterion will be higher than those obtained with less than perfect measures. The decrease in magnitude of the validity coefficient associated with measurement error of the predictor, the criterion, or both, is called *attenuation*. As with range restriction, there are statistical procedures that provide an estimate of what the validity coefficient would be if it had been obtained by using measures that were perfectly reliable (i.e., $r_{xx} = 1.00$).

SAMPLING ERROR Criterion-related validity coefficients are obtained from people who have been hired and are used to assess the accuracy of inferences that are made about individual applicants. The validity coefficient based on a sample is an estimate of what the coefficient is in the entire population; usually, it is impractical or impossible to measure the validity coefficient directly in the population. Estimates of the validity within a population may vary considerably between samples; estimates from small samples are likely to be quite variable.

◆ ◆ ◆
BIAS AND FAIRNESS

BIAS

In discussing reliability, we noted that measurement errors could be made in a consistent, or predictable, fashion. In the time clock example, five minutes were added to each worker's arrival time. What if the clock had added five minutes only to the arrival times of female employees? The observed scores are still reliable, but now they validly represent the true arrival times for male employees, but not females. The clock is biased in measuring arrival times of female employees. *Bias* refers to systematic errors in measurement, or inferences made from measurements, which are related to group membership characteristics such as age, sex, or race (Jensen, 1980). For example, the human resources manager assigns higher know-how scores to females, when in fact there are no differences in cognitive ability between men and women. Inferences, or predictions, drawn from the biased measurements are themselves biased. Figure 3.3 illustrates a hypothetical situation where the cognitive ability scores of females are higher, on average, than those for the males, reflecting some type of systematic error. This is the same scatterplot given in Figure 3.1 (page 97) but with the data for Ms. F and Mr. E, and Ms. J and Mr. H, reversed. Therefore, it will have the same regression line as given in Table 3.1 on page 96. Now, Ms. F's job performance score is predicted to be 6.91 versus 5.11 previously; Ms. J's is predicted to be 6.31 versus 5.71. The regression line, using the biased cognitive ability measure as a predictor, overestimates the likely job performance of the female employees and underestimates that of males. If this regression line were used to make hiring decisions (e.g., "We want employees who will obtain performance scores of 6 or better, so hire only applicants with cognitive ability scores of 8 or higher"), the predictions of successful job performance would be biased in favour of the female applicants. There are other, more complicated types of bias that might occur in a set of measurements (Sackett and Wilk, 1994). However, the statistical procedures needed to establish bias are often compli-

FIGURE 3.3 **Cognitive Ability and Job Performance — II**

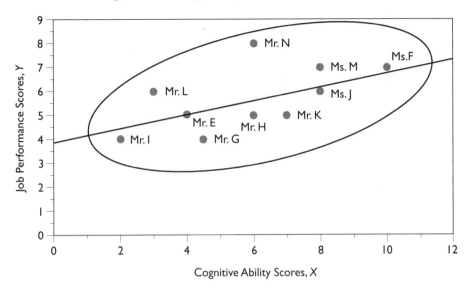

cated and difficult to carry out. Nonetheless, the question of bias can be answered through empirical and objective procedures.

FAIRNESS

The concept of *fairness* in measurement refers to the value judgments people make about the decisions or outcomes that are based on measurements. An unbiased measure or test may still be viewed as being unfair either by society as a whole or by different groups within it. Canada is a bilingual country composed of French and English language groups. Suppose a completely unbiased cognitive ability test were used to select people for the Canadian civil service and that all the francophone applicants scored well above the highest scoring anglophone. Such cognitive ability scores would predict that francophones do better on the job than anglophones; only francophones would be hired for the civil service. This outcome would very likely be judged as unfair by English-speaking Canadians even though it would be the empirically correct decision. Canadians might expect their civil service to represent both official language groups. In fact, political considerations might require that the civil service be proportional to the two linguistic groups. Issues of fairness cannot be determined statistically or empirically. Fairness involves perceptions. An organization may believe it is fair to select qualified females in place of higher ranking males in order to increase the number of women in the organization; on the other hand, the higher ranking males who were passed over might not agree. Achieving fairness often requires compromise between conflicting interests (Gottfredson, 1994; Sackett and Wilk, 1994).

In addition to the concerns about the impact of tests on different groups, fairness issues also include the reaction of applicants to testing and personnel selection decisions. It is important from business, ethical , and legal standpoints to have tests that are scientifically sound; it is also important to have procedures that are perceived as fair. From a business perspective, the adverse reactions to selection tests and procedures may impair the ability of an organization to recruit and hire the best applicants, thereby reducing the utility of the recruitment and selection process. From an ethical view, the perceived fairness of the testing procedures may negatively affect the unsuc-cessful candidates. From a legal perspective, the perception of unfairness may lead unsuccessful applicants to pursue discrimination charges against the prospective employer in various legal arenas (Gilliland, 1993). Serious consideration should be given to the perception of a test or selection proce-dure from the applicant's perspective prior to its adoption. This does not mean that an employer should discard scientifically valid procedures because they may be perceived as unfair; there is far more risk borne by an organiza-tion that makes employment decisions on the basis of unproven methods. In the final analysis, fairness is a question of balance.

♦ ♦ ♦
UTILITY ANALYSIS

At this point, the human resources manager's boss might ask whether using scientific procedures for selection is worthwhile. After all, the validity proce-dures outlined in this chapter take time and money to implement with no guarantee that they will be free of bias or that they will be perceived as fair. Furthermore, validity coefficients that have not been adjusted to account for range restriction, attenuation, and sampling error mostly fall in the range from 0.30 to 0.40, accounting for 16 percent or less of the variability in outcome measures. These are legitimate questions. The manager must be able to demonstrate that scientific selection produces benefits or advantages to the organization that exceed the cost of operating the selection system. Utility analysis is a method of evaluating selection systems by determining the net gains that accrue to the organization from their use.

TAYLOR-RUSSELL UTILITY MODEL

Taylor and Russell (1939) developed a procedure to demonstrate the practical effectiveness of selection systems. The procedure relied not only on the validity coefficient but also on two other conditions that influenced the worth of the system, the selection ratio and base rate. The *selection ratio* is the proportion of job applicants selected for positions in the company. *Base rate* is the proportion of applicants who would be successful had all the applicants been hired. The base rate can be estimated from available employment data. For the performance data in Table 3.1, a company considers any employee who obtains a score of 6 or above to be a success. Figure 3.4 shows that five of the employees are at or above this level of performance; therefore, the base rate is 0.50. Half the workers hired through the current

FIGURE 3.4 Cognitive Ability and Job Performance — III

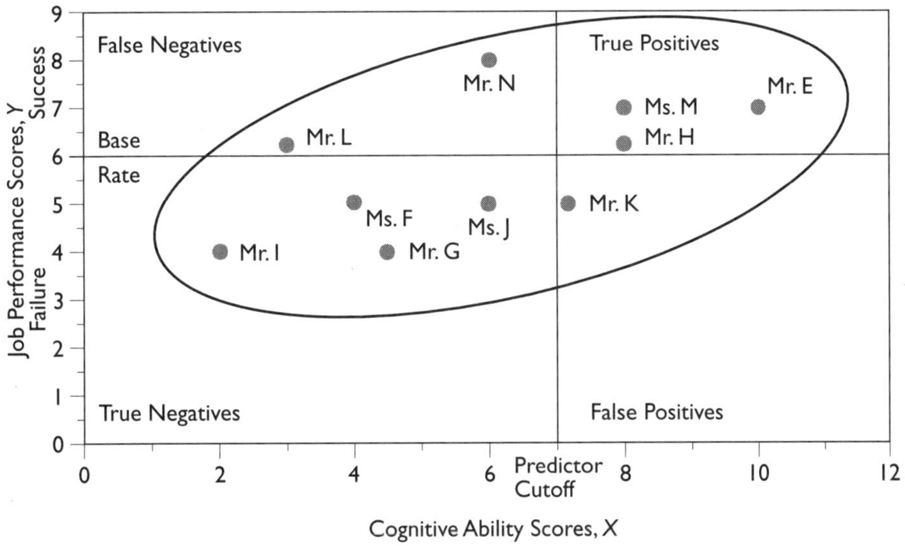

Base Rate = .50

Selection Ratio = .40

Validity = .56

selection system are satisfactory. What if only four positions were open when these people originally applied for work, and selection had been based on cognitive ability as measured through the know-how interview? The selection ratio would be 0.40 (i.e., 4 out of 10 applicants are hired). Using the regression line previously established for this group, cognitive ability scores equal to or greater than 7 predict performance scores that are equal to or greater than 6. Selecting the four applicants with the highest cognitive ability scores would lead to the employment of Mr. E, Ms. M, Mr. H, and Mr. K.

The intersection of the lines representing the base rate and selection ratio divide the scatterplot into four quadrants, representing four different outcomes of the selection process. *True positives* represent those applicants predicted to be a success who actually are successful, in this case Mr. E, Ms. M, and Mr. H. *False positives* are those predicted to be successful who turn out to be unsatisfactory employees, in this case Mr. K. *False negatives* are those who were predicted to be unsatisfactory but would be successful if hired, in this case Mr. L and Mr. N. *True negatives* are those predicted to be unsatisfactory and would be so if hired, in this case Ms. F, Mr. G, Mr. I, and Ms. J. (These four outcomes are discussed in greater detail in Chapter 10.) Taylor and Russell defined the *success rate* as the proportion of applicants hired through the selection system who are judged satisfactory. Three of the four people hired fall into this category, producing a Success Rate =0.75. If the success rate is greater than the base rate, as it is here (0.75 v. 0.50), the selection system is considered to be useful since it leads to a greater proportion of successful hires than would otherwise be the case.

The success rate is determined by the specific base rate, selection ratio, and validity that applies in any given situation. Changing the selection ratio, effectively moving the cutoff line to the left or right in Figure 3.4, or the base rate, moving the base rate line up or down, would alter the number of people falling in each quadrant and would have an impact on the success rate. A different validity, changing the orientation or shape of the oval, would also affect the success rate. Taylor and Russell produced a series of tables, which estimate the success rate for any given combination of validity, base rate, and selection ratio.

BROGDEN/CRONBACH/GLESER UTILITY MODEL

The Taylor-Russell model evaluates the worth of a selection system in terms of an increase in the percentage of successful workers that are hired through the system. It assumes that workers fall into only two categories: successful or unsuccessful. However, most workers vary in the degree of success they exhibit in doing their jobs. Those who are more successful are more valuable employees because they increase the overall productivity of an organization. Can this overall increase in productivity, or utility, be established for selection systems? If so, then comparison of the utility figures reflect the relative worth of different selection systems. Higher utility values indicate that the selection process has added well-qualified, more productive workers to the organization. Over the years several researchers have developed a formula for calculating the utility of a selection test or system (Brogden, 1949; Cronbach and Gleser, 1965):

$$u = nr_{xy}sd_{yz}z_x - c$$

where u = the increase in utility or productivity in one year from hiring n employees through the selection system;

n = the number of employees hired with the selection system;

r_{xy} = the criterion-related validity coefficient

sd_y = the standard deviation of job performance

z_x = the average, standardized predictor score of the employees hired through the selection system; and

c = the total costs involved in obtaining the new employees, including pro-rated costs associated with development of the system.

This formula shows that the benefit that accrues from each person hired through the selection system is related not only to the size of the validity coefficient but also to the standard deviation of job performance of the employees and the average predictor score of the hired employees. A large standard deviation suggests that there is great variability in job performance among the workers. A selection system, for any validity coefficient, will be more valuable in this situation, since the outcome of the selection process may result in hiring someone who is either exceptionally good or exceptionally bad. If all the workers, once hired, perform at relatively the same level, the selection system will have less impact on productivity. The average standardized score on the predictor, which is related to the selection ratio, indicates the extent to which top candidates were hired,. Z scores closer to zero suggest that people of average ability were hired, while Z scores greater than

1.0 suggest that on average the best candidates were selected. The best candidates should add more value to the organization. The net benefit is obtained by subtracting the cost of developing and operating the selection system. Costs can be quite variable, ranging from a few dollars to administer a paper and pencil test to several million to develop a system to select jet pilots.

Different estimation procedures can be used to express sd_y as a dollar value, which then allows a dollar figure to be placed on the actual productivity gain (Boudreau, 1991), although not everyone agrees with the appropriateness or need to do this (Latham and Whyte, 1994). The dollar-valued gain in productivity can be considerable when a large number of employees are being hired, giving rise to questions about the credibility of such values to people outside the human resources field. For example, Cronshaw (1986) showed that the use of a selection test battery by the Canadian Forces resulted in a gain of close to $3 million per year for the 417 people selected for a clerical/administrative trade group. If this figure is multiplied by the number of years an average person remains in this job category, the utility increases to over $51 million. Nonetheless, the utility formula, either in dollar or non-dollar form, allows a comparison of different selection systems in terms of the productivity they bring to an organization. If nothing else, the Brogden-Cronbach-Gleser model demonstrates the significant gains that may accrue through a scientifically based selection system.

◆ ◆ ◆
SUMMARY

Science produces information that is based on accepting as true only that objective information that can withstand continued attempts to cast doubt on its accuracy. The accuracy of scientific statements is examined empirically through methods that can be observed, critiqued, and used by others. Scientific information is dynamic and constantly evolving. One goal of personnel selection is to use scientifically derived information to predict which job applicants will do well on the job. Scientific procedures allow for the measurement of important human characteristics that may be related to job performance. The reliability and validity of the information used as part of personnel selection procedures must be established empirically. The methods used to establish reliability and validity can be quite complex and require a good statistical background. As a scientific process, any personnel selection system must be able to withstand attempts to cast doubt on its value; utility analysis provides a means of examining the net benefits that accrue to an organization from selecting people with scientific procedures.

EXERCISES

1. Measure the length of your classroom without using a measuring tape or ruler. Describe the standard of measurement you chose to use. What are the difficulties inherent in using a standard such as the one you chose?

2. Have at least three different people measure the length of the room using your standard of measurement. How similar are their measurements? What does this imply about the accuracy of your measure? What does this imply about the accuracy of the observers?

3. Choose a specific job held by one of the people in your group. After discussing the job, choose one characteristic that you think is crucial to performing that job.. How would you measure both the characteristic and job performance? Use Figure 3.2 to help you specify the conceptual and measurement levels.

4. Describe a procedure that could be used to establish the validity of your characteristic as a predictor of job performance.

5. Assume that Figure 3.4 represents the relationship between your predictor and a measure of job performance. Discuss why you would not want to set the predictor cutoff extremely high. What would an extremely high predictor cutoff mean in terms of recruitment?

References

Ackerman, P.L., and L.G. Humphreys. 1990. "Individual Differences Theory in Industrial and Organizational Psychology." In M.D. Dunnette and L.M. Hough, eds. *Handbook of Industrial and Organizational Psychology*, Vol. 1. 2nd ed. Palo Alto: Consulting Psychologists Press, 223–82.

Binning, J.F., and G.V. Barrett. 1989. "Validity of Personnel Decisions: A Conceptual Analysis of the Inferential and Evidential Bases." *Journal of Applied Psychology* 74: 478–94.

Boudreau, J.W. 1991. "Utility Analysis for Decisions in Human Resource Management." In M.D. Dunnette and L.M. Hough, eds., *The Handbook of Industrial and Organizational Psychology*, Vol. 2. 2nd ed. Palo Alto: Consulting Psychologists Press, 621–745

Brogden, H.E. 1949. "When Testing Pays Off." *Personnel Psychology* 2, 171–83.

Cronbach, L.J. 1971. "Test Validation." In R.L. Thorndike, ed. *Educational Measurement*, 2nd ed. Washington, DC: American Council of Education.

Cronbach, L., and G. Gleser. 1965. *Psychological Tests and Personnel Decisions*. Urbana, IL: University of Illinois Press.

Cronshaw, S.F. 1986 . "The Utility of Employment Testing for Clerical/Administrative Trades in the Canadian Military. *Canadian Journal of Administrative Sciences* 3, 376–85.

Gilliland, S.W. 1993. "The Perceived Fairness of Selection Systems: An Organizational Justice Perspective." *Academy of Management Review* 18, 694–734.

Gottfredson, L.S. 1994. "The Science and Politics of Race-norming." *American Psychologist* 49, 955–63.

Jensen, A.S.R. 1980. *Bias in Mental Testing*. New York: Free Press.

Kerlinger, F.N. 1986. *Foundations of Behavioral Research*, 3rd ed. New York: Holt, Rinehart and Winston.

Latham, G.P., and G. Whyte. 1994. "The Futility of Utility Analysis." *Personnel Psychology* 47, 31–46.

"The Reform Party's Days of Discontent." 1996. *Maclean's*, May 20, 21–22.

Nunnally, J.C., and I.H. Bernstein. 1994. *Psychometric Theory*, 3rd ed. New York: McGraw-Hill.

Sackett, P.R., and S.L. Wilk. 1994. "Within-Group Norming and Other Forms of Score Adjustment in Pre-employment Testing." *American Psychologist* 49, 929–54.

Sackett, P.R., and J.R. Larson, Jr. 1990. "Research Strategies and Tactics in Industrial and Organizational Psychology." In M.D. Dunnette and L.M. Hough, eds. *Handbook of Industrial and Organizational Psychology*, Vol. 1, 2nd ed. Palo Alto: Consulting Psychologists Press, 419–90.

Schmidt, F.L., and J.E. Hunter. 1977. "Development of a General Solution to the Problem of Validity Generalization." *Journal of Applied Psychology* 62, 529–40.

Taylor, H.C., and J.F. Russell. 1939. "The Relationship of Validity Coefficients to the Practical Effectiveness of Tests in Selection: Discussion and tables." *Journal of Applied Psychology* 23, 565–78.

Whitehead, A.N. 1967. *Science and the Modern World*. New York: Free Press.

4

Organization

and

Job Analysis

♦ ♦ ♦

CHAPTER GOALS

This chapter begins with a discussion of organizational analysis and its relevance to the recruitment and selection of employees and ends with a discussion of several job analysis techniques. After reading this chapter you should

♦ be able to describe the purposes of organizational analysis and its relation to human resources recruitment and selection;

♦ understand organizational structures and the evolution of organizations from hierarchical to vertical process-based structures;

♦ be familiar with three levels of analysis in any organization;

♦ recognize some useful tools for conducting organizational, process, and job analyses;

♦ be able to describe guidelines for conducting analyses employing a variety of job analysis techniques; and

♦ recognize processes for identifying personnel specifications to be used in recruitment and selection of human resources.

♦ ♦ ♦

ORGANIZATION ANALYSIS: A MACRO PERSPECTIVE ON RECRUITMENT AND SELECTION NEEDS

Canadian organizations have faced growing challenges to productivity and survival during the past two decades, issues discussed in detail in Chapter 11. Contributing factors include government deregulation, increasing global competition, free trade, rapidly changing technology, and consumers who have come to expect more for their money. One result has been the explosion of schemes for improving organizational performance. From the quality audits and quality circles of the late 1970s through the current total quality philosophy of the 1980s and 1990s, quality improvement programs have taken firm hold in Canadian organizations. Unfortunately, as many organizational consultants have discovered, "piecemeal approaches that are assumed to be *the* answer are as dangerous as no response at all" (Rummler and Brache, 1990, 2).

Inefficient improvement programs, including those in human resources recruitment and selection, can be avoided if the organization is viewed as a dynamic system. Function rather than structure is critical to the organizational systems model, and the organization is defined as a set of interactive functions rather than a collection of discrete departments. This model proposes that the organization exists to fulfill its strategic goals; it is made up of subsystems (e.g., departments and functions) that produce outputs contributing to the achievement of those goals.

The automobile is a useful analogy to a dynamic system that lends itself to easy examination. The subsystems that taken together make up the total system include the internal combustion system, the electrical system, the fuel system, the drive train, the exhaust system, and the cooling, brake, and lubrication systems. No single one of these subsystems makes up the total system *automobile*, nor does an automobile simply comprise the total collection of these subsystems. That is, we could dump these subsystems together in a pile and have nothing more than a heap of unsightly junk. Whether we are describing automobiles or organizations, it is the interactions and connections between each of the subsystems that make a healthy operating system. And, like an automobile, an organization functions within a physical environment (e.g., the physical plant and the external environment) that merits consideration when describing the system or problem solving within it. Unlike the automobile, however, the organization also functions within a cultural environment that adds another layer of unique constraints on its functioning.

Mechanical systems typically require little human intervention; the automobile may be started up by a human and proceed to idle on the spot with no further human mediation (at least until it runs out of fuel). Under these conditions the automobile is best described as an input-throughput-output system (i.e., fuel is input into the system, is processed through the system, and exits the system as an output called exhaust). To progress from point A to point B, however, more complex human activity is required.

Human behaviour drives operating systems (automobiles and organizations) while simultaneously placing unique constraints on how those systems function. Because individuals are responsible for system operation at every level, and human behaviour varies with individuals and situations, organizational effectiveness can be directly linked to the effectiveness of subsystems and individuals within those subsystems (Katz and Kahn, 1978). A dynamic systems view leads the analyst to focus on the organization's overall strategic goal when intervening within any part of the system or its component subsystems. The key objective of this approach is to promote performance at all levels that contributes to optimal outputs from the organizational system.

The recruitment and selection functions of human resources departments make two major contributions to the organization. First, they exist to maximize the probability of making accurate selection decisions about applicants, thus placing individual performers within each operating subsystem of the organization. Second, in participating in these placement decisions, they directly influence the level of functioning of every other subsystem in the organization. It should be noted here that human resources departments are often actively involved in quality of worklife issues. Although the debate about the nature of the relationship between job performance and job satisfaction has yet to be settled, research has suggested that good work performance tends to lead to enhanced quality of worklife as indicated by the amount of job satisfaction experienced by individual employees (e.g., Wanous, 1974). Additionally, job satisfaction is moderately correlated with absenteeism; thus, it is to the benefit of the organization and the individual job incumbents to select those who are likely to perform successfully. In order for recruitment and selection specialists to make the best possible decisions, an organizational analysis should provide the backdrop for all human resources initiatives.

PURPOSE OF ORGANIZATION ANALYSIS

Organization analysis, the study of the organizational system and its components (subsystems), serves the following functions:

1. Identification of an organization's overall goals.
2. Description of the environmental constraints in which the organization operates.

3. Definition of the functions of and relationships between organizational components.

4. Assessment of the capabilities of the system and its components relative to the strategic goals.

5. Identification of gaps in the system that must be addressed in order to promote optimal system functioning.

Information obtained through organizational analysis can provide a valuable context for the operation of human resources programs. When the guiding principles of the organization are laid out as goals, and the environment in which the organization operates is defined, recruitment and selection processes can effectively contribute to the long-term survival of the organization. That is, human resources recruitment and selection programs no longer function solely to attract people to fill positions; human capital is assessed in an organization analysis as an essential component of system capabilities and is addressed on a system-wide level when gaps are evident. The following sections address how organization analyses are conducted and how the information gained is used to address system needs.

CHARTING ORGANIZATIONAL RELATIONSHIPS

The traditional view of organizations is evident in the organizational chart. Typically, such charts show a top-down view of the departments and positions that make up organizations. Figure 4.1 presents a generic organizational chart. The CEO is placed at the top of the chart; a collection of senior managers report directly to the top. Each senior manager may be responsible for one or more departments. Within each of these departments exists a department manager to whom function or area supervisors report. Each supervisor is responsible for many employees. This view of the organization tends to promote *chart management* rather than the management of critical processes and human performance systems (Rummler and Brache, 1990). It is a structural view of the organization, which fails to capture the functional links between the departments and between individuals within those departments.

Hierarchical charts have dominated organization design since the onset of the Industrial Revolution. Weber (1947) concluded that top-down authority protected the organization from abuse of power and thus improved both organizational functioning and individual employee well-being.

FIGURE 4.1 **Conventional Organizational Chart**

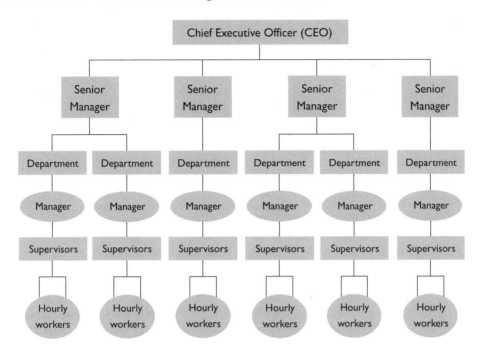

Organizational theory held that the "people actually doing the work have neither the time nor the inclination to monitor and control it and that they lack the depth and breadth of knowledge required to make decisions about it" (Hammer and Champy, 1993, 53).

The vertical view of the organization, where authority flows from the top down, is becoming a liability. Kiechel (1993) identified trends in organizational design that are rapidly accelerating. Three of these trends have the potential to significantly influence job analyses and recruitment and selection of human resources:

◆ The average company will become smaller, employing fewer people.

◆ The traditional hierarchical organization will give way to a variety of organizational forms, the network of specialists foremost among these.

◆ Work itself will be redefined: constant learning, more high-order thinking, less nine-to-five. (39)

As the Canadian marketplace becomes more competitive, and technology continues to evolve, many organizations have responded by re-engineering their organizational structures. Downsizing and rightsizing have become the nomenclature of the '80s and '90s. A recent article in *Fortune* magazine notes that "corporate restructuring fever has held pitch for over a decade now— some 400 000 hapless folks got the boot during 1995 alone" (Labich, 1996, 65). Data from Statistics Canada show that although the total Canadian labour force grew by 4.2 percent from 1990 to 1995, unemployment increased by 22.2 percent during the same period (Statistics Canada, 1996). Further, although public demand for products and services has continued to grow, fewer people are now employed in goods manufacturing, primary industries, construction, and trades. As the traditional hierarchical structure gives way, organizations are more often seeking employees who can adapt to constantly changing dynamic systems rather than hiring for a given set of skills or job expertise (Longo, 1995). One large organizational consulting group (Deloitte and Touche, 1995, 1) asserts that:

> In a world of ever-shorter product cycles and nimble global competitors who can quickly copy new technology innovations, it's the three T's—talent, training and teamwork—that win. There's only one differentiable element in global competition anymore—who's got the better people.

Empowerment of employees and a process-based view of organizational performance means that individuals are now placed in positions where decision-making and control over job processes is part of their daily work experience. Organizations are getting leaner and smarter, and the role of recruitment and selection programs is evolving alongside. The shift from task-based to process-based thinking is placing new pressures on human resources specialists to "move beyond valid job-based predictors because the work to be done changes constantly" (Cascio, 1995, 932). Modified job analysis procedures that capture redefined forms of work will necessarily evolve to complement, and perhaps in some cases replace, task-based job analysis techniques (Kiechel, 1993; May, 1996).

An alternative view of organizational structure has been evolving since the 1970s. A dynamic systems view of the organization (e.g., Gilbert, 1978;

Katz and Kahn, 1978; Rummler and Brache, 1990) charts not the departments and reporting relationships, but the functional relationships that exist between departments. It is a process-based way of looking at the organization that facilitates analysis of the changing face of organizations as they move toward the 21st century. Figure 4.2 shows how the functional relationships within departments of an organization and between the organization and its external customers can be charted using a Total Performance System approach (Brethower, 1982). The overall organization is functionally described as an input-processing-output system, with human intervention inherent in every component. Similarly, each department or function is

FIGURE 4.2 **Total Performance Diagram of a System and Subsystems**

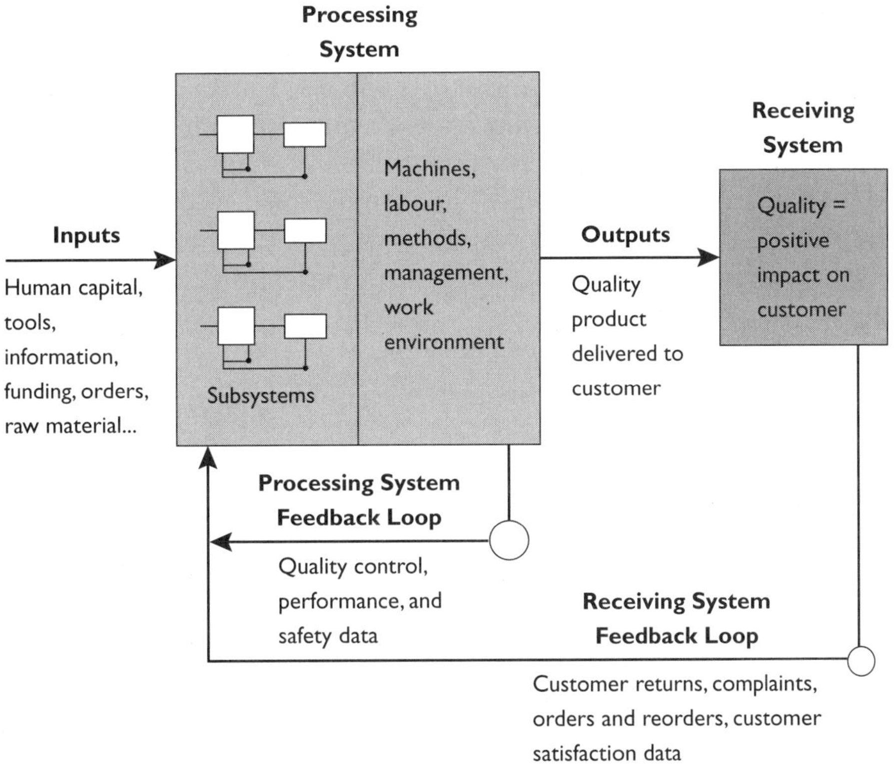

Source: Adapted from Brethower, 1982 (cf. Redmon and Agnew, 1991, and Redmon and Wilk, 1991).

129

viewed as a processing system with its own inputs, outputs, and receiving systems. Inputs into the system (e.g., information, human capital, and tools) are processed via machines and human performance, with the support of management systems and specific production methods. Internal quality control feedback consists of ongoing measurement and charting of system performance, usually related to the quality of the products and services generated in the processing system and the human performance that generates them. Each processing subsystem produces outputs that serve as inputs into other subsystems within the organization. All of this occurs in an environmental context that supports the organization by requiring and purchasing its services and products.

Consider Tom's Landscaping Service, a small company that provides lawn and garden care and landscaping services to home and small business owners (Devries, 1995). Suppose that Tom has hired a consultant to complete an analysis of his organization. The consultant produced Total Performance diagrams similar to those depicted in Figure 4.2. Tom's Landscaping Service delivers completed services to its receiving system, the external customers, through its subsystem functions that interact to produce quality outcomes. The *sales* subsystem of Tom's produces sales orders by contacting potential customers identified through market data, following up on referrals from previous and current customers, and responding to new customer requests. Thus, sales people work within their own processing subsystem to produce outputs (service orders) that are received by operations. Clearly, interactions between functions and departments are equally as important as the activities that go on within departments.

◆ ◆ ◆
THREE LEVELS OF ANALYSIS

Organizations comprise three levels: the organizational or strategic level, the process or subsystem level, and the job level (Gilbert, 1978; Rummler and Brache, 1990). An organizational system is defined by the sum of the interactions between its subsystems. One overall mission defines the purpose of the organization, and each subsystem is justified by how its objectives contribute to the achievement of that mission (Churchman, 1979). Subsystem outputs comprise the total of all products and services contributed by each job within a subsystem. Each of the three levels of analysis can be functionally charted using the Total Performance System approach (Brethower, 1982), and each are considered subsequently in detail.

LEVEL I: THE ORGANIZATION LEVEL

The focus at the organizational level is the company's relationship with the ultimate customer (i.e., the consumer who buys the final product or service), which is summarized in a strategic goal. The strategic goal for Tom's Landscaping Service is "to provide top service (no complaints from customers about the workers' care of their lawns) on a dependable basis at a reasonable price. They may not always be able to charge less than the larger companies but they would provide higher quality service and dependability than their larger counterparts could" (Devries, 1995, 78). Tom's is a comprehensive strategic goal that describes not only the specific output (service) but also includes a statement of quality (top quality) and competitiveness in the marketplace (reasonable rates). An organization analysis pinpoints factors at this level that directly influence performance toward the goal, and thus, the satisfaction of the ultimate customer. Analysis at the organizational level considers four components (Gilbert, 1978; Rummler and Brache, 1990):

1. Organizational missions and goals define the crucial outputs of the organization that are necessary to ensure survival;

2. Standards and measures of organizational productivity are used to define exemplary performance contributing to those outputs and to track system results;

3. Organizational culture and structure is concerned with the reward systems operating in the organization and how those rewards flow through the organization to influence performance; and

4. Deployment of human capital and other resources considers how resources are dispersed throughout the system and how this influences progress toward or away from the strategic goal.

The resulting *big picture* provides the reference point for all processes and activities that occur within organizational subsystems. Conducting business at process and job levels, while ignoring this referent, can jeopardize the organization's long-term survival. An organization's overall performance may be poor, while performance at process and job levels appears healthy, because of management's focus on processes and people without viewing them in the larger organizational context (Rummler and Brache, 1990). Under these conditions, processes and jobs are managed as individual entities, linked only by reporting relationships rather than being linked by one common goal. The selection and placement process within a healthy organization will link recruitment, hiring, placement, and promotion decisions within the context of the strategic goals of the organization.

MEASUREMENT AND RELEVANCE TO RECRUITMENT AND SELECTION

Strategy-driven organizations view themselves as functional entities. Zemke and Gunkler (1982) assert that there are three prerequisites for treating an organization as an entity. First, a measurement system that tracks organizational results and provides information regarding individual and subsystem performance is in place. Second, a feedback system is needed for making organizational performance and outcome information available at all levels, including those of subsystems and individuals. Information flows both up and down in this type of organization. Finally, the organization must establish contingent relationships between organizational results and rewards for individual behaviour. Thus, the organization assuming a dynamic systems vantage establishes links between behaviour and results and between results and the values and expectations of those in the receiving system—the ultimate customers. The strategic goal functions as the rule that explicitly states the link between system results and its impact on the receiving system (e.g., to deliver quality service at affordable prices). The strategy-driven organization directs the performance of individuals and subsystems accordingly. Because the dynamic system strives for constant improvement within a rapidly changing market and culture, it is insufficient to define the strategic goal at one point in time and take steps toward achieving it. In searching for appropriate organization-level requirements, the organization as a dynamic system defines the overall strategic goal, implements steps toward achieving the goal, measures performance and outputs and their impact on the receiving system, and refines goals and processes based on impact data.

The define-implement-test-refine cycle can be broken down into several discrete steps. First, determine current performance levels in relation to the organizational strategy and specify desired performance levels. That is, describe what the operation looks like now, and what it would look like were it performing optimally. In this step, the major missions of the organization are defined as accomplishments that lend themselves easily to measurement. Gilbert's analysis (1978) leads us to the conclusion that the qualifications of every good description of the overall goal of an organization can be summed up by four words: accomplishment, control, overall, and numbers. He proposes four questions that can be used to determine if the mission stated is truly the overall goal that will guide the organization toward success:

1. Is it an *accomplishment*, and not just a description of behaviour? If the mission has been described in behavioural terms, it has not been identified.

2. Do those assigned the mission have primary *control* over it? Or does good performance principally depend on others?

3. Is it a true *overall objective*, or merely a subgoal?

4. Can a *number* be put on it—that is, can it be measured?

If you can answer "Yes" to each of these questions then you have identified an overall mission upon which to guide organizational performance. The strategic goal of Tom's Landscaping Service, to provide top quality service on a dependable basis at a reasonable rate, passes each of these criteria. It is stated as an accomplishment that can be detected in the absence of the individual performers. It is within the control of Tom and the management team to ensure that the tools, human resources, and other raw system inputs are adequate for generating the desired outcome. It is stated in terms of an overall objective; that is, the one most important thing that the company accomplishes is to provide their service in such a manner as to have a positive impact on the customer. Finally, top quality service and reasonable rates can be reliably tracked and measured.

The next step is to determine measurement systems that will track progress toward goal achievement. Measures are chosen that report on organizational outcomes at regular and frequent intervals. Key variables are tracked and fed back into the system in meaningful ways. Figure 4.2 on page 129 shows two sources of data that control organizational performance: the internal quality control and the external receiving system feedback loops. Measures of performance are taken internally to detect deficiencies in the system before they reach the customer. Customer feedback data are collected to track customer satisfaction in order to continually improve system and subsystem processes.

Next, internal and external feedback data are made available to all members of the organization. Even individuals at the worker level are made aware of relevant system, subsystem, and individual performance levels. Finally, the organization establishes a system wherein individuals are rewarded for both individual performance and organizational results (Zemke and Gunkler, 1982). Recall that human performance constitutes unique constraints on system functioning. Thus, performance of the organizational system can be directly linked to the performance of individuals within organizational subsystems. The strategy-driven organization that assumes a dynamic systems vantage realizes that it must control performance at the individual level in order to achieve the primary organizational goal.

Where does the human resources recruitment and selection process fit into this define-implement-test-refine cycle? When data from the internal and external feedback loops indicate that the desired organizational performance is not occurring, the analyst seeks to determine if the source of the problem is a deficiency in job design, information, tools or raw materials; selection, placement or training; or incentives for motivating human performance (Brethower, 1982; Gilbert, 1978). While human resources subsystems can vary in the extent of their size and power within organizations, they typically exert some influence over a major source of organizational performance. When designing and implementing recruitment and selection programs to fill jobs within specific subsystems, human resources specialists must always link their own subsystem goals to the overall organizational goal. Losing sight of the goal can result in less than optimal recruitment and selection policies and practice.

CAUTIONARY NOTES ON CONDUCTING ORGANIZATION ANALYSIS The reader might be wondering at this point "How do I know what to measure?" or "How do I go about measuring it?" Once again, the strategic goal plays a role. If the goal as stated has passed the accomplishment, control, overall, and numbers criteria, then the measures will be easy to identify. But don't get caught in the data trap! There is a tendency when starting out on an organizational analysis to want to measure everything. The result is lots of numbers and little information. A good set of measures provides information on critical dimensions of performance that tell the people in the organization where they are going and where they have been. Good measures are directly related to standards for performance that are linked to system results and their impact on the receiving system. Consider again Tom's Landscaping Service. Let's assume that Tom measures organizational performance along three important dimensions: service delivery, quality, and profit. Service delivery measures suggested by Tom's quality criteria provide Tom with an indicator of service success. He measures quality by rating attractiveness and neatness on a checklist and expresses the quality index as the ratio of attractiveness over timeliness (i.e., how much time elapsed between the customer's initial order and completion of the job). Tom also measures the cost of service delivery by computing the employee compensation for each job, the cost of rework for inferior jobs, and the cost of raw materials required for each job. He relates the cost passed on to the customer to the typical price obtained in the current market. His data tell him that although he is slightly more expensive than the typical landscaping firm, the quality of the jobs delivered is superior. His company expends very little to rework inferior jobs and spends more than the typical on employee compensation (he hires highly qualified individuals and pays them well). Finally, Tom inspects his balance sheets to assess the financial health of his organization. Exemplary delivery of quality service must be balanced against a profit margin high enough to keep Tom in business. Tom's company uses a few carefully chosen measures of organizational performance and gleans a great deal of useful information from these measures. His company is successful in part because he tracks organizationally important variables that are directly linked to customer values and expectations.

LEVEL II: THE PROCESS LEVEL

Processes are the means by which an organization produces outputs to fulfill its strategic goals. A process is "a collection of activities that takes one or more kinds of input and creates an output that is of value to the customer" (Hammer and Champy, 1993, 35). Customers can be those in internal receiving systems or they can be the ultimate customers that purchase the product or service. At this level, the focus is on the inter-relationships between components of the organization. Processes do not occur within single departmental structures; they are input-throughput-output systems that are best described by what gets done and how. The systems analyst focuses on strategic goals even when intervening at the process level. All interventions, including those in human resources selection, are guided by their relationship to the overall goal. With function in mind, the analyst asks

"What is the process?" and "What does the process accomplish?" All subsystem processes in the organization have process goals that are specific to them. In a healthy system, accomplishment of those goals contributes to the overall strategic goal. Similar to strategic goals, subsystem goals are stated in terms of accomplishments, overall objectives, control, and numbers or measures.

An additional criterion at this level is reconciliation (Gilbert, 1978); that is, is the subsystem goal reconcilable with other system goals, or does it conflict with them? A good subsystem goal is reconcilable with the goals of all other subsystems in the organization and with the overall strategic goal. Attainment of any of the subgoals does not have adverse impact on the achievement of desired subsystem or strategic results. If, for example, the goal of *sales* is to generate as many customer orders as possible and the goal of *operations* is to complete the job in a timely manner, then achievement of Tom's strategic goal is in jeopardy. The goal of the sales subsystem is in conflict both with the operations subsystem and with the overall organizational goal that specifies quality service at reasonable rates. Further, the operations subsystem goal will also be in conflict with the overall strategic goal if some quality criterion is not specified. A reconcilable subsystem goal might state that "sales will generate x number of orders per time period, given data from operations specifying their current work load and job completion projections." A reconcilable operations objective would be "to complete jobs in a timely manner while remaining within quality specifications." Achievement of these subsystem goals will then contribute to attaining the overall goal of the organization.

Processes in any organization follow normal business activities but are difficult to detect and trace if a structural view of the organization is taken. Hammer and Champy (1993) suggest that processes go unmanaged because of the traditional structural approach to defining organizations. People are put in charge of managing departments, but rarely is anyone put in charge of managing a process from beginning to end. They further suggest that processes should be given names that express their beginning and end. Thus, the product development process should be called "concept to prototype" (118). Similarly, the human resources process could be called "recruitment to promotion." Identifying the process in terms of its logical beginning and end permits the analyst to chart the process as it plays out in the organization. The next section describes how processes are traced using a functional approach rather than a structural one.

PROCESS MAPPING Process mapping can be a useful intermediate step between organization analysis and job analysis. It permits the analysts, often a cross-functional team, to assess how different functions are involved in a single process. This information can be used by the team to improve processes and by human resources specialists to guide recruitment and selection initiatives. Process mapping serves a function similar to organizational charting in that it provides a picture of the way work gets done. Process mapping is best completed by a team of individuals representing all areas that participate in the process. Two general steps in process mapping are as follows (Hammer and Champy, 1993; Rummler and Brache, 1990):

1. Identify all functions, departments, and specialty areas involved in the process.

2. Trace the process through all its steps from initial inputs to the final output.

Once the process has been mapped, the team can see how different functions, departments, and personnel are involved in producing the final output. Gaps in the system, if they exist, become evident as missing or extra steps readily stand out (Rummler and Brache, 1990; Scholtes, 1988). Next, an *ideal process* map can be produced to be used as a guide for process improvement. In the ideal map (i.e., what the process would look like in the perfect-case scenario), the team identifies all functions, departments, or work areas that should be involved in the process, and the most effective links between these areas are drawn. The ideal map can provide objective guidance to support recruitment and selection strategies. Human resources deficiencies and surpluses are made evident when the map of the current process is compared with that of the ideal process. Those who have considerable experience with process mapping will realize that human resources deficiencies and surpluses are not always readily evident. It may take the team several iterations of mapping and observing workflow to pinpoint areas of shortage and surplus.

Suppose that in response to internal quality control data and customer complaints, Tom's Landscaping Service (Devries, 1995) put together a cross-functional team to map the order-to-delivery process. Figure 4.3 shows the

FIGURE 4.3 Process Map for Tom's Landscaping Service

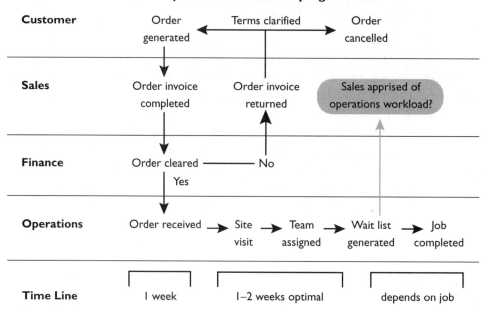

map that the team generated. This map shows the functions involved from the start to the end of this process. Starting with the customer, the order is generated and a service order invoice is completed in sales. If this order is cleared through finances, it is passed on to operations; if it is not, the order is returned to sales so the terms can be clarified with the customer. An order received by operations results in a site visit by the operations manager, who determines the exact nature of the job. A team of landscapers is assigned to the job based on the information gathered at the site visit. The team leader then places the order on a wait list and jobs are completed in turn. This process map highlighted a critical gap in the system: There were more orders coming in than the operations teams could handle in a timely manner. The cross-functional team concluded that there were two possible solutions. Sales could be apprised of the workload in operations and turn down orders accordingly. This solution would mean that an additional line on the process map would connect the operations back with the sales, indicating that sales would receive the wait list data from operations. It would also mean that those customers would give their business to another firm. Or, additional personnel could be hired so that jobs would not sit on wait lists prompting customers to complain or to go elsewhere for service. Tom's financial advisors would then be consulted to confirm whether it makes good business sense to purchase the extra equipment necessary and to hire additional landscapers to handle the extra business. If so, the human resources process recruitment-to-placement would be invoked to seek out new individuals to be hired by Tom's.

IMPACT OF PROCESS-LEVEL REQUIREMENTS ON INDIVIDUAL AND ORGANIZATIONAL PERFORMANCE More Canadian employees than ever are members of process teams, and individuals are less likely than ever to be linked to an easily identifiable collection of discrete job tasks. According to Hammer and Champy (1993, 70):

> *A task-oriented, traditional company hires people and expects them to follow the rules. Companies that have reengineered don't want employees who can follow rules; they want people who will make their own rules. As management invests teams with the responsibility of completing an entire process, it must also give them the authority to make the decisions needed to get it done.*

The implications of this changing view of organizational performance for the recruitment and selection subsystems are far-reaching. They include the need for valid predictors of the behaviours required under a process model of job performance, and these predictors must be acceptable from a human rights perspective (see Chapter 2). It is no longer sufficient to assess a candidate's education, experience, and skills. The prospective employee's ability to make good decisions and to generate usable ideas, to work in a team environment, and to work under conditions of minimal supervision are becoming equally important in the re-engineered organization (Cascio, 1995; Hammer and Champy, 1993). We will explore these issues further in considering analysis at the job level of an organization.

LEVEL III: THE JOB LEVEL

A job is defined as a collection of positions that are similar in their significant duties (e.g., supermarket cashier, anesthetist); a position consists of a collection of duties assigned to individuals in an organization at a given time (Cascio, 1982; Harvey, 1991). Jobs and positions are among the basic building blocks of any organization and selection of individuals to fill these positions has a significant impact on the success of the organization. The unit of analysis at the job level is human performance and events that affect it. In the early part of this century, this meant that people performed a set of tasks that were specifically related to a job. The view of efficiency experts such as Frederick Taylor was that these tasks should be highly organized and distributed among specialized workers (Haber, 1964). Operations research focused on identifying problems, designing models for testing, and deriving solutions to work problems based on these job models. Human behaviour was considered to be a constant, and employees were paid to produce an output under a given set of operational constraints. Organizational culture and the modern business environment have evolved and human behaviour is now considered to be an important variable in determining system functioning. Employees are now paid to think and make decisions as well as to produce outputs.

Individual employees and managers are the means by which processes function, whether poorly or effectively. Among the variables that are critical to performance at the job level are recruitment, selection, and promotion of individual employees, assessment and communication of job responsibilities, development and application of standards for performance, and implementation of feedback and reward systems and training programs (Rummler and Brache, 1990). Analysis at the job level involves identifying the goals and the major responsibilities of a job.

IDENTIFICATION AND MEASUREMENT OF JOB-LEVEL REQUIREMENTS Jobs can be mapped and analyzed just as organizations and processes can be mapped, and jobs have major objectives to be accomplished. At the job level, these objectives are defined in terms of the major responsibilities of the job. The requirements for success on the job are described as the levels of performance and the quality of relevant outputs that are achieved in relation to specified standards. Figure 4.4 shows the contribution of individual job outputs to subsystem outputs. Each individual within the processing system is responsible for one or more job responsibility and task. Those tasks collectively produce the results that are generated by the processing system. Feedback loops within the processing system tell each individual how he or she is performing relative to specified standards.

FIGURE 4.4 Contribution of Individual Job Outputs to Subsystem Outputs

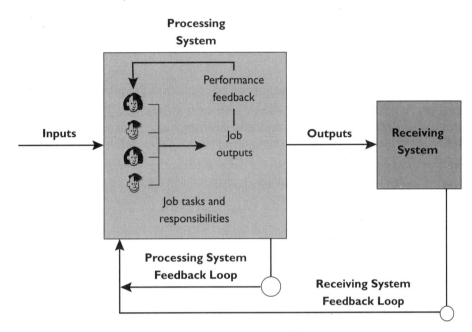

Daniels (1994) defines feedback as "information about performance that allows an individual to adjust his or her performance" (99). He cites internal feedback deficiencies as "a major contributor to virtually all problems of low performance" (100). For performance feedback to be meaningful, objectives for performance and results at the job level must be consistent with and contribute to process and organizational level goals (Gilbert, 1978; Rummler and Brache, 1990). In a healthy organization, job objectives are linked to process goals, subsystem process goals are aligned with the overall strategic goal of the organization, and strategic goals are linked to receiving system values and expectations.

Objectives identified at the job level are more specific than those at the subsystem level, but must adhere to the same standards of employability. Using Gilbert's criteria, they should be stated in terms of an accomplishment rather than a behaviour, should be in the primary control of the performer, should describe overall objectives for the job, should be reconcilable with other job objectives and subsystem goals, and should be measurable. Although job level objectives are more specific than subsystem goals, they are not necessarily easier to identify. The variables identified by Kiechel (1993) that are relevant to the recruitment and selection functions at the process level also affect job level variables. Because companies are downsizing, organizations are shifting toward flatter and less hierarchical structures, and work itself is being redefined; jobs are becoming more complex. Thus, the analyst looking to identify major responsibilities and tasks inherent to specific jobs will find that a functional rather than a structural approach better serves the purpose. The following sections describe some common means for analyzing the content of jobs and consider job analysis in the changing culture of the world of work.

◆ ◆ ◆
JOB ANALYSIS

Job analysis refers to the process of collecting information about jobs "by any method for any purpose" (Ash, 1988). The information collected from a job analysis can be used toward many ends (e.g., classifying and describing jobs, developing employee appraisal systems, designing jobs, and developing training programs). In the context of employee recruitment and selection, the results of the analysis specify the requirements of the job that are subsequently used to establish employee selection programs. Harvey (1991, 73) contends that

> it is critical that the term job analysis *be applied only to procedures that* collect *information describing verifiable job behaviors and activities; it should* not *be used to denote the wide assortment of procedures that make inferences about people or otherwise* apply *job analysis data (e.g., to infer personal traits that might be necessary for successful job performance).*

Job analysis techniques generally fall into two categories: work-oriented and worker-oriented (Harvey, 1991; McCormick, 1979; McCormick and Jenneret, 1991; McCormick, Jenneret, and Mecham, 1972). In work-oriented job analysis, the emphasis is on work outcome and description of the various tasks performed to accomplish those outcomes. These methods produce "descriptions of job content that have a dominant association with, and typically characterize, the 'technological' aspects of jobs and commonly reflect what is achieved by the worker" (McCormick et al., 1972, 348). The descriptions of tasks or job duties generated via work-oriented methods are typically characterized by their frequency of occurrence or the amount of time spent on them, the importance to the job outcome, and the difficulty inherent in executing them (e.g., Gael, 1983; Ghorpade, 1988). Because task inventories generated via work-oriented techniques are developed for specific jobs, or occupational areas, the results are highly specific and may have little or no relationship with the content of jobs in other fields (McCormick and Jeanneret, 1991).

Alternatively, worker-oriented job analysis methods focus on general aspects of jobs that describe perceptual, interpersonal, sensory, cognitive, and physical activities. Worker-oriented methods generate descriptions "that tend more to characterize the generalized human behaviors involved; if not directly, then by strong inference" (McCormick et al., 1972, 348). These techniques are not limited to describing specific jobs; they are generic in nature and the results can be applied to a wide spectrum of task-dissimilar jobs (Harvey, 1991; McCormick, 1979; McCormick and Jeanneret, 1991; McCormick et al., 1972). The changes in the world of work described above, from a task- to process-based way of thinking, highlight the usefulness of worker-oriented job analysis procedures in meeting the new demands placed on human resources specialists.

Whether work- or worker-oriented, Harvey (1991) proposes three criteria that should characterize any job analysis method: First, the goal of job analysis should always be the description of observable work behaviours and analysis of their products. Second, the results of a job analysis should describe the work behaviour "independent of the personal characteristics or attributes of the employees who perform the job" (75). Positions in an organization exist independently of the incumbents that fill those positions; in job analysis it is the job (i.e., the collection of positions) that is being analyzed, not the performance of the individual incumbents. Worker specifications (i.e., the knowledge, skills, abilities, and other personal attributes—KSAOs) necessary to perform successfully on the job are inferred in a separate process using the results of a job analysis. Finally, the analysis must be verifiable and replicable. That is, the organization must be able to produce evidence of both the validity and the reliability of each step in the job analysis process.

Although there are no laws that specifically require a job analysis prior to implementing recruitment and selection programs, employment decisions must be based on job-related information (Sparks, 1988). Job analysis is a legally acceptable way of determining job relatedness, and has been endorsed in U.S. case law. In 1975 the United States Supreme Court made a precedent setting decision when it criticized the Albermarle Paper Company for its failure to use a job analysis to demonstrate the job relatedness of its selection procedures (*Albermarle Paper Co. v. Moody*). According to Harvey (1991), "Albermarle established job analysis as something that virtually *must* be done to defend challenged employment practices" (120). Additionally, even though the *Uniform Guidelines on Employee Selection* (1978) are not law, the U.S. courts have granted them significant status in guiding administrative interpretations of the job analysis-job relatedness link (Levine, 1983; Sparks, 1988). The *Uniform Guidelines* represent a joint agreement between several U.S. government departments and agencies (Equal Employment Opportunity Commission, Civil Service Commission, Department of Labor, and Department of Justice) outlining professional standards for employee selection procedures. The *Uniform Guidelines* emphasize the criticality of valid job analysis procedures in developing selection programs. Although these legal precedents and guidelines originate in the United States, Canadian human rights commissions and courts will continue to recognize them as professional standards unless it is established that Canadian legal precedent and professional practice deviate substantially from those of the United States (Cronshaw, 1988). Thus, job analysis both aids the organization in determining what KSAOs should be included in its selection measures, and is an essential step in protecting the organization should its selection procedures be challenged in court (Ash, 1988; Levine, Thomas, and Sistrunk, 1988).

SURVEY OF JOB ANALYSIS TECHNIQUES

Although the various existing job analysis techniques differ in the assumptions they make about work, they follow the same logical process when applied to the recruitment and selection of human resources. First, work activities are described in terms of the work processes or worker behaviours that characterize the job. Next, machines, tools, equipment, and work aids are defined in relation to the materials produced, services rendered, and worker knowledge applied to those ends. Work measurements and standards are used to describe work performance. The job context is characterized in terms of physical working conditions, work schedules, social context and organizational culture, and financial and non-financial incentives for performance. Finally, personnel specifications are inferred by linking the job requirements identified in the analysis with the education, experience, skills, and personal attributes required for successful job performance (McCormick, 1979).

In preparing for a job analysis, the first step should be to collect existing information describing the target job. The analyst uses organizational charts, legal requirements (e.g., the job *clinical psychologist* may be governed through legal statutes at the provincial level), job descriptions, union regulations, and previous data from related job analyses to learn about the job. In addition, job-related information can be found in the National Occupational Classification system (NOC, 1993). The NOC systematically describes occupations in the Canadian labour market based on extensive occupational research. (See Boxes 4.1 and 4.2.) Such information, when gathered and studied in advance, will prove invaluable for organizing and conducting the ensuing analysis.

Attention should be given to what techniques will be employed for gathering job information. Gael (1988) notes that, depending on the objective of the job analysis, some techniques are better suited than others for providing job information. Analyses typically involve a series of steps, often beginning with interviews or observations that provide the information to construct a task inventory or to complete a structured questionnaire. Ideally, the job analyst employs a combination of strategies to arrive at a comprehensive and accurate description of the job in question (Cascio, 1982; Harvey, 1991), although analysts operating within the very real constraints of time and funding often use a single method. Each analysis method contributes slightly different information and, by using a combination of methods, potential gaps in the results are minimized. A discussion of these techniques follows.

INTERVIEWS The interview is perhaps the most commonly used technique for gathering job facts and establishing the tasks and behaviours that define a job. This method involves questioning individuals or small groups of employees and supervisors about the work that gets done. The interview may

BOX 4.1 OCCUPATIONAL DESCRIPTION FOR VETERINARIANS

Veterinarians prevent, diagnose and treat diseases and disorders in animals and advise clients on the feeding, hygiene, housing and general care of animals. Veterinarians work in private practice or may be employed by animal clinics and laboratories, government or industry.

Examples of titles classified in this unit group

Small Animal Veterinary Specialist

Veterinarian

Veterinary Inspector

Veterinary Pathologist

Veterinary Physiologist

Zoo Veterinarian

Main duties

Veterinarians perform some or all of the following duties:

- Diagnose diseases or abnormal conditions in animals through physical examinations or laboratory tests
- Treat sick or injured animals by prescribing medication, setting bones, dressing wounds or performing surgery
- Inoculate animals to prevent diseases
- Advise clients on feeding, housing, breeding, hygiene and general care of animals
- May supervise animal health technologists and animal care workers
- May be responsible for overall operation of animal hospital, clinic or mobile service to farms
- May conduct veterinary research
- May enforce government regulations in disease control and food production including animal or animal-based food inspection.

Employment requirements

- Two to four years of pre-veterinary university studies or, in Quebec, completion of a College program in health science and
  A four-year university degree in veterinary medicine
  and
  Completion of national certification examinations are required.
- Provincial licensure is required.
- In Quebec, membership in the professional corporation for veterinarians is mandatory.
- Entry into research positions may require post-graduate study.

Additional information

- The duties of veterinarians performing research may be similar to those of some biologists.

Classified elsewhere

- *Animal Health Technologists (3213)*
- *Biologists and Related Scientists (2121)*

Source: National Occupational Classification (1993), Human Resources Development Canada. Reproduced with the permission of the Minister of Public Works and Government Services Canada, 1996.

BOX 4.2 OCCUPATIONAL DESCRIPTION FOR PAINTERS, SCULPTORS, AND OTHER VISUAL ARTISTS

Painters, Sculptors and Other Visual Artists create original paintings, drawings, sculptures, etchings, engravings and other artistic works. They are usually self-employed. This group also includes art instructors and teachers, who are usually employed by private art schools.

Examples of titles classified in this unit group

Art Instructor

Artist

Ink Sketcher

Painter

Portrait Painter

Sculptor

Silkscreen Artist

Main duties

A summary of the main duties for some occupations in this unit group follows:

◆ Painters create drawings, paintings and other original artwork using oils, pastels, watercolours, charcoal, ink and other materials.

◆ Sculptors create sculptures, statues and other three-dimensional artwork by shaping, carving and fabricating materials such as clay, stone, wood or metal.

◆ Art instructors and teachers teach students in the techniques and methods of drawing, painting, sculpting and other forms of artistic expression.

Employment requirements

◆ Creative ability and talent, as demonstrated by a portfolio of work, are required. Art programs are offered at universities, colleges and private art schools.

◆ Art instructors and teachers may be required to have a university degree or college diploma in a field related to art.

Classified elsewhere

◆ *Artisans and Craftspersons (5244)*

◆ *Graphic Designers and Illustrating Artists (5241)*

Source: National Occupational Classification (1993), National Resources Development Canada. Reproduced with the permission of the Minister of Public Works and Government Services Canada, 1996.

be structured or unstructured, although for job analysis purposes, a structured format is recommended. The results of a job analysis interview may stand on their own, as in a formal integrated report, when there are few incumbents working within a small geographical area. Or, they may provide the necessary information for completing a task inventory, structured questionnaire or other analytic technique (Gael, 1983, 1988).

Because it is such an important step in most job analyses, the interview should be well planned and carefully conducted. McCormick (1979) and others (Fine, Holt, and Hutchinson, 1974; Gael, 1988; Gatewood and Feild, 1990; Levine, 1983) offer many valuable guidelines for conducting interviews. Adhering to these criteria will help both the interviewer and the person being interviewed remain at ease and obtain useful job information.

1. **Announce the job analysis well ahead of the interview date.** The impending job analysis and its purpose should be well known among employees and management.

2. **Participation in interviews should be voluntary, and employees should be interviewed only with the permission of their supervisors.** The job analyst avoids creating friction within the organization and is sensitive to the use of coercion in obtaining information. In general, when analysis interviews are free from organizational politics, they can be completed in a timely manner with valid, uncontaminated results.

3. **Interviews should be conducted in a private location free from status earmarks.** It would be unwise, for example, to conduct interviews with hourly workers in the company president's office. The job analyst is a non-partisan party whose primary objective is to accurately describe the content of jobs; interviewees should feel comfortable and able to provide truthful information about their work and the conditions under which it is done.

4. **Open the interview by establishing rapport with the employee and explaining the purpose of the interview.** Interviews are often associated with anxiety provoking events such as job and promotion applications and even disciplinary action. The experienced interviewer takes time at the outset to create a non-threatening environment and alleviate any fears that interviewees might have.

5. **Ask open-ended questions, using language that is easy to understand, and allow ample time for the employee's responses.** Most people given the opportunity will talk in great detail about the work they do. The good analyst avoids rushing or intimidating people, does not talk down to them, and takes a genuine interest in the interviewee's responses.

6. **Guide the session without being authoritative or overbearing.** Keep the interview on topic and avoid discussions concerning worker-management

relations and other unrelated topics. When discussions become tangential, the analyst can bring them back on track by summarizing relevant details and referring to the interview outline.

7. **Explain to the employees that records of the interviews will identify them only by confidential codes.** The names of interviewees and other personal information should be protected. When confidentiality is ensured, more accurate information will be obtained.

The job analyst should record the incumbent's or supervisor's responses, either by taking notes or by tape recording the interview. Trying to remember what was said following the interview is difficult at best and likely to produce inaccurate information. Recall that the purpose of the interview is to obtain information about the work that the employee does, thus questions should elicit information describing important job tasks, physical activities involved in the job, environmental conditions (physical and social) under which the work occurs, and typical work incidents.

An interview outline prompts the interviewer to ask important questions about the job. The interviewer may start out asking: "What are the main things that you do in your job?" Based on the response, and on the interviewer's previous knowledge of the job, the interviewer then probes for more detail (Gael, 1988; Ghorpade, 1988). The tasks that make up each job area are delineated and the result of the interview should be a clear description of critical job domains and their related elements. Interview outlines can vary from presenting a few informal prompts to listing very structured questions to be addressed in a specific order. In general, the more specific the interview outline is, the more reliable will be the information obtained from interviewees.

While there are no hard and fast rules concerning how many people should be interviewed, the job analyst is wise to demonstrate that the collection of incumbents interviewed is representative of the employees whose job the analysis reflects. For example, when conducting a job analysis for meeting planning consultants employed in a large travel company, the analyst may obtain a stratified sample that reflects the proportion of males and females in the position. Other demographic variables such as race and ethnicity, age, physical handicaps and abilities, and native language would also be considered in a representative sample of interviewees. Representativeness is important for two reasons. First, interviewing a range of employees will generate more accurate information concerning the job. Second, if the job analysis is challenged in court, the analyst must be able to defend the procedure. A charge of unfair discrimination will be hard to defend if the analyst cannot demonstrate that the job analysis results were obtained from a sample representative of those who actually do the work (Thompson and Thompson, 1982). Supervisors should always be included in the pool of interview respondents, as they have a unique perspective of how jobs are performed and the standards for acceptable performance.

One advantage of the interview method is that the job is described by those who know it best: the employees who do the work and their immediate supervisors. And, although interviews should be well structured, they enable interviewees to contribute information that may be overlooked by other analysis techniques.

There are, however, certain disadvantages to job analysis interviews. First, they can be expensive and time consuming and may be impractical for jobs with a large number of incumbents. Interviews take a great deal of time to conduct and may require a substantial number of interviewees to be truly representative of the job incumbent pool. Individual interviews are more time consuming and more expensive to conduct than group interviews, but the benefits of individual interviews can outweigh the relative costs. Individual employees, free from immediate social controls, are likely to respond with greater openness than those interviewed in a group. Thus, the information obtained from the individual interview may be more accurate than that obtained from the same people interviewed together. A second disadvantage of this technique is that workers may be prone to distorting the information they provide about their jobs, particularly if they believe that the results will influence their pay (Cascio, 1982). This distortion can be overcome by making the purpose of the interview clear, and by interviewing multiple incumbents and supervisors.

DIRECT OBSERVATION Martinko makes the case that "the most effective way to determine what effective job incumbents do is to observe their behavior." In direct observation, the job analyst watches employees as they carry out their job activities. This allows the analyst to come into direct contact with the job; thus the data are obtained firsthand as contrasted with the "more remote types of information generated by questionnaires and surveys" (Martinko, 1988, 419).

Direct observation is most useful when the job analysis involves easily observable activities (Cascio, 1982). Analyzing the job *poet* through direct observation would likely produce little of value, whereas the job landscaper lends itself more readily to direct observation. Before conducting direct observations, the analyst will already have learned about the job by studying existing documents. Next, the job analyst determines the nature of the job by asking: "Does the job involve easily observable activities?" and "Is the work environment one in which unobtrusive observations can be made?" If the answer to both questions is "Yes" then direct observation may be a viable analysis method.

In direct observation, systematic observations of employee activities are made and data can be recorded either in narrative format or using a customized checklist or worksheet (Cascio, 1982; Martinko, 1988). Different jobs and environments will require different observation methods. A landscaper's job, one that does not occur within a complex social context, might best be observed and recorded by using a tally sheet such as that shown in Figure 4.5. The job of residential counsellor, in which the job tasks are heavily influenced by dynamic social conditions, will require a recording format that enables the observer to identify important activities and the conditions under which they occur. An example of a recording sheet used in observing residential counsellors at work can be found in Figure 4.6. The form enables the observer to collect information about the job by defining the conditions under which a particular activity occurs and listing the tools and aids

FIGURE 4.5 Frequency Tally Sheet

Observation record for landscaper Date: _15–03–96_ Start time: _10:30 am_ End time: _11:07 am_
Observer: _Keltie_ Employee ID: _734_

Tasks (planting trees)	Check if done	Time spent
1. Measure area & mark spot	x	5 min
2. Dig hole	x	16 min
3. Move shrubbery	—	—
4. Lift trees (manually)	x	<1 min
5. Lift trees (winched)	—	—
6. Fill hole	x	7 min
7. Rake area	x	5 min

FIGURE 4.6 Work Activity Recording Sheet

Observation record for residential counsellor

Employee ID: _735_   Observer: _Faiz_   Date: _15 Feb 1996_

Condition	Activity	Tools	Time
Resident arrives home from school	Counsellor helps resident remove snow clothes	No special tools	5 min
Physiotherapy program	Counsellor leads resident through exercises	Walker, leg splints, physiotherapy program instructions	20 min
After meal	Medication delivery to residents	Med recording forms, medication instructions	15 min

employed in the activity. Both recording formats permit the observer to record valuable qualitative and quantitative data.

In preparing for observations, the analyst might ask: "How many observations are enough?" or "How long should observations be?" These questions are addressed in planning the job analysis observations and, once again, there is no rule book one can turn to for the answers. As with the individual and group interviews, a representative sample of workers is needed. If the organization or department is small (e.g., Modern Builders with only three employees in the job *electrician*), samples from all workers can be obtained. If, however, the organization or department is large (e.g., New World Residential Centres with 10 homes employing over 120 residential counsellors), a sample of workers consisting of at least 10 to 15 percent of the staff can be observed (McPhail, Jeanneret, McCormick, and Mecham, 1991). Observation times should be stratified so that all shifts are covered, and all work conditions are observed, ensuring that important patterns in worker activities are evident and extraneous information is eliminated. When observing at New World Residential Centres, for example, an analyst would want to observe morning, afternoon, and evening shifts during weekdays and weekends, as activities during these periods can change substantially. Similarly, when observing shift workers in a manufacturing plant, activities may change during peak and down times and shift and day considerations will influence the observation schedule.

There are a variety of technological aids available to the observer. Audio and video recording, for example, can facilitate the observation process. Each has its advantages and disadvantages. Audio tapes can augment observer notes with important verbal behaviour of the worker, but they are rarely useful observation tools on their own. Important information may be lost because of poor recording quality and background noise, or because many of the behaviours of interest may be non-verbal (Martinko, 1988). Video recording provides a permanent product of the verbal and non-verbal components of the observation session, which the analyst can review in private for later data collection. When the work area is small and a camera can be placed unobtrusively, video taping is an option to consider. But, while it may be easier to make unobtrusive observations in some settings using a video tape, the video cannot follow workers around in large work areas without someone at the controls. Another disadvantage, reactivity to observation, may be greater during video taped sessions than during observation sessions employing live observers. Martinko also concludes that video taping can be expensive and may require a skilled technician to produce quality tapes.

The analyst conducting direct observation sessions should be aware that regardless of the observation technique employed, his or her presence may change the behaviour of the employees. Imagine yourself at work; a strange individual with a clipboard begins to write down everything you do. Knowing you are being watched, you may respond by doing your work according to what you think the observer is looking for rather than doing it as you would in the normal day-to-day routine. This effect can be minimized when the analyst blends into the surroundings (e.g., by choosing an unobtrusive observation position) and when the employees have been informed of the purpose of the observations and are only observed with their explicit permission.

In addition to direct observation, the job analyst may ask incumbents to monitor their own work behaviour (Harvey, 1991; Martinko, 1988). Martinko describes several advantages that self-monitoring may have over other observation procedures. First, it is less time-consuming and less expensive because the job incumbents observe and record their own behaviour. Second, self-monitoring can be used when the conditions of work do not facilitate direct observation by another person as in potentially dangerous or sensitive work. Finally, self-monitoring can provide information on otherwise unobservable cognitive and intellectual processes involved in the job. The potential shortcomings of self-monitoring are that incumbents may not be reliable observers of their own behaviour, the self-monitoring task is an additional duty to be completed above the normal workload, and some amount of training may be required in order to generate valid and reliable results from self-generated data.

STRUCTURED JOB ANALYSIS QUESTIONNAIRES AND INVENTORIES

Structured questionnaires and inventories require workers and other subject matter experts to respond to written questions about their jobs. Respondents are asked to make judgments about activities and tasks, tools and equipment, and working conditions involved in the job. These can be off-the-shelf questionnaires and inventories that are amenable for use in a variety of jobs, such as the worker-oriented Position Analysis Questionnaire (PAQ) (McCormick, Jeanneret, and Mecham, 1989), or, they can be developed by the analyst for the specific job and organization in question using the critical incident technique (Flanagan, 1954), functional job analysis (Fine et al.,1974; Fine and Wiley, 1971), or other inventory method.

Position Analysis Questionnaire The PAQ is a structured job analysis questionnaire that focuses on the general behaviours that make up a job. It assumes that all jobs can be characterized in terms of a limited number of human abilities. The PAQ includes 195 items, called job elements; the first 187 describe general work activities, and the remaining items relate to compensation. The job elements are organized into six dimensions:

1. *Information input* assesses the sources of information a worker uses on the job.

2. *Mental processes* statements refer to the types of reasoning, decision making, planning, and information processing behaviours used by the employee.

3. *Work output* items relate to the physical activities engaged in and the tools used by the worker.

4. *Relationships* with other persons measure the types of interpersonal relationships inherent in the job.

5. *Job context* elements measure the physical and social environment in which the work takes place.

6. *Other job characteristics* measure other conditions of work not falling into the other five categories (McCormick et al., 1989).

Each of the six dimensions is subdivided into sections made up of items related to particular job facets (i.e., components of job dimensions). Facets of information input, for example, include visual sources of job information, non-visual sources of job information, sensory and perceptual processes, and estimation activities. Items used to assess visual sources of job information ask respondents to rate the extent to which they use written, quantitative, and pictorial materials, visual displays, mechanical devices, and so on. With this method, the job analyst reviews background job information, conducts extensive interviews with incumbents, observes the job, and rates the extent to which each item of the questionnaire applies to the target job (McPhail et al., 1991). Each item is rated using a specified response scale. For example, the response scale accompanying the facet *visual sources of job information* is:

Extent of Use

0   Does not apply

1   Nominal/very infrequent

2   Occasional

3   Moderate

4   Considerable

5   Very substantial

(McCormick et al., 1989, 3)

"Extent of use" measures the degree to which an item is used by the worker. The five other scales employed are importance to this job, amount of time (spent doing something), possibility of occurrence (of physical hazards on the job), applicability (of an item to the job), and other special codes used for a small number of job elements (McCormick et al., 1989).

The PAQ can be completed by trained job analysts, personnel professionals, or job incumbents and supervisors, although trained job analysts produce the most accurate and reliable results in the least amount of time (McPhail et al., 1991). Researchers have concluded that the quality of job information obtained via the PAQ is partially dependent upon the readability of the instrument. Ash and Edgell (1975) assessed the readability of the

PAQ using four indexes. These authors concluded that the PAQ requires at least a college-level reading ability for both the directions and the questionnaire items, and that "the questionnaire as presently constituted probably should not be routinely given to job incumbents and supervisors except in those areas requiring much higher levels of education than 10–12 years" (766). The authors of the *Position Analysis Questionnaire: Job Analysis Manual* (McPhail et al., 1991) recognize that although some organizations have obtained useful job information from having incumbents and supervisors complete the questionnaire, some of the items have unique definitions that may not be readily apparent to those employees.

The job analyst begins the PAQ process by reviewing available information about the job, and by observing the work, the work environment, and the equipment used on the job. Job description questionnaires administered to a large sample of employees may also be used to gather information. Finally, interviews with a sample of incumbents and supervisors provide the detailed information required to accurately complete the PAQ. An interview guide can be found in the PAQ manual (McPhail et al., 1991) and is recommended for use by novice job analysts. The authors warn that the interview should not be conducted "as an oral administration of the PAQ. The analyst's goal in the interview is to gain enough information about the job to enable him or her to respond to all of the PAQ items at some later time" (12). When complete information about the job is obtained, the job analyst assigns ratings to each of the PAQ items; one PAQ answer sheet is completed for each individual interviewed.

Because the PAQ is a standardized job analysis tool, data from single or multiple positions may be used (McCormick, Mecham, and Jeanneret, 1977; Mecham, McCormick, and Jeanneret, 1977). Ratings from the 195 PAQ items are sent to PAQ Services, Inc. for computer processing. Job dimension scores and estimates of required aptitudes to perform the job are derived, based on statistically determined relationships. Attribute profiles were generated during the development of the PAQ using a sample of industrial psychologists who rated the relevance of 76 human attributes (e.g., verbal comprehension, movement detection) to each of the job elements assessed by the instrument (McCormick, 1979). For employee selection purposes, the final analysis of PAQ data identifies individual attributes that serve as employee specifications, which can subsequently be used in selection of new employees.

There are several advantages to using the PAQ. First, it can be used with a small number of incumbents yet generates valid results, and it is standardized, thereby permitting easy comparisons between jobs. Second, it is a straightforward process to get from PAQ results to selection procedures. Finally, the PAQ has been rated as one of the most cost-efficient job analysis methods (Levine, Ash, and Bennett, 1980). The primary disadvantage is that because it is a worker-oriented technique, the PAQ does not quantify what work actually gets done on the job (Gatewood and Feild, 1990; McCormick, 1979). Considering the change in the world of work, from task- to process-based modes of thinking, this later disadvantage may well be an advantage.

Task Inventories Task inventories are work-oriented surveys that break down jobs into their component tasks. A well-constructed survey permits workers to define their jobs in relation to a subset of tasks appearing on the inventory (Christal and Weissmuller, 1988). Drauden (1988) indicates that certain task inventory methods were developed in response to the *Uniform Guidelines* criteria for job analysis. According to these criteria, job analysis should assess: (1) the duties performed, (2) the level of difficulty of job duties, (3) the job context, and (4) criticality of duties to the job. An inventory comprises task statements that are objectively based descriptions of what gets done an a job. Tasks are worker activities that result in an outcome that serves some specified purpose (Levine, 1983; McCormick and Jeanneret, 1991). These inventories are typically developed for specific jobs or occupations in contrast to worker-oriented methods that permit application of instruments to a wide variety of unrelated jobs.

Functional Job Analysis Fine and his colleagues (Fine, 1988; Fine et al., 1974) distinguish between what a worker does and what is accomplished in the Functional Job Analysis (FJA) method. They define task statements as "verbal formulations of activities that make it possible to describe what workers do *and* what gets done so that recruitment, selection ... and payment can be efficiently and equitably carried out" (Fine et al., 1974, 4). In FJA, well written task statements clearly describe what an employee does so that an individual unfamiliar with the job should be able to read and understand each task statement. Task statements contain four elements: (1) a verb describing the action that is performed; (2) an object of the verb that describes to whom or what the action is done; (3) a description of tools, equipment, work aids, and processes required for successful completion of the task; and (4) an expected output describing the result of the action (Fine

TABLE 4.1 TASK STATEMENTS DESCRIBING RESPONSIBILITIES OF RESIDENTIAL COUNSELLORS			
Who performs what? (verb)	To whom or what? (object)	To produce or achieve what? (output)	Using what tools, aids, equipment, and processes?
Counsellor observes and records frequency of behaviours	group home resident	to determine cause of undesirable behaviours	using record sheets customized data forms, video tapes, live observation
Counsellor meets with, talks to, describes data to, answers questions	parents and group home staff and management	to explain results of analysis and describe proposed intervention	using data collected during observations, mediator techniques

Source: Adapted from Fine, Holt, and Hutchinson, 1974.

et al., 1974; Levine, 1983). Taken together, task statements describe all the essential components of the job. Although recommendations vary for the optimal number of task statements that define a job, from as little as 6 to 12 (Gatewood and Feild, 1990) to as many as 30 to 100 (Levine, 1983), one is well advised to keep in mind the purpose of generating task statements: When conducting a job analysis to support a human resources selection program, the task statements should be specific enough to be useful in pinpointing employment specifications, but not so specific as to be cumbersome. Generally, 20 to 30 task statements are sufficient for this purpose.

Task statements should be carefully edited for inclusion in the task inventory. Fine and his colleagues (1974) suggest that

> ... the most effective way of testing whether or not Task Statements communicate is for a group of analysts to compare their understandings of the tasks and to reach an agreement on their meaning. The broader the range of experience represented by the editing group, the more likely the Task Statements are to be complete, accurate, and clearly stated, and the less likely the information in them is to be dismissed as merely a matter of opinion. Group editing can increase the

objectivity of tasks analysis and, therefore, the reliability of Task Statements. (9)

Once the inventory is made it is distributed to a sample of job incumbents and other experts who are asked to rate the tasks on several scales including: (1) *data, people, and things,* which describes the way in which the worker interacts with sources of information, other people, and the physical environment; (2) *worker function orientation,* which describes the extent of the worker's involvement with data, people, and things; (3) scale of worker instructions, which describes the amount of control a worker has over the specific methods of task performance; and (4) general educational development scales, which assess the abilities required in the areas of reasoning, mathematics, and language (Fine, 1973; Fine et al., 1974; Gatewood and Feild, 1990). Later work by Fine (1988) indicates that workers are asked to rate tasks on the inventory according to whether or not they perform the task and, if desired, to indicate the frequency, criticality, and importance of the task to the job. The usefulness of the latter three ratings, he notes, is dubious. "The critical issue is really whether the task needs to be performed to get the work done. If it is necessary, then it is important and critical, and frequency does not matter" (1029).

Generating Employee Specifications Once a task inventory is completed by the incumbent sample, the results can be summarized according to the mean rating each item received. McCormick (1979) points out that there is no easy formula for determining job requirements from task inventories. Gatewood and Feild (1990) suggest that the analyst sets a cutoff point for mean ratings (e.g., 3 on a 5-point scale) and for standard deviations (e.g., 1), which are computed for each item scored by the respondents. Items with a mean rating of ≥3 and a standard deviation of ≤1 would, according to this rule, be included in the list of job requirements. Finally, they suggest that at least 75 percent of employees must indicate that they perform the task. Thus, any task statements receiving a score of 3 or higher, a standard deviation of 1.0 or less (lower standard deviations are associated with more agreement among raters), and which at least 75 percent of employees engage in are included in the final task inventory that describes the job. The final inventory determines the content of the measures to be used in the new selection program.

TABLE 4.2 A TASK ANALYSIS INVENTORY TO ASSESS THE JOB "MEETING PLANNER"

Job Tasks	Frequency of performance	Criticality of performance	Difficulty of execution	Importance for new hire
Researches pricing structure of potential hotel meeting facilities in order to determine the sites that are within the negotiable price range of the client	[ ]	[ ]	[ ]	[ ]
Prepares reports for clients summarizing hotel, air, and ground transportation vendor offers				

Frequency	Criticality	Difficulty	New Hire
1 = never	1 = not at all critical	1 = not at all difficult	1 = not at all important
2 = seldom	2 = somewhat critical	2 = somewhat difficult	2 = somewhat important
3 = occasionally	3 = moderately critical	3 = moderately difficult	3 = moderately important
4 = frequently	4 = very critical	4 = very difficult	4 = very important
5 = most of the time	5 = extremely critical	5 = extremely difficult	5 = extremely important

It is good practice to have the incumbents rate the knowledge, skills, and abilities (KSAs) associated with each task after the final inventory is generated, as it is the KSAs that will be ultimately sampled with the subsequent selection measures. Gatewood and Feild (1990, 347) proposed these definitions of knowledge, skills, and abilities in order to make inferences concerning employee specifications for a job:

- **Knowledge:** A body of information, usually of a factual or procedural nature that makes for successful performance of a task.

- **Skill:** An individual's level of proficiency or competency in performing a specific task. Level of competency is typically expressed in numerical terms.

- **Ability:** A more general, enduring trait or capability an individual possesses at the time when he or she first begins to perform a task.

KSAs are rated with respect to their necessity to the job, whether they are required upon entry to the job, and the difficulty inherent in obtaining them (i.e., the experience or education that is required). Table 4.3 presents a sample task statement with its component KSAs described.

TABLE 4.3 TASK STATEMENT AND COMPONENT KSAS FOR THE JOB "MEETING PLANNER"

Task Statement:

Summarizes information in report form from potential hotel, air, and ground transportation vendors in order to convey information to clients and facilitate comparisons between vendor offers and bids for service using meeting and travel reference guides.

Knowledge

K1. Knowledge of service offers from vendors.

K2. Knowledge of negotiated goods and services agreements from vendors.

K3. Knowledge of facility and travel reference guides.

K4. Knowledge of vendor pricing structures and policies.

Skills

S1. Skill in typing 40 words per minute without error.

Abilities

A1. Ability to use *Meeting Facilities Guide.*

A2. Ability to use *Official Airlines Guide.*

A3. Ability to use *SABRE* and *Apollo* airline reservation systems.

A4. Ability to compile information from several sources.

A5. Ability to record information through writing, Dictaphone, or word processor.

Task inventories are advantageous in that they are efficient to use with large numbers of employees, and are easily translated to quantifiable measures. On the other hand, they can be time-consuming to develop and thus can be expensive. Motivating incumbents to participate in the rating process may also be a problem with long inventories (Cascio, 1982). When the task inventory procedure and analysis is well planned, the results can be extremely valuable in developing human resource selection programs.

CRITICAL INCIDENT TECHNIQUE Critical incidences are examples of effective and ineffective work behaviours that are related to superior or inferior performance. This method, which generates behaviourally focused descriptions of work activities, was originally developed as a training needs assessment and performance appraisal tool (Bownas and Bernardin, 1988). Ghorpade notes that it is also commonly employed as a means of generating employee specifications based on critical job behaviours. The first step in this method is to gather a panel of job experts, usually consisting of people with several years experience who have had the opportunity to observe both poor and exemplary workers on the job. The job of the panel is to gather critical incidents. Flanagan (1954) defined an incident as an observable human activity that is sufficiently complete to facilitate inferences and predictions about the person performing the act. Panel members describe incidents including the antecedents to the activity, a complete description of the behaviour, the results of the behaviour, and whether the results were within the control of the worker. After the incidents are gathered, they are translated into dimensions that are expressed as KSAOs by the panel. The incidents represent real behaviours of both exemplary and inferior workers, thus it is assumed that they provide a logical basis for determining employee specifications (Ghorpade, 1988).

WORKER TRAITS INVENTORIES Worker traits inventories are not job analysis techniques according to Harvey's strict criteria (1991). Recall, Harvey strongly asserted that the term job analysis "should *not* be used to denote the wide assortment of procedures that make inferences about people or otherwise *apply* job analysis data (e.g., to infer personal traits that might be necessary for successful job performance)" (73). These methods are mentioned here because they are widely used to infer employee specifications from job analysis data, and are commonly included in the job analysis literature.

The Threshold Traits Analysis System (Lopez, 1988) is designed to identify worker traits that are relevant to the target job. This method assumes that work behaviours encompass the position function, the worker traits, and the resulting job performance. According to Lopez, a trait is "a set of observable characteristics that distinguishes one person from another" (881). Supervisors, incumbents, and other subject matter experts rate the job according to the relevancy of 33 worker traits (e.g., stamina, perception, oral expression, adaptability to pressure, and tolerance). Traits are also rated with respect to the level of trait possession necessary to perform the job, and the practicality of expecting potential incumbents to possess the traits upon hiring.

The Ability Requirements Scales (ARS), now called the Fleishman Job Analysis System (FJAS), were developed as a system for identifying employee characteristics that influence job performance. It assumes that job tasks differ with respect to the abilities required to perform them successfully, and that all jobs can be classified according to ability requirements.

Fleishman and his colleagues (Fleishman and Mumford, 1988; Fleishman and Quaintance, 1984) have identified through factor analysis a collection of 52 ability categories. Categories range from oral comprehension to multilimb coordination to night vision. Administration of the ARS requires that 20 or more subject matter experts, including job incumbents, supervisors, and others, be presented with a job description or task list. The experts are asked to rate the extent to which each ability is required for the job. Ratings on the ability scales are then averaged to identify the overall ability requirements essential to the job.

A third worker trait technique is the Job Element Method (JEM), which attempts to distinguish between superior and inferior workers on the basis of job-related abilities. Elements describe the range of employee specifications commonly called KSAOs (Primoff and Eyde, 1988). The JEM procedure requires supervisors and other subject matter experts to generate a list of elements required for job performance. Elements (e.g., accuracy for a grocery store cashier) are broken down into sub-elements (e.g., ability to determine cost of items, press register keys, and make change) that exhaustively describe the job. The expert panel is subsequently asked to rate the elements and sub-elements on four scales: (1) *barely acceptable* measures whether or not minimally acceptable employees possess the ability; (2) *superior* asks whether the ability distinguishes superior workers from others; (3) *trouble likely if not considered* asks whether or not the ability can be safely ignored in selecting employees; and (4) *practical* asks whether or not workers can be expected to have an ability.

RATING JOB ANALYSIS METHODS

Much research has considered the efficacy of various job and worker trait analysis techniques for generating employee specifications. Levine and his colleagues (Levine, Ash, Hall, and Sistrunk, 1983) assessed seven job analysis methods for their effectiveness for a variety of organizational purposes and for their practicality. Job analysis experts were asked to rate the Threshold Traits Analysis, Ability Requirements Scales, Position Analysis Questionnaire, Critical Incident Technique, Functional Job Analysis, and the Job Elements Method, all of which have been discussed in this chapter. Additionally, the Task Inventory with the Comprehensive Occupational Data Analysis Program (TI/CODAP) was assessed. For purposes of identifying personnel requirements and specifications, the seven methods rated in the following order: (1–5) Threshold Traits Analysis, Job Elements Method, Functional Job Analysis, Ability Requirements Scales, and Position Analysis Questionnaire; (6–7) TI/CODAP and Critical Incident Technique. The first five ratings were not significantly different from each other, meaning that they were rated as equally acceptable for identifying personnel requirements. All five were rated significantly higher than the TI/CODAP and the Critical Incident Technique.

Job analyses must meet legal requirements if challenged in court, thus the respondents were asked to rate each of the job analysis methods in terms of how well they stand up to legal and quasi-legal requirements. TI/CODAP and Functional Job Analysis ranked highest, followed closely by the PAQ. The Job Elements Method, Critical Incident Technique, Threshold Traits Analysis, and the Ability Requirements Scales ranked fourth through seventh respectively. Hence, the highest ranking method for meeting legal requirements scored as one of the least preferred methods for identifying personnel requirements and specifications. Functional Job Analysis was highly ranked by job analysis experts on both of these important aspects of use.

Regarding practicality, Levine and colleagues (1983) assessed the versatility, standardization, user acceptability, amount of training required for use, operational practicality, sample size requirements, off-the-shelf usability, reliability, cost of use, quality of outcome, and amount of time required for completion for each of seven job analysis methods. The PAQ received consistently high ratings (i.e., above 3 on a 5-point scale) on all items except the amount of training required. Functional Job Analysis was next with high ratings on all scales with the exception of training, cost, and time to completion. In terms of overall practicality scores, these methods were followed by the JEM, the Threshold Traits Analysis, Ability Requirements Scales, and TI/CODAP. The Critical Incident Technique received the overall lowest ratings on practicality measures. The TI/CODAP and PAQ rated highest for reliability, followed by Functional Job Analysis.

Other researchers have assessed job analysis techniques to determine whether or not different results are produced when different subject matter experts are used. Mullins and Kimbrough (1988) found that different groups of subject matter experts produced different job analysis outcomes using the critical incident technique. They also determined that performance levels of subject matter experts influenced analysis outcomes. These results are inconsistent with previous studies that found no difference in job analysis outcomes relative to performance levels and the authors suggest that the complexity of the job may mediate the performance level/analysis outcome relationship. In a similar study, Schmitt and Cohen (1989) found that when using a task inventory, people with different occupational experience produced different outcomes, as did males and females. No difference was found for experts of different races.

Job analysis researchers have also questioned the relationship between the amount of information analysts are given about a job and the quality of analysis outcomes (Harvey and Lozada-Larsen, 1988). They concluded that differential accuracy of analysis results is a function of the amount of information provided for the analysts. Specifically, analysts having the job title and job description were more accurate in their analyses than those given only the job title. The authors make an important conclusion that should be considered when preparing for a job analysis (460):

> *Our results indicate that the amount of job descriptive information available to raters has a significant effect on job analysis accuracy. Raters with more detailed job information are consistently more accurate than those given only a job title.*

◆ ◆ ◆

SUMMARY

In the world of work, jobs are rapidly evolving due to changing technology and organizational practices. For many workers, this means that the tasks performed today may be radically different from those required a few months from today. Task and job instability creates a growing need for hiring people with an already-learned set of skills and with the ability to make decisions and adapt to changing organizational demands. As a result, human resources professionals may increasingly find the need to combine organization, process, and job analysis techniques in novel ways, while remaining within acceptable legal limits in making recruitment and selection decisions. This chapter demonstrates how human resources functions should tie their process goals to those of the overall organization. Conducting job analyses against a backdrop of process and organization analyses can enhance the effectiveness of the human resources function.

A wide variety of techniques is available for analyzing jobs. While some focus primarily on the work that gets done, others focus on generic human behaviours that are relevant to all work. Which of these techniques to use is a decision based on the goal of the analysis, the resources available to the analyst, and the needs of the organization. No one method will be completely acceptable for all selection needs in an organization. Job analysts must themselves be adaptable in the methods they apply. Employing a process analysis to the needs of the human resources functions in an organization can help the analyst in making wise choices concerning which tools best serve the current needs of the system.

THE FUTURE OF JOB ANALYSIS

Approaches to job analysis are evolving as the world of work changes. Longo (1995) argues that one side effect of re-engineering and flattening organizations is the disappearance of the job as a stable collection of tasks. In the context of these changes, May (1996,1) addressed some current issues surrounding ways that job analysis remains of value to organizations as a relevant descriptive tool. She states

> Traditionally, job analysis provides detailed information regarding tasks and activities performed in a specific job. Often this information is used to document job boundaries and assign tasks and responsibilities. The resulting products, namely job descriptions and job specifications, are then used to inform human resource functions such as selection and performance management. Job analysis captures the content of jobs as they are described at one point in time. What happens to the usefulness of this technique when the content of jobs changes, sometimes frequently?

Not only do jobs change frequently in the modern market, but approaches to defining work and jobs are also evolving rapidly. Post-job, or "dejobbed," organizations have resulted as new technology in re-engineering and quality management has taken hold. The post-job organization is one that hires people to work well and adaptively, not to fit a job slot. In such an organization, responsibilities are assigned based on the demands of current projects rather than on the basis of previous work patterns (Longo, 1995). In this type of organization, traditional work-based approaches to job analysis are clearly not adequate for determining who will "work well."

Kiechel (1993) confirms that the nature of work is being redefined. This means that the "shelf-life of job analysis results is only as long as the duration of the current job configurations" (May, 1996, 1). If organizations are to survive this trend, then they must adjust their practices accordingly. Human resources practitioners are responding by looking for new ways to select incumbents based on work-related competencies in addition to specific job knowledge and skills. May aptly concludes that

> *Job analysis will continue to be useful if: 1) organizations consist of jobs that are structured around specific tasks and are relatively stable, 2) organizations are collecting data for the purpose of legal compliance and defensibility, and 3) organizations can use modified approaches to job analysis to capture new forms of work.*

Trends in job analysis reflect the shift from structurally based to process-based views of work and organizations. These trends, as summarized by May (1996), include

♦ obtaining job information from customers, technical experts, and those who design work, as well as from job incumbents and supervisors;

♦ describing how the work or job is expected to change in the future and the KSAOs that will be required for the new work;

♦ focusing on collections of tasks or work functions rather than on specific and isolated tasks;

♦ using tools borrowed from other areas of organizational practice, such as flowcharting and process charting, to capture the dynamics of work as it occurs in the organizational context.

Kiechel (1993) takes note that "the average number of employees per company increased until the 1970s, it has been decreasing since then" (40). He contends that we are moving toward modular corporations that are pared down to core competencies. This view, combined with May's discussion (1996) of the evolution toward rapidly changing jobs and organizations that demand flexibility of their workers, suggests that the need for new approaches to job analysis is now an organizational reality. In order to recruit, select, and promote flexible workers who are able to make their own rules and adjust to the changing demands of work, human resources specialists are faced with the ever increasing need to adjust their methods to ensure that people are hired based on the needs of the organization, while remaining within legal boundaries.

C A S E   A

Paper Manufacturing

Martin is the president of a large paper manufacturing company. He states that the purpose of his organization is to sell quality paper products at a lower price than his competitors while still making a profit. "This is really in our control as long as we can keep our manufacturing costs down and our overall productivity up. That means we have to set up production so we reinforce productivity but not at the expense of the worker. In my estimation you can't meet the overall goal of the organization if you take advantage of employees. There are side effects for pushing people too hard, although many managers don't understand that."

"I am an advocate of Performance Management (PM) style of running the company. We want to pay people for what they do and create an environment in which they can be most effective. Right now we are having some manage-

ment conflict because many managers are not following the strategies that have been set up to realize our mission. I really wanted to base performance appraisals on objective measures of performance from my job to the janitor's but some of my key players are fighting these changes. I hope this is out of ignorance and fear rather than an inherent desire to destroy the company."

The company is composed of two main divisions: necessity items and luxury items. Two-thirds of the products are manufactured out of the necessity division and the other third is from luxury. Lucy is the head of the luxury line and has been sweating bullets over sales due to a dwindling economy. However, her division has still been able to add a few new customers each month, and has been excellent at holding on to the current clients. Lucy has fewer people in her division, but she also has fewer supervisors per employee than her necessity counterpart. She has a customer service and customer satisfaction program, and each one of her sales representatives are responsible for sales—which includes attracting new customers, keeping old customers, and asking customers how they can serve their needs better. These strategies Lucy believes are compatible with the overall goal of the company.

Anne is the overall head of the necessity division, with Jeff in charge of food paper products and Todd in charge of writing paper products. Anne reports that

she spends most of her time refereeing disputes between Jeff and Todd. Both men constantly compete with one another and refuse to share ideas. Anne states that she is continually coming up with compromises but this is starting to take up so much of her time she can't get her "real" work done. Whenever she tries to confront the situation she is met with yelling, blaming, or "It's not fair." She admits that she has been trying to run everything herself and has been sending out memos rather than talking to either man face to face.

Source: Devries, 1995, 79.

C A S E   B

East Side Eatery

Stan is the proud owner of East Side Eatery. He has owned the place for the past five years, and until recently it has been a financial success. Stan tells you that his number one concern is customer satisfaction. With Stan, you get more than you pay for. "Here we surpass customer expectations. Our goal is to provide great food, great service, and a unique environment in which to dine. Complimentary wine for those who have to wait with reservation. Anything extra that is not specified in the menu is a perk to most of my patrons," exclaims Stan as he glows with pride. (You're thinking that Stan is pretty dramatic but wonder if his philosophy is effective.) Stan tells you

that the motto of all the employees is "We aim to please." (Where does he get these people?)

You used to frequent Stan's eatery and have always been satisfied with the food—but you are shocked at Stan's motto for you don't remember leaving the eatery with that feeling. It's been four months since you've eaten in this restaurant and now you are remembering why. The service here is poor, at best. You've been waiting over 20 minutes and you had a reservation ("Where is my glass of wine?"). Once you are finally seated at a table (which looks as though someone squeezed it in at the last moment) it is another five minutes before you get your menu ("Give it to me the first time and you won't have to come back Knucklehead," you mentally scream at the waiter). Ten minutes after you get your menu your waiter returns to take your order. You are interested in the special—boneless chicken, but the waiter can give you no information on how it is prepared (other than, "You know, they take out the bone."). Obviously, you stick to an old standby rather than risk the mystery chicken.

When your meal finally does arrive (20 minutes after you ordered it) you are impressed with the food. Even the salad is good here. It is aesthetic in appearance with a plethora of unusual vegetables and not a speck of iceberg lettuce to be found. As you munch on your salad you watch the employees as they "work." Most of them are laughing and talking but a bit too loudly for the atmosphere. Food is placed on a counter from the kitchen but often sits there for five minutes or more before it is picked up, patrons have to request beverage refills and tables are only cleared as they are needed, not as customers leave. Stan has told you that he has specified the behaviors that he wants to see his employees display. "Greet every customer within 10 seconds of entering the restaurant, those who have reservations and have to wait should be offered free drinks, when the waitresses or waiters are busy the hostess or host will provide drink refills, menus, and any other assistance. The people who bus the tables can also fill in to assist the waitpersons. Here we all work together to make this one of the best eateries in town. Can't ask for much more than that, can you?" (You can ask for it but it doesn't mean you'll get it.) "Since the employees' performance is specified I don't need to hire a manager for everyone already knows what to do."

Source: Devries, 1995, 66.

E X E R C I S E S

1. Draw a chart of an organization that you are involved in (e.g., your employer, university, or volunteer organization). The chart should specify who is ultimately in charge of the organization (e.g., the company president or a board of governors) and how authority flows through it. Label each position or group of positions and place them in hierarchical or vertical positions relative to each other.

2. Chart the functional relationships between divisions presented in Case A (Paper Manufacturing). Present the overall organizational system in a Total Performance System diagram: label relevant system inputs, processing steps, outputs, and the receiving

system; identify processing and receiving system feedback mechanisms where they exist or are proposed; include the major divisions as subsystems within the main processing system. Note where conflicts exist between and within each of the major divisions.

3. Make a customer service process map from the information provided in Case B (East Side Eatery). The map should include information on what happens from the time customers enter the restaurant until they pay for their meals and leave. Label the organizational divisions that are responsible for different stages of the customers' experiences and the products and services each of those divisions provide. Next, identify any gaps in the service system and draw a second process map of what the ideal service flow would look like according to Stan's descriptions.

4. Using the form presented in Figure 4.6, observe someone at work or monitor your own work for a short time period (e.g., 15–30 minutes). Record the conditions and activities as they change, describe the activities that the worker engages in, the tools used, and the amount of time spent on each activity. Do not choose a job that does not lend itself to direct observation. If you are observing another person at work, get permission before doing so.

5. Prepare a brief outline for conducting a job analysis interview. Use the outline to interview an incumbent or supervisor. You may choose to interview a parent or sibling about his or her work, a co-worker or supervisor from your workplace, or a classmate. Make careful notes during the interview and write up a point-form summary of the major job tasks as described by the interviewee.

References

Ash, R.A. 1988. "Job Analysis in the World of Work." In S. Gael, ed., *The Job Analysis Handbook for Business, Industry and Government*. Vol. 1. New York: Wiley, 3–13.

Ash, R.A., and S.L. Edgell. 1975. "A Note on the Readability of the Position Analysis Questionnaire (PAQ)." *Journal of Applied Psychology* 60: 765–66.

Bownas, D.A., and H.J. Bernardin. 1988. "Critical Incident Technique." In S. Gael, ed., *The Job Analysis Handbook for Business, Industry and Government*. Vol. 2. New York: Wiley, 1120–37.

Brethower, D.M. 1982. "Total Performance Systems." In R.M. O'Brien, A.M. Dickinson, and M. Rosow, eds., *Industrial Behavior Modification*. New York: Pergamon Press.

Cascio, W.F. 1982. *Applied Psychology in Personnel Management*. 2nd ed. Reston, Virginia: Reston Publishing.

Cascio, W.F. 1995. "Whither Industrial and Organizational Psychology in a Changing World of Work?" *American Psychologist* 50: 928–39.

Christal, R.E., and J.J. Weissmuller. 1988. Job-Task Inventory Analysis. In S. Gael, ed., *The Job Analysis Handbook for Business, Industry and Government*. Vol. 2. New York: Wiley, 1036–50.

Churchman, C.W. 1979. *The Systems Approach*. New York: Dell.

Cronshaw, S.F. 1988. "Future Directions for Industrial Psychology in Canada." *Canadian Psychology* 29: 30–43.

Daniels, A.C. 1994. *Bringing Out the Best in People*. New York: McGraw-Hill.

Deloitte & Touche LLP. 1995. *U.S. Manufacturers Need Top Talent to Meet Challenge of Global Competition*. [Online]http://www.dttus.com/dttus/hot/hotlist.htm.

Devries, J. 1995. *The Effects of Systems-Centered versus Individual-Centered Training on the Analysis of Organizational Problems*. Western Michigan University. Unpublished doctoral dissertation.

Drauden, G.M. 1988. "Task Inventory Analysis in Industry and the Public Sector." In S. Gael, ed., *The Job Analysis Handbook for Business, Industry and Government*. Vol. 2. New York: Wiley, 1051–71.

Fine, S.A. 1973. "Functional Job Analysis Scales: A Desk Aid." *Methods for Manpower Analysis*. No. 7. Kalamazoo,

MI: W.E. Upjohn Institute for Employment Research.

Fine, S.A. 1988. "Functional Job Analysis." In S. Gael, ed., *The Job Analysis Handbook for Business, Industry and Government*. Vol. 2. New York: Wiley, 1019–35.

Fine, S.A., A.M. Holt, and M.F. Hutchinson. 1974. "Functional Job Analysis: How to Standardize Task Statements." *Methods for Manpower Analysis*. No. 9. Kalamazoo, MI: W.E. Upjohn Institute for Employment Research.

Fine, S.A., and W.W. Wiley. 1971. *An Introduction to Functional Job Analysis*. Washington, DC: Upjohn.

Flanagan, J.C. 1954. "The Critical Incident Technique." *Psychological Bulletin* 51: 327–58.

Fleishman, E.A., and M.D. Mumford. 1988. "Ability Requirements Scales." In S. Gael, ed., *The Job Analysis Handbook for Business, Industry and Government*. Vol. 1. New York: Wiley, 917–35.

Fleishman, E.A., and M.K. Quaintance. 1984. *Taxonomies of Human Performance: The Description of Human Tasks*. Orlando, FL: Academic Press.

Gael, S. 1983. *Job Analysis: A Guide to Assessing Work Activities*. San Francisco, CA: Jossey-Bass.

Gael, S. 1988. "Interviews, Questionnaires, and Checklists." In

S. Gael ed., *The Job Analysis Handbook for Business, Industry and Government*. Vol. 1. New York: Wiley, 391–418.

Gatewood, R.D., and H.S. Feild. 1990. *Human Resources Selection*. 2nd ed. New York: Dryden Press.

Ghorpade, J.V. 1988. *Job Analysis: A Handbook for the Human Resource Director*. Englewood Cliffs, NJ: Prentice-Hall.

Gilbert, T.F. 1978. *Human Competence: Engineering Worthy Performance*. New York: McGraw-Hill.

Haber, S. 1964. *Efficiency and Uplift: Scientific Management in the Progressive Era 1890–1920*. Chicago, Illinois: University of Chicago Press.

Hammer, M., and J. Champy. 1993. *Reengineering the Corporation*. NY: HarperBusiness.

Harvey, R.J. 1991. "Job Analysis." In M.D. Dunnette and L.M. Hough, eds., *Handbook of Industrial and Organizational Psychology*. Vol. 1. Palo Alto, CA: Consulting Psychologists Press, 71–163.

Harvey, R.J., and S.R. Lozada-Larsen. 1988. "Influence of Amount of Job Descriptive Information on Job Analysis Rating Accuracy." *Journal of Applied Psychology* 73: 457–61.

Katz, D., and R.L. Kahn. 1978. *The Social Psychology of Organizations*. New York: Wiley.

Kiechel, W., III. 1993. "How We Will Work in the Year 2000." *Fortune*, May 17: 38–52.

Labich, K. 1996. "How to Fire People and Still Sleep at Night." *Fortune*, 65–72.

Levine, E.L. 1983. *Everything You Always Wanted to Know About Job Analysis*. Tampa, Florida: Mariner Publishing.

Levine, E.L., R.A. Ash, and N. Bennett. 1980. "Exploratory Comparative Study of Four Job Analysis Methods." *Journal of Applied Psychology* 65: 524–35.

Levine, E.L., R.A. Ash, H. Hall, and F. Sistrunk. 1983. "Evaluation of Job Analysis Methods by Experienced Job Analysts." *Academy of Management Journal* 26: 339–48.

Levine, E.L., J.N. Thomas, and F. Sistrunk. 1988. "Selecting a Job Analysis Approach." In S. Gael, ed., *The Job Analysis Handbook for Business, Industry and Government*. Vol. 1. New York: Wiley, 339–52.

Longo, S.C. 1995. "After Reengineering—'Dejobbing'?" *CPA Journal* 65: 63.

Lopez, F.M. 1988. "Threshold Traits Analysis System." In S. Gael, ed., *The Job Analysis Handbook for Business, Industry and Government*. Vol. 1. New York: Wiley, 880–901.

Martinko, M.J. 1988. "Observing the Work." In S. Gael, ed., *The Job Analysis Handbook for Business, Industry and Government*. Vol. 1. New York: Wiley, 419–31.

May, K.E. 1996. "Work in the 21st Century: Implications for Job Analysis." *The Industrial Psychologist*. [On-line] http://cmit.unomaha. edu/tip/ TIPApr96/may.htm.

McCormick, E.J. 1979. *Job Analysis: Methods and Applications*. New York: AMACOM.

McCormick, E.J., and P.R. Jeanneret, 1991. "Position Analysis Questionnaire (PAQ)." In S. Gael, ed., *The Job Analysis Handbook for Business, Industry and Government*. Vol. 1. New York: Wiley, 825–42.

McCormick, E.J., P.R. Jeanneret, and R.C. Mecham. 1972. "A Study of Job Characteristics and Job Dimensions as Based on the Position Analysis Questionnaire (PAQ)." *Journal of Applied Psychology* 56: 347–67.

McCormick, E.J., P.R. Jeanneret, and R.C. Mecham. 1989. *Position Analysis Questionnaire*. Palo Alto, CA: Consulting Psychologists Press.

McCormick, E.J., R.C. Mecham, and P.R. Jeanneret. 1977. *Technical Manual for the Position Analysis Questionnaire (PAQ) (System II)*. Logan, Utah: PAQ Services.

McPhail, S.M., P.R. Jeanneret, E.J. McCormick, and R.C. Mecham, 1991. *Position Analysis Questionnaire: Job Analysis Manual* (revised edition). Palo

Alto, CA: Consulting Psychologists Press.

Mecham, R.C., E.J. McCormick, and P.R. Jeanneret. 1977. *Users Manual for the Position Analysis Questionnaire (PAQ) (System II)*. Logan, Utah: PAQ Services.

Mullins, W.C., and W.W. Kimbrough. 1988. "Group Composition as a Determinant of Job Analysis Outcomes." *Journal of Applied Psychology* 73: 657–64.

National Occupational Classification. 1993. Minister of Supply and Services Canada, LM-247-12-92E.

Primoff, E.S., and L.D. Eyde. 1988. "Job Element Analysis." In S. Gael, ed., *The Job Analysis Handbook for Business, Industry and Government*. Vol. 1. New York: Wiley, 807–24.

Redmon, W.K., and J.L. Agnew, 1991. "Organizational Behavior Analysis in the U.S.: A View from the Private Sector." In P.A. Lamal, ed., *Behavior Analysis of Societies and Cultural Practices*. Washington. DC: Hemisphere.

Redmon, W.K., and L.A. Wilk. 1991. "Organizational Behavior Analysis in the U.S.: Public Sector Organizations." In P.A. Lama, ed., *Behavior Analysis of Societies and Cultural Practices*. Washington. DC: Hemisphere.

Rummler, G.A., and A.P. Brache. 1990. *Improving Performance: How to Manage the White Space on the Organization Chart*. San Francisco, California: Jossey-Bass.

Schmitt, N., and S.A. Cohen. 1989. "Internal Analyses of Task Ratings by Job Incumbents." *Journal of Applied Psychology* 74: 96–104.

Scholtes, P.R. 1988. *The Team Handbook*. Madison, WI: Joiner Associates.

Sparks, C.P. 1988. "Legal Basis for Job Analysis." In S. Gael, ed., *The Job Analysis Handbook for Business, Industry and Government*. Vol. 1. New York: Wiley, 37–47.

Statistics Canada. 1996. *Canada at a Glance: Labour Market*. [On-line]. http://www.statcan.ca/Documents/ English/Faq/Glance/ labour.htm

Thompson, D.E., and T.A. Thompson. 1982. "Court Standards for Job Analysis in Test Validation." *Personnel Psychology* 35: 872–73.

"Uniform Guidelines on Employee Selection Procedures." 1978. *Federal Register* 43: 38290–315.

Wanous, J.P. 1974. "A Causal-Correlational Analysis of the Job Satisfaction and Performance Relationship." *Journal of Applied Psychology* 59: 139–244.

Weber, M. 1947. *The Theory of Social and Economic Organization*. A.M. Henderson and T. Parsons, trans. New York: Oxford University Press.

Zemke, R.E., and J.W. Gunkler. 1982. "Organization-Wide Intervention." In L.W. Fredericksen, ed., *Handbook of Organizational Management.* New York: Wiley.

5

The Relevance
of Criteria

◆ ◆ ◆

CHAPTER GOALS

This chapter provides the foundation for the measurement of job-related performance as an integral part of the recruitment and selection process. It links job performance not only to individual competencies but also to organization goals and values. Measures of job performance are used as criteria in selecting new employees and as a means of evaluating current employees. The last part of the chapter reviews several performance measurement techniques. After reading this chapter you should

- understand the importance of developing and using scientifically sound measures of job performance in selection and assessment;

- know how organizational goals influence both individual and group performance;

- understand the relationship between individual performance measures, criteria, and performance dimensions related to a job;

- appreciate the technical aspects of measuring job performance;

- be familiar with the strengths and weaknesses of different types of performance rating systems; and

- understand the features that a performance appraisal system should have in place to satisfy human rights concerns.

◆ ◆ ◆

THE RELEVANCE OF CRITERION MEASURES TO RECRUITMENT AND SELECTION

The New York City-based Colgate-Palmolive Company has operations in nearly 200 countries throughout the world, including Canada. It recruits and hires people from around the world. Its workforce consists of people from different cultures and different backgrounds. In order to remain a successful, competitive global enterprise, Colgate must be capable of sustaining organizational excellence. Colgate has chosen to do this through its selection process, which is based on the identification and communication of Colgate's values, vision, and strategic goals. Colgate accomplished this by setting up *competency-development* teams, which identified the skills and experiences that were required for each job level within each function. For example, a team composed of financial officers from various Colgate operations identified the skills and experiences needed to perform successfully as an associate accountant, senior accountant, or supervisor of accounting. These skills and experiences, or competencies, are then used to select people, to identify their training needs, and to assess their performance (Anfuso, 1995). In effect, Colgate integrates its strategic goals with individual performance through the recruitment and selection process. It seeks to hire people who have the competencies needed to perform at a successful level to maintain Colgate's organizational excellence.

When Colgate or other companies go to the marketplace to recruit and hire, they know what they are looking for in terms of competencies as well as what they expect in the way of performance from the people they hire. Job applicants may only have a vague or very general idea about the job for which they've applied and the competencies that it requires. This idea may be shaped by a job description in a want ad, word of mouth, or by an expectation associated with a job title (e.g., senior accountant). As part of the recruitment and hiring process, applicants want to learn more specific information about their prospective job. They want to know the set of duties, behaviours, or tasks that they will be asked to perform if they are hired, and they want to know what competencies they must have to perform those duties. They also want to know the performance level that will be needed to maintain organizational excellence and how that performance will be measured. Employers must be able to answer these questions if they are to compete successfully in the labour market, to recruit and to select the most appropriate job candidates.

Colgate's goal is to hire top performing employees who will maintain organizational excellence. Before Colgate's competency-development teams could identify the skills and experiences, they had to know the behaviours performed in different jobs. Based on their knowledge gained through experience in the job, and assisted by human resources professionals, the members of the competency-development teams defined a set of behaviours and established the level of performance required for organizational excellence. Once the behaviours were established, the knowledge, skills, abilities, and experience related to those behaviours could be identified. This is the same situation as presented in Chapter 3 where a human resources manager links cognitive ability to higher levels of job performance (see Figure 3.2, Line A, p. 104). The competency-development team (subject matter experts) is actually carrying out a job analysis based on organizational goals. Box 5.1 presents a procedure that can be used to identify goal-based competencies. Although the procedure presented in Box 5.1 starts with identification of job behaviours, the subject matter experts could just as easily have first specified the competencies related to organizational excellence and then determined the job behaviours expected of someone who has those competencies. This is the approach British Petroleum uses to select employees for its global workforce (Moravec and Tucker, 1992).

BOX 5.1 A JOB ANALYSIS BASED ON ORGANIZATIONAL GOALS AND OBJECTIVES

1. Convene a panel or team of subject matter experts, that is, people who are most knowledgeable about the job in question;
2. Ask the panel to examine the job in the context of the organization's goals;
3. Ask the panel to identify the individual competencies (knowledge, skills, ability, experience) that are related to organizational excellence and to successful attainment of organizational goals;
4. Ask the panel to list all of the specific job behaviours that should be expected from someone with the desired competencies;
5. Use the identified job-related behaviours as a measure of performance.

An increasing number of Canadian organizations have realized the economic benefits that result when they select employees who have the competencies or characteristics that predict excellent or superior performance of goal-related job behaviours. The Ontario Lottery Corporation, the Ontario Ministry of the Solicitor General and Correctional Services, Goodyear Canada, Guardian Insurance Company of Canada, and University Hospitals of Alberta all have implemented core competency strategies that link performance measurement with recruiting and staffing processes.

Developing measurable processes is crucial to the success of the recruitment and selection function. At some point, a human resources manager must be capable of determining whether a job applicant possesses the required competencies; at another point, the human resources manager must be capable of measuring the performance associated with the competencies. The human resources manager must validate the hiring strategy.

To validate the hiring system, the human resources manager must measure the level of competencies possessed by any job applicant. Chapters 7, 8, and 9 examine the different techniques that have been developed over the years to make these assessments, both those which are routinely used (résumés, interviews) and those which are less familiar (employment tests). Often overlooked by human resources managers is the need to measure performance as well. As the Canadian companies noted earlier recognize, performance measurement is an integral part of the recruiting and selection system. Chapter 7 provides a model showing this integration. Before proceeding further with this chapter, you may want to skip ahead to Chapter 7 and review Figure 7.3, p. 282, which presents this integrated model.

Measuring performance is easier said than done. The organization, or its human resources manager, must decide what performance to measure and the level of performance needed to attain organizational excellence. Job performance is behaviour, the observable things people do, that is relevant to the goals of an organization. As we've seen in the last chapter on job analysis, rarely if ever does a job involve the performance of only one specific behaviour. Measures of job performance are called criteria when used in the selection of job applicants; they are the performance standards for judging success or failure on the job.

Choosing a criterion or performance measure may be rather complex. Suppose you are the human resources specialist in charge of selecting petroleum engineers for British Petroleum. You are responsible for recruiting and selecting men and women who will perform successfully as engineers. Do you recruit and select people on the basis of their job-related technical skills, or do you also consider leadership qualities, business awareness, planning and organizational ability, communication and interpersonal skills, initiative, and problem solving ability? British Petroleum identified all of these job dimensions, through job and organizational analysis, as related to success. What, then, constitutes successful performance by a petroleum engineer? What if someone is judged to be a success as a leader but a failure in the technical aspects of engineering, or vice versa? Are any of these performance dimensions more important than others? Should we combine performance across all dimensions or always consider each dimension separately? These are some of the criterion-related issues that must be addressed when an organization develops an integrated selection and recruitment system. How these questions are answered establishes not only how we define and measure job-related performance but also who the organization will recruit and hire.

THE CRITERION PROBLEM

Most efforts directed at improving selection systems have focused on improving the measurement of job-related competencies; until recently, relatively less thought has been given to improving the measurement of job performance. Most organizations rely on criterion-related validity studies to defend the appropriateness of their selection systems before human rights and other tribunals. No matter how accurately the organization measures competencies, the criterion-related validity will still be low without improvement in performance measurement. Unfortunately, many human resources managers do not appreciate the linkage between selection and performance measurement. Performance measures are often chosen because the pressure of getting things done leads to choosing the most convenient measure at hand and hoping it will turn out all right. The criterion problem is really one of choosing a measure or set of measures that best captures the essence of the complex job-related performance in question such as that encountered by British Petroleum.

Successful companies like Body Shop Canada and Coors Brewing recognize the important role that performance measurement plays in developing strategies for effective recruitment and selection. Rather than simply choosing a measure and hoping it works, the first step is to specify the job performance in terms of measurable behaviours; the next step is to find valid measures of those behaviours. The criterion or performance measure must be a valid indicator of job performance as determined by job and organizational analysis. There is an important difference in contemporary approaches to establishing criteria. Companies such as Sun Microsystems are not only looking to hire people who have the competencies needed for successful job performance, they also link the required performance to organizational goals and values. Desired job-related behaviours and outcomes are those that secure organizational goals; increasingly, companies are looking for a fit between the person and the organization.

◆ ◆ ◆
LINKING ORGANIZATION PERFORMANCE TO GROUP AND INDIVIDUAL PERFORMANCE

Canadian organizations, particularly manufacturers, are increasingly concerned about attaining a competitive advantage over their competition. They face problems of global competition, competition with cheap wage economies or economies where taxation is low, and a workforce whose growth is slowing. They also must deal with periodic downturns in the economy.

Manufacturing industries can deal with their local and world-wide problems in a number of ways, including increasing productivity. "Working smarter" has become a catch-phrase of the 1990s. Much of the effort to increase productivity has produced problem-driven, quick-fix solutions, which have focused on individual performance while ignoring organizational productivity. Many factors affect organizational productivity. One organization may be more productive than another for reasons that have nothing to do with human resources; for example, the nature of the product, the technology used in manufacturing the product, and the market position of the company at a given time. Nonetheless, human resources interventions, such as implementing valid selection and performance appraisal systems, do lead to increased levels of individual productivity (Guzzo,1988).

WHAT IS PRODUCTIVITY?

There is no common, widely shared definition of productivity (Mahoney, 1988). The definition of productivity depends upon an organization's goals and values. Economists define productivity as the relationship between outputs of goods and services and the inputs of basic resources—labour, capital goods, and natural resources. Human resource specialists focus on the performance and effectiveness of personnel at an individual level and consider the fit between the individual and the organization. Often organizational productivity is not simply an aggregate of productivity measures taken over individuals; it also includes the idea of outputs relative to organizational goals.

ORGANIZATIONAL GOALS: LINKING INDIVIDUAL PERFORMANCE AND AGGREGATE PRODUCTIVITY

Individuals affect productivity through behaviours that directly contribute to the organization's goals. In the case of British Petroleum, technical skills, leadership qualities, business awareness, planning and organizational ability, communication and interpersonal skills, initiative, and problem solving ability were linked to organizational effectiveness. These performance factors or dimensions are related to achieving British Petroleum's goals. Differences between workers at British Petroleum on any or all of these factors will result in different levels of individual productivity. Recruiting and selecting workers who excel on these job dimensions leads to organizational productivity at British Petroleum. Organizational productivity is influenced to a considerable degree by such factors as organizational culture and climate, management practices including performance evaluation and reward schemes, individual attitudes and values, and consensus about organizational goals that may exist between the individual and the supervisor, and the supervisor and the manager. The level of organizational productivity may depend on the degree to which employees, supervisors, and managers share the same attitudes, values, and goals (Vancouver and Schmitt, 1991). Obviously, the differences across organizations, reflected in their goals and values, will lead to different levels of organizational productivity.

ORGANIZATIONAL GOALS

The measurement of productivity is closely tied to the goals and values of the organization. Different subgroups or individuals within an organization may not share the same goals or values. For example, managers may view productivity increases as a means to their own advancement while a worker may believe that increased productivity will only lead to demands for more productivity. Often, employees at all levels are unaware of the organization's goals. Organizational goals must be clearly stated and linked to specific individual performance. An organization should measure employee behaviour that is directed toward accomplishing its goals and not simply measure some aspect of employee behaviour because the behaviour is easy to measure. Once relevant goals have been defined, the next step is to define the set of behaviours that are necessary for reaching the goals. As we discussed in Chapter 4, organizational analysis provides the human resources specialist with a set of tools that can be used to assess the work environment in terms of the characteristics of the organization, while job analysis provides information about a specific job. Both must be used together to identify appropriate criteria for measuring job performance in a specific organizational environment.

◆ ◆ ◆

IDENTIFYING APPROPRIATE CRITERIA: ORGANIZATIONAL GOALS AND VALUES

SPECIFYING THE JOB PERFORMANCE DOMAIN

As we've seen, British Petroleum identified seven specific performance dimensions that were essential to its organizational effectiveness. A different company with different goals (e.g., Ontario Lottery Corporation) would have different performance dimensions and different performance measurement systems or criteria. A multi-million dollar project designed to develop an integrated selection and performance evaluation system for use with the U.S. army suggests that the job dimensions defined through different organizational goals may have a common, underlying structure (Campbell, 1990).

Job performance is behaviour (i.e., the observable things people do) that is related to accomplishing the goals of an organization. The job performance domain is a name given to the set of all behaviours that are relevant to the goals of the organization, or the unit, in which a person works. The goals pursued by an organization are value judgments on the part of those empowered to make them. Goals are defined for employees who hold specific positions within the organization. Individual performance must contribute to achieving the organizational goals. The activities or behaviours needed to accomplish goals may vary considerably from job to job, or across levels in organizations. It becomes a matter of *expert* judgment whether particular actions or behaviours are relevant for particular goals. Performance is *not* the consequence or result of action, it is the action itself (Campbell, 1990). This is the concept of the performance domain presented in Figure 3.2, p. 104. This concept is consistent with the job and organizational analysis procedure outlined in Box 5.1 (p. 181), which is designed to focus directly on criteria performance related to job objectives and goals, and to identify the competencies needed to maintain organizational effectiveness.

THE JOB PERFORMANCE DOMAIN

The behaviours that people are expected to do as part of their job appear to fall into eight *job dimensions* or job components, which together specify the job performance domain. These eight job dimensions, as identified by Campbell, are as follows:

1. **Job-specific task proficiency** reflects the degree to which an individual can perform technical tasks that make up the content of the job. A petroleum engineer and an accountant must perform different behaviours as part of their specific jobs. Within jobs, individuals may vary in their level of competence. One engineer may be more technically proficient than another, just as one accountant may be more technically proficient than some other accountants.

2. **Non job-specific task proficiency** reflects the degree to which individuals can perform tasks or behaviours that are not specific to any one job. Both the engineer and accountant may have to have a good understanding of the business environment in which their company operates.

3. **Written and oral communication task proficiency** is the degree to which an individual can write or speak, independent of the correctness of the subject matter. Both the engineer and accountant make oral reports to people they deal with on the job; both also make written reports on the work they perform.

4. **Demonstrating effort** reflects the degree to which individuals are committed to performing all job tasks, to working at a high level of intensity, and to keep working under adverse conditions. How willing are the engineer or accountant to work overtime to complete a project? Do they begin their workdays earlier than expected? Can they be relied upon to give the same level of effort day in and day out? Do they show initiative?

5. **Maintaining personal discipline** characterizes the extent to which negative behaviours are avoided. Does either the engineer or accountant drink on the job? Do they follow the appropriate laws, regulations, or codes

that govern their professions? Do they show up for scheduled assignments?

6. **Facilitating peer and team performance** is the degree to which an individual supports co-workers, helps them with job problems, and keeps them working as a team to achieve their goals. Is the engineer or accountant available to give the others a helping hand? Does either offer new trainees the benefit of their experience? Do they keep their colleagues focused on completing the work team's goals?

7. **Supervision/Leadership** includes behaviours that are directed at influencing the performance of subordinates through interpersonal means. Does either the engineer or accountant set goals and performance standards for people they direct? Do they use whatever influence is at their disposal, including authority to reward and punish, to shape the behaviour of subordinates?

8. **Management/Administration** includes all other performance behaviours involved in management that are distinct from supervision. Do the engineer and accountant contact clients and arrange appointments; do they schedule work in the most efficient manner; do they complete all the paper work related to a project?

Job-Specific Task Proficiency, Demonstrating Effort, and Maintaining Personal Discipline are likely to be major performance components of every job (Campbell, 1990); however, not all eight dimensions have to be present in every job. There are few, if any, management skills required by an assembly line worker in an auto plant; on the other hand, the seven performance dimensions identified by British Petroleum fit nicely into this framework. The pattern of differences in these eight dimensions can be used to classify jobs and is consistent with the job classification schemes used by the U.S. *Dictionary of Occupational Titles* and the *Canadian Classification Dictionary of Occupations*.

What determines individual differences on these eight job performance components? That is, why does one petroleum engineer perform more efficiently than another? Campbell proposes that these job dimensions are influenced by three factors: *declarative knowledge, procedural knowledge and skill,* and *motivation*. Declarative knowledge is knowledge about facts and things including knowledge of rules, regulations, and goals. Procedural knowledge and skill is attained when declarative knowledge, knowing what to do, is combined with knowing how to do it. One petroleum engineer knows all about drilling techniques but lacks the appropriate skills to perform successfully on an oil rig. Procedural knowledge and skill includes cognitive, psychomotor, physical, perceptual, interpersonal, and self-management skills. Motivation is defined in terms of choice to perform, level of effort, and persistence of effort. Job performance is some combination of these three factors; performance cannot occur unless there is both a choice to perform at some level and at least a minimal amount of knowledge and skill.

CONTEXTUAL PERFORMANCE

Contextual performance involves activities or behaviours which are not part of a worker's job, but which remain important for organizational effectiveness. While job performance is closely related to underlying knowledge, skills, and abilities, contextual performance supports the organizational, social, and psychological environment in which the job is performed. Contextual activities are not related to a specific job or role but extend to all jobs in an organization. Contextual performance often reflects organizational values. For example, many Canadian companies actively support worthwhile causes as part of their desire to be good corporate citizens and may expect their employees to contribute time or money to these projects. The United Way campaign is one fundraising activity that enjoys strong corporate support. Volunteer fundraising activities on the part of employees are not related to specific jobs but may advance the goals of the organization.

Contextual performance appears to fall into five major categories (Borman and Motowidlo, 1993):

1. Persisting with enthusiasm and extra effort as necessary to complete own task activities successfully;
2. Volunteering to carry out task activities that are not formally part of one's own job;
3. Helping and cooperating with others;
4. Following organizational rules and procedures;
5. Endorsing, supporting, and defending organizational objectives.

Contextual performance activities may represent important criteria for jobs in many organizations because of their relationship to organizational effectiveness. Not all of these contextual performance dimensions may have the same degree of relevance or importance across organizations. Organizations are likely to emphasize those that are most compatible with their values and goals. Contextual performance is not a substitute for job performance, it represents *additional* factors that may be considered in developing personnel selection criteria. Contextual performance, by itself, does not get the job done. An increasing number of North American companies such as Apple Computer, GE, Honeywell, and 3M assess how well employees fit the organization in addition to how well they can do the job (Bowen, Ledford, and Nathan, 1991).

◆ ◆ ◆
CRITERION MEASUREMENT

Once job and organization analyses have identified the major performance dimensions, the next step is to measure employee performance on those dimensions. How will we measure job task proficiency, supervision, or helping and cooperating with others? We can think of these job dimensions as labels that are constructed to describe different aspects of job performance. Before we can measure any job dimension we have to define that dimension in terms of specific, measurable activities or behaviours. For example, supervision includes giving orders to subordinates, accomplishing organizational goals, teaching employees the proper way to do a job, among many other things. One person may be better at "giving orders to subordinates" than "teaching subordinates"; our view on that person's supervisory performance will depend on which of these behaviours we include in our measure of supervisory performance. Smith (1976) established general guidelines to help identify effective and appropriate performance measures.

Relevancy requires that a criterion measure is a valid measure of the performance dimension in question. Suppose we develop a measure of supervision based on the number of "subordinate orders" given by a supervisor. This measure might be relevant to one aspect of supervision, but it is also deficient in not measuring the "teaching subordinates" component of supervision. Additionally, the total number of subordinate orders given by any one supervisor may be influenced by factors beyond the supervisor's control such as the quality of the supervisor's employees and the nature of the supervisory position. As a criterion measure, the number of subordinate orders may be contaminated in that it is measuring things other than the supervisor's performance. *Criterion relevance* is the degree to which the criterion measure captures behaviours that constitute job performance. *Criterion deficiency* refers to those job performance behaviours that are not measured by the criterion. *Criterion contamination* is the degree to which the criterion measure is influenced by, or measures, behaviours that are not part of job performance.

Reliability involves agreement between different evaluations, at different periods of time and with different, although apparently similar, measures; that is, the criterion measure must meet scientific and professional standards of reliability. Reliability is the degree to which observed scores are free from random measurement errors (i.e., the dependability or stability of the measure). Criterion or performance measures are subject to the same errors as any other kind of measurement. There is no such thing as error-free criterion measurement; some criteria, however, are more reliable than others. Reliable criterion measures will tend to produce similar scores when the same behaviour is measured on more than one occasion. The reliability of any criterion measure must be established, as part of its use in a personnel selection system, through the procedures discussed in Chapter 3.

Practicality means that the criterion measure must be available, plausible, and acceptable to organizational decision-makers. The number of subordinate orders must mean something to those responsible for assessing supervision. It must also be a number that is readily available at little cost. It must also be a plausible indicator of individual performance. That is, the criterion measure must have meaning and credibility for those who will use the measurements in making decisions. There is a danger of being seduced by practicality and choosing criteria, which, while readily available, do not meet standards of validity and reliability. These two requirements cannot be traded off in favour of practicality.

◆ ◆ ◆
DEVELOPING CRITERIA MEASURES

There are several issues that must be considered as part of the process of developing a criterion or a set of criterion measures. The resolution of these issues influence which measures are selected as criteria and when measurements are made.

MULTIPLE, GLOBAL, OR COMPOSITE CRITERIA

THE ULTIMATE CRITERION The first issue is one that has generated a great deal of controversy over the years; namely, how many criteria should be measured? In large part this controversy arises through misunderstanding of the job performance domain. At one time, criterion research was dominated by a concern to find the ultimate criterion for a given job. The ultimate criterion is the concept of a single criterion measure that could reflect overall job success. The idea of an ultimate criteria implies that job performance is a unitary concept, that one measure could be found that assessed a person's overall job performance. Even Thorndike (1949), who developed the idea, recognized that an ultimate criterion would rarely, if ever, be found in practice, "A really complete ultimate criterion is multiple and complex in almost every case. Such a criterion is ultimate in the sense that we cannot look beyond it for any higher or further standard in terms of which to judge the outcomes of a particular personnel program" (121). Unfortunately, many who followed Thorndike did not heed his advice and wasted considerable time in trying to find ultimate measures of job performance. It is unlikely that you will ever find one measure that will tell you everything about performance in a specific job.

GLOBAL VERSUS MULTIPLE CRITERIA Job analysis procedures used by most organizations are inductive; the job analyst infers the dimensions that make up the overall job performance domain from specific empirical data. Other approaches, such as those used by Colgate-Palmolive or British Petroleum, deduce performance dimensions from organizational goals with the help of job analysis data. As we've seen, British Petroleum identified technical skills, leadership qualities, business awareness, planning and organizational ability, communication and interpersonal skills, initiative, and problem solving ability as important job dimensions and assessed potential employees on each dimension. If there is a need to compare the relative performance of petroleum engineers, is it appropriate to combine the scores on each dimension into an overall composite score, or should a new criterion be developed to measure overall, global performance?

Many practitioners, heavily influenced by the controversy surrounding the search for ultimate criteria, would answer "No." They emphasize that the multidimensionality of job performance requires the use of multiple, independent, criteria to measure performance. They believe that independent criteria, reflecting independent performance dimensions, should not be combined into an overall, composite measure of job performance. Combining *leadership qualities* and *initiative* to understand the engineer's performance would be, to use Smith's (1976) analogy, like adding toothpicks to olives to understand a martini. Neither did they believe it was appropriate to obtain a separate, overall measure of performance because such a global criterion measure would lose the rich information contained in the multiple performance dimensions. More recently, this position has changed. The choice of a criterion measure should be determined by its intended purpose, "...if you need to solve a very specific problem (e.g., too many customer complaints about product quality), then a more specific criterion is needed. If there is more than one specific problem, then more than one specific criterion is called for. But in most situations, a global measure will serve quite well." (Guion, 1987, 205).

COMPOSITE VERSUS MULTIPLE CRITERIA We have emphasized the multi-dimensionality of job performance with the requirement of assessing those different dimensions through multiple criterion measures. Nonetheless, there may be times when a single, all-inclusive criterion measure is needed as part of making employment decisions and no global criterion measure is available. Not everyone agrees that it is inappropriate to combine individual criterion measures into a single composite (Landy, 1989). There seems to be general agreement on how to proceed. Since performance measures will be used for a variety of purposes, it makes sense to collect each criterion measure separately or in its multiple, uncollapsed form. That information can be combined to compute a composite criterion as needed for different administrative decisions. The weights assigned to the separate performance measures in creating a composite measure should reflect the priority of the different performance dimensions as set by the organization's goals. Implicit in this position is recognition that the priority of organizational goals may change over time. If separate performance measures have been maintained, it is a relatively straightforward exercise to recompute the composite to reflect the new organizational, and economic, realities. Caution is in order; creating a composite averages performance across all the performance dimensions. Performance on one dimension may be so critical that deficiencies cannot be made up by excellent performance on other dimensions. In this case, a composite criterion is inappropriate.

CONSISTENCY OF JOB PERFORMANCE

In discussing reliability as a requirement for criterion measurement, we assumed that the employee's behaviour was more or less consistent at the time the observations were made. Of course, people's job performance may change over time. This is a substantially different issue than the random, daily fluctuations in performance. Changing performance levels may affect criterion measurements.

TRAINING VERSUS JOB PROFICIENCY CRITERIA Do you obtain the same criterion results if you measure performance very soon after a person is placed in a job as opposed to several months or years later? Generally, early performance in a job involves informal learning or systematic training. Workers are continually evaluated during training or probationary periods. Performance measures taken during early training will be very different from those taken later when workers are more proficient. Criterion measurements taken during training periods may produce validity coefficients that overestimate the selection system's ability to predict later job proficiency (Ghiselli, 1966). Nonetheless, the convenience of short-term performance measures, rather than their relevance to long-term performance, dictates their use as criteria. Training criteria remain very popular performance measures.

TYPICAL VERSUS MAXIMUM JOB PERFORMANCE Maximum performance occurs in situations where individuals are aware that they are being observed or evaluated, or where they are under instructions to do their best. Their performance is measured over a short time period when their attention remains focused on performing at their highest level. Typical performance is the opposite of maximum performance; it consists of a situation in which individuals are not aware that their performance is being observed and evaluated, in which they are not consciously attempting to perform to the best of their ability, and in which performance is monitored over an extended period of time. There is very little relationship between performance under typical and maximum performance situations, for either inexperienced or experienced workers. Performance measures taken during training are measures of maximum performance and may be inappropriate if a selection system is to predict long-term typical performance. Motivational factors play a larger role in typical, everyday performance. In maximum performance, motivation is probably at high levels for everyone; in typical performance situations in the actual work setting, motivation is likely to differ among individuals (Sackett, Zedeck, and Fogli, 1988).

DYNAMIC VERSUS STABLE CRITERIA Employee performance appears to decrease over time regardless of the employee's experience or ability. These changes may reflect the effects of many personal, situational, and temporal factors. Early job performance may be limited only by ability and experience since every new employee is motivated to do well, while later job performance may be influenced more by motivation (Deadrick and Madigan, 1990).

SUMMARY Early job performance, which may occur under more rigorous scrutiny than later performance, is ability-driven and a better estimate of what individuals can maximally achieve rather than how they will typically perform on the job. Performance will decrease over time, generally reflecting changes in motivation. Training criteria are acceptable performance measures for estimating maximum performance, but will overestimate typical performance. To be safe, several performance measures should be taken at different times when validating selection systems.

◆ ◆ ◆
JOB PERFORMANCE CRITERIA

It is very unlikely that any two workers doing the same job will perform at exactly the same level. Factors such as knowledge, skill, and motivation are likely to cause variation in job performance within and between workers. Most likely any two petroleum engineers hired by British Petroleum would not perform at the same level on all of the critical job dimensions; nor is it likely that any one engineer would perform at the same level on all dimensions. Every employee has strengths and weaknesses. How do we actually measure these differences in performance between employees on the relevant job dimensions? What do we actually use as the criterion data necessary for validating selection systems? The remainder of this chapter reviews some of the more common criterion measures and measurement techniques. If you have previously studied Performance Appraisal, you will recognize many of these methods. Performance appraisals or evaluations often provide the answers to the above questions. These different criteria have been grouped into five broad categories.

OBJECTIVE MEASURES: PRODUCTION, SALES, AND PERSONNEL DATA

Objective production, sales, and personnel data, also known as *hard criteria* or ancillary measures, are often used as performance measures. These data are produced by the workers in doing their jobs, or are related to observable characteristics or behaviours of the workers. They are called objective measures because they represent the actual number of things produced or number of sales made. The assigned number does not depend upon the subjective judgment of another person. The number of audits completed by an accountant at Colgate-Palmolive is known for any given period; the quality of those audits may be reflected in the number of errors detected by a higher level review. In this case both the quantity and quality (number that are error free) of audits are objective measures related to the actual job performance of the accountant. If the quality of the audit rested on the judgment or perception of the accountant's supervisor that the audits met acceptable, professional standards, quality would then constitute a subjective measure. Production or sales measures generally involve quantity, quality, and trainability, which is the amount of time needed to reach a specific performance level. Table 5.1 lists examples of production and sales criteria.

PERSONNEL DATA Using personnel data as criteria involves the use of objective measures that are not directly related to actual production or sales but which convey information about workplace behaviour. Criteria derived from personnel data tend to be global in nature and may tell more about contextual performance than the worker's actual performance on specific job dimensions. Personnel data may be better measures of organizational behaviours than job performance. Absence data are routinely collected and stored in each worker's file and are often used as criteria. Absence measures likely tell more about employee rule-following behaviour than how well they perform their jobs (i.e., when they do show up for work). In addition to absence data, information on job tenure, rate of advancement or promotion within the organization, salary history, and accident history have been used as criteria. Table 5.1 also presents examples of personnel data used as criteria. Criteria should be selected because they are reliable, relevant, and practical. While most objective measures may meet the test of practicality, they may not necessarily be reliable or relevant. While quantity may be measured with a fair degree of accuracy, the consistency of the information may

TABLE 5.1 EXAMPLES OF OBJECTIVE MEASURES OF JOB PERFORMANCE*

Production or Sales Measures

Quantity
- Number of items produced
- Volume of sales
- Time to completion
- Number of calls processed each day
- Average size of sales orders
- Words typed per minute
- Speed of production

Quality
- Number of errors
- Dollar cost of errors
- Number of customer complaints
- Number of spelling and grammatical mistakes
- Degree of deviation from a standard
- Number of cancelled contracts

Trainability
- Time to reach standard
- Rate of increase in production
- Rate of sales growth

Personnel Data

Absenteeism
- Number of sick days used
- Number of unscheduled days off work
- Number of times late for work

Tenure
- Length of time in job
- Voluntary turnover rate
- Involuntary turnover rate

Rate of Advancement
- Number of promotions
- Percent increase in salary
- Length of time to first promotion

Accidents
- Number of accidents
- Cost of accidents
- Number of days lost to accidents
- Number of safety violations

*These are measures that have been used over time; inclusion on this list does not necessarily mean that these are the best objective measures of individual or group performance.

depend on the time of the measurement or the duration over which it was taken.

CONTAMINATION AND DEFICIENCY OF OBJECTIVE MEASURES Objective measures may be influenced by factors beyond a worker's control. Insurance companies use the total dollar value of insurance sold in a month to measure an agent's performance. One agent may sell more insurance in a month than another because one's territory includes a compact city district populated by upper-income professionals while the other's includes a sparsely populated rural county of low-income farm workers. Both the opportunity to make sales, and the amount of insurance sold, may have more to do with the sales territory than the sales ability of either of the agents. The total dollar value of insurance sold may not measure how safely the agents drove to their territories, the oral communication skills needed to explain the complex insurance policies, or how accurately they completed the necessary paperwork to initiate the policy and to bill for its premiums. Successful performance of these other job dimensions may have as much to do with the long-term success of the insurance company as the dollar sales volume. Using personnel data, such as absenteeism, turnover, rate of advancement, salary history, and accidents as criteria leaves an organization open to criticism of criterion deficiency or contamination. The practicality and convenience of objective data do not justify their use. Before production, sales, or personnel data can be used as criteria, their reliability and validity as measures of job performance dimensions must be established. Objectiveness does not exempt criteria from this process.

SUBJECTIVE MEASURES: RATING SYSTEMS

It is relatively easier to find objective measures for jobs that involve people in the actual production of goods and services. As a person's job becomes removed from actual production or sales work, it becomes more difficult to associate objective measures to the employee's performance. Upper level jobs in an organization may involve more administration, leadership, team building, and decision making, dimensions which are not easily measured in objective terms. The issues of criterion relevance, deficiency, and contamination become even more serious. How should Colgate-Palmolive evaluate the performance of the accountant's supervisor? Most likely, the supervisor's

own manager, peers, and perh...
judge, the supervisor's performanc...
doubt, performance ratings are the most i...

RATING ERRORS A rating system is simply a proc...
tify an opinion or judgment. A rating system must s...
ments for measurements we discussed in Chapter ...
measurement system, ratings are open to error. Leniency, centr...
and severity errors are types of errors made by judges who restri...
ratings to only one part of the rating scale. Some raters may assign o...
extreme ratings; some may give only very positive ratings (*leniency*) while
others give only very negative ones (*severity*), others may judge all performance to be average and not assign extreme ratings in either direction
(*central tendency*). Most students can identify teachers who have a reputation
for giving mostly A's or F's, extreme ratings, or those who pass everyone with
a C. *Halo errors* occur when a judge's ratings over several job dimensions are
influenced by the rating the judge first assigned to a particularly important
dimension. After assigning a very high rating on "leadership," a rater may feel
that the same score is warranted for "effort," particularly since the judge may
have little experience with the employee on this dimension. Halo errors are
often the result of the following type of thinking, "If I rated her excellent on
Leadership, she must be excellent on Effort as well. Besides, if I give her a
low rating on effort, or say I have no basis for judging her effort, my boss who
will review this assessment may think I'm not doing my job. So, I know she's
excellent on Leadership; she's probably excellent on Effort. I'll give her an
Excellent rating on Effort." These types of rating errors introduce the
personal biases of the raters into the measurement process and reduce the
likelihood that the assigned ratings are appropriate measures of the performance under review.

REDUCING RATING ERRORS Over the years many different aspects of both
raters and rating systems have been examined in an attempt to reduce rating
errors. While rating errors can never be eliminated, they can be reduced.
Rating errors can be reduced by (1) defining the performance domain;
(2) adopting a well-constructed rating system; and (3) training the raters in
using the rating system. We've already discussed the first item; before dealing with rater training, we will briefly review different types of rating
systems.

RELATIVE RATING SYSTEMS

Relative Rating Systems compare the overall performance of one employee with that of others. These techniques provide global assessments as the rater compares overall performance rather than performance on each job dimension. The use of a single overall rating avoids the problems with rating errors over the set of dimensions. The trade-off for avoiding these errors is the loss of performance information on specific job dimensions. As we discussed previously, global criteria may not always be the most appropriate to use. There are three basic types of relative rating systems: rank order, paired comparison, and forced distribution methods.

RANK ORDER In rank ordering, the rater arranges the employees in order of their perceived overall performance level. For a group of 10 workers, the best performer would be assigned rank 1 and the worst, rank 10. There are two problems with this procedure. Raters may have a good idea of who are the best and worst performers but often have difficulty discriminating, that is assigning ranks, between the remaining employees. Secondly, because the system is relative, it does not tell whether any or all of the workers are performing above or below acceptable levels. In other words, an employee may be rated the third best accountant but, in absolute terms, may not meet acceptable performance standards.

PAIRED COMPARISONS In this method, the rater compares the overall performance of each worker with that of every other worker that must be evaluated. In rating four employees, their supervisor compares every possible pair of workers: Employee #1 v. Employee #2, Employee #1 v. Employee #3, and so on. The workers are then ranked on the basis of the number of times they were selected as the top rated performer over all the comparisons. One problem with the procedure is the large number of comparisons that often have to be made. With four workers, a supervisor must make six comparisons; for 10 workers, the number of paired comparisons increases to 45. Making a large number of paired comparisons becomes tedious leaving some raters to rush through the procedure. While this technique does guarantee that all employees being rated are given due consideration, it still does not provide information on absolute performance levels.

FORCED DISTRIBUTION This system attempts to provide absolute information within a relative rating context. Rather than rank workers from top to bottom, the system sets up a limited number of categories, which are tied to performance standards. For example, the rater may be given a scale with the categories Excellent, Above Average, Average, Below Average, and Poor to evaluate each worker overall or on specific job dimensions. So far, this procedure resembles that used by an absolute graphic rating scale procedure; the difference is that the rater is forced to place a predetermined number or percentage into each of the rating categories. Generally, raters assign workers to categories on the basis of a normal frequency distribution, which assumes most workers to be Average with only a few judged Excellent or Poor. This technique is quite good at controlling leniency, central tendency, and severity errors; however it does not reduce halo effects. Often raters oppose systems like this, which require them to label a given percentage of their subordinates into extreme categories, on the grounds that this distorts the true state of affairs. They may feel that the number of poor or excellent performers working for them does not match the quota the system has allocated to those categories. Forced systems work best when only gross discriminations are required between workers.

ABSOLUTE RATING SYSTEMS

Absolute Rating Systems compare the performance of one worker to an absolute standard of performance. These methods provide either an overall assessment of performance or assessments on specific job dimensions. A rating scale is developed for each dimension that is to be evaluated. Over the years, a variety of formats have been developed to assess performance in absolute terms. While these rating scales may have important qualitative differences, they usually lead to the same administrative decisions. One rating system may provide more effective feedback while supervisors are more likely to favour another and support its use. The ratings assigned to employees by either rating system are likely to be highly correlated, once measurement errors are taken into account. The particular ratings scale format may not make much difference in the relative order of scores derived for each employee. However, different rating formats may not have the same degree of validity or meet relevant legal requirements (Greene, Bernardin, and Abbott, 1985). A review of several of the more popular ratings formats follows.

Graphic Rating Scales can be produced to assess an employee on any job dimension. The scale usually consists of the name of the job component or dimension, a brief definition of the dimension, a scale with equal intervals between the numbers placed on the scale, verbal labels or anchors attached to the numerical scale, and instructions for making a response. Figure 5.1 presents samples of relatively good and poor scales that have been designed to rate Effort. The presence or absence of these elements helps to distinguish between these two samples. The poor scale presented in Figure 5.1 (a) does not provide the rater with a definition of Effort. It is left for each rater to define this term in a different way, leaving open the possibility that the definitions are so variable, the raters will not be assessing the same dimension. The good example in Figure 5.1 (b) provides a definition of the performance dimension. There is no guarantee that the raters will not use other interpre-

FIGURE 5.1 Examples of Rating Scales

a) Effort

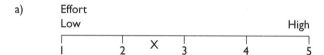

b) Effort — Consider the amount of energy brought to the job. Will subordinate personal convenience to complete work in a professional manner.

1	2	③	4	5
Poor	Below Average	Average	Above Average	Excellent

c) Effort — Reflects the degree to which individuals are committed to performing all job tasks, to working at a high level of intensity, and to continue working under adverse conditions.

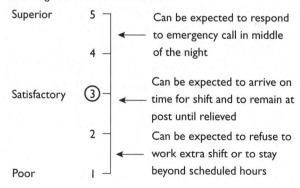

tations of Effort in making their ratings (or that this is the best way to define effort), but at least they have had to consider the standardized definition. The poor example contains very general anchors at each end of the scale but provides no information on what constitutes High or Low effort. Again each rater may use a different reference point to characterize the effort of the person being rated. The anchors in the good example provide benchmarks to help understand the differences between various degrees of effort. Finally, the poor example allows the rater such latitude in making a response that the person in charge of reviewing the completed assessments may have difficulty knowing what rating was given. In the poor example, does the x indicate a rating of 2 or 3? In the good example, there is no doubt about which response was intended.

*Trait-Based Rating Scale*s are graphic rating scales, which ask the rater to focus on specific characteristics of the person being reviewed. The rater judges the extent to which a worker possesses traits such as dependability, leadership, friendliness, and so on. In most cases the traits are either very poorly defined or extremely vague. Furthermore, the traits under assessment rarely are chosen because they are job-related. The failure to demonstrate the relevance of the chosen traits to job dimensions is a fatal flaw, which makes such appraisal systems next to worthless. Nonetheless, trait-based performance measurement systems continue to be used. Partly, this is due to the ease with which such a scale can be concocted, and the apparent cost savings of using one general performance measure across all jobs that are being evaluated. Organizations that use such systems in decision making run the risk of justifying the validity of such performance ratings in costly litigation before various tribunals.

Checklists present the rater with a list of statements that may describe either work behaviours or personality traits. Sometimes the list is restricted to behavioural statements only. The rater goes through the list and identifies those statements that apply to the employee being evaluated. With behavioural checklists, the rater is describing what the worker does. Since some behaviours may be more valuable to an organization, weights can be assigned to the different statements. Generally, the weights are developed through a job analysis or by people who are very familiar with the job. The rating for an individual is obtained by adding the weights of those statements that have been identified for that person. This approach is known as the Method of Summated Ratings. A second checklist method is the Forced Choice

Procedure in which a rater is given several statements and is asked to select one that most or least typifies the employee. By forcing the rater to choose from among a group of all positive or all negative statements, the format tends to reduce leniency, central tendency, and severity errors. On the whole, raters detest using the Forced Choice Procedure, particularly when they believe that several statements apply equally well to the worker. A further limitation of the Forced Choice Procedure is its failure to provide an easily understood performance measure that can be interpreted in terms of job dimensions. One purpose of any evaluation is to provide the worker with feedback on their performance, to identify strengths and weaknesses. This is difficult to do if the performance measure is not readily understood by either the rater or the person being measured.

Critical Incident Methods require raters to observe the job behaviour of an employee and to record those behaviours displayed by the worker that are critical to effective or ineffective performance. The technique forces the rater to concentrate on the behaviour, not traits or characteristics, of the worker. The critical incidents are identified through interviews with people knowledgeable about the specific job. The critical incidents are then given to an observer who checks off those that are displayed by the worker while performing the job. This method is essentially the same as a Summated Checklist Method. Box 5.2 contains a series of critical incidents for a security dispatcher related to the job dimensions of Job Specific Task Proficiency, Demonstrating Effort , and Maintaining Personal Discipline. These critical incidents were collected as part of a job analysis for the security dispatcher position at a Canadian university. The dispatcher's supervisor would mark off those behaviours present in the dispatcher's job performance.

BOX 5.2 CRITICAL INCIDENTS FOR A SECURITY DISPATCHER

Job Specific Task Proficiency
- Properly secures lost and found articles
- Controls visitor access to buildings
- Monitors multiple surveillance devices

Demonstration of Effort
- Reports early for shift to hear debriefing from preceding shift
- Remains at post until relieved
- Volunteers for overtime when needed

Personal Discipline
- Follows safety procedures
- Does not take unauthorized breaks
- Maintains proper demeanor during stressful situations

Mixed Standard Rating Scales are variations on critical incident checklists. Three critical incidents, similar to those presented in Box 5.2, are selected for each job dimension being reviewed. The items represent excellent, average, and poor performance, respectively. The items are randomly presented on a checklist without labelling the job dimensions and raters are asked to indicate whether the employee's behaviour is better, worse, or the same as the behaviour presented in the statement. A score is assigned to each job dimension on the basis of the pattern of ratings for each dimension. For example, if a security dispatcher were judged to perform better than that given in the statement they would be given a score of 7, while a dispatcher judged to perform worse on all three statements would be given a score of 1. Other weights would be assigned to the remaining possible patterns. While the mixed standard rating scale does reduce rating errors, it tends to introduce another: many raters make logically inconsistent responses to the set of three statements within each dimension. The time needed to construct Mixed Standard Rating Scales, coupled with the inconsistent responding of those who use it, argue against its wide scale use. It can be very useful, however, in those organizations willing to spend time and money improving the scales to eliminate the inconsistent responding.

Behaviourally Anchored Rating Scales (BARS) use empirically derived critical incident job behaviours to anchor the values placed on a rating scale. Although this procedure sounds simple, it is actually quite complex and time-consuming. An example of a BARS designed to measure Effort is presented in Figure 5.1 (c). To construct this scale, a group of workers most familiar with the job uses a critical incident procedure to identify specific job dimensions. A second, independent group generates behavioural examples of excellent, average, and poor performance on each dimension identified by the first group. A third group is given the dimensions identified by the first group and the behavioural items generated by the second and asked to match items to dimensions. This step is called *retranslation* and represents an attempt to establish the content validity of the items. A fourth group then takes the valid items and assigns each a value from the measurement scale that represents its level of performance. Items with low variability in assigned scale values are retained for the scale. The resultant scale is tested and refined before being adopted for general use (Smith and Kendall, 1963). BARS is the Rolls-Royce of rating scales (and perhaps as costly). It has the advantage of being, arguably, the best rating procedure in use today. It integrates job analytic information directly to the performance appraisal measure. It also involves a large number of people in the development of the measure. Generally, these people, supervisors and workers, support the process and become committed to its success.

Behaviour Observation Scales (BOS) are very similar to BARS in that the starting point is an analysis of critical job incidents by those knowledgeable about the job to establish performance dimensions (Latham and Wexley, 1981). Once the list of behaviours that represent different job dimensions is constructed, supervisors are asked to monitor the frequency with which employees exhibit each behaviour over a standardized time period. Next, the frequency data are reviewed through an *item analysis* where the response to each item is correlated to a performance score for a dimension. This performance score is obtained by summing all the items that belong to a particular dimension. Only those items that attain high correlations with the total score are retained for the performance appraisal measure. This procedure assures a high degree of internal consistency for each dimension.

An example of a BOS scale used in evaluating the performance of a security dispatcher is presented in Table 5.2. Several differences are apparent in comparison to a BARS designed to measure the same dimension. First, there is no attempt to integrate the critical incidents into one overall scale. Second, there are no behavioural anchors attached to the scale, rather the rater judges the frequency with which each employee displays the critical behaviours. Latham and Wexley (1981) recommend using a five-point scale where the numbers are defined in terms of frequencies; for example, they would assign the value 1 if the worker displayed the critical behaviour 0–64 percent of the time, 2 for 65–74 percent, 3 for 75–84 percent, 4 for 85–94 percent, and 5 for 95–100 percent. In this way, the rater assesses the frequency of engaging in actual critical behaviours as opposed to rating the employee in terms of a behavioural expectation that the worker might not have had an opportunity to perform.

BOS generally take less time and money to develop than BARS. The BOS development procedure requires participation of supervisors and workers leading to their greater acceptance of the system. Nonetheless, there are some weaknesses to this procedure. One major problem lies with the rating scale. A rating of 1 suggests poor performance since the critical behaviour is displayed less than 65 percent of the time. Consider using this scale to rate the hitting and fielding performance of a major league baseball player. A ball

TABLE 5.2 BEHAVIOURAL OBSERVATION SCALE USED TO EVALUATE A SECURITY DISPATCHER

Job Specific Task Proficiency

Properly secures lost and found articles

	Almost Never	1	2	3	4	5	Almost Always

Controls visitor access to buildings

	Almost Never	1	2	3	4	5	Almost Always

Monitors multiple surveillance devices

	Almost Never	1	2	3	4	5	Almost Always

Ensures confidentiality and security of information

	Almost Never	1	2	3	4	5	Almost Always

Activates appropriate emergency response teams as needed

	Almost Never	1	2	3	4	5	Almost Always

Total Score _____

6–16	17–19	20–21	22–23	24–25[*]
Very Poor	Unsatisfactory	Satisfactory	Excellent	Superior

[*] Performance standards are set by management

player who hits the ball 30 percent of the time is called a millionaire; the BOS would classify him as a failure. A major leaguer who successfully fielded the ball 85 percent of the time would soon be out of a job; the BOS would classify his performance as excellent. The frequency with which a behaviour occurs may have different interpretations depending on the behaviour. Frequency measures also do not capture the importance or criticality of the behaviour. The captain of the Titanic almost always missed hitting icebergs. Another very serious problem with the BOS is that the demands it makes on human memory may exceed the available capacity. Raters may not be able to remember accurately the specific behavioural information required by the BOS and may end up making global judgments (Murphy and Cleveland, 1995).

Management By Objectives (MBO) is a performance measurement system that emphasizes completion of goals that are defined in terms of objective criteria such as quantity produced or savings realized. MBO starts with the identification of organizational goals or objectives and uses these to specify goals for each employee's job performance. Before any goals can be set, the job-related behaviours must first be identified through a job analysis. The employee plays an important role in this process. Once the job is understood by both the employee and supervisor, both meet to develop a mutually agreeable set of goals that are outputs of the employee's job. Once the goals are established, the supervisor uses them to evaluate the employee's performance. Over the review period there are several meetings between employee and supervisor to review progress. At the end of the review period, there is a final meeting to assess whether the employee met the established goals and to set the goals for the next review period. Strengths of this system involve the linkage between organizational and individual goals, frequent analysis and discussion of the employee's progress toward meeting the goals, and immediate feedback about performance. The employees know, from the objective criteria, whether they are performing up to expectations. Because the system is based on objective or hard criteria, the system suffers from all the problems inherent in the use of that type of performance measure.

IMPROVING RATINGS THROUGH TRAINING AND ACCOUNTABILITY

RATER TRAINING Training raters in the use of the rating system helps to reduce rating errors and to increase the reliability of the measurements (Day and Sulsky, 1995). A training program for raters ensures that all the raters are operating from a common frame of reference. Raters should have the same understanding of the rating system's instructions; they should have the same interpretation of the performance dimensions that are to be evaluated; and they should know how to use the rating system's measurement scale. Training programs can also include information on the types of rating errors that occur and how to avoid them. Some programs include information on how to improve observation of work behaviour. Although training programs can become quite elaborate, involving role-playing and use of demonstration video tapes, many rater training sessions consist of workshops built around explanation of the rating system accompanied by practice rating sessions.

RATER ACCOUNTABILITY Apart from training, the factor that has the most impact on rating accuracy is rater accountability. In 1996, the Alberta Court of Queen's Bench ordered Purolator Courier Ltd. to pay a former employee $100 000 in a wrongful dismissal suit that centred on the appropriateness of the employee's performance evaluation (Gibb-Clark, 1996). Rating accuracy increases when raters are called upon to explain or to justify the ratings they make. Accountability can be built into a system by requiring the rater to provide the employee who is being rated with feedback from the appraisal. Many supervisors are uncomfortable doing this, particularly when the feedback is negative. However, if feedback is not given, the employee can neither benefit from the appraisal by improving performance nor challenge evaluations that are suspect. In the Purolator Courier case, the trial judge was most concerned that the employee had not been given assistance to meet increased expectations.

Most organizations that undertake performance appraisals require both the rater and the employee to review, and to sign, the completed rating form. Employees, however, cannot be forced to sign rating forms with which they disagree. Accountability is also established by building into the rating system a mechanism for the formal review of all performance appraisals. By monitoring all evaluations, a review panel can assess whether any one rater's assessments appear to significantly deviate from those obtained from the other raters. Knowing that their ratings will be reviewed can lead raters to play it safe by giving everyone an acceptable evaluation (i.e., making a central tendency error). On the other hand, raters under this type of system can usually justify any extreme ratings they give to employees. Organizations that cannot justify their performance evaluations may suffer both public and financial embarrassment.

WHO DOES THE RATING?

SUPERVISOR RATINGS Most workplace assessments are traditionally carried out by an immediate supervisor or manager. In recent years, organizations have started to recognize that this may not be the best practice. They have started to obtain ratings from other co-workers and subordinates. Some organizations also ask the worker to perform an appraisal of their own performance. Each of these groups provides information about the employee's performance from a different perspective and some may not see the total scope of the employee's job performance (Murphy and Cleveland, 1995).

PEER RATINGS Co-workers tend to provide more lenient reviews than supervisors. As part of a class project, suppose the professor requires each member of the group to evaluate each other with respect to certain criteria related to the project. Would you assign a very lenient grade in the expectation that the other students will evaluate you similarly, or would you assign a grade that reflects your honest judgment of how others contributed to the project? If you knew your grade was based on this peer evaluation, would group performance be enhanced or hindered? Most organizations avoid involving co-workers in the assessment process out of fear that doing so will lead to hostility between co-workers, to increased competitiveness among the co-workers, and to a breakdown in team functioning. Nonetheless, evaluations from co-workers or peers can be quite reliable and valid sources of information about an employee's job performance.

SUBORDINATE RATINGS Ratings by subordinates of their supervisor are relatively rare, although some large companies such as Ford Motor Company (Bernardin and Beatty, 1984) do obtain such ratings as part of reviewing managerial performance. Subordinate ratings, however, are very common in universities where a professor's teaching performance is evaluated through student evaluations, and where faculty routinely evaluate the performance of their supervisors (department heads, deans, presidents). Student evaluations of teaching performance are used by a professor's peers in evaluating that professor for promotion or tenure. While the students would be in a good position to observe teaching effectiveness, they might not be the best persons to evaluate the professor's research productivity, or administrative work on committees. There are two related concerns about subordinate ratings; either the subordinates will give lenient ratings to influence their own treatment ("If I rate my professor highly, I'm more likely to get a good grade") or the supervisor will attempt to manipulate the subordinate ratings through altering performance expectations ("I'll give them an easy test so they all pass and, perhaps they'll remember this gift when they evaluate my teaching").

SELF-RATINGS What if your professor asked you to evaluate your own performance on the group project? How would your evaluation compare with those of other students in your group and your professor? Generally, self-appraisals are the most lenient of all, although there appears to be less halo error. That is, while people tend to give ratings that accurately reflect differences in their performance on different job dimensions, all the ratings tend to be inflated. Self-appraisals are used to get employees thinking about their performance and as the basis for discussion, rather than as part of a formal review process.

CLIENT OR CUSTOMER RATINGS An increasing number of organizations ask customers or clients to rate the performance of employees with whom they have interacted. For example, Sun Life of Canada asks customers to rate the performance of sales people in terms of the service they provided to the customer. Other companies such as Ford and Honda's Acura division also obtain information from an employee's internal clients. Internal clients include anyone who is dependent upon the employee's work output. For example, the manager of an engineering division might be asked to evaluate the human resources manager in charge of recruiting engineers for the division. Both internal and external customers can provide very useful information about the effectiveness of an employee or a team of employees (Belcourt, Sherman, Bohlander, and Snell, 1996). This information provides a unique view of the employee's performance from individuals who are directly involved with the employee, but who at the same time are neither subordinate nor superior to the employee.

360-DEGREE FEEDBACK The 360-degree feedback procedure uses information obtained from supervisors, peers, subordinates, self-ratings, and clients or customers to provide the employee with feedback for development and training purposes. As noted above, the information provided by these different sources is likely to disagree to some extent. The difference in information suggests that no one evaluation is the right one. Supervisors do accept upward feedback from subordinates when that feedback is not the only information used to evaluate them. Information from non-traditional rating sources should be balanced with that from more traditional sources (Murphy and Cleveland, 1995).

NON-TRADITIONAL METHODS FOR MEASURING PERFORMANCE

Following a decline in use during the 1970s, ratings have regained popularity with the development of rating systems that focus on behaviours related to the job's performance domain. New performance measurement systems developed over the past several years, however, offer alternative methods for obtaining criteria data. In most cases, these procedures are adapted from techniques used in personnel selection. Figure 5.2 illustrates the relationship between these different types of criterion categories and the eight performance dimensions defined by Campbell (1990). The lines connecting dimensions and categories, based on empirical evidence, suggest that ratings have been used for every performance dimension. The alternative measures presented in Figure 5.2 are briefly described here.

JOB KNOWLEDGE/SKILL TESTING Job knowledge or skill testing procedures include paper and pencil tests as well as "walk through" procedures, which require an individual to demonstrate knowledge or general skills such as manipulating controls or equipment to achieve a desired outcome. Constables in the Royal Canadian Mounted Police (RCMP) must pass a job knowledge examination before they can compete for promotion to higher ranks. These types of measures reflect a worker's requisite skill or knowledge to perform a task; they do not indicate the worker's proficiency or what the worker will or can do. Since these measures are "tests," the same issues arise as when they are used as predictors; particularly, they must not lead to adverse impact against subgroups. These procedures and issues will be discussed in later chapters.

HANDS-ON TESTING AND SIMULATION There are two categories containing related techniques differing in the degree to which they attempt to reproduce actual, critical work behaviours. In *hands-on testing*, workers perform one or more tasks associated with their job. The testing may take place either through formal observation of normal job tasks, or off-site where the worker is asked to perform using normal job equipment and techniques. This latter case is really a type of work samples test where the employee is asked to produce a sample of job-related behaviour. Similarly, *simulations* attempt to duplicate salient features of the work site and to measure job proficiency under realistic conditions (Murphy, 1989). In qualifying for promotion, RCMP constables must successfully complete a job situation exercise which simulates conditions encountered as part of the job. Work samples testing and simulation have been used primarily as predictor measures rather than criteria or, in the case of simulation, as a training method (e.g., flight simulators). When used to measure performance, hands-on methods appear to produce reliable scores on critical, job-related tasks. These new evaluation procedures are generally complex, expensive to develop, and demanding to

FIGURE 5.2 Criterion Measures Related to Campbell's Performance Dimensions

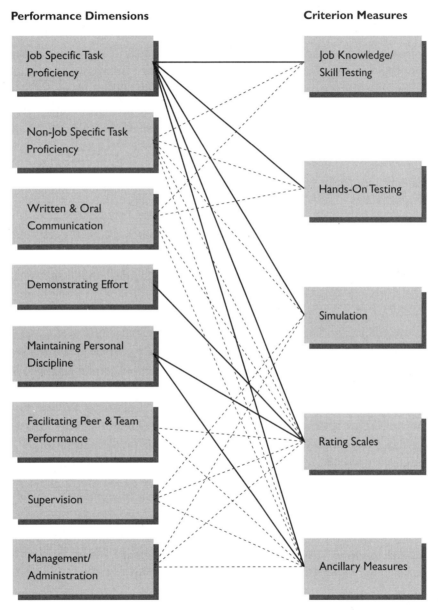

Performance Dimensions

Job Specific Task Proficiency

Non-Job Specific Task Proficiency

Written & Oral Communication

Demonstrating Effort

Maintaining Personal Discipline

Facilitating Peer & Team Performance

Supervision

Management/ Administration

Criterion Measures

Job Knowledge/ Skill Testing

Hands-On Testing

Simulation

Rating Scales

Ancillary Measures

Note: Heavy lines indicate the three dimensions thought to be present in all jobs.

administer, raising the issue of their practicality arises in most situations. Nonetheless, they may have immense potential for use in validation research.

HUMAN RIGHTS AND PERFORMANCE APPRAISAL

Ever since *Griggs* v. *Duke Power Co.*, 401 U.S. 424 (1971), personnel practices in the United States and Canada have been increasingly subject to review by the judiciary or human rights tribunals. Although the Canadian legal precedents have occurred more recently, they have been influenced by U.S. case law (Cronshaw, 1986, 1988). Reviews of U.S. decisions related to criterion-related validity studies and performance measurement systems emphasize that the defensibility of criterion measures rests upon the ability to demonstrate that performance measures are job-related (Barrett and Kernan, 1987).

The absence of a job analysis as part of criterion development will likely cast suspicion on any performance measurement system subject to judicial review (Landy, 1989). In *B.L. Mears et al* v. *Ontario Hydro* (1984), a tribunal under the Ontario Human Rights Commission decided that black employees were unfairly ranked for layoffs, compared to white employees, through the use of vague and undefined criteria (e.g., productivity, safety, quality of work, attendance, and seniority). Additionally, the ranking system was informal as no written records of productivity or quality of work were kept. In reviewing U.S. court decisions involving performance appraisal systems, Barrett and Kernan (1987) also note the requirement for written documentation regarding performance measurements. They go on to advise employers to maintain a review mechanism through which employees can appeal performance assessments they believe to be unfair or discriminatory.

Increased critical examination of performance measurement practices by Canadian human rights commissions and courts will mean strict adherence to accepted professional standards of criterion development (Cronshaw, 1988). These standards will include those that apply in the United States unless it can be shown that professional standards in Canada seriously deviate from those in the United States, or that Canadian legislation or case law has established practices that vary from U.S. standards. At present neither of these conditions hold. The most explicit statement on criteria is contained in the *Uniform Guidelines* (1978), which were jointly developed by the U.S. Equal Employment Opportunity Commission, Civil Service Commission,

Department of Labor and Department of Justice (Uniform Guidelines, 1978, 38300-01):

> *Whatever criteria are used should represent important or crucial work behavior(s) or work outcomes... The bases for the selection of the criterion measures should be provided, together with references to the evidence considered in making the selection of criterion measures. A full description of all criteria on which data were collected and means by which they were observed, recorded, evaluated, and quantified should be provided. If rating techniques are used as criterion measures, the appraisal form(s) and instructions to the raters should be provided as part of the validation evidence or should be explicitly described and available. All steps taken to insure that criterion measures are free from factors which would unfairly alter the scores of members of any group should be described.*

The research presented in this chapter, standards of professional practice, and reviews of legal decisions suggest that the following steps must be included in a performance measurement system that will satisfy human rights requirements.

1. Conduct a job and organization analysis to describe the job performance domain that is necessary for successful completion of the organization's goals.

2. Select criteria that are valid, reliable, and practical measures of the job performance dimensions. Document the development of the criteria and measurement scales as well as their validity.

3. Identify the performance standards, goals, or expected results that will be used to evaluate employees on the selected criteria. These standards should be made known to employees in understandable terms at the beginning of the review period.

4. Train people in the use of the performance measurement system, particularly when they will be called upon to make judgments about employee

performance. This training should include a review of the criteria, the measurement scales, and the standards.

5. Provide written instructions to all assessors on the proper use of the measurement system, particularly if the system involves the use of rating procedures.

6. Provide feedback from the performance evaluation to the employees. Assist those employees who receive poor evaluations to improve their performance. Raters should be trained in the effective use of feedback.

7. Establish a formal review mechanism, which has responsibility for the appraisal system and for any appeals arising from the evaluation process.

8. Document all steps in the development of the appraisal system and its use, as well as all decisions affecting employees that result from using the performance measurement data.

◆ ◆ ◆
SUMMARY

Any criteria chosen for use must be valid, reliable, practical, and capable of withstanding legal challenge. A construct validation strategy such as that outlined by Campbell (1990) will help to satisfy legal requirements. Once job-related performance dimensions have been identified, the type of criterion measure that most validly represents each performance dimension should be selected. Most likely, there will be different measures for different performance dimensions. There is no evidence to suggest that any one type of measure is inherently more sound than any other; in particular, rating systems, if properly developed, will provide data that are as reliable as other types of measures. Current research suggests that training criteria are acceptable performance measures for estimating maximum performance. However, to obtain a better understanding of possible changes in validities over time, repeated measures of performance should be taken over time. Data from the various criterion measures should be collected in an uncollapsed form and formed into composites when necessary. The weighting of composites should reflect the priority assigned by the organization to the different goal-related behaviours. All the procedures used in establishing the performance dimensions, their measures, and data collection and analysis should be documented.

EXERCISES

[Note: These exercises can be carried out for any occupation, but teaching is used since it is an occupation with which the student analysts will have some familiarity.]

As consumers, students are concerned about the quality of instruction they receive in the classroom. Over time a large number of teaching evaluations have been developed by colleges and universities to assess teaching performance. Many of these forms suffer from all the defects of graphic rating scales. For this exercise:

1. Obtain a copy of the teaching assessment form used by your institution and critique it using the information presented in this chapter.
2. Use the job analysis procedure presented in Box 5.1 (p. 181) to determine the critical tasks and job dimensions related to teaching. Your subject matter experts should include both professors and students. Keep in mind that you are focusing on teaching only, and not other aspects of the performance domain for the job of professor. (As an alternative, you may start with the eight performance dimensions identified by Campbell and have the subject matter experts determine their relative weight and then provide critical behaviours for each.)
3. For each job dimension, use the behaviours that you identified for that dimension to construct a behaviourally anchored rating scale of the type shown in Figure 5.1 (c). You do not have to follow all the steps required to construct a BARS, but you should at least have your subject matter experts rate the different behaviours for their importance.
4. Compare your scale with the one in use in your institution. Which one would you prefer to use? Which would your professor prefer? Why?

References

Anfuso, D. 1995. "Colgate's Global HR Unites under One Strategy." *Personnel Administrator* 74: 44–52.

Barrett, G.V., and M.C. Kernan. 1987. "Performance Appraisal and Terminations: A Review of Court Decisions since Brito v. Zia with

Implication for Personnel Practices." *Personnel Psychology* 40, 489–503.

Belcourt, M., A.W. Sherman Jr., G.W. Bohlander, and S.A. Snell. 1996. *Managing Human Resources*. Toronto: Nelson Canada.

Bernardin, H.J., and R. Beatty. 1984. *Performance Appraisal: Assessing Human Behavior at Work*. Boston: Kent-PWS.

Borman, W.C., and S.J. Motowidlo. 1993. "Expanding the Performance Domain to Include Elements of Contextual Performance." In N. Schmitt, W.C. Borman, and Associates, *Personnel Selection in Organizations*. San Francisco, CA: Jossey-Bass. 71–98.

Bowen, D.E., G.E. Ledford Jr., and B.R. Nathan. 1991. "Hiring for the Organization, Not the Job." *Academy of Management Executive* 5: 35–51.

Campbell, J.P. 1990. "Modelling the Performance Prediction Problem in Industrial and Organizational Psychology." In M.D. Dunnette and L.M. Hough, eds., *The Handbook of Industrial and Organizational Psychology*, Vol. 1, 2nd ed. San Diego: Consulting Psychologists Press, 687–732.

Cronshaw, S.F. 1986. "The Status of Employment Testing in Canada: A Review and Evaluation of Theory and Professional Practice." *Canadian Psychology* 27: 183–95.

Cronshaw, S.F. 1988. "Future Directions for Industrial Psychology in Canada." *Canadian Psychology* 29: 30–43.

Day, D.V., and L.M. Sulsky. 1995. "Effects of Frame-of-Reference Training and Ratee Information Configuration on Memory Organization and Rater Accuracy." *Journal of Applied Psychology* 80: 156–67.

Deadrick, D.L., and R.M. Madigan. 1990. "Dynamic Criteria Revisited: A Longitudinal Study of Performance Stability and Predictive Validity." *Personnel Psychology* 43: 717–44.

Ghiselli, E.E. 1966. *The Validity of Occupational Aptitude Tests*. New York: Wiley.

Gibb-Clark, M. 1996. "Court Orders Purolator to Pay Fired Employee." *The Globe and Mail*, May 4: B3.

Greene, L., H.J. Bernardin, and J. Abbott. 1985. "A Comparison of Rating Formats after Correction for Attenuation." *Educational and Psychological Measurement* 45: 503–15.

Guion, R.M. 1987. "Changing Views for Personnel Selection Research." *Personnel Psychology* 40: 199–213.

Guzzo, R.A. 1988. "Productivity Research: Reviewing Psychological and Economic Perspectives." In J.P. Campbell and R.J. Campbell, eds. *Productivity in Organizations*. San Francisco, CA: Jossey-Bass.

Landy, F.L. 1989. *Psychology of Work Behaviour*. 4th ed. Pacific Grove, CA: Brooks/Cole.

Latham, G.P., and K.N. Wexley. 1981. *Increasing Productivity through Performance Appraisal*. Reading, MA: Addison-Wesley.

Mahoney, T.A. 1988. "Productivity Defined: The Relativity of Efficiency, Effectiveness, and Change." In J.P. Campbell and R.J. Campbell, eds. *Productivity in Organizations*. San Francisco, CA: Jossey-Bass.

Moravec, M., and Tucker, R. 1992. "Job Descriptions for the 21st Century." *Personnel Administrator* 71: 37–44.

Murphy, K.R. 1989. "Dimensions of Job Performance." In R.F. Dillon and J.W. Pelligrino, eds. *Testing: Theoretical and Applied Perspectives*. New York: Praeger, 218–47.

Murphy, K.R., and J.N. Cleveland. 1995. *Understanding Performance Appraisal: Social, Organizational, and Goal-Based Perspectives*. Thousand Oaks, CA: Sage.

Sackett, P.R., S. Zedeck, and L. Fogli. 1988. "Relations Between Measures of Typical and Maximum Job Performance." *Journal of Applied Psychology* 73: 482–86.

Smith, P.C. 1976. "Behaviours, Results, and Organizational Effectiveness: The Problem of Criteria." In M.D. Dunnette, ed., *Handbook of Industrial and Organizational Psychology*. Chicago: Rand McNally, 745–76.

Smith, P.C., and L.M. Kendall. 1963. "Retranslation of Expectations: An Approach to the Construction of Unambiguous Anchors for Rating Scales." *Journal of Applied Psychology* 47: 149–55.

Thorndike, R.L. 1949. *Personnel Selection: Test and Measurement Technique*. New York: Wiley.

"Uniform Guidelines on Employee Selection Procedures." 1978. *Federal Register*, 43: 38290–315.

Vancouver, J.B., and N.W. Schmitt. 1991. "An Exploratory Analysis of the Person-Organization Fit: Organizational Goal Congruence." *Personnel Psychology* 44: 333–52.

6

Recruitment: Identifying, Contacting, and Attracting the Talent Pool

CHAPTER GOALS

This chapter reviews the role played by recruitment in human resources planning. We present this topic from the perspective of both the job seeker and the employing organization. After reading this chapter you should

- understand the link between recruitment and selection;
- appreciate the strategies used by job seekers to investigate jobs and organizations;
- understand how a job seeker's interests and values influence job search strategies;
- appreciate how job candidates use characteristics of the job and organization in making choices between jobs;
- know the role that accurate expectations play to improve the fit between a person and an organization;
- know why a realistic job preview may benefit both the job seeker and the organization;
- be aware of the internal and external factors that influence an organization's recruitment strategy;
- understand the linkage of recruitment to job and organization analysis;
- be able to design and implement a recruitment action plan; and
- be aware of the different methods that can be used to recruit internal and external job applicants.

◆ ◆ ◆
THE ORGANIZATION AND JOB FROM THE CANDIDATE'S PERSPECTIVE

Figure 6.1 presents a simplified view of the human resources management system, which serves as the framework for our discussion. In this model, recruitment is an outcome of human resources planning. The decision to recruit candidates for jobs in an organization is based on 1) an assessment of the internal and external factors affecting the organization; 2) an organization analysis based on those factors; and 3) a job analysis that identifies worker behaviours and characteristics that will identify candidates who are qualified for the position. The ultimate goal of a job-related selection system is to bring people into the organization who will perform at above average levels and who will increase the productivity of the organization.

Only within the last 20 years has recruitment received serious attention for the important role it plays in the selection process. Previously, recruitment was simply a means of attracting a large enough pool of candidates from which the organization could select the best qualified (Guion, 1976). Hardly any consideration was given to the possibility that candidates were using the recruiting process to select the organization. Job applicants are not passive organisms. During the recruitment and selection process, they form opinions about the organization, the selection process, the people they meet, and the desirability of working in the organization. Because of their experience, many candidates conclude that they do not want to work in a particular organization, or that they will not fit in; they may also form other attitudes, which last through their early work experience (Rynes, 1993). In the long run such *self-selecting out* may be in the interests of both the applicant and the organization, if that decision is based on accurate information and a realistic perception of the job and the organization. On the other hand, if these early decisions are based on inaccurate information, both the candidate and the organization may be worse off.

In many ways recruitment is the first step in the selection process. People apply for jobs in organizations on the basis of their interest in the job, and their belief that they have the required knowledge, skills, abilities, and other talents needed to do the job well. They also hope that the organization will provide a hospitable environment in which to spend the better part of their working day. Obviously, this is an idealized view of the world; in bad economic times when jobs are at a premium, people may change their

FIGURE 6.1 Recruitment as Part of the HR Planning Process

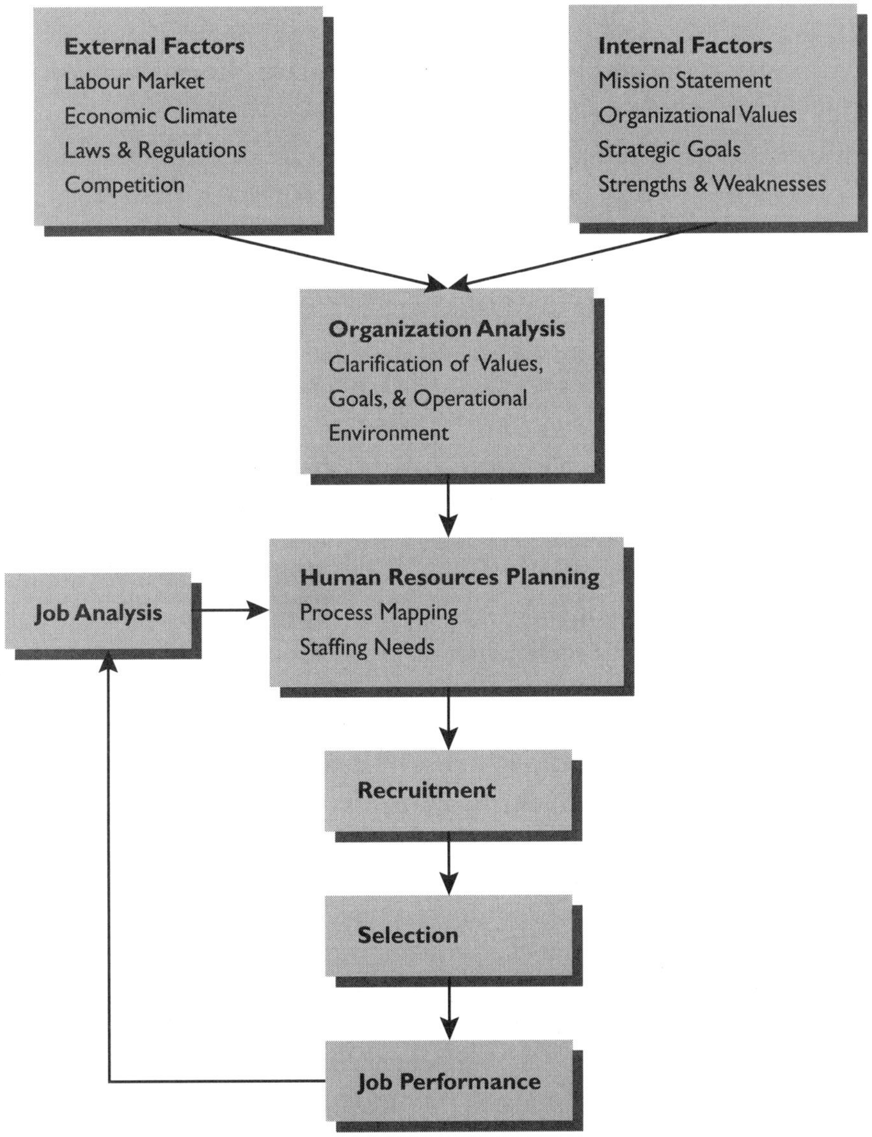

External Factors
Labour Market
Economic Climate
Laws & Regulations
Competition

Internal Factors
Mission Statement
Organizational Values
Strategic Goals
Strengths & Weaknesses

Organization Analysis
Clarification of Values,
Goals, & Operational
Environment

Job Analysis

Human Resources Planning
Process Mapping
Staffing Needs

Recruitment

Selection

Job Performance

perceptions of jobs and organizations, as well as their willingness to work in either. In hard economic times, people may value the security of having a job and the income it provides above everything else. Security and income, although important considerations, are not always the most influential factors in attracting applicants to jobs or organizations.

INVESTIGATING THE ORGANIZATION

Individuals become job applicants after forming an opinion on the desirability of working in a particular job within a specific organization (Schwab, Rynes, and Aldag, 1987). The strategies and information that people use in arriving at such decisions are by no means clear. Some people undertake extensive searches before applying for a job with an organization. They consult a variety of published documents for information about the organization, including annual reports and stories about the company and its employees in newspapers and business periodicals. With the advances of technology, many of these documents can be located quite readily through computer searches of CD-ROM databases or through access to archives located on the company's home page on the Internet. Job applicants also seek out employees of the organization or friends or acquaintances who have experience in it to obtain personal views on what it's like to work for the company and what the employees are like as co-workers. Often, the nature of supervision in the organization is an important concern to the candidate.

It is unlikely that any candidate, no matter how thorough their search for information, will get a complete picture of what life is like in the organization. One of the characteristics of the recruitment process is a mutual search for information about each other by the candidate and the organization. At some point an individual forms an impression of the organization and decides to apply for a job. Many well-qualified individuals may not pursue jobs based on their impression that they and the organization are incompatible. Of course, some individuals are more concerned with finding any job and make no effort to find out information about the organization beforehand.

INVESTIGATING THE JOB

Candidates investigate the job as well as the organization. Box 6.1 presents a summary of job attributes that candidates consider as part of their job search. The relative importance of these attributes depends on a person's age, sex, career interests, and previous work experience (London and Stumpf, 1982). Pay and the nature of the work to be done as part of the job rank consistently near the top in importance for all job seekers. Applicants for managerial and professional positions place emphasis on opportunities for advancement and promotion, while blue-collar candidates are more concerned with job security (Heneman, Schwab, Fossum, and Dyer, 1989). Ultimately, the values and interests of the job applicant influence the relative importance of these different attributes. Unfortunately, many candidates fail to take the last step in their investigation: an examination of their own interests, values, and talents.

BOX 6.1 INFLUENTIAL JOB ATTRIBUTES

All Candidates

Pay

Nature of Work

Opportunities for Knowledge and Skill Development

Recognition

Good Interpersonal Relations with Co-workers

White-Collar Job Candidates

Opportunity for Advancement

Opportunity for Promotion

Geographic Location of Work

Responsibility

Opportunity to be Creative

Blue-Collar Job Candidates

Job Security

(The order of listing does not imply order of importance, which may depend on many other factors).

Source: Adapted from Heneman et al. (1989), and London and Stumpf (1982).

INTERESTS AND VALUES

A person's interests and values determine whether that individual applies for a specific job. People who dislike sitting in an office all day are unlikely to apply for jobs as accountants, even if they have the appropriate qualifications. Such people, however, might pursue jobs as managers of wildlife preserves, even though they do not meet all of the requirements. Interests and values are strong factors in guiding career or job choice decisions.

Interests and values do not indicate whether a person is qualified for a job. Interests and values only suggest the type of work a person may find satisfying. Nonetheless, the degree of satisfaction with a job is one of the many factors that influence job turnover, especially in good economic times when jobs are plentiful (Carsten and Spector, 1987).

VOCATIONAL COUNSELLING Most new job seekers are unsure of their interests and career goals. Vocational guidance counsellors assist job seekers in identifying groups of jobs that are compatible with their values and interests. One technique that guidance counsellors use as part of this process is to have the person complete a value or interest inventory. These are self-report measures, which require individuals to complete a systematic series of questions about their likes and dislikes. The scores from these measures are compared with normative data that have been collected from actual incumbents in many different types of jobs and professions. The individuals are advised of those occupations where job incumbents hold interests similar to their own.

Interest Inventories Many of the measures that are used to assess vocational interest are based on vocational theories developed by Holland (1973). According to Holland, six major themes can be used to classify both vocational interests and related jobs. Holland proposed that in North America most people can be categorized in terms of some combination of six basic personality types:

◆ *Realistic* types perceive themselves as having mechanical and athletic ability but lacking ability in human relations; they tend to value money, power, and status; they prefer working in technical and skilled occupations such as farmer, and metal or machine worker.

◆ *Investigative* types perceive themselves as scholarly, intellectually self-confident, and possessing mathematical and scientific ability but lacking in leadership; they tend to value scientific and intellectual activities; they prefer working in scientific occupations such as chemist, engineer, and medical technologist.

◆ *Artistic* types perceive themselves as expressive, nonconforming, original, introspective, independent, and disorderly; they tend to value artistic and musical activities and aesthetic qualities; they prefer working in artistic, literary, and musical occupations such as photographer, writer, and music teacher.

- *Social* types perceive themselves as liking to help others, understanding of others, having teaching ability and lacking mechanical and scientific ability; they tend to value social activities and problems; they prefer working in educational and social welfare occupations such as a member of the clergy, social worker, and counsellor.

- *Enterprising* types perceive themselves as aggressive, popular, self-confident, sociable, possessing leadership, but not scientific abilities; they tend to value political and economic achievement; they prefer working in sales and managerial occupations such as sales person, buyer, and office manager.

- *Conventional* types perceive themselves as conforming, orderly, and having clerical and numerical ability; they tend to value business and economic achievement; they prefer working in office and clerical occupations such as accountant and bookkeeper.

Holland proposed that occupational environments are dominated by a given type of person and thus the environments can also be categorized by combinations of these six types. People search for environments that are compatible with their own values and interests and let them exercise their skills and abilities on problems that they find satisfying. Ultimately, the person's work performance is determined by an interaction of personality and environment, with the best performance occurring when there is a match between both. For example, an individual who is categorized as a Conventional type is more likely to be satisfied working as an accountant in an occupational environment dominated by Conventional types than as a photographer working in an Artistic environment. An interest inventory does not assess the individual with respect to the knowledge, skills, or abilities that are needed to work as an accountant or a photographer; it only assesses the compatibility of interests. Holland's theory is much more complex than what can be presented here, with most interests and occupations related to a combination of the six basic types.

Interest inventories, those based on Holland's theory or others (Box 6.2), are useful tools in the hands of a trained vocational counsellor; they identify lines of work or occupations that individuals may never have considered. Interest inventories are most useful when the individual responds openly and honestly. They are of little value if an individual fakes answers to convince the counsellor or someone else that he or she should, or should not, pursue a certain career.

BOX 6.2 COMMONLY USED INTEREST INVENTORIES

Canadian Occupational Interest Inventory

General Occupational Interest Inventory

Jackson Vocational Interest Survey

Kuder Preference Record, Vocational

Minnesota Importance Questionnaire

Self-Directed Search

Sixteen Personality Factor Questionnaire

Strong Interest Inventory

Vocational Preference Inventory

IDENTIFYING KNOWLEDGE, SKILLS, ABILITIES, AND OTHER ATTRIBUTES

Potential job applicants must also have a good idea of the knowledge, skills, abilities, and other attributes (KSAOs) they possess and their compatibility to those required for the job they are seeking. Job advertisements and other recruiting materials generally give the individual guidance about the needed KSAOs; candidates must decide on their own whether they meet those qualifications. Many job applicants do not have an accurate perception of their own strengths and weaknesses; neither do they know how to present vital information to prospective employers. People apply to many jobs for which they are not qualified. In Chapter 7, we will review several steps that employers take, based on the candidates' applications and résumés, to screen out individuals who do not meet the basic job requirements. Vocational guidance counsellors can help job seekers, both new and experienced, avoid futile applications by helping them to identify their abilities, skills, and other talents. Many of the tests used by employers to identify knowledge and skills are also available for use by qualified counsellors. Vocational counsellors have a good understanding of the level of abilities or skills needed in certain jobs and can help candidates determine if their applications for those jobs have a realistic chance of meeting with success. They can also assist job seekers in presenting themselves to prospective employers by helping them to write letters and résumés that are well-organized, which will create a favourable impression of the candidate.

INTENSITY OF THE JOB SEARCH

Job seekers pursue employment with different levels of intensity. Some take a very casual, passive approach and apply only for those positions that meet their ideals. They may not do a very thorough or systematic job search, but may simply rely on formal advertisements or job announcements. They do not take the time to find out anything about the organization, the job, or themselves. They do not make an effort to use resources such as vocational counsellors to assist in the job search. Other applicants spend several hours per day job hunting by examining all possible sources of information, including social networks, news groups on the Internet, and friends and relatives. They apply for any position that falls within their area of interest. These applicants also investigate the organization and have a good perception of the job and their own strengths and weaknesses. The more intense the job search, the more likely an individual will find a job placement (Zadny and James, 1977).

Two factors, financial need and self-esteem, influence job search intensity. Individuals with greater financial need pursue jobs with greater intensity. Studies done on unemployment compensation systems consistently show that higher unemployment benefits, as well as lengthier benefit periods, are related to longer periods of unemployment. The higher benefit levels may reduce the financial consequences of unemployment and allow job seekers to hold out for a better job (Schwab et al., 1987). Regardless of financial considerations, some people are achievement-oriented; being unemployed lowers their self-esteem and self-worth. Having a job is an important part of their identity. Whatever the reasons, the intensity of the job search effort increases the likelihood of attracting job offers and of finding a job (Schwab et al., 1987).

BOX 6.3 A JOB SEARCH STRATEGY

1. Determine your values and interests.
2. Determine your knowledge, skills, abilities, and other talents.
3. Determine the jobs or occupation in which you are interested and for which you qualify.
4. Begin an intensive and systematic search for jobs in your designated occupations.
5. Thoroughly investigate all available jobs uncovered by your search.
6. Thoroughly investigate the organizations in which those jobs are available.
7. Determine if there is a fit between yourself, the job, and the organization.
8. Pursue all available jobs where there is a fit.

◆ ◆ ◆
JOB CHOICE MODELS

Successful job searches end with offers of employment. The successful applicant may be in the enviable position of having to choose between several offers. How do job applicants make such decisions, and more importantly, what are the implications of these decision strategies for recruitment efforts? Box 6.1 presents several job attributes that job applicants believe are important. How does an applicant compare these attributes when deciding between competing offers? If an applicant wants to find a job that provides both excellent pay and opportunity for advancement, which job will the applicant choose when Job A provides excellent pay but no opportunity for advancement and Job B provides opportunity for advancement but poor pay?

EXPECTANCY THEORY

Expectancy theory (Vroom, 1964) is a widely studied theory of work motivation, which has also been used as a framework to study how job candidates make job choices. The theory proposes that a job candidate's decision to join an organization is based on the candidate's belief about the likelihood that a job will bring with it valued attributes. The theory proposes that candidates will choose the job with the highest expected value. This score is based on adding together the perceived value for each attribute, weighted by its likelihood. If the score for Job A is higher than for Job B, the candidate will choose Job A.

Expectancy theorists disagree on whether candidates evaluate all job attributes or only a limited number. Regardless of the number of attributes involved, expectancy models differ in assuming whether candidates evaluate job attributes sequentially or simultaneously. They also differ in assuming whether candidates attempt to find a job that maximizes the expected value, or whether candidates accept a job as soon as they find one that meets a minimum expected value (Schwab et al., 1987). On the whole, expectancy models provide a reasonably good framework for understanding job choice decisions (Wanous and Coella, 1989).

JOB SEARCH/JOB CHOICE

The job search/job choice model (Soelberg, 1967) proposes that candidates follow four steps in making a job choice decision. The four steps in Soelberg's model integrate many of the points already discussed in this chapter.

BOX 6.4 AN ILLUSTRATION OF EXPECTANCY THEORY

Values for Job Attributes

Suppose that job candidates assign values that range from –5 to +5 to different job attributes. Candidate X assigns a value of +5 to pay and +3 to opportunity for advancement. [Note: In reality there are more than two attributes to evaluate for any position].

Likelihood of Obtaining the Desired Outcome

Candidate X believes there is an 80 percent chance that Job A will provide excellent pay but only a 60 percent chance of opportunity for advancement. In evaluating Job B, Candidate X comes to expect a 40 percent chance of excellent pay and an 80 percent chance of advancement.

Weighted Expectancy Score

For Job A, Weighted Expectancy Score = $[(+5 \times .80)+(+3 \times .60)] = 4.8$
For Job B, Weighted Expectancy Score = $[(+5 \times .40)+(+3 \times .80)] = 4.4$

Decision

Expectancy theory predicts that the candidate will pursue the job with the highest score when all the attributes, weighted by their perceived value and likelihood, are added together. Therefore, candidate X should choose Job A.

1. The candidate identifies an occupation based on his or her values and perceived qualifications.

2. The candidate plans a job search.

3. During the job search and job choice stage, a candidate examines all possible job choices until one is found that meets the candidate's minimum standards on a selected number of job attributes. Each attribute is examined sequentially; high scores on one attribute do not compensate for low scores on another. If one attribute is perceived to be deficient, the job is not accepted. (In expectancy models, high scores on one attribute compensate for low scores on another since all scores are added together.) Once a minimally acceptable job is found, the candidate attempts to find at least one other minimally acceptable job before making a choice.

4. Before making a commitment to accept a job, the candidate attempts to verify the information used in making the initial job choice decision.

While the job search/job choice model is very appealing, there is insufficient empirical evidence on which to judge its soundness (Wanous and Coella, 1989).

IMAGE MATCHING

Tom's (1971) image matching theory proposes that job candidates compare their own self-image to their image of an organization and choose to work for the organization whose perceived image closely matches their own. This approach is very similar to Holland's argument that candidates seek occupational environments that are congruent with their interests. For example, a computer designer, whose self-image is that of a laid back, easy-going person, would be less likely to take a job at IBM (which might be perceived as a straight-laced, buttoned-down organization) and more likely to take a job at Apple Computers (which might be perceived as a more informal, easy-going organization). Whether these perceptions are correct is irrelevant; what matters is the match between the candidate's perception of self and the organization.

Like job search/job choice theory, Tom's model has generated very little research on which to judge its soundness. The few studies that have investigated this theory tend to support its premise (Wanous and Coella, 1989). It remains an interesting alternative by proposing that candidates make job choices through a simultaneous comparison of organizations rather than through a comparison of job attributes, and that they make choices on the basis of an image match rather than seeking the best job.

IMPLICATIONS FOR RECRUITMENT

REDUCING INFORMATION OVERLOAD All of the job choice models require the job candidate to handle and process large amounts of information about jobs and organizations. Candidates may experience information overload and try to cope with this situation by either ignoring additional information or by only paying attention to selected pieces of information. Either way, important information about the job and organization is lost. Job candidates can only base their decisions on information that they have retained. This limitation offers suggestions on how organizations should present information to job candidates.

ACCURACY AND CONSISTENCY OF INFORMATION Organizations must recognize that candidates have a limited capacity to retain information. It is of no benefit to present candidates with an extensive amount of information when most of it will be lost in a very short time. Organizations should limit their information flow to a reasonable level while at the same time making sure that the candidate becomes aware of important features of the job and its environment. The information that a candidate receives from an organization should be consistent. Candidates may use the behaviour of organization representatives as signals or indicators about the organization's climate, efficiency, and attitude toward employees (Schwab et al., 1987). While the organization cannot control the message a candidate receives about it from external sources, it can ensure that all information and materials received from the organization and its representatives are accurate and consistent. This does not mean that a company should insist that only positive information is presented about itself. As we will discuss shortly, it may be more desirable in the long run to convey accurate information, even if some of that material is negative.

REPETITION Job seekers often distort information they receive to make it support decisions they make or want to make. Information theory suggests that repetition is an effective communication strategy to ensure that important information is accurately received. Important information should be presented to the candidate by several different information sources. The sources chosen to present important information on job and organizational attributes must be seen by the candidate as reliable and credible. These sources represent the organization and are used by the candidate to form an image of it. Organizations must give serious consideration not only to the content of information presented to candidates but also to the context in which it is presented. The organization must take extreme care in preparing recruiting materials, selecting advertising media, and choosing the recruiters who will interact with job applicants.

IMAGE ADVERTISING In making a job choice, candidates evaluate the organization as well as the job. As part of an initial job search, job seekers may not even consider applying for jobs in organizations that have a negative image. Job seekers may decide against smaller companies with little or poor public visibility. To counteract such perceptions, or to create an accurate perception, organizations often initiate activities designed to enhance their image and reputation. Image advertising seeks to raise the profile of organizations in a positive manner to attract interest from job seekers (Magnus, 1985). A good example of image advertising is the "No life like it" advertising campaign used by the Canadian Forces to create a positive image about the military lifestyle. The campaign is directed at attracting the attention and interest of individuals who might not normally consider a military career because of misperceptions.

An organization that is having trouble attracting qualified candidates should investigate how it is perceived by job candidates and take corrective action, if necessary. Image advertising must present an accurate and consistent picture of the organization. Image advertising that creates misperceptions will lead to mismatches in the fit between person and organization. Image advertising should be designed to improve the attractiveness of the organization on the basis of an accurate representation of its characteristics.

◆ ◆ ◆
THE PERSON-ORGANIZATION FIT

Up to this point we have discussed the job search and job choice process from the job candidate's perspective. Obviously, there is another player involved in this process. No matter how desirable or compatible a job and organization appear to the candidate, it is all for naught unless the candidate receives an offer of employment. While the candidate seeks to learn as much as possible about the job and organization, the organization, through its representatives, is seeking to learn as much as it can about the candidate. At the same time, both the candidate and the organization are trying to appear as attractive as possible to each other. The organization wants to have a choice of top candidates while the candidate wants to have a choice of job offers. The job candidate and the organization are each trying to determine if the other is the right fit. The decision of each is based upon the exchange of information that takes place over the recruitment process. If the job candidate does not make an adequate investigation of the job or organization, or if the organization does not represent itself accurately, the probability of a person-organization mismatch increases. Mismatches can be quite costly in terms of absenteeism, low productivity, and turnover. A major goal of any recruitment campaign should be to improve the chance of making a good fit between candidates and the organization.

COMMUNICATION AND PERCEPTION

Based on information that was available or obtained during the recruitment process, the candidate and the organization form a perception of each other. If the perceptions of both are positive ("This is the right candidate," "This is the right job for me"), a job offer is made and accepted. If the perceptions of one do not match those of the other, a job offer is either not made, or if made, not accepted. Figure 6.2 presents the possible outcomes from this process. In all cases, there is a possibility that the perceptions formed by both the candidate and the organization are wrong. Candidates, particularly, develop overly positive perceptions of the organization (Wanous and Colella, 1989).

Perceptions are based on communication. During the recruiting process both the candidate and the organization try to control the flow of information from one to the other. One party may not wish to share some information with the other. An organization may fear losing top quality candidates by revealing that it is not the perfect workplace; candidates may fear losing a job offer by admitting they do not plan to stay with the organization for a long period of time. Both may misrepresent their attributes or characteristics. An organization may exaggerate the chances for promotion to attract a

FIGURE 6.2 Matching the Candidate's and Organization's Perceptions: Job Offer Outcomes

		Candidate's Perception of the Organization	
		Positive	Negative
Organization's Perception of the Candidate	Positive	Job offer made by organization and accepted by candidate.	Job offer made by organization and rejected by candidate.
	Negative	Job offer not made by organization but would have been accepted by candidate.	Job offer not made by organization and would not have been accepted by candidate.

candidate; candidates may exaggerate their experience. Both the organization and the candidate evaluate each other during the recruitment process (Rynes, 1993). Inaccurate, incomplete, or distorted information leads to misperceptions and inaccurate decisions. A primary goal of recruitment should be to increase the accuracy of the perceptions that each party holds about the other.

ACCURATE EXPECTATIONS

By developing a systematic job search strategy, job candidates will come into contact with information on jobs and organizations. Many of the initial expectations that candidates develop are based on the accuracy of this preliminary information, as well as the more extensive information that accumulates during the recruiting process. For example, accuracy of information received from the recruiting source and the organization directly influenced the length of time that Canadian students stayed in seasonal jobs as well as their commitment to the organization and their job satisfaction (Saks, 1994). Organizations have no control over whether candidates search for any information, or which information they select and use in forming an opinion about the job or organization. Candidates actively evaluate the merits of any message they receive (Wanous and Colella, 1989). Organizations do, however, have control over the accuracy and the completeness of the information they present when recruiting job candidates. During the United States' war with Iraq, many military personnel who were recruited into the U.S. reserve forces were shocked and outraged to learn that they were liable for combat duty; they claimed that they had never been made aware of such a possibility before signing on (Buckley, Fedor, and Marvin, 1994).

Recently, courts in both Canada and the United States have held employers accountable for the accuracy of information they present to job candidates as part of the recruiting process. False promises and misrepresentations made in recruiting candidates to work for a company may result in a damage award. Employees who believe that they were misled about the nature of their working conditions or their working environment are likely to take legal action against their employers to the extent that they are injured through reliance on the false or misleading statements (Buckley et al., 1994).

CREATING ACCURATE EXPECTATIONS

Four factors play a very influential role in creating accurate expectations that candidates hold about prospective jobs: (1) the source of the information, (2) the media used to deliver the information, (3) the content of the information, and (4) the nature of the job candidates who receive the information (Popovich and Wanous, 1982).

SOURCE OF INFORMATION In describing a job or position, the organization should present information to job candidates that accurately describes the job and its context. As discussed in previous chapters, the best way to obtain this information is through organization and job analysis. The information obtained through these means serves as a good basis for recruiting materials and other information presented to job candidates. Year-end reports, shareholder reports, technical manuals, and other documents are also good sources of accurate information. In particular, annual reports offer an insight into the mission, values, and goals of the organization.

COMMUNICATION MEDIA There is an extensive array of media that organizations can use to contact job seekers. We will take a more detailed look at some of the more prominent recruitment media, and their effectiveness, later in this chapter. In choosing recruitment media, organizations should consider the effect of the communication channel, itself, on the recruitment process. Both Wanous and Colella (1989) and Rynes (1991) summarize empirical research on the effectiveness of recruiting media. Those reviews suggest that media differ in effectiveness in relation to the criteria used to measure the effectiveness. Job applicants who are recruited through referrals from people in the organization are less likely to quit than job candidates who are recruited through newspaper advertisements; on the other hand, job applicants who walk in off the street may perform at higher levels than referrals. At present, there is little theoretical understanding of the relationship between recruitment sources and organizational outcome measures, thus limiting the usefulness of this empirical information in constructing recruitment programs. Perhaps the best advice is to use a broad approach; use as many different types of communication media as the organization can afford, including newer technologies such as job postings on the Internet or an organization's home page on the World Wide Web. These newer technologies offer the potential for quick, two-way interaction between job candidates and the organization of the type that may be very effective in promoting accurate communication (Wanous and Colella, 1989).

CONTENT OF INFORMATION The content of information provided throughout the recruitment process is the most important factor in creating accurate job expectations (Breaugh and Billings, 1988). Breaugh and Billings propose that the content of the recruitment message should be

◆ Accurate—job candidates should be given both positive and negative information about the job and the organization.

◆ Specific—job candidates should be given detailed information that will allow them to make an informed decision.

◆ Broad—job candidates should be given information about a wide range of job and organizational attributes, and not only information related to a narrow range of topics.

◆ Credible—job candidates must believe that the information they receive is reliable and accurate;

◆ Important—job candidates should be given information that is important to their decision-making, which they are unlikely to receive through other means

NATURE OF THE JOB CANDIDATES The organization must know something about the audience that will receive the information. This includes knowledge of the social and demographic characteristics of the target group. For example, the written materials used as part of the recruitment process should be readable by the potential job applicants. Written recruiting materials that require a college or university reading level might not be understood by job candidates with less education; this could create a problem if the job only requires a high-school education. Conversely, materials written at a lower level might present the wrong image when trying to attract college and university graduates. In the case of recruiting people with very specialized expertise, the recruitment materials may contain specialized terms that will only be understood by people with the appropriate background. In this way, they act to screen out inappropriate applicants.

In addition to being understood, the content of the message should be presented in a manner compatible with its intended audience. The materials should encourage interest in the job and company on the part of the candidate. This is more likely to happen if the material addresses the needs and interests of its target group.

The organization should also know the sources of information that its target audience is likely to use. Professionals who are looking for a job may use the services of a private employment agency, or search job advertisements in professional newsletters or journals. Blue-collar job seekers may rely on classified ads in the local newspaper or the services of Canada Employment Centres. Cost is always a factor in determining choice of media; nonetheless, limited job advertising compromises an employer's ability to mount a defence against charges of discriminatory hiring practices. If the organization only recruits carpenters by placing job ads in male-oriented magazines, it runs the risk of not attracting female applicants and of not hiring female carpenters. Female carpenters could argue that the recruiting process was designed to limit female applications by not advertising the position in media of interest to female carpenters. If a lawsuit by female carpenters were successful on these grounds, the organization might be liable for substantial damages.

REALISTIC JOB PREVIEWS

Recruitment programs can be designed to increase the accuracy of the expectations that job candidates hold about the job and the organization. One such program, Realistic Job Previews (RJPs), is very effective in improving the fit between the job candidate and the organization. The primary goal of RJPs is to reduce turnover among newcomers to an organization by providing job candidates with accurate information about the job and the organization (Wanous, 1980). Other hoped-for outcomes of the RJP are (1) that the job candidates will develop realistic perceptions of what it is like to work in the organization; (2) that they will view the organization in a more credible light; and (3) that, if they accept the job offer, they will be more satisfied with their job and committed to the organization.

Rather than have a candidate accept a job on the basis of unrealistic expectations, only to quit after discovering a mismatch with the organization, RJPs give the candidate an accurate preview of the job before the job offer is accepted. In this way, candidates who discover a mismatch self-select out, or remove themselves from the competition, saving themselves the aggravation of having made a bad decision and the organization the cost of hiring and training them. There are some concerns, however, that the realism

BOX 6.5 DEVELOPING AND IMPLEMENTING REALISTIC JOB PREVIEWS IN A RECRUITMENT PROGRAM

1. Initiate RJPs to avoid future problems, not current problems.
2. The diagnosis of organizational problems that prompt the introduction of an RJP does not have to be highly structured.
3. An RJP should evaluate or judge conditions as well as simply describing them.
4. RJPs should concentrate on a few major issues and make in depth presentations on those items rather than trying to cover every possible issue.
5. Proportional to what the job is really like, RJPs should include moderately negative information but not extremely negative information.
6. RJPs should include the presentation of audiovisual materials.
7. The people appearing in RJP materials should be actual employees rather than actors.
8. The RJP should take place relatively early in the recruitment process.
9. The RJP should be implemented as a matter of policy and not left to the wishes of individuals handling the recruiting.
10. The results of any evaluation of an RJP program should be made available to any interested parties, including competitors.

Source: Based on Wanous, 1989.

also discourages very qualified candidates from accepting job offers from the organization (Rynes, 1991).

The Canadian Forces (CF) uses RJPs as part of its recruitment program. The program was designed to reduce early attrition of new recruits by improving the person-job fit; the RJP is carried out throughout the Canadian Forces as a matter of policy. The RJP is embedded in a comprehensive counselling system designed to match the goals, interests, and abilities of applicants to the characteristics and conditions of service associated with specific trades in the Forces (Wilson, 1980). By using advertising media, the Canadian Forces raises the interest of potential applicants in the military as a career and attracts them to recruiting centres. The applicant is met by a recruiting officer who presents the candidate with brochures and information on the CF and determines initial suitability of the candidate for a career in the CF. Applicants who pass this first screen then view an Orientation Video, which depicts the careers of two actual candidates from recruitment through basic and trades training, and on to their first job postings. The video provides a realistic preview of life in the Forces in general and includes information on both the positive and negative aspects of military life. For example, it may portray the personal and social support offered to members of the CF and their families as well as the hazards and physical demands of military duty (Ellis and Angus, 1985).

Following the orientation video, the candidate meets with a military career counsellor and has an opportunity to raise any questions or concerns stimulated by it. At this point, the candidate must make a decision about whether to continue the process by completing an application form and a series of ability and aptitude tests. Candidates are next shown up to five Trade/Lifestyle Videos for entry-level positions for which they qualified through ability and aptitude testing. These videos are based on interviews with personnel from each trade they represent; they contain both verbal descriptions and live action footage of what it is like to work in that trade in a military environment. The speakers not only provide a description of what the trade is like but also express their views about their work. Following these videos, the candidate meets once again with a military career counsellor to review all aspects of the different trades and the military lifestyle. If the candidate remains interested in one of the selected trades, and if there is an appropriate vacancy in that specialty, the candidate is given an offer to enrol in the Canadian Forces (Ellis and Angus, 1985).

RJPs remain one of the most intriguing aspects of the recruiting process. They appear to lead to accurate expectations on the part of job candidates, to reductions in turnover, and to improvements in job satisfaction and in organizational commitment. However, much of the research leading to these conclusions has methodological flaws, which prevent making any definitive conclusions about their general effectiveness (Rynes, 1991). RJPs are only one means of producing a person-organization match. Before embarking on an extensive RJP program, serious consideration should be given to some of the less expensive ways to improve the accuracy of information presented to job applicants.

◆ ◆ ◆
RECRUITMENT STRATEGY

The first part of this chapter presented an overview of the job recruitment process from the perspective of both the job candidate and the organization. The remaining sections of this chapter focus on the more practical aspects of the recruiting process. Recruitment takes place in a human resources context, which is influenced by both internal and external factors as well as the more immediate needs of the job and the organization. Figure 6.1 illustrates the role that these factors play in recruiting. These factors raise a number of issues, which must be addressed when developing a recruitment strategy.

EXTERNAL FACTORS

All recruitment is influenced by two factors over which the organization has little control: (1) the labour market, and (2) the legal environment (Rynes, 1991).

LABOUR MARKETS AND RECRUITING Organizations must develop a recruiting campaign that makes sense in the context of a specific labour market. Labour markets impose different constraints than do economic conditions. The overall nature of the economy may influence an organization's decision to hire or not to hire, but once a decision to hire is made, the nature of the labour market determines how extensively the organization will have to search to fill the job with a qualified candidate. Toyota Canada was in the enviable position of having more than 50 000 people apply for 1200 positions that were being created as part of an expansion at its Cambridge, Ontario plant. (See Box 11.1, p. 475) The jobs paid $20 per hour plus benefits in a geographic area that had an 8.3 percent rate of unemployment. Toyota had 11 000 applications on file before it ran a single advertisement or it had posted the jobs with Canada Employment Centres (Keenan, 1996).

When qualified labour is scarce, the organization must broaden its recruiting beyond its normal target population. This includes going beyond normal recruiting channels to attract applicants it might not seek in more favourable times. For example, if there is a shortage of chartered accountants, the organization may take a look at hiring finance majors with a background in accounting who they believe will develop into the position with some additional training. The organization may also recruit outside its normal territory, emphasizing those geographic regions with high unemployment rates or low economic growth. In favourable labour markets, the organization may only advertise the accounting position in one or two professional journals. In a poor market, it may decide to use a variety of media to attract as

244

many qualified applicants as possible. With poor labour markets, the organization may make the job more attractive by improving salary and benefits, training and educational opportunities, and working conditions. In poor markets, the organization may spend additional resources to overcome the shortage of qualified applicants and to increase the attractiveness of the organization and the job as a place of employment. These considerations become even more important when the organization must compete with its rivals for scarce human resources. Recruiting when the labour market is poor is an expensive proposition.

PART-TIME LABOUR MARKETS AND RECRUITING In response to today's global economy, more and more companies are employing low-wage, entry-level workers on a part-time basis. Temporary or contingent jobs have shown tremendous growth over the last decade. Nearly two million people go to work each day in North America on a part-time basis. North American retailing giants such as Sears, Walmart, and K-Mart have made working part time their industry norm. Recruiting and retaining the best part-time workers present unique problems to companies choosing to go this route. Workers who receive lower pay and benefits are less likely to feel committed to their organization or to go out of their way to get the job done. Many part-time workers are unskilled and poorly educated. Companies such as Whirlpool have responded to the need to recruit part-time workers by restructuring their pay and benefits as well as providing training and educational opportunities for them, others such as Taco Bell have attempted to restructure the work environment to meet the needs of their part-time employees (Greengard, 1995). Increasingly, temporary work is serving as a training ground for more permanent positions. A recent survey found that over two-thirds of temporary workers reported that they gained new skills while in their temporary positions. On the other hand, ever greater numbers of skilled professionals and retired workers are taking jobs on a part-time or contract basis (Flynn, 1995). Organizations who depend on part-time workers will need to develop recruiting methods to attract and retain contingent employees.

Companies that need workers on a temporary or short-term basis often turn to temporary help agencies to provide them with contingent workers. In these cases, the workers are employees of the temporary help firm, not of the organization in which they do their work. Investigations in both Canada (Galt, 1992) and the United States (Castro, 1993) suggest that some temporary help agencies may be willing to accommodate their client organizations' requests that the agency not send blacks, people with accents, or unattractive women. Often, the client organizations have the mistaken notion that since they are not the legal employer, they are immune to charges of discrimination and free from any employment equity obligations. By allowing temporary workers on their premises and directing their work, the client organization can be subject to discrimination claims, unless it can show that the assignment based on group membership was a bona fide occupational requirement (Ryan and Schmit, 1996).

THE LEGAL ENVIRONMENT Any organizational recruitment program must comply with the legal and regulatory requirements that apply to its operation. Chapter 2 presented some of the landmark cases and legislation that govern employment in Canada. In the United States, employment laws and regulations are assumed to affect both recruitment practices and outcomes (Rynes, 1991). It is likely that Canadian employment legislation has similar effects on recruitment in Canadian organizations. The most important considerations are employment equity and pay equity legislation. Any recruitment campaign that intentionally or unintentionally excludes members of groups that are protected under human rights legislation runs the risk of being declared discriminatory, with the organization subject to penalties and fines. The best defence against charges of systemic discrimination is to document that every attempt has been made to attract members from the protected groups. In Canada, employment equity legislation seeks to eliminate discrimination in the workplace for women, disabled people, native people, and visible minorities. Organizations may be called upon, particularly if they wish to do business with the federal government, to demonstrate that they have actively sought to recruit members from these four groups. Good faith recruitment efforts mean that the organization must use a variety of communication channels to get its message to members of different groups and to present its recruiting message in a way that interests different audiences. The recruitment effort must make members from these groups feel welcome within the organization, even when they are working there on a temporary basis.

INTERNAL FACTORS

While it is clear that different organizations take different approaches to recruiting new employees, very little is known about how organizational characteristics produce differences in recruiting practices, processes, or outcomes. Partly, this is the result of most research focusing on job seekers rather than the employing organizations (Rynes, 1991). There are many possible organizational characteristics that could influence a job seeker's perception of the organization during the job search phase (e.g., the type of industry, size of the organization, profitability, growth, and financial trends). These characteristics may influence both the number and quality of applicants who apply for a position with the organization. They may also influence how the organization recruits candidates and how competitive the organization is in making offers to the best applicants (Rynes, 1991).

BUSINESS PLAN A company's business plan has a major impact on its recruiting strategy. An organization's business plan includes a statement of its mission and philosophy, a recognition of its strengths and weaknesses, and a statement of its goals and objectives for competing in its economic environment. A business plan addresses those aspects of the external environment that affect how the organization does business. An organization's business plan influences the degree to which the organization fills vacancies with internal or external applicants (Rynes, 1991). Rarely do organizations fill entry-level positions with internal candidates; however, it is quite common to bring someone in from the outside to fill a vacant position. Organizations differ in their approach to staffing these positions. Some insist, as a matter of organizational policy, that internal candidates be given preference as a means of motivating employees (recall that advancement is a recruiting factor) and ensuring that the successful candidate knows and shares the organizational philosophy, values, and goals. In some cases, collective agreements with employees may require that internal applicants be given first consideration for positions for which they are qualified. Other organizations insist that external candidates be given preference for jobs in order to expose the company to new ideas and to new ways of doing business. Still other organizations may insist that the best candidate be given the job offer, regardless of whether they are an internal or external applicant.

JOB LEVEL AND TYPE Both the type of occupation and the nature of the industry in which it is involved may influence an organization's recruiting strategy (Rynes, 1991). In some industries or occupations people are recruited in a particular way, not so much because that method is very effective, but because it is the norm. It is how recruiting is done for that type of work, and how it is expected to be done. For certain executive level positions, vacancies are never advertised but given to a consulting company to carry out an executive search. Such "headhunting" firms generally have a list of potential executive candidates that they have developed over time through contacts in many different organizations. The search firm knows the organization and works to find a match with one of its candidates. Rarely, if ever, are such firms used to recruit production or service workers; vacancies for these types of positions are filled from candidates who respond to local newspaper advertisements or job postings with Canada Employment Centres, or who are referred by other employees, as was the case with the 55 000 applicants for the production jobs at Toyota Canada (Keenan, 1996).

ORGANIZATION AND JOB ANALYSES

Job and organization characteristics play a major role in the recruitment process. Chapter 4 described procedures that allow organizations to identify these characteristics. Organization analysis provides an organization with a means of clarifying its values and goals and assessing the internal and external environments in which it operates. Job analysis provides the organization with an understanding of the expectations, behaviours, and tasks that are associated with a specific job. Job analysis also provides the organization with an understanding of the knowledge, skill, ability, or other talents that are needed to perform the job successfully. Both organization and job analyses provide information that helps to increase the person-organization fit. The information produced by these analyses helps the organization's human resources team produce a recruitment strategy.

TRANSLATING ORGANIZATION ANALYSIS DATA INTO THE RECRUITING STRATEGY Without a doubt, there are major differences in how organizations recruit personnel. Recruiting strategies reflect the organization's culture, values, and goals, as does all the information provided to job applicants. These materials, which should accurately represent the organization's culture, values, and goals, also influence who is recruited. As we saw previously, Colgate-Palmolive and British Petroleum recruit applicants who match their goals and values. IBM Canada also ties its recruiting initiatives to achieving organizational goals. In 1995, it hired about 800 new employees based on achieving its objectives of growth, customer satisfaction, and a high performance culture. Different organizational goals lead to different recruitment strategies. Similarly, an organization's philosophy and values influence whether it actively seeks to recruit women and members of minorities, or whether its approach to employment equity is one of minimal compliance. Organization analysis helps to clarify these issues.

In developing recruiting strategies, one must decide whether to concentrate recruiting efforts on internal or external candidates. Organization analysis reveals the likelihood of finding suitable internal candidates and the extent to which qualified internal candidates can fill the job openings, by providing an inventory of skills and abilities that exist within the company as well as indicating the potential for advancement among current employees. In conjunction with job analysis, this information gives a good indication of the likelihood of finding the right internal people for the job and the need for external recruiting. Unfortunately, relatively few companies inventory their employees' skills and abilities; such inventories are expensive to develop and to maintain.

TRANSLATING JOB ANALYSIS DATA INTO RECRUITING MATERIALS One of the most important pieces of information candidates rely on throughout the recruiting process is a description of the job and worker requirements. Recruiting information should give applicants a clear idea of the duties and tasks that form part of the job and the resources that they will need to do the job. It is very difficult to recruit job applicants without knowing the essential characteristics of the position or the requirements of the workers. Job descriptions that are up-to-date and based on a job analysis lead to accurate expectations on the part of the job candidate. Box 6.6 presents a job description for a security dispatcher at a university, which was derived from a Critical Incident job analysis.

Both applicants and recruiters should have a clear idea of the qualifications needed by people in the position. Often recruiters are told to seek the "best person" for the job, instead of being told to find the "best qualified person" for the job. Perhaps the best applicant for the security dispatcher's position is a graduate of the police academy who has worked for several years as a desk sergeant with the city police. Without knowing exactly what the

BOX 6.6 JOB DESCRIPTION OF A UNIVERSITY SECURITY DISPATCHER

The Security Dispatcher plays a vital role as part of the Campus Security team. The Security Dispatcher receives, analyzes, and collects vital information from various devices such as emergency telephone lines and surveillance equipment. The Security Dispatcher facilitates and coordinates appropriate responses between university and emergency response teams such as Campus Security, fire department, Metro Police, and others. The Security Dispatcher works in conjunction with the Manager of University Security, the Warrant Officer in charge of Commissionaires, and the Assistant Director of Residence Security.

The Security Dispatcher provides general information, processes requests for assistance (help desk and telephone calls), monitors all surveillance equipment, operates and organizes all recording and communications equipment, and records all incidents, complaints, and information requests in the shift log. The Security Dispatcher is responsible for proper storage and distribution of security equipment. The Security Dispatcher is also responsible for recording, storing, and returning of lost and found items.

The Security Dispatcher has a strong team commitment and is responsible for providing guidance and leadership for all veteran and new team members. The Security Dispatcher performs all responsibilities and duties in a polite and efficient manner, particularly when dealing with the public. Also, the Security Dispatcher remains knowledgeable on all policies and duties related to the position.

Previous work experience, first aid courses, and any type of security training is highly desirable. In view of the above-mentioned responsibilities, the Security Dispatcher must possess a sense of integrity, good written and oral communication skills, general knowledge of campus layout and services, and a general understanding of the role campus Security plays within a university environment.

security dispatcher did, the university could spend a lot of money hiring someone who was overqualified for the position.

HUMAN RESOURCES PLANNING

Human resources planning "is a process of developing and implementing plans and programs to ensure that the right number and type of individuals are available at the right time and place to fill organizational needs" (Dolan and Schuler, 1994, 90). This planning process is based on analysis of the organization's business plan, resulting in a forecast of the number and type of employees required to meet the plan's objectives. Through organization and job analyses, the planning process identifies the human resources needed to carry out the business plan, both those resources that exist within the organization and those that must be secured through a recruiting program. Human resources planning develops an action plan to eliminate any discrepancy between the supply and demand for human resources. With respect to the recruitment process, human resources planning must provide answers to the following questions:

♦ Based on our business plan, how many positions will we need to staff?

♦ Based on the job analysis, what is the nature of the position that must be filled?

♦ Based on the job analysis, what qualifications (knowledge, skills, abilities, experience) must job candidates possess to do the job successfully?

♦ Based on organization analysis, what percentage of the positions can, or should, be staffed with internal candidates?

♦ Based on the labour market, is there an available supply of qualified external candidates?

♦ Based on the labour market, how extensively will we have to search for qualified applicants? Will we have to search beyond our normal geographic boundaries? Will we have to take special measures to locate our target applicant population? What sources or methods should we use to reach the potential applicants?

♦ Based on legal considerations, what are our goals with respect to employment equity?

♦ Based on the business plan, organization analysis, and job analysis, what information and materials will we present to job candidates?

Answers to these questions form the organization's recruiting strategy (i.e., its plan for staffing the organization). The human resources management team must also have a plan for implementing the strategy.

RECRUITMENT ACTION PLAN

TIMING OF RECRUITMENT INITIATIVES In many organizations, recruiting occurs in response to need. An employee leaves for one reason or another and, if the position is retained, must be replaced either through internal or external hiring. In cases like this, there is little organizational control over timing. Delays in hiring may lead to delays in production, with unrealistic demands placed on the remaining employees. The recruitment goal is to hire someone qualified to do the work as soon as possible, even if hiring at a later date may have found someone who was better qualified for the position. In other organizations where there is a systematic turnover of employees, recruiting may follow a well-defined pattern. This pattern occurs most often in large organizations, which recruit heavily from among college and university graduates. The availability of such graduates in the spring of each year often determines when organizations implement their recruiting strategy; it influences when they send information to campus employment centres, place advertisements in campus newspapers, visit the schools, meet with the potential applicants, extend invitations to visit the organization, and make their job offers. Figure 6.3 represents a typical time line for these activities.

FIGURE 6.3 **Recruiting Time Line**

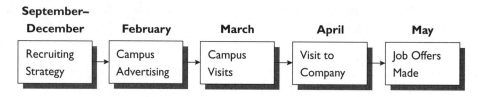

If an organization is late in recruiting, top candidates may have already accepted offers from the competition. To remain competitive, the organization must synchronize its recruiting to when the best candidates are available. This means that the human resources team must have a good working knowledge of the labour market.

In competing for qualified candidates, particularly when supply is weak, organizations are starting to incorporate in their recruiting strategies knowledge of how job candidates evaluate jobs and make choices. There is evidence to suggest that job seekers prefer early job offers as a way of reducing anxiety and uncertainty about other offers; there is also evidence to suggest that more qualified candidates generate offers earlier and more easily than less qualified candidates (Rynes, 1991). If this is so, then organizations may have to begin recruiting as early as possible if they want to hire the most qualified candidates. Instead of waiting until the spring to recruit college and university graduates, a company may begin the process earlier in order to make job offers before the end of the fall semester. Some organizations are also beginning to pursue college and university students before they enter the job market. Companies often use summer job placements, internships, or cooperative education as early recruitment programs (Rynes, 1991). These strategies are designed to have candidates accept an early job offer that meets their minimum standards rather than waiting to make a choice between competing offers.

The timing of events within a recruiting program is important. The process outlined in Figure 6.3 can extend over a considerable period of time, with several candidates evaluated for each vacancy. Job candidates do not put a halt to their job search activities while waiting for a decision. An organization that does not provide candidates with timely feedback about their progress through the recruitment and selection process may risk losing top candidates. Job seekers may take lack of contact as a lack of interest and accept an early offer from a less preferred company. Job candidates may not put a halt to job search activities even after accepting an early offer from an organization. They may continue to receive interest from other companies that were late off the mark in recruiting, and if they receive an attractive offer, they may change their minds about accepting the first offer. Maintaining contact with the candidate after an offer is accepted helps to forestall such reversals.

LOCATING AND TARGETING THE APPLICANT POOL In an ideal world, an organization could search as broadly as possible until it found the most suitable applicant. However, extensive recruiting is an expensive proposition, which few organizations can afford. It is also questionable whether the benefits of extensive recruiting overcome its associated costs. A more effective plan is to target recruiting efforts on a specific pool of job applicants who have the appropriate knowledge, skills, abilities, and other talents needed to perform the job. This applicant pool may be concentrated in one geographic area or spread widely throughout the nation. The human resources team must know where to find the appropriate applicant pool.

If a company wants to hire electronics technicians, it makes more sense to concentrate on recruiting graduates from electronics training programs or from areas where there is a concentration of electronics technicians rather than searching broadly throughout the country. The human resources team must know which colleges or institutes offer training in electronics; they must know where electronics industries are concentrated. If a company were recruiting experienced miners, it would be more appropriate to target Cape Breton as a source for this applicant pool rather than Metropolitan Toronto. On the other hand, recruiting upper level executives might require a nation-wide search to find the best candidate.

Targeting a specific applicant pool allows the organization to tailor its message to that group, to understand where that applicant pool is likely to be located, and to attract applications from that pool. In limiting its recruiting to a target applicant pool, however, an organization must be careful not to systematically exclude members of protected groups.

◆ ◆ ◆
RECRUITMENT METHODS

Once the target applicant pool has been identified and located, the human resources team must choose the most appropriate methods for reaching all members of internal and external applicant pools, including members of protected groups. The following sections describe some of the more popular recruiting methods that have been used to contact members of different applicant pools.

INTERNAL CANDIDATES

Internal candidates provide the organization with a known source of labour. Many of the activities carried out as part of human resources planning provide the organization with information about the best qualified internal applicants.

JOB POSTINGS Job postings refer to internal advertisements of job vacancies. The advertisements can take the form of notices posted on bulletin boards, ads placed in company newsletters, announcements made at staff meetings, or notices circulated through departments. The intent of the posting is to make internal employees aware of the vacancy and to allow them an opportunity to apply for the position. As a matter of policy, some organizations seek to fill positions through internal sources before going to the external market. Other organizations may have agreed, through a collective agreement with employees, to give first consideration to internal candidates for any vacant position that falls under the collective agreement. In these cases, the jobs are posted for a period of time in specified locations. Internal postings generally provide information on the job, its requirements, and compensation associated with the position.

Job postings provide an excellent means of discovering talented people within the organization and providing them with an opportunity for advancement within the organization. Knowing that good performance will be awarded through advancement has a positive effect on employee motivation. Job postings make the vacancy known to all employees; this is an important consideration when implementing employment equity programs throughout different levels of the organization. However, there are disadvantages to job postings. Internal postings lengthen the time needed to fill the position; external searches generally do not begin until after all internal candidates are first evaluated. Internal candidates who are unsuccessful may become less motivated, or may initiate a job search outside the organization. Placing an internal candidate in a vacant position sets off a sequence of events that brings with it a degree of instability and change: the position the employee leaves must itself be posted and filled. The effects of filling the first position with an internal candidate reverberate through several layers of the organization before the process comes to an end.

REPLACEMENT CHARTS Organizations expect that vacancies will occur through death, illness, retirement, resignation, or termination. As part of the human resources planning function, organizations develop a succession plan for filling vacancies with existing employees. Organizations have a good idea of the talent in higher level positions that can step in to fill a vacancy, either on a short-term or long-term basis. Replacement charts, like organizational charts, list each job with respect to its position in the organizational structure, particularly its relationship to positions above and below it. The replacement chart lists the incumbent for the position and the likely internal replacements for the incumbent. The chart includes information on the present job performance of each potential successor (e.g., "excellent performer"), an assessment of their readiness to step into the position (e.g., "needs more experience in present position), and a rank ordering of each as the incumbent's replacement. Replacement charts provide a quick, visual presentation of an organization's human resources, but they give little information beyond that of a candidate's performance and promotability. Replacement charts are limited by the constraints imposed by the organizational chart. Employees are evaluated for positions one level above theirs in the chain of command; they are not evaluated for positions that are horizontal or lateral to theirs.

HUMAN RESOURCES INFORMATION SYSTEMS Human resources planning often involves the creation of a comprehensive computerized database, which contains the job analysis information on each position, including information on the required knowledge, skills, abilities, and other attributes (KSAOs). This computerized inventory also contains information on employee KSAOs, along with their work histories, experiences, and results of performance evaluations. Internal candidates for a vacant position may be found through a computer match of the person's characteristics with those required by the job. The match does not give any indication of interest in the position or motivation to take on the new job. It is simply a first cut of employees who qualify for the position.

NOMINATIONS Nominations are the least systematic internal recruitment method. They occur when someone who knows about a vacancy nominates another employee to fill it. In most cases, supervisors nominate one or more of their employees for a vacant position. Presumably, the supervisor nominates those employees whose KSAOs match those needed by the job. This process often results in very good employees not being nominated for a position. Supervisors or managers may use the nominating process to rid themselves of a problem employee or someone with whom they have poor interpersonal relations. Nominations also leave the organization open to charges of discriminatory promotion practices. For example, in replacing a manager, the other senior managers who are male may fail to nominate any women for the position. The women employees who were passed over may ask whether the failure to nominate women was due to lack of qualified female employees, or to male bias against female managers.

EXTERNAL CANDIDATES

Organizations do not have a dependable supply of external applicants. The sources they use to attract external applicants have to be more creative and varied than those for internal candidates. The following section reviews some of the more common means used to reach external candidates.

JOB ADVERTISEMENTS Organizations spend a considerable part of their recruiting budgets on advertising vacant positions. The advertisements identify who the employer is and include basic information on the job and compensation, the requirements needed for the job, and how to apply (including closing dates for applications). The ad may also contain information on the organization's employment equity program. The ad should not include any statements that could lead to charges of discrimination (e.g., "The ideal applicant will be between 25 and 30 years old"), unless those statements can be supported as bona fide occupational requirements.

Job advertisement campaigns should be designed with the target applicant pool in mind:

- Who are we trying to reach? Who is our target applicant pool?
- How large is the applicant pool and what portion of it do we need to reach to obtain a reasonable number of applicants?
- How many applicants do we need to fill the position with qualified people?
- What type of ad content will attract the target applicant pool's attention?
- What advertising media are likely to reach the target applicant pool?

The answers to most of these questions are very complex and depend on consideration of many factors including the nature of the organization, the job, and the target applicant pool. One of the most important decisions is choosing the media for the advertising campaign.

Newspapers are perhaps the most common media for job advertisements. They offer a quick and flexible means of contacting potential applicants. Newspapers need only two or three days of lead time before an ad is published. The ad can be placed in the Classifieds section listing employment opportunities or prominently displayed in another section of the paper. Often managerial and professional positions are advertised in a newspaper's business section. Newspapers have specific geographic distribution areas. An organization can choose to advertise locally in a paper that serves the immediate area of the organization, or it can advertise in papers such as *The Globe and Mail*, which have a national distribution. Of course, the increased distribution comes at an increase in cost. Blue-collar positions tend to be advertised locally, with managerial and professional positions advertised nationally. Newspaper ads run for a very short period of time; they attract the interest of people who are actively searching for a job and who happen to see the advertisement before it disappears.

Professional periodicals and trade journals allow the organization to reach very specialized groups of applicants. Many professional or trade associations publish newsletters or magazines that are distributed to each member. These publications carry job advertisements. The association, and the distribution of its publication, may be international, national, or regional. Publications of this type are the best means of reaching people with specific skills or qualifications. Ads in these types of publications can be quite expensive and often require a long lead time before the ad appears. For example, an advertisement appearing in the March issue of a newsletter may have had an early January deadline for ad copy. With the recent growth in the World Wide Web, many professional and trade associations have reduced the publication lag by placing the job ads that are carried in their publications on-line as they are received.

Radio and television job advertising, in comparison to print media, has not been used extensively. These media offer the potential to reach large numbers of the target applicant pool. Radio and television advertising directors have detailed demographic information on the audience for specific shows and can place the advertisement during shows likely to be watched by the target applicant pool. Nonetheless, organizations appear reluctant to use these sources for job advertisements and limit their use to image advertising. The cost of such advertising, particularly on a national scale, may be quite high even for a 15- or 30-second commercial. The short duration of most commercials prevents the inclusion of essential job information. When radio and television advertising is used, the focus of the ads is to stimulate interest in the organization and to motivate the potential applicant to seek additional information from another recruiting source. This approach is used in the radio and television advertising of the Canadian Forces. While much of the ad content is devoted to image advertising, the ads always end with a phone number or address through which interested people may obtain more detailed information.

Public displays attempt to bring job vacancies to the attention of the target applicant pool through the use of advertisements that range from Help Wanted notices to display ads placed in buses, subway stations, and trains. Service and retail employers rely on Help Wanted signs posted in their windows or near service counters to attract job applicants. Most positions advertised through these types of notices are at the entry level and do not require extensive skills or abilities on the part of the applicant. These ads are directed at recruiting employees from among the employer's normal range of customers. Display ads in public transportation stations and vehicles attempt to reach a broader population than help wanted ads, but like those notices, they are also directed at attracting people for low skill or ability entry-level positions. These ads simply advertise the availability of jobs with an organization and provide those who are interested with a means of contacting the organization to obtain more specific information. Public display ads tend to be low in cost relative to the number of people that they reach. For example, one ad inside a bus may be seen by several thousand commuters over a month's display.

Direct mail advertising attempts to bring the organization's recruiting message directly to members of the target applicant pool. The potential employer sends each person on the mailing list recruiting information about the organization and the job, reaching both those who are actively seeking jobs and those who may become interested through reading the materials. The keys to this type of advertising are the acquisition or development of a mailing list consisting of names and addresses of the target applicant population, the attractiveness of the recruiting materials, and the ease with which follow-up contacts can take place. Often mailing lists can be obtained from various professional associations. In Canada, many rural communities have had trouble in recruiting medical practitioners. In response to this need, several communities have started active recruitment campaigns involving direct contact with potential graduates of medical schools, where the target applicant population is easy to identify and locate (LeBlanc, 1996).

Special recruiting events involve bringing a large number of potential job candidates into contact with an organization that is seeking to fill positions. Two well-established events used successfully to attract job seekers are open houses and job fairs. In an open house, an organization invites potential job applicants within its community to visit the company facilities, to view demonstrations or videos about the company and its products, and to meet the organization's employees informally over refreshments. Open houses work best when an organization has several jobs to fill and when there are tight labour markets. In a job fair, several organizations seeking to hire from the same target applicant pool arrange to recruit in conjunction with an ongoing event. For example, a trade or professional association may invite employers to hold a job fair as part of its annual convention. The employers who pay a fee to participate have access to all the convention delegates, both those who are actively seeking jobs and those who may become interested through meeting an organization's representative. The convention delegates represent the ideal target applicant pool. The job seekers make contact with organizations while the employers meet many prospective employees in a short period of time, at relatively low cost. The disadvantage is information overload, where the candidate is bombarded with too much information from too many organizations.

Employee referral is word-of-mouth advertising that relies on current employees telling their friends and relatives about job vacancies within their company. This is a low or no cost method of advertising. It assumes that the employees know other people with skills and abilities similar to their own, that the employees refer people with good work habits and attitudes similar to their own, and that current employees are the best representatives of the organization. In some companies, employees are paid a bonus for each successful referral. The greatest concern with using this method is the probability that it may produce charges of discriminatory hiring practices. In referring friends and relatives, employees are likely to refer individuals from their own ethnic, racial, or gender groups; this could work against meeting employment equity goals.

WALK INS In the external methods described above, the organization makes every attempt to contact members of the target applicant pool. The recruitment is initiated by the employer. Walk-in recruitment is initiated by the job seeker who visits an organization's personnel office and requests to fill out an application for employment, even though the company may not have any job vacancies. The *write-in* method is a variation of this approach; rather than visiting the company, job seekers send a copy of their résumés to the company. The company usually holds the applications for a period of time (e.g., three months), in case vacancies do occur. Walk-in and write-in methods are inexpensive ways to fill entry-level positions. In the past, these methods were rarely used to recruit professionals or managers, but with the prevalence of corporate downsizing, where supply exceeds demand, more professional and technical positions are being filled by walk-ins.

EMPLOYMENT AGENCIES Employment agencies are independent organizations that attempt to find a match between a person and a job. Their success depends on the willingness of both the job seeker and the organization to use their services. There are three major types of employment agencies.

Canada Employment Centres (CECs) are publicly funded employment agencies operated throughout the country by Human Resources Development Canada. As soon as employers voluntarily notify their local CEC of job vacancies, the position is posted at the CEC's Job Information Centre. The posting is also included in the CEC's National Job Bank, which lists vacancies that are available throughout the country, in case job seekers wish to relocate. Prospective applicants scan the job postings and meet with a job counsellor to determine if their skills and abilities fit those required by any of the jobs. When matches occur, the counsellor refers the applicant to the company's personnel department where additional screening takes place. To facilitate matches, the CECs offer vocational guidance counselling, and interest, skill, and ability assessment to job seekers. At present, CECs charge neither the job seeker nor the employer any fees for their services. The effectiveness of CECs is somewhat mixed; most of their job placements are in sales, clerical, and service industries with very few in managerial and professional occupations.

Private employment agencies act in much the same fashion as CECs. They provide many of the same services to both job seekers and organizations who are seeking to hire, except they charge a fee for their services. Their primary function is to place people in jobs. Most provinces regulate employment agency fees and prohibit the agency from charging the job seeker for placing them with an employer. Their fees are paid by the employing organization, usually in the form of a commission tied to a percentage of the job candidate's starting salary. The employment agency may use any of the recruiting methods we've discussed, but they tend to rely on walk-ins, newspaper advertising, and lists of potential job seekers compiled over time. Employment agencies tend to have a fair degree of success in finding both skilled and managerial workers.

Executive search firms are private employment agencies that specialize in finding executive talent. Executive search firms charge the organization for their services whether or not they are successful in filling a position. The major difference between search firms and employment agencies is that search firms rarely advertise positions, although they will do so if requested by their clients. Rather, they seek out candidates who are not actively seeking jobs through an extensive list of contacts that they have developed over time. Their main supply of talent comes from executives who are already employed by other organizations; consequently, these search firms are known as "headhunters." The major disadvantages of using search firms are their cost and the likelihood that some firms develop specific recruiting philosophies that lead them to look for the same type of executive to fill all positions.

Temporary Help Agencies are similar to private employment agencies except that they specialize in providing organizations with short-term help. In most cases, the worker remains employed by the temporary help firm, but carries out duties under the direction and control of the temporary help firm's client organization. These agencies provide clients with temporary help, contract workers, seasonal and overload help in certain specialized areas such as secretarial help, computer experts, labourers, or executives, among others. Temporary help agencies rely on inventories of talent pools that they have developed over the years and they are capable of filling their clients needs within a reasonable amount of time. However, as discussed previously, the client organizations may be liable for any discrimination claims incurred through the control and direction of the temporary employee.

RECRUITING AT EDUCATIONAL INSTITUTIONS Technical schools, colleges, and universities are common sources of recruits for organizations seeking entry-level technical, professional, and managerial employees. Many schools provide their students with placement services, which assist the recruiting efforts of visiting organizations. Recognizing educational institutions as a good source of target applicants, organizations have well-established campus recruiting programs, which involve both campus advertising and campus visits by company recruiters. Campus recruiting is one of the most popular ways in which graduates find their first job. It is also an expensive proposition in terms of both time and money. It becomes even more expensive considering that on average about 50 percent of recruits may leave the organization within the first years of employment (Dolan and Schuler, 1994). Many research studies have tried to identify factors that produce successful recruiting campaigns at educational institutions. At one time, the characteristics of the recruiter were thought to be of utmost importance, but reviews of recent studies on this topic suggest there is little, if any, relationship between recruiter characteristics and the success of a recruiting program (Rynes, 1991). A more likely determinant is the choice of campuses an organization decides to visit (Boudreau and Rynes, 1987).

BOX 6.7 EXECUTIVE SEARCH FIRMS

Why use an executive search firm?
- To obtain suitable candidates who otherwise might not have applied
- To maintain objectivity
- To avoid conflicts of interest between parties involved in the search
- To eliminate administrative burdens related to the search

What does an executive search firm do?
- Anything, within reason, that the client wants
- Obtains description from the client of the type of person being sought
- Develops a profile of suitable applicants
- Develops and places advertisements, if necessary
- Contacts potential candidates directly
- Searches résumé banks
- Facilitates interview process
- Conducts reference checks
- Conducts hiring negotiations

What does an executive search cost?
- Fees: As a rule of thumb, 30 percent of the candidate's gross starting salary
- Expenses: As high as 15 percent of gross starting salary
- Fees and expenses are generally negotiable
- Hiring is guaranteed: If the new employee does not work out by the end of the first year, a replacement is found without cost

How long does an executive search take to complete?
- Three to four months

THE INTERNET/WORLD WIDE WEB The newest recruitment method involves use of the Internet by both job candidates and organizations. At present there are more than 1000 World Wide Web (WWW) sites around the world devoted to human resource topics. Increasingly, these sites are used by organizations to place advertisements for job openings and by candidates to place their files in résumé banks. In addition, organizations list job vacancies on their corporate home pages, provide digital application forms, and encourage e-mail responding. Corporations can couple their job listings with a wealth of information about the company, making it easier for candidates to develop an impression of its culture and values.

Universities and colleges also have started to place the résumés of their graduates on their home pages for prospective employers to browse. The

University of Western Ontario's job placement site on the WWW records 200 000 to 250 000 visits a month. Private recruitment agencies, such as the Career Exchange Opportunities Group, also operate Web sites. These high-tech employment centres expand the job search to the entire world and attract higher quality applicants at lower cost (Cukier, 1996).

The Web appears to suit all types of jobs, although managerial and professional jobs appear to be particularly well-suited. People who search the Net for jobs must be familiar with the technology and have the capability to access the Net. As the Internet spreads, the diversity of jobs advertised on Web sites will most certainly increase. Most of these sites, such as *Atlantic Canada Careers* or *Canadian Résumé Centre*, can be found by using the search engines that come with various Internet software packages.

INTERNAL VERSUS EXTERNAL RECRUITMENT

Table 6.1 summarizes the advantages and disadvantages of different recruitment methods. Internal recruitment has the advantage of dealing with

TABLE 6.1 COMPARISON OF INTERNAL AND EXTERNAL RECRUITMENT METHODS

Methods	Advantages	Disadvantages
Internal Recruitment		
Job Postings	Inexpensive. Rewards performance. Discovers talent.	Time-consuming. Produces instability. Demoralizing process.
Replacement Charts	Based on known human resources.	Limited by organizational chart and structure.
Information Systems	Known KSAO database linked to job.	Expensive. Rarely used by companies.
Nominations	Based on known human resources.	Random process. May lead to discrimination.
External Recruitment		
Newspaper Ads	Quick & flexible. Specific market.	Expensive. Short lifespan for ads.
Periodicals/Journals	Targets specific groups or skills.	Long lead time for ad. Expensive.

TABLE 6.1 (continued)

Methods	Advantages	Disadvantages
Radio & TV	Mass audience. Targets specific groups. Image advertising.	Very expensive. Short ad duration. Provides little information.
Public Displays	Inexpensive.	Provides little information.
Direct Mail	Targets specific groups and skills. Can provide much information.	Expensive & inefficient. Requires mailing list. Often not read.
Special Events	Useful for filling multiple jobs. Relatively inexpensive. Targets job pool.	Shares job pool with competition. Information overload/stress.
Employee Referrals	Inexpensive.	May lead to discrimination and inbreeding.
Walk-Ins	Inexpensive.	Random process. Inefficient.
Canada Employment Centres	Inexpensive. Job-KSAO fit.	Success limited to certain occupational categories.
Private Employment Agency	Person-job fit.	Expensive.
Executive Search Firm	Known talent pool.	Very expensive.
Temporary Help Agency	Access to short-term labour pool. Few recruiting demands.	Exposure to risk of discrimination claims. Mostly unskilled and poorly educated talent pool.
Recruiting at Schools	Known talent pool. Pre-trained applicants.	Time-consuming. Very expensive.
Internet	Inexpensive. Mass audience. Specific audience.	Random process. Unknown audience.

known quantities. Internal job applicants already have realistic expectations of life in the organization. They are, or should be, aware of the organizational goals and values. Likewise, the organization is familiar with the internal applicant's work history and performance record. Internal recruitment is also relatively inexpensive. Most middle level jobs in an organization are filled through this means. External recruitment, on the other hand, is mostly used to staff jobs at either the entry or executive levels. External recruitment brings needed skills and competencies to an organization and prevents organizations from becoming "inbred." It exposes companies to new people, new ideas, and new ways of doing things. External recruitment may be the only means through which employment equity programs succeed. External recruitment can be very time-consuming and expensive.

◆ ◆ ◆
EVALUATING RECRUITING EFFORTS

We started this chapter with the proposition that recruitment is simply a means of attracting a large enough pool of candidates from which the organization could select those it thought were the best qualified to fill job vacancies. It is quite obvious that recruiting can be very expensive. Organizations that engage in recruiting should be concerned that their money and time are well spent. They should want to know whether the job advertisements paid off in more applications; whether better qualified candidates were hired; what it cost to recruit the new employees; whether the new recruits are more productive or have a more positive attitude about the organization; and whether they stay with the organization for a longer period of time. Unfortunately, many companies do not bother to ask these questions or to evaluate their recruiting efforts. Their primary criteria for judging the success of recruiting appears to be whether the vacant jobs were filled. Very few organizations track the performance and behavioural outcomes of people recruited into the organization or the costs associated with the recruiting campaign, including advertising costs (Rynes and Boudreau, 1986).

Recruiting should not be taken at face value but evaluated on the basis of specific criteria. Recruiting efforts should be evaluated separately from the evaluation of the selection system. The criterion measures that an organization uses to evaluate its recruiting program should be consistent with the goals that were set for that effort. If the organization wanted to recruit the best possible candidates that were available, it would be unfair to evaluate the recruiting program on the cost that it took to find those candidates. The appropriate measure would be whether the best possible candidates were hired. If the organization used recruiting to generate a large applicant pool, then an appropriate criterion measure might be the number of applications that were received rather than the quality of the people hired. There are many different criterion measures that can be used to evaluate recruiting efforts. Box 6.8 lists criterion measures that have been used to investigate the effectiveness of different recruitment methods (Rynes, 1991; Wanous and Colella, 1989). These criteria can be grouped into three broad categories: behavioural measures, performance measures, and attitudinal measures.

Noticeably absent from Box 6.8 are any measures that are based on cost or an integration of cost and benefits. As discussed in Chapter 3, utility analysis provides a mechanism for applying cost-benefit analysis to human resources decisions. Boudreau and Rynes (1985) adapted utility analysis to incorporate the effects of recruitment, including financial and economic factors, and the effects associated with changes in the size and quality of the applicant pool, the number of applicants processed, and the average qualification level of those hired. Improved recruitment altered the benefits that could be expected from improved selection procedures because recruitment produced a more qualified and less diverse applicant pool. Boudreau and

---

BOX 6.8 EXAMPLES OF CRITERIA USED TO EVALUATE RECRUITING METHODS

Behavioural Measures

Turnover

within 6 months

within 12 months

within 24 months

Absenteeism

Performance Measures

Performance Ratings

Sales Quotas

Performance Potential

Attitudinal Measures

Job Satisfaction

Job Involvement

Satisfaction with Supervisor

Commitment to Organization

Perceived Accuracy of Job Descriptions

Source: Rynes, 1991; Wanous and Colella, 1989.

Rynes concluded that the most effective procedure was an integrated recruitment-selection strategy. Boudreau (1991) demonstrates the use of utility analysis to evaluate the effectiveness of different recruiting approaches in conjunction with selection models.

There is one final criterion, employment equity, that should be considered as part of evaluating any recruitment efforts. The organization must review whether its recruiting campaign has produced an increased presence of qualified women, visible minorities, native people, and disabled people in its workforce. In the context of Canadian employment equity legislation, recruiting efforts must be judged on this basis as well as the more traditional outcome measures.

◆ ◆ ◆
SUMMARY

Recruitment is the first step in the personnel selection process, but, unlike other aspects of the personnel process, it is a situation where actions and decisions of the job seeker play a major role. A recruitment process, no matter how brilliantly conceived, is a failure if it does not attract job applicants. Recruitment campaigns are a success when they understand the recruitment process from the job seeker's point of view. The recruitment process must take into account the strategies that job seekers use to investigate jobs and organizations. The recruitment process should provide job candidates with information they need about the job and the organization to make appropriate job choices.

Recruitment campaigns should be based on the principle of improving the fit between job candidates and the organization. Organizations can help to achieve this by presenting an accurate image of both the job and the organization to job seekers. The organization should use communications in a way that develops accurate expectations and perceptions on the part of job applicants. One method that appears capable of doing this is a realistic job preview.

In developing a recruitment strategy, human resources planners must consider both the internal and external constraints on the organization. All recruitment is influenced by external factors over which the organization has little control (e.g., the labour market and the legal environment), as well as internal factors that it can influence (e.g., its business plan and values).

Recruitment strategies and materials, which are grounded in organization and job analysis, establish both realistic expectations among job applicants and the availability of qualified internal and external job candidates. Every recruitment strategy must contain an action plan, which schedules recruiting initiatives and provides a means of identifying and locating the target applicant pool. The action plan must also identify the appropriate methods for contacting the target applicant pool. The action plan should also include a method for evaluating the effectiveness of the recruitment campaign.

E X E R C I S E S

1. Choose an organization in your community. Schedule a meeting with its human resources manager (or designate). Using the material in this chapter as a guide, interview the manager on the organization's recruiting efforts (e.g., determine the role that job and organization analysis played in developing the strategy); ask whether the organization considers how potential applicants would react to the recruiting materials; and so forth. Prepare a report on the organization's recruiting strategy and its effectiveness.

2. Examine the organization's recruiting program (the one chosen for Exercise 1) from a job candidate's perspective. With the assistance of the human resources manager, locate a recently hired employee; interview that employee with respect to job search strategy, perceptions of the organization and the job, their perceptions of the recruiting process, what influenced their decision to take the job, and whether their views have changed after being in the organization for a period of time. Prepare a report summarizing this interview.

3. Using the information presented in this chapter and the information obtained from your interviews in Exercises 1 and 2, develop a comprehensive recruitment strategy for the organization based on the job of the person whom you interviewed.

4. How did the organization advertise the position? Identify the best ways for reaching the target applicant pool for this job.

5. Prepare an advertisement for the position of the person whom you interviewed. Compare the costs of running this advertisement in some of the commonly used media discussed in this chapter.

References

Boudreau, J.W. 1991. "Utility Analysis for Decisions in Human Resource Management." In M.D. Dunnette and L.M. Hough, eds., *Handbook of Industrial and Organizational Psychology*, Vol. 2, 2nd ed. Palo Alto: Consulting Psychologists Press. 399–444.

Boudreau, J.W., and S.L. Rynes. 1985. "The Role of Recruitment in Staffing Utility Analysis." *Journal of Applied Psychology* 70: 354–66.

Boudreau, J.W., and S.L. Rynes. 1987. "Giving it the Old College Try." *Personnel Administrator* 32: 78–85.

Breaugh, J.A., and R.S. Billings. 1988. "The Realistic Job Preview: Five Key Elements and their Importance for Research and Practice." *Journal of Business and Psychology* 2: 291–305

Buckley, M.R., D.B. Fedor, and D.S. Marvin. 1994. "Ethical Considerations in the Recruiting Process: A Preliminary Investigation and Identification of Research Opportunities." *Human Resource Management Review* 4: 35–50.

Carsten, J.M., and P.E. Spector. 1987. "Unemployment, Job Satisfaction, and Employee Turnover: A Meta-Analytic Test of the Muchinsky Model. " *Journal of Applied Psychology* 72: 374–81.

Castro, J. 1993. "Disposable Workers." *Time*, 141(March 29): 43–47.

Cukier, W. 1996. "Job Hunting in Cyberspace." *The Globe and Mail*, April 16: C9.

Dolan, S.L., and R.S. Schuler. 1994. *Human Resource Management: The Canadian Dynamic.* Toronto: Nelson Canada.

Ellis, R.T., and R.J. Angus 1985. *Matching CFCIS Vocational Preference Checklist Items with Probability of Adjustment to Entry-Level CF Trades: A Research Plan.* (Technical Note 17/85). Willowdale, Ontario: Canadian Forces Personnel Applied Research Unit.

Flynn, G. 1995. "Contingent Staffing Requires Serious Strategy." *Personnel Journal* 74 (April): 50–58.

Galt, V. 1992 ."Agencies Still Refer Whites Only." *The Globe and Mail*, September 8: B1.

Greengard, S. 1995. "Leveraging a Low-Wage Work Force." *Personnel Journal* 74 (January): 90–102.

Guion, R.M. 1976. "Recruiting, Selection, and Job Placement." In M. Dunnette, ed., *Handbook of Industrial and Organizational Psychology*. Chicago: Rand-McNally. 777–828.

Heneman, H.G., D.P Schwab, J.A. Fossum, and L.D. Dyer. 1989. *Personnel/Human Resource Management*. Homewood, IL: Irwin.

Holland, J.L. 1973. *Making Vocational Choices: A Theory of Careers*. Englewood Cliffs, NJ: Prentice-Hall.

Keenan, G. 1996. "Toyota Swamped in Rush for Jobs." *The Globe and Mail*, February 21: A1, A7.

LeBlanc, S. 1996. "Guarantee of Extra Cash not Luring Doctors to Rural Areas." *The Halifax Mail-Star,* March 1: A1, A2.

London, M., and S.A. Stumpf. 1982. *Managing Careers*. Reading, MA: Addison-Wesley.

Magnus, M. 1985. "Recruitment Ads at Work." *Personnel Journal* 64: 4–63.

Popovich, P., and J.P. Wanous. 1982. "The Realistic Job Preview as a Persuasive Communication." *Academy of Management Review* 7: 57–578.

Ryan, A.M., and M.J. Schmit. 1996. "Calculating EEO Statistics in the Temporary Help Industry. *Personnel Psychology* 49: 167–80.

Rynes, S.L. 1991. "Recruitment, Job Choice, and Post-Hire Consequences." In M.D. Dunnette and L.M. Hough, eds., *Handbook of Industrial and Organizational Psychology*, Vol. 2, 2nd ed., Palo Alto: Consulting Psychologists Press, 399–444.

Rynes, S. L. 1993. "Who's Selecting Whom? Effects of Selection Practices on Applicant Attitudes and Behaviour." In N. Schmitt, W.C. Borman et al., eds., *Personnel Selection in Organizations*. San Francisco, CA: Jossey-Bass, 240–274.

Rynes, S.L., and J.L. Boudreau. 1986. "College Recruiting in Large Organizations: Practice, Evaluation, and Research Implications." *Personnel Psychology* 39: 729–57.

Saks, A.M. 1994. "A Psychological Process Investigation for the Effects of Recruitment Source and Organization Information on Job Survival." *Journal of Organizational Behavior* 15: 225–44.

Schwab, D.P., S.L. Rynes, and R.J. Aldag. 1987. "Theories and Research on Job Search and Choice." In K.M. Rowland and G.R. Ferris, eds., *Research in Personnel and Human Resource Management*, Vol. 5. Greenwich, CT: JAI Press, 129–66.

Soelberg, P.O. 1967. "Unprogrammed Decision Making." *Industrial Management Review* 8: 19–29.

Tom, V.R. 1971. "The Role of Personality and Organizational Images in the Recruiting Process." *Organizational Behavior and Human Performance* 6: 573–92.

Vroom, V.H. 1964. *Work and Motivation*. New York: Wiley.

Wanous, J.P. 1980. *Organizational Entry: Recruitment, Selection, and Socialization of Newcomers*. Reading, MA: Addison-Wesley.

Wanous, J.P. 1989. "Installing a Realistic Job Preview: Ten Tough Choices." *Personnel Psychology* 42: 117–33.

Wanous, J.P., and A. Colella. 1989. "Organizational Entry Research: Current Status and Future Directions." In K.M. Rowland and G.R. Ferris, eds., *Research in Personnel and Human Resource Management*, Vol. 7, Greenwich, CT: JAI Press, 59–120.

Wilson, F.P. 1980. *Towards a More Systematic Counselling Model for the Canadian Forces* (Working Paper 80–3). Willowdale, Ontario: Canadian Forces Personnel Applied Research Unit.

Zadny, J.J., and L.F. James. 1977. "A Review of Research on Job Placement. *Rehabilitation Counselling Bulletin* 21: 150–58.

7

Selection I:
Applicant
Screening
and
Selection

◆ ◆ ◆

CHAPTER GOALS

This chapter introduces procedures that provide information for making hiring decisions. It places employment selection in the context of labour markets, the legal environment, and organizational constraints. It establishes organization and job analysis as the foundation for employee selection and reviews some of the common procedures used to screen job applicants: biographical data, résumés, screening interviews, and reference checks. After reading this chapter you should

◆ understand the role that human resources planning, organization analysis, and job analysis play in selection;

◆ know the relationship between job analysis and the predictor and criterion measures that are used in selection;

◆ know the difference between employee screening and employee selection;

◆ know the advantages and disadvantages of using four very common screening devices: biographical data, application forms, résumés, screening interviews, and reference checks; and

◆ understand the psychometric properties of each of these common screening procedures along with any legal considerations pertinent to their use in making employment decisions.

◆ ◆ ◆

HR PLANNING, ORGANIZATION AND JOB ANALYSIS, AND SELECTION

Human resources planning identifies an organization's staffing requirements and develops an action plan for recruiting an adequate supply of qualified job applicants. Figure 6.1 on p. 225 presented factors that influenced this planning process, including organization and job analysis. Once the job applicants are in hand, the organization must decide which individuals, if any, to hire. The goal of the organization is to hire those applicants who are not only capable of performing the job, but who will also perform at above average levels. Hiring the best qualified applicants increases the productivity of the organization. Selection involves collecting information from job applicants to determine those who possess the most knowledge, skills, abilities, or other talents linked to successful job performance. This sounds like a rather straightforward task, but those factors that affect recruiting also influence the selection of job applicants.

In practice, there are some exceptions to hiring the most productive worker. Some organizations choose to hire people who they believe will be satisfied and content with the work they are given, and who will likely spend their working life in one job with that organization. This orientation arises, mostly, in conventional assembly line jobs where the employee's performance is controlled by the flow of the line. Here, the company is more concerned with turnover and absenteeism, outcomes that can have an effect on the flow of the assembly line. It wants to hire those applicants who will come to work every day and who will stay in the job for a relatively long time period. The company must be capable of identifying applicants who are likely to exhibit these behaviours.

LABOUR MARKETS AND SELECTION

A favourable labour market will produce a large number of job applicants and will allow the organization to be more selective in its hiring. On the other hand, unfavourable labour markets may lead the organization to select applicants it might otherwise not consider. Figure 7.1 represents these two market conditions under which a company is trying to fill 10 positions. When there are many job applicants, the organization has the luxury of setting higher selection standards. A smaller proportion of job applicants qualifies for positions in the company. Figure 7.1(a) represents a situation where approximately 20 percent of 100 applicants meet the minimal requirements that have been established for the position. For the moment, let's assume that offers are made to the highest ranked candidates in descending order until all 10 positions are filled and that half of all offers are rejected. The selection ratio of .20 will produce just enough qualified candidates who accept the offers. Figure 7.1(b) represents an unfavourable market where

FIGURE 7.1 The Influence of Labour Markets on the Selection Process

Favourable Labour Market

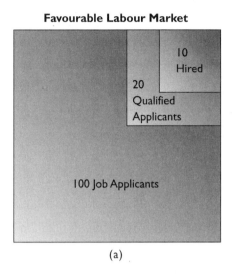

(a)

Unfavourable Labour Market

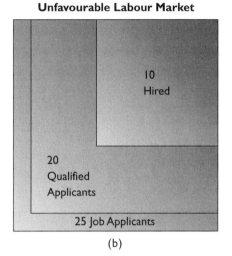

(b)

there are only 25 applicants. A selection ratio of .20 would not produce a sufficient number of qualified applicants. The company could either intensify its recruiting efforts to attract more applicants, as discussed in Chapter 6, or lower the requirements for the position. To obtain 20 candidates who meet the lower standards, the company could set the selection ratio at .80.

EFFECT OF UNFAVOURABLE LABOUR MARKETS ON SELECTION The performance of the 10 people hired under the unfavourable market conditions is likely to be lower, on average, than that of the 10 hired under favourable conditions. Under the unfavourable labour conditions, more of the applicants who are hired are likely to be unsatisfactory performers. Figure 7.2 illustrates this relationship; it presents the relationship between a predictor, cognitive ability scores, and a criterion measure of job performance for all job applicants as a scatterplot, the oval area (see Figure 3.3 on p. 111 for a review). In Figure 7.2, the cutoff score on the predictor has been set to represent a selection ratio (SR) of either .20 (Line A) or .80 (Line B). Job candidates who score above the predictor cutoff and are hired but who turn out to be job failures (their performance falls below the Base Rate) are False Positives. With a selection ratio of .20, False Positives fall into area a; when

FIGURE 7.2 **The Effect of Reducing Selection Standards on Job Performance**

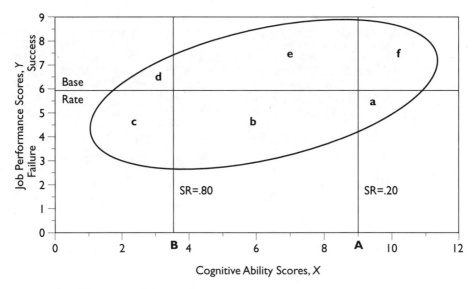

A and B represent Selection Ratios

	A	B
True Positives	f	e + f
False Positives	a	a + b
True Negatives	b + c	c
False Negatives	d + e	d

the selection ratio is set at .80, the False Positives fall into the larger area a+b. Nonetheless, selection still provides a benefit. If all the applicants were hired without any selection at all (i.e., setting the selection ratio at 1.00), there would be even more False Positives (area a+b+c).

LEGAL ENVIRONMENT AND SELECTION

Selection programs and practices must operate within the legal context described in Chapter 2. They may not discriminate, have adverse effect, or have adverse impact on members of protected groups. Selection programs that intentionally or unintentionally exclude job applicants through the use of characteristics or factors that are protected under human rights legislation run the risk of being declared discriminatory, with the organization subject to penalties and fines. Chapter 2 outlined a procedure to determine if selection practices meet legal scrutiny. All information that is gathered as part of the selection process must be job-related and must be obtained through procedures that themselves are non-discriminatory. Additionally, selection procedures must be sensitive to employment equity needs; they must produce the best qualified candidates within the context of any agreed upon employment equity programs.

BUSINESS PLANS AND SELECTION

An organization's goals, values, and philosophy influence selection procedures. The business plan identifies the proportion of positions to be filled by internal candidates. Internal candidates may be assessed through different procedures than job applicants from outside the organization. The organization likely has performance data on the internal candidate and may already have used it to develop replacement charts for each position in the organization. Internal candidates who have a history of poor performance are unlikely to be selected for another position. An assessment centre, which will be discussed in Chapter 8, is a selection procedure commonly used to evaluate internal candidates for promotion or transfer to other positions in the company. Some organizations require all employees at certain organizational levels to go through the assessment procedure as a way of identifying employees with potential for upper level managerial positions (Cascio and Ramos, 1986). Ford Motor Company uses an assessment centre to identify students for entry into a college and university sponsorship program with a view to eventual recruitment. The students are selected on the basis of having met four competency dimensions which Ford believes are needed for future job success (Payne, Anderson, and Smith, 1992). The four competency or job dimensions that reflect Ford's organizational goals are

1. Business awareness
2. Interactive awareness
3. Work structure
4. Drive and enthusiasm

APPLICANT REACTIONS TO SELECTION PROCEDURES Job level and type influence selection just as they do recruitment. An organization may believe that certain selection procedures are inappropriate for one type of job but very appropriate for another, even though the selection procedure is equally valid for both. An executive search may involve review of a candidate's accomplishments and several interviews with people in the organization. A search for an entry level manager might involve candidates taking an extensive series of employment tests in addition to being interviewed. Although the testing may be very appropriate at the executive level as well, the organization's culture dictates that such testing is not done beyond the entry level. The personnel specialist must meet not only technical and legal standards in developing a selection system, but also the demands of the organizational culture in which it will operate (Smither, Reilly, Millsap, Pearlman, and Stoffey, 1993).

ORGANIZATION AND JOB ANALYSIS AND SELECTION

Organization and job analysis play important roles in the development and evaluation of selection systems. They provide the raw data for assessing the internal and external environments in which the organization operates and for understanding the expectations, behaviours, and tasks that comprise a specific job. Job analysis data help identify the knowledge, skill, ability, or other attributes (KSAOs) required to perform the job in question. The information produced by organization and job analysis provides the basis for designing a selection strategy that is both job-related and defensible before the courts or other tribunals.

◆ ◆ ◆

TRANSLATING ORGANIZATION AND JOB ANALYSIS DATA INTO SELECTION MEASURES

Taking into account the factors discussed above, the human resources specialists must develop a procedure for selecting the most appropriate candidates. The selection procedures must be job-related, non-discriminatory, and legally defensible. Selection procedures that follow from a job analysis have the potential for meeting these requirements and for leading to hiring decisions that are in the best interests of both the organization and the candidate.

A SELECTION MODEL Figure 7.3 presents a model of a selection system based on job analysis. In this model, job analysis information is used to identify both the performance domain and the KSAOs or competencies associated with performance of critical job or competency dimensions. As discussed previously, job analysis information is used to identify tasks and behaviours that form part of a job and the requirements that are necessary to perform those tasks and behaviours. Examination of the job dimensions and critical tasks leads human resources specialists to make inferences about the KSAOs required to perform successfully in the job. These inferences are based on empirical evidence demonstrating validity between the job dimensions and KSAO constructs in other situations. This proposed relationship between the performance domain and the KSAO constructs is represented by Line A in Figure 7.3. This is the same relationship expressed by Line A in Figure 3.2 (p. 104).

The KSAOs and job dimensions linked by Line A are abstractions; they cannot be measured directly. These constructs must be used to develop predictor and criteria data before they can be used to select job candidates. Chapter 5 discussed the process of defining the performance domain and developing related criterion measures. Line D represents this process in Figure 7.3, as it also does in Figure 3.2. In establishing a selection system, the identification and development of the performance domain and related criteria is just as important to the success of the system as the proper development of the predictor side of the model. Unfortunately, in practice not enough attention is paid to developing adequate criterion measures. Criterion measures may be used because they are available rather than because they appropriately represent the competencies or performance domain of interest (Binning and Barrett, 1989). Table 5.2 (p. 207) presents sample items from a rating scale developed through a job analysis used to evaluate the performance of employees in the security dispatcher position described in Box 6.6 (p. 250).

The human resources specialist must also translate the KSAO constructs into measurable predictors. Review the security dispatcher job description presented in Box 6.6. That description is based on a job analysis and presents critical job behaviours and tasks as well as job requirements. The fact that the security dispatcher sends, receives, processes, and analyzes information suggests that the applicant should have a fair degree of cognitive ability. The fact that the security dispatcher must be capable of operating a

FIGURE 7.3 Job Analysis, Selection, and Criterion Measures of Performance: A Systems Approach

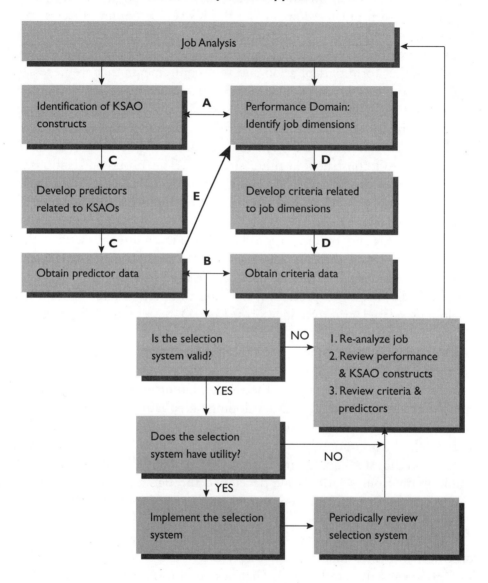

variety of electronic equipment suggests that the applicant should have experience operating such equipment. Similarly, the job description suggests that applicants should remain calm under stress, have good interpersonal skills, have good written and oral communication skills, and have specific knowledge of the university campus. The human resources specialists must determine how each of these KSAOs will be assessed. With respect to cognitive ability, the human resources team may decide to use an employment test to assess the general cognitive ability of each applicant and specific ability tests to assess communication skills (see Chapter 8). Information about past work history and experience may come from an application form or the candidate's résumé, while information about the candidate's ability to deal with people and with stress may be determined through an interview. The predictors that are chosen must validly represent the KSAO constructs that are linked to the performance domain. This relationship is represented by Line C in Figure 7.3, as well as in Figure 3.2. The validity of the predictor measures is established through either content or construct validity procedures. Either expert judgment or empirical evidence must support the use of a predictor measure as representative of a KSAO construct.

Keep in mind that the goal of selection is to identify job candidates who have those behaviours required for success on the job. On the basis of predictor data obtained through an assessment of job applicants, the human resources team predicts which of those applicants will turn out to be successful when placed in the job. This prediction is represented by Line E in Figure 7.3, and in Figure 3.2. In most organizations this relationship is inferred through establishing a correlation at the measurement level between the predictor and criterion measures; Line B represents criterion-related validity in Figures 7.3 and 3.2. If the relationship in Line E cannot be established through either criterion-related, content, or construct validity, the human resources team must begin the process again. This may include redoing the job analysis, but more often than not it only involves a review and refinement of the predictor and criterion measures. The work of the human resources team does not end once they establish the validity of the selection system. The final step is to demonstrate that selection based on the valid predictors has utility; that is, the predictors lead to the selection of job applicants who increase organizational productivity. Several methods for assessing utility were described in Chapter 3. Finally, even with a system that has utility, the selection system should be reviewed periodically; jobs and organizations change over time.

SELECTING APPLICANTS The remainder of this chapter introduces materials that are used to sort job applicants into acceptable and unacceptable categories. These materials include items that are familiar to everyone who has applied for a job: application forms (including weighted application forms and biographical data), résumés, screening interviews, and reference checks. These items are used in some form during the preliminary stages of selection by almost every organization. Chapter 8 continues with a review of selection testing and Chapter 9 concludes with a more in depth discussion of the employment interview. These procedures, from the most basic to the most sophisticated, must satisfy both psychometric and legal concerns when used to hire employees.

♦ ♦ ♦
APPLICANT SCREENING

Screening involves the use of job-related information obtained from job applicants to identify those who meet the minimum requirements that have been established for a position. Screening procedures, such as those presented here, are designed to cut down the number of job applicants. Candidates who fall short of the minimum standards are eliminated at this point and receive no further consideration. Selection, on the other hand, involves a more extensive assessment of those applicants who meet the minimum requirements to identify those candidates who are most likely to excel in the position. Consider the 50 000 plus applications that Toyota Canada received for its 1200 positions. (See Box 11.1, p. 475.) Should all 50 000 applicants be put through an extensive selection process? Many of those applicants will not have the required training or skills needed to compete for the positions; a review of information supplied by the candidates on their application forms or résumés can separate the applicants into two groups: those who meet the minimum requirements, and those who do not. Even then, screening a large number of applications can be expensive. If it takes about 10 minutes to review an application and/or résumé before making a decision, it will take about 8300 person hours, or about 200 people each working one 40-hour week, to sort the applications! If those doing the sorting are paid at least the same wages as those hired, $20 per hour, the screening process will cost Toyota Canada over $160 000. Suppose the screening process identified 5000 Toyota applicants as qualified for the 1200 jobs. Which ones should be hired? A comprehensive assessment of the 5000 remaining applicants may result in a merit list; making job offers in a top-down order from the list will be the most productive hiring strategy, even taking into account the cost of assessing the 5000 applicants (Murphy, 1986). Think of what the costs would be if all initial 50 000 applicants were subject to a much more elaborate selection process!

RECRUITMENT, SCREENING, AND SELECTION

Figure 7.4 diagrams the relationship between recruiting, screening, and selection in terms of different questions that are asked at each of these steps. Recruitment seeks to find enough applicants; screening identifies whether those candidates who applied meet minimum requirements; and selection reviews each qualified candidate to find those who will be most successful in the job if they are hired.

Caution must be exercised when screening job applicants. The screening devices are designed to provide a quick and relatively inexpensive sort of applicants into acceptable and unacceptable categories. Usually, the criteria on which these decisions are made are subjective; the decision-maker often has to interpret what an applicant meant by writing a specific statement or what a person's job experience and training actually are. The screening procedures are open to errors, both false positives and false negatives. Over the complete selection process, applicants who pass through the initial screening round as false positives are likely to be eliminated through more extensive testing. The false negatives, those who met the qualifications but were eliminated, are gone forever. Applicants who find themselves in this position may turn to the courts if they believe the initial screening procedures discriminated on grounds that were unrelated to job performance. Screening instruments that are used without consideration of their psychometric properties and without regard for the legal environment leave employers open to litigation. The next section reviews some of the most common methods used to screen job applicants.

FIGURE 7.4 **The Relationship Between Recruitment, Screening, and Selection**

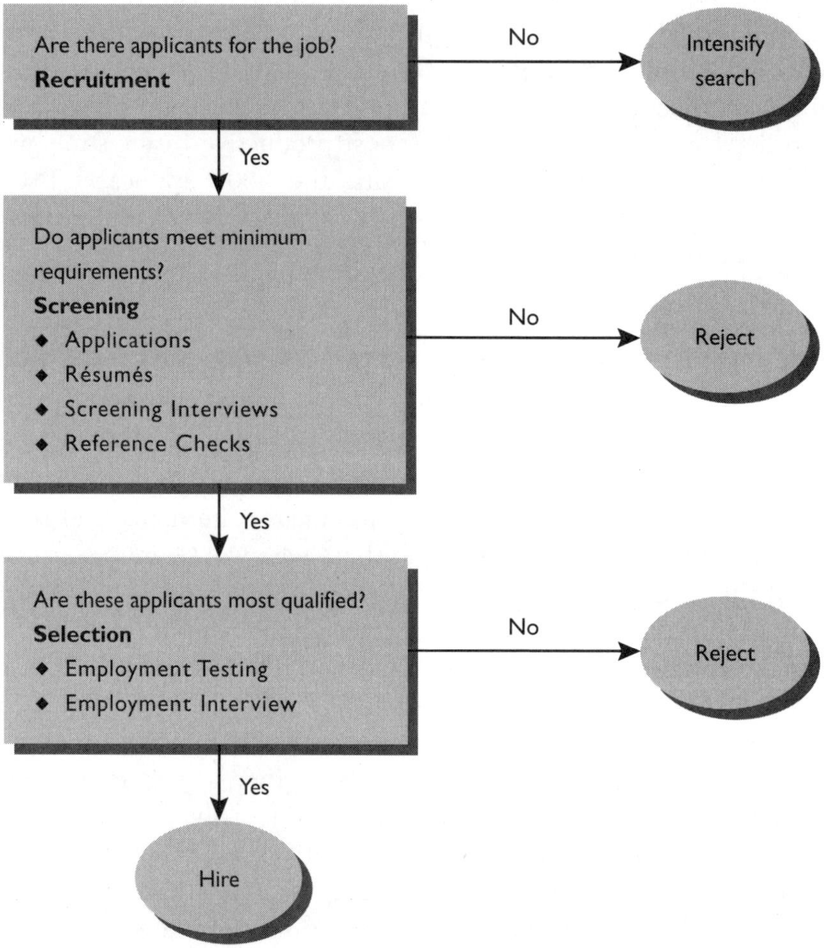

Are there applicants for the job?
Recruitment
→ No → Intensify search

↓ Yes

Do applicants meet minimum requirements?
Screening
◆ Applications
◆ Résumés
◆ Screening Interviews
◆ Reference Checks
→ No → Reject

↓ Yes

Are these applicants most qualified?
Selection
◆ Employment Testing
◆ Employment Interview
→ No → Reject

↓ Yes

Hire

SCREENING METHODS

Application forms, résumés, interviews, and reference checks are the most common screening procedures used in selection. These procedures all seek to make a prediction about the applicant's future job performance from past life or work events. If the biographical data obtained through these procedures is related to the future job, the predictions may have some validity.

Some of these procedures are better than the others in predicting future job success. Screening procedures, when properly developed, identify those applicants who meet minimum qualifications. Following screening with more comprehensive selection procedures identifies those applicants who will enhance organizational productivity. Unfortunately, many employers make hiring decisions based on screening procedures alone without requiring a more extensive assessment of the acceptable applicants. They may not be aware of the benefits of more rigorous selection procedures; they may believe that they do not have the expertise needed to use such procedures; or they mistakenly believe that the traditional screening procedures do not have to meet the same legal requirements as selection tests.

APPLICATION FORMS

Information obtained from application forms is one of the oldest ways of determining whether job applicants meet minimum job requirements. Filling them out is a hurdle, which the applicant must overcome before moving on to more rigorous, and expensive, examination. For example, applicants for a security dispatcher position may be required to have passed a course on CPR (cardiopulmonary resuscitation). Applicants who do not have such training can be identified through a question on the application form and screened out of the competition. Similarly, information on other job requirements such as minimum level of education, specialized training, or credentials can be obtained through a few well-chosen questions on the application blank. Employers often overlook the fact that before any item on an application blank can be used to screen applicants, its job-relatedness must first be established through a job analysis. For example, CPR training must be shown to be related to the work of a security dispatcher. It is not sufficient to believe that applicants "ought" to have a particular level of education, or to have graduated from a specific type of training program. The job-relatedness must be demonstrable to withstand charges of discriminatory hiring practices. Few employers recognize the need to demonstrate the job-relatedness of information they collect during the application process.

HUMAN RIGHTS CONSIDERATIONS Employers cannot ask for information that is prohibited on discriminatory grounds under human rights legislation (see Table 2.1, p. 38) unless it can be established that the information is a bona fide occupational requirement. Many employers routinely collect information through application forms that will not be used to make a hiring decision, but which is required by the human resources department once the employee is hired. The justification for collecting this data is expediency; if the applicant is hired, the personnel office will already have the necessary personal information on file. Some employers unwittingly collect information on application forms that will leave them open to charges of discriminatory hiring practices; for example, applicants may be asked their social insurance number, date of birth, sex, marital status, number of dependents, name of next of kin, health status, and so on. Having obtained this information before making a hiring decision, an employer may have to prove that it was not used in making the hiring decision. It is far better to collect this information from applicants only after they have been hired. Box 7.1 presents an application blank that was designed specifically for the security dispatcher position described in Box 6.6 on p. 250. This form requests only the most minimal information. There is always the temptation to collect as much background data as possible about a candidate through the application form on the grounds that this may help the human resources manager prepare to interview the candidate. However, once irrelevant information is in hand, there is a temptation to use it in making a decision.

Before putting any item on an application form, the human resources manager should ask the following questions:

- What is the purpose of having the item on the form?
- Is there a better way to obtain the information elicited by the item?
- How will the information be used?
- Is it more appropriate to obtain the information only after making a job offer?
- Does the item constitute a discriminatory hiring practice?
- Is the item job-related?
- Has the validity of the item as a screening device been established?

WEIGHTED APPLICATION FORMS

Each item on an application form provides information about the candidate. Only rarely is any one item sufficient to screen out a candidate. Candidates for a staff lawyer position that involved the actual practice of law would need

BOX 7.1 JOB APPLICATION FORM: SECURITY DISPATCHER

Part I: Personal Data

Name: _____

Address: _____

_____

      City   Province   Postal Code

Home Phone: _____ Work Phone: _____

Are you legally eligible to work in Canada? Yes _____ No _____

Have you ever been convicted of a criminal offence for which you have not been pardoned? Yes _____ No _____

Languages Spoken: <u>English</u>: Yes _____ No _____ <u>French</u>: Yes _____ No _____
Languages Read: <u>English</u>: Yes _____ No _____ <u>French</u>: Yes _____ No _____

Do you wish to work Full-Time _____ Part-Time _____?

Have you ever worked for us before? Yes _____ No _____ If yes, when?_____

If hired, when are you available to begin work? _____

Part II: Education and Training

Highest grade or year completed (check all that apply to you):

    High school   _____   Diploma received? Yes _____ No _____
    Technical/Trade School _____   Diploma received? Yes _____ No _____
    Community College   _____   Diploma received? Yes _____ No _____
    University   _____   Degree received? Yes _____ No _____

Program or areas studied (check all that apply to you):

    Security _____ Computer _____ Clerical _____ Management _____
    Communications _____ Electronics _____ Criminology _____
    Public Relations _____ Other (please specify) _____

Do you currently possess a valid First-Aid Certificate? Yes _____ No _____

Do you currently possess a valid CPR Certificate? Yes _____ No _____

BOX 7.1 (continued)

Part III: Employment History

List in order your last three employers, starting with your most recent employer.

1. Name and Address: _____
   _____

   Supervisor's Name and Title: _____

   Dates Employed: From _____ To _____

   Reasons for leaving: _____

   Describe the work you did, including title of job, duties, and responsibilities:
   _____
   _____

   May we contact this employer? Yes _____ No _____

2. Name and Address: _____
   _____

   Supervisor's Name and Title: _____

   Dates Employed: From _____ To _____

   Reasons for leaving: _____

   Describe the work you did, including title of job, duties, and responsibilities:
   _____
   _____

   May we contact this employer? Yes _____ No _____

3. Name and Address: _____
   _____

   Supervisor's Name and Title: _____

   Dates Employed: From _____ To _____

   Reasons for leaving: _____

   Describe the work you did, including title of job, duties, and responsibilities:
   _____
   _____

   May we contact this employer? Yes _____ No _____

ices

of persons (excluding relatives) whom you may wish us to
ɔur job performance.

_____

_____

_____

_____

3. _____

_____

Part V: Applicant's Certification

Please read the following carefully before signing.

I certify that the information I have given on this form is accurate and complete to the best of my knowledge. I understand that, should I be hired, intentionally making false statements on this form will be considered sufficient grounds for dismissal.

Date: _____

Signature of Applicant: _____

Skills — skills

Mitch Van Rassel
Partner

Thank you,
RJ PROFESSIONALS

Poster Desired - change to positive

Date Available, how ever / yes

on

to have passed the bar exam. That credential would be sufficient to screen out candidates who had graduated from law school but had yet to be called to the bar. However, an organization might consider hiring such a candidate if the position did not involve actual practice. Many organizations hire lawyers to provide advice or to do research without expecting them to practice law. In this latter case, passing the bar exam is certainly relevant and provides some information for making a screening decision, but it cannot screen out any candidate by itself. That item must be considered in the context of other information obtained from the application blank.

COMBINING INFORMATION FROM APPLICATION FORM ITEMS How should the information from the application form be combined to make a decision when there is no single item that screens out candidates? Can information from the application form be used to make a prediction about job success or failure? In most cases, the person responsible for making the decision examines the application and makes a subjective decision. Much like a clinical psychologist making a diagnosis, the recruiter or human resources manager examines all the information and comes to a conclusion about a particular applicant based on personal experience and knowledge. There is an alternative to this subjective procedure; the manager develops a scoring key for responses that the applicants make to items on the form. In the case of two lawyers applying for a job, those who have not passed the bar exam might be given a score of 0, while those who have passed are scored 1. Similarly, weights are assigned to responses to other items; adding all of the assigned weights together produces a total score on the application form for each job candidate. The weights are not assigned arbitrarily; they reflect the difference between successful and unsuccessful workers on some criterion measure. There are several different methods that can be used to develop the set of weights (Telenson, Alexander, and Barrett, 1983).

Like any selection instrument, the weighted application form must exhibit good psychometric properties. Weighted application forms are developed in relation to a criterion measure of performance established for current and previous employees. If an employer were concerned with the level of absenteeism among security dispatchers, number of days absent would serve as a criterion measure. The human resources manager would define the acceptable number of days absent in a year, and then divide the current and previous security dispatchers into two groups, those who fall above and below that value. Then, the applications on file for security dispatchers are reviewed, and the frequency of responses for each item on the application form is recorded separately for the low and high absenteeism groups. For example, 80 percent of security dispatchers with only a high-school education fall into the good attendance category while the remaining 20 percent with only a high-school education fall into the poor attendance group. The difference between these two percentages, 60 percent (i.e., 80 – 20 = 60), is used to derive a statistical weight that is then applied to answers of "high-school graduate" to the " highest level of education" question. In the case of university graduates, if 60 percent have a low absenteeism rate, with 40 percent having a high rate, a weight based on 20 percent would be applied to "university graduate" answers to this item. This weighting procedure is called the *vertical percentage method*. In this way, applicants who had only a high-school education would be given a higher score (.60) than university graduates (.20).

The *horizontal percentage method* considers the percentage of successful employees in all categories defined by an application form item. If 75 percent of employees with technical/trade diplomas and 70 percent of those with community college degrees fell into the low absenteeism group, the horizontal percentage method would find the lowest common denominator across all four educational response categories. University degree holders would be given a score of 1.00 (i.e., .60/.60); community college graduates, 1.17 (i.e., .70/.60); technical/trade school graduates, 1.25 (i.e., .75/.60); and high-school graduates, 1.67 (i.e., .80/.60). In this way, those with only a high-school degree would get the highest score and those with a university degree, the lowest. Once the weights have been determined using one of the accepted weighting procedures, an overall score is obtained by adding together the weights from all the items. Finally, the overall score is correlated with the criterion measure to determine the validity of the weighted application form.

VALIDITY OF WEIGHTED APPLICATION FORMS On the whole, well-constructed weighted application forms are very good predictors of several different types of work behaviour (e.g., absenteeism, accidents, turnover, among others, Cascio, 1976). Weighted forms are also easy and economical to use (Lee and Booth, 1974). There are some problems with using this approach. First, criterion measures such as turnover, absenteeism, and accident rates that are typically used to validate weighted application forms may not adequately represent a job's complex performance domain. (Recall the discussion on criterion development in Chapter 5.) However, Ghiselli's (1966) analysis of validity data suggests that weighted application forms also predict both training success and job proficiency. Second, it takes data from a large number of employees to obtain percentages that are good estimates of the appropriate weights. It may take several years to collect the necessary data; there is the risk that changes in the job, the applicants, or the organization over that period may produce weights that represent neither the first- or last-hired employees. However, a recent meta-analysis suggests that weighted application forms that include biographical information may have a greater degree of stability than previously thought (Rothstein, Schmidt, Erwin, Owens, and Sparks, 1990). Finally, while weighted application forms provide the basis for very good empirical predictions (Mitchell and Klimoski, 1982), they do not offer any understanding of why those relationships exist (Guion, 1967).

BIOGRAPHICAL DATA

Application forms require job candidates to make a report about their past experiences and accomplishments. As presented in Box 7.1, a typical application form addresses a very narrow range of job-related items. Owens (1976; Owens and Schoenfeldt, 1979) extended this approach to a much broader range of biographical topics in developing the Biographical Information Blank (BIB). The BIB includes questions about what was done to the job applicant by others (e.g., parents, teachers, co-workers) and what kinds of experiences the applicant has had in the past. Applicants report this information by answering a series of multiple-choice or short answer questions. Biodata items touch upon the applicant's health, family background, socioeconomic status, hobbies, as well as interests, attitudes, and values. Box 7.2 presents an example of a BIB that was developed for use with job candidates for a managerial position. The information obtained from the BIB is scored to produce either a total score, overall, or a score for specific sets of items or factors. Like the weighted application form, the BIB must be validated before it can be used to select job applicants. The Canadian insurance industry has used biodata as part of its selection procedures since 1942. The Life Insurance Marketing Research Association (LIMRA), on behalf of the Canadian industry, has developed a BIB for use exclusively in Canada. This

BOX 7.2   AN EXAMPLE OF A BIOGRAPHICAL INFORMATION BLANK

Name _____

Address _____

Number of Dependents _____

How long have you lived at your current address?_____

Do you consider your net worth to be low___moderate_____or high___?

Have you ever been turned down for a loan? Yes_____ No_____

How many credit cards do you have?_____

Highest level of education completed:

   High School_____ Vocational School_____ College_____

   University_____Post Graduate_____

What educational degrees do you have? B.A._____ B.Sc.___B.Comm._____

   MBA_____ Master's_____ Other_____

What subjects did you major in?_____

What was your grade point average in university? A____ B___ C___ D___

Did you graduate with honors? Yes_____ No_____

Did you receive any awards for academic excellence? Yes____No____

Did you receive any scholarships? Yes_____No_____

List the extracurricular activities you participated in during school:

_____

Did you find school stimulating_____ boring_____?

Did you hold a job while attending school? Yes_____ No_____

How did you pay for your post-high school training? (Check as many as appropriate)

Parents paid_____ Loans_____ Scholarships_____Paid own way_____

Have you ever held a job where you earned commissions on sales? Yes___ No____

   If "Yes," were your commissions low_____ moderate____ high_____?

In five years from now, what do you expect your salary to be?_____

Do you enjoy meeting new people? Yes_____ No_____

How many social phone calls do you receive a week?_____

Do people count on you to "cheer up" others? Yes____No____

How many parties do you go to in a year?_____

Do you enjoy talking to people? Yes_____No_____

Rate your conversational skills:

   Excellent_____ Very Good_____ Good_____ Fair_____ Poor_____

How often do you introduce yourself to other people you don't know?

   Always_____ Sometimes_____ Never_____

Do you enjoy social gatherings? Yes_____No_____

Do you go to social gatherings out of a sense of duty? Yes___No____

How many times a year do you go out to dinner with friends? _____

Do you enjoy talking to people you don't know? Yes____No____

What non-work-related social activities are you engaged in?

_____

What are your hobbies?

_____

What sports, recreational, or physical activities do you engage in?

_____

How confident are you in your ability to succeed?

   Very Confident_____ Confident_____ Somewhat Confident_____

biodata instrument conforms to Canadian human rights legislations and is sensitive to the Canadian cultural context.

BIB DIMENSIONS The BIB, which is also known as a life history or personal history inventory, is based on the view that past behaviour is the best predictor of future behaviour. Understanding how a job applicant behaved in the past through examination of related BIB items allows a prediction of that applicant's future interests and capabilities. Statistical analyses of different BIB forms suggests that the BIB items cluster on 13 to 15 major dimensions (Owens, 1976). Although the comparability of dimensions across different BIBs may be questionable (Klimoski, 1993), rational comparison of the different biodata factors suggests that the following eight dimensions may be common to all life event inventories (Owens, 1976):

◆ School Achievement—academic success and positive academic attitude.

◆ Higher Educational Achievement—holding a degree from a post-secondary school.

◆ Drive—motivation to be outstanding, to attain high goals, to achieve.

◆ Leadership and Group Participation—involvement in organized activities and membership in groups.

◆ Financial Responsibility—financial status and handling of finances.

◆ Early Family Responsibility—an "own family" orientation.

◆ Parental Family Adjustment—happy parental home experience.

◆ Situational Stability—mid-life occupational stability.

These dimensions appear to be relatively stable and offer an explanation of why certain applicants may be more successful than others. That is, a relationship between a particular item on the BIB and a criterion measure is not as important to predicting future behaviour as the relationship of the dimension represented by the item and the criterion. Knowing that the applicant is high in *drive* and *financial responsibility* is more important than knowing an applicant's precise goals or financial status.

BIB AS A MEASURE OF PERSONALITY An argument can be made that the dimensions underlying biodata or personal histories actually reflect different aspects of the job applicant's personality. In fact, biodata dimensions correlate well with personality-related dimensions of the *Strong Interest Inventory*

(Owens, 1976). As well, life event or personal history inventories have been used to develop measures of personality. The *Assessment of Background and Life Experiences* (ABLE) measures six different personality constructs through biodata information. A major study conducted for the U.S. Army showed that the ABLE constructs successfully predicted important job-related criteria such as technical proficiency, general soldiering proficiency, effort and leadership, personal discipline, and physical fitness and military bearing (Hough, Eaton, Dunnette, Kamp, and McCloy, 1990). Chapter 8 presents a more extensive discussion of the use of personality tests in selection.

FAKING THE BIB Often managers express concern that job applicants are less than honest in completing a BIB or life events history, particularly when it comes to reporting negative information. Available evidence on the degree of accuracy in applications is mixed. Cascio (1975) reviewed over 100 biodata inventories completed by job applicants for positions with a Florida police department. Cascio compared the answers that applicants gave to 17 items on the BIB to the actual event. On average, there was an exceptionally high correlation (.94) between the applicant's answer and the true state of affairs. This research suggests that if applicants believe their answers may be verified, they will be more likely to tell the truth. Obviously, this is more likely to happen when the BIB items ask for factual, objective information that can be checked. However, some distortion should be expected. Goldstein (1971) found that specific types of information reported on traditional application forms was inaccurate in up to 25 percent of the cases that he studied. Unfortunately, accuracy of application forms and BIBs has not been extensively examined. This last figure is consistent with the degree of inaccuracy or misrepresentation, 33 percent, found in application materials supplied by the job candidate ("Looking at Job Applications," 1994). Unfortunately, the rate of misrepresentation or inaccuracy may be increasing as the competition for jobs increases.

VALIDITY OF BIODATA Validation research on biodata produces results similar to that for the weighted application form. Biodata is a very good predictor of certain types of job behaviours (e.g., absenteeism, turnover, job proficiency, supervisory effectiveness, and job training) in a wide range of occupations (Asher, 1972; Ghiselli, 1966, Rothstein et al., 1990). Nonetheless, there are major concerns that must be addressed before biodata can be used as part of the selection process. Foremost among these are legal considerations. Many BIB items (e.g., marital status, family background) request information that is protected under human rights legislation. A case might be made to use these types of items if they are job-related (Cascio, 1976); however, the employer would bear the onus of establishing their worth as a predictor. Many other items on a BIB delve into areas that are not protected by legislation, but which raise issues of privacy. Many job applicants feel that it is inappropriate to share information on their financial status or the number of credit cards they carry with a prospective employer. As we discussed in Chapter 6, job applicants form perceptions of the organization and its values, which influence their decisions to accept job offers (Rynes, 1993). The use of a BIB that included items that give the appearance of discrimination and of invading privacy may have the unintended effect of losing highly qualified candidates. In fact, potential job applicants who completed application forms with discriminatory items reacted more negatively to the organization than when those items were removed from the form. The potential applicants believed that the organization, in the first case, was less attractive as a place to work, that they would be less likely to pursue a job with the company and to accept one if offered, and that they would be less likely to recommend the organization to friends. They also came to believe that the organization treated its employees unfairly (Saks, Leck, and Saunders, 1995). In the United States, each item on a BIB must be shown not to have an adverse impact on members of protected groups (*State of Connecticut v. Teal* 457 U.S. 440, 1981); Canadian human rights legislation requires that any information used in the hiring process be job-related. The human resources manager must decide if the benefits of using a BIB outweigh the potential hazards, or if it can be replaced by an equally valid but less intrusive selection instrument.

The Canadian insurance industry has shown that having a BIB comply with human rights legislation does not sacrifice its predictive validity. The biodata form developed by LIMRA has been the subject of extensive validation research. Criterion-related studies carried out by LIMRA show that the Canadian biodata form successfully predicts which job applicants will survive for at least a year and produce sales in the top half of all agents with a company. LIMRA also estimated the utility of the biodata form; in current dollars, each agent hired through the process returned a net profit of around $25 000.

RÉSUMÉS

A résumé is another source of biographical information produced by job applicants. The intent of the résumé is to introduce the job applicant to the organization through a brief, accurate, written self-description. The information contained on most résumés overlaps with the information requested by the employer through application blanks or biographical inventories. One difference is that on the résumé applicants voluntarily provide biographical information about themselves. They believe this information is job-related and that it will lead a potential employer to decide that they meet the minimum job requirements and are worthy of further consideration. A second difference is that job applicants may include information on the résumé that the employer might rather not have seen. Although it is not as common as it was a few years ago, some job applicants still list information about their citizenship or national origin, height, weight, marital status, or other characteristics that, if used as part of selection, run afoul of employment legislation. It might be extremely difficult for an employer to prove that such prohibited information did not influence an employment decision. Another important difference is that résumés are unstandardized. The uniqueness of each applicant's résumé makes the use of standardized scoring techniques difficult, if not impossible. Nonetheless, all of the psychometric and legal considerations that apply to application forms and biodata apply equally to the use of résumés in selection. Information obtained from the résumé must be job-related and non-discriminatory.

FIRST IMPRESSIONS In addition to providing specific biographical information, the résumé presents a first impression of the applicant. The recruiter or human resources manager may form an image of the applicant based on characteristics of the résumé itself. The résumé's style, neatness, organization, layout of information, and the vocabulary and phrases used throughout convey information about the candidate, in addition to the facts presented within the résumé. In essence, the human resources manager may believe that these characteristics reflect different aspects of the applicant in much the same way as a projective personality test (see Chapter 8).

WRITING A RÉSUMÉ Many job applicants have difficulty writing a good résumé. Vocational guidance counsellors and employment counsellors often provide help in writing résumés as part of the services they offer. As well, most libraries have many references on writing effective job résumés. There are a few basic points to consider in preparing a résumé. It should include the applicant's name, address, and phone numbers, education and training, employment history, references, and a brief statement of employment goals and objectives. Information on hobbies, interests, and other pursuits should be included only if it is relevant to the career goals. For example, a candidate for a forest ranger position may want to note an interest in hiking. The résumé should be well-organized and laid out to emphasize the different types of information it covers. The type and size of the font should not discourage someone from reading the résumé. It should be typed, or produced with a laser-quality printer. Incorporating features such as unusual type fonts, small point type, excessive italics, or single line spacing which make the résumé difficult to read, generally guarantees that it will not be read. Box 7.3 presents an example of a standard résumé. This example is intended to identify the major features of a résumé and to present that information in an organized manner.

SCREENING BASED ON RÉSUMÉS In today's labour market, where many candidates are competing for a limited number of jobs, a voluminous number of résumés, as in the case of Toyota Canada, make screening much more difficult. Organizations have had to develop procedures for systematically processing candidates on the basis of their résumés. Wein (1994) reports the following pre-employment screening procedure:

♦ Think of what the company needs for excellent job performance in terms of its job performance criteria.

♦ Screen out those résumés that do not include a stated job objective or career goal.

♦ Read each résumé with reference to the company's job performance criteria.

♦ Check résumés for work experience, chronology, and history.

♦ Examine surviving résumés for concrete accomplishments and identifiable skills.

♦ Look at résumés one more time for appearance.

HONESTY AND THE RÉSUMÉ Job applicants should feel free to customize their résumés to include their own unique attributes or experiences. However, it is important to be honest and to avoid exaggeration in presenting

BOX 7.3 AN EXAMPLE OF A RÉSUMÉ

Résumé

Dominique Kelly   March 1, 1996
1255 Main Street
Anywhere, Nova Scotia
B1M 3D7

Phone: (902) 555-1001
Fax: (902) 555-1002
e-mail: domkelly@bluenose.freenet.ca

Career Objective

Law enforcement, corrections, or security officer.

Education

1990   Graduated from Bluenose Senior High School
1992   Graduated from Bluenose Community College
        Degree: Associate of Arts
        Major: Law enforcement and administration

Employment History and Experience

1992 – Present   Guard, Bluenose Armoured Car Services
1990 – Present   Corporal, Bluenose Regiment, Reserve Forces

Awards and Honours

1992   President's Medal for Academic Achievement, Bluenose Community College

Special Skills

Certified lifeguard and water safety instructor.

Interests

Sports: Hunting, target shooting, and swimming.
Member: Bluenose Ground Search and Rescue Team

References

Mr. John Smith, Supervisor   Prof. Jane Osgoode
Bluenose Armoured Car Services   Bluenose Community College
Anywhere, Nova Scotia   Anywhere, Nova Scotia
B1M 4D8   B2K 1X9
(902) 555-2034   (902) 555-7462

qualifications or accomplishments. If facts are checked later and they seem to have been distorted to the applicant's benefit, either job loss or severe embarrassment results. Box 7.4 lists some prominent Canadians whose résumés included misleading statements about their credentials ("Little stretches," 1996).

With an increasingly competitive labour market, job candidates may be more prone to fudging the truth about their credentials. There is often a very fine line between presenting yourself in the best possible light and intentionally misrepresenting your background. Human resource managers must learn how to read between the lines of résumés. Here are some points to look for when examining a résumé:

◆ Unexplained gaps in work or education chronology;

◆ Use of qualifiers such as "knowledge of," "assisted in" to describe work experience;

◆ Listing schools attended without indicating receipt of a degree or diploma;

◆ Failure to provide names of previous supervisors or references;

◆ Substantial time periods in a candidate's work history listed as "self-employed" or "consultant";

◆ Style in place of substance—using flashy paper or fonts on the résumé.

Such characteristics should serve as a warning signal to examine the résumé closely and to undertake a thorough reference check before proceeding further with the application.

SCREENING INTERVIEWS

In North America, the interview is the most popular selection device; it is used nearly universally (Rowe, Williams, and Day, 1994). The interview, a face-to-face interaction between two people, is designed to allow one of the parties to obtain information about the other. In employment, the employer's representative is called the interviewer while the job applicant is called the interviewee or applicant. This traditional terminology does not convey the complex, dynamic, interactive nature of the interview. It is used only as a matter of convenience to identify each of the parties involved in the interview, since both attempt to obtain information about the other through the interview process. Each, at times, is both an interviewer and an interviewee.

BOX 7.4 PROMINENT CANADIANS WHO FUDGED THEIR RÉSUMÉS

Jane Fulton—Deputy Minister of Health, Alberta

Government commissioned report concluded Ms. Fulton was guilty of overstating about twelve of her accomplishments. She retained her position.

Ralph Klein—Premier of Alberta

His 1993 campaign literature said he had graduated from high school when he had dropped out.

Jocelyne Bourgon—Clerk of the Privy Council of Canada

She did not quite have the MBA degree people thought she had at the time of her appointment. She retained her position.

Jag Bhaduria—Member of Parliament

Used the initials LL.B (Int.) after his name which suggest the possession of a law degree, which he did not have. Still serving as a Member of Parliament but dropped from the Liberal Caucus.

Kim Campbell—Former Prime Minister of Canada

Her résumé made the doubtful claim that she was fluent in German, Russian, and Yiddish. Lost next election; no longer active in politics.

Terry Popowich—Vice-President, Toronto Stock Exchange

He claimed to have an MBA from the London School of Economics. He was fired after it was discovered that he did not have one.

Source: *Halifax Daily News*, April 5, 1996.

SCREENING FOR ORGANIZATIONAL FIT In our discussion of recruitment in Chapter 6, we described how job applicants use their initial interview with a recruiter to obtain information about the organization, just as the interviewer takes the opportunity of the interview to find out information about the applicant that is not apparent from an application form or résumé. The interview has considerable value as a recruiting device and as a means of initiating a social relationship between a job applicant and an organization (Rowe et al., 1994). The selection interview is used to present information, mostly favourable, about the organization as an employer, with the hope of increasing the odds that an applicant will accept a forthcoming job offer. The job applicant uses the occasion of the interview to learn more about the company as an employer and to make inferences about its values and philosophy in deciding if there is a fit (Gati, 1989). Without a doubt, interviewing that is done as part of the recruitment process serves as a screening mechanism. Job applicants who do not meet the recruiter's and the organization's standards do not proceed further. Today, organizations such as Goodyear Canada and Guardian Insurance Company of Canada are using the initial screening interview to determine whether job candidates possess competency in core performance areas that have been related to corporate mission statements and corresponding strategic plans. As noted previously, Ford Motor Company selects students for sponsorship through universities and technical colleges on the basis of how well the students fit four competency dimensions that were related to successful job performance. These core competencies and performance areas are identified through procedures discussed in Chapter 5. This initial assessment also includes screening based on those values believed necessary to achieving the company's strategic goals. Successful Canadian organizations recognize that selection and performance measurement go hand in hand.

IMPROVING THE INTERVIEW—A PREVIEW For almost as long as it has been used as a selection device, the interview has suffered criticism for poor reliability and validity. However, more recent work by Latham (1989) and Janz (1982) shows that both the reliability and validity of the interview can be substantially improved by structuring job analysis information into interview questions. The work of these two Canadian psychologists on the employment interview is described in more detail in Chapter 9. That chapter examines the use of the interview in the final stages of the selection process as part of deciding which candidates are the most qualified. The remainder of this section reviews the role of the interview in the earlier stages of the selection process as a screening device to decide if a job applicant meets minimum requirements.

THE TYPICAL SCREENING INTERVIEW Screening interviews typically consist of a series of free-wheeling, unstructured questions that are designed to fill in the gaps left on the candidate's application form and résumé. Such traditional interviews take on the qualities of a conversation and often revolve around a set of common questions like those presented in Box 9.1,

p. 378 (e.g., "What is your greatest accomplishment?"). These questions cover the applicant's personal history, attitudes and expectations, and skills and abilities. The information obtained by many of these questions probably would have been better left to a well-constructed application form. Skilful interviewees often have learned how to give socially desirable answers to many of these frequently asked questions. While some distortion is to be expected in the answers an applicant makes during an interview, there is no reason to believe that those inaccuracies, intentional or otherwise, occur with greater frequency than inaccuracies in biodata and résumé information. There is very little direct evidence on the rate or percentage of misinformation that takes place over the course of an interview. As with applications and biodata, when interview questions focus on verifiable events related to past work or educational experiences, accuracy will likely increase.

SCREENING INTERVIEW FORMAT The interviewer often obtains better information from a screening interview by following an interview guide. Following a set of preplanned questions or topics during the interview, in addition to reviewing the applicant's file before the interview begins, will improve the reliability or consistency of information gathered through the interview (Schwab and Henneman, 1969). The format for this type of interview begins with some opening remarks by the interviewer to put the applicant at ease. This generally involves an exchange of pleasantries and personal information, including information on the interviewer's role in the organization. The interviewer states the purpose of the interview and how the information will be used. The interviewer will also mention whether any information presented during the interview will be held in confidence or shared with others. The interviewer will also note whether any notes or recordings will be made during the interview. Following these clarifications, the interview questions concentrate on the applicant's past work history, education and training, and general background. The applicant is given an opportunity to ask questions about the job and company as well as about issues raised during the interview. In closing, the interviewer outlines the timeline for the decision process and when applicants are likely to hear the outcome. After the applicant leaves, the interviewer prepares a summary of the interview by completing either a written narrative or a rating form.

DECISIONS BASED ON THE SCREENING INTERVIEW The interviewer is frequently required to make inferences about an applicant's personal qualities, motivation, overall ability, attitude toward work, and potential not only for doing the job but also for fitting into the organizational culture. Organizations that use screening interviews often require the interviewer to rate specific attributes or characteristics of the applicant either in addition to, or instead of, making an overall recommendation. Table 7.1 presents a sample

TABLE 7.1 AN EXAMPLE OF A POST-INTERVIEW SUMMARY

Widget Manufacturing
Interview Summary

Applicant's Name _____ Date _____

Position _____ Interviewed By _____

Ratings: 0–Unacceptable; 1–Poor; 2–Satisfactory; 3–Good; 4–Excellent

	Rating	Comments
Previous Experience	0 1 2 3 4	
Neatness/Grooming	0 1 2 3 4	
Communicating	0 1 2 3 4	
Interpersonal Skills	0 1 2 3 4	
Adaptability	0 1 2 3 4	
Maturity	0 1 2 3 4	
Emotional Stability	0 1 2 3 4	
Leadership Potential	0 1 2 3 4	
Ability to Work with Others	0 1 2 3 4	
Planning/Organizing	0 1 2 3 4	
Attitude toward Work	0 1 2 3 4	
Realistic Expectations	0 1 2 3 4	
Overall Impression	0 1 2 3 4	

Total Score _____

Recommendation: _____ Unacceptable/Notify applicant of rejection
_____ Applicant is acceptable for position
If acceptable, arrange for the following:
_____ Employment Testing
_____ Selection Interview

form used to rate applicants following a screening interview. The traits or attributes that interviewers are asked to rate vary among organizations. They range from the very specific (e.g., attitude toward working irregular hours) to the very general (e.g., initiative).

In discussing realistic job previews used by the Canadian Forces as part of its recruiting strategy, we noted that applicants first meet with a recruiting officer who determines their initial suitability for a military career. The recruiter engages in a brief interview with the applicant after reviewing the candidate's application form. Following the screening interview, the recruiter makes a recommendation on the candidate's suitability. No further action is taken on those who are judged unsuitable for the military. Those applicants who pass the screening interview proceed to more extensive testing as well as the job preview. Microsoft Canada makes similar use of a screening interview to discover computer science graduates whose thinking is fast, flexible, and creative. The Microsoft interview includes questions related to computer science knowledge, and also brain-teaser type questions about balloons that move in mysterious ways. More than the right answer, Microsoft Canada is looking for an ability to think creatively and a display of an inquiring mind. Only about 25 percent of applicants from one of Canada's leading computer science programs make it through the final stages of the screening interview (Carpenter, 1995).

IMPRESSION FORMATION Interviewers use both the verbal and non-verbal behaviour displayed by job applicants in forming an impression of the applicant (Dreher and Sackett, 1983; Rynes and Miller, 1983; Webster, 1982). Similarly, the applicant uses the interviewer's verbal and non-verbal behaviours to form an impression of the interviewer, and the organization, in judging the probability of receiving a job offer and the desirability of accepting it and in working for the organization. Box 7.5 lists common behaviours displayed by applicants during an interview that lead to either positive or negative impressions on the part of the interviewer. While there is no guarantee that presenting all the positive behaviours and avoiding all the negative ones will lead to the next step in the selection process, doing so should increase the likelihood of such an outcome.

VALUE OF THE SCREENING INTERVIEW Considerable time and energy have been spent on investigating the effectiveness of the interview. In recent years, however, the selection interview has received much more attention than the

BOX 7.5 INTERVIEW DO'S AND DONT'S

Applicant Behaviours that Influence Positive Impressions

1. Being on time for the interview.
2. Being prepared for the interview by
   ♦ having done homework on the company
   ♦ anticipating common interview questions
3. Making direct eye contact with the interviewer.
4. Remaining confident and determined throughout the interview regardless of how the interviewer's cues suggest the interview is going.
5. Providing information about strong points when answering questions.
6. Answering questions quickly and intelligently.
7. Demonstrating interest in the position and organization.

Applicant Behaviours that Influence Negative Impressions

1. Presenting poor personal appearance or grooming.
2. Displaying an overly aggressive, know-it-all attitude.
3. Failing to communicate clearly (e.g., mumbling, poor grammar, use of slang).
4. Lacking career goals or career planning.
5. Overemphasizing monetary issues.
6. Evasiveness, or not answering questions completely.
7. Lacking maturity, tact, courtesy, or social skills.

screening interview. Past reviews of the employment interview (Harris, 1989; Webster, 1982) suggest that it is a useful screening device. Interviewers who screen for production or clerical workers generally develop a stereotype of an acceptable applicant and quickly decide whether the applicant fits that mould. The remainder of the interview generally involves the interviewer seeking information from the applicant either to confirm or to contradict the interviewer's impression. Negative information, particularly when it occurs early in the interview, is difficult to change and tends to influence the outcome more than positive information. Training interviewers may reduce some types of errors they make in rating applicants, but there is no evidence that this reduction affects the quality of the overall judgments made by the interviewer.

CAUTIONS Using the interview as a screening device brings with it the potential for introducing discriminatory practices into the hiring process.

Interviews, even those that are highly structured, are conversations between individuals. Something is said that provokes a response. In opening an interview with small talk or chit-chat, interviewers often delve into the personal background of the applicant. They may ask questions about marital status, child-care arrangements, birthplace or birth date, or the applicant's name that relate to national or ethnic origin. Table 2.1 (p. 38) shows that information of this type is clearly prohibited. Should a job applicant who has been asked these questions be turned down, the onus will be on the employing organization to show that the reason was lack of job-related requirements and not discriminatory hiring practices. Interview questions should follow the same rule of thumb as application blanks: Is the information obtained from this question job-related? If you cannot answer yes, don't ask the question.

REFERENCE CHECKS

Job applicants are often asked to provide the names of personal references as well as the names of their supervisors from previous jobs. It is understood that these individuals will be contacted and asked for their views on the applicant. These people may be asked questions that range from those that simply seek to verify information presented by the applicant to those that ask them to make judgments about the traits, characteristics, and behaviours of the applicant. Consequently, the term *reference check* may be applied to vastly different procedures, which have different levels of reliability and validity. In assessing the worth of reference checks, it is necessary to keep in mind the specific procedure that was actually used. Regardless of the specifics, reference checks normally take place last in the screening process; references are sought only on those applicants who have survived the previous screens.

POPULARITY AND VALIDITY OF PERSONAL REFERENCES Along with biodata, the résumé, and the interview, references are the most commonly used screening devices. Unlike biodata, reference checks do not enjoy a good reputation and add little of value to the screening process (Baxter, Brock, Hill, and Rozelle, 1981). One of the most comprehensive investigations into references (Goheen and Mosel, 1959; Mosel and Goheen, 1958; 1959) suggested that ratings based on references from the applicant's past supervisors did not predict performance ratings given by the applicant's current supervisor; neither did the references identify factual information that would have led to judging the applicant unsuitable for the position. In effect, the information in the reference was more of a statement about the referee, the person writing the reference, than the applicant. Unfortunately, the validity of personal references has not improved over time. Canadian human resource consultants now routinely warn corporate clients to be leery of making hiring decisions on the basis of personal references (Dankel, 1991; Kabay, 1993). Predictions about future job success based on references have not been overly successful.

REASONS FOR POOR VALIDITY OF PERSONAL REFERENCES There appear to be several reasons for the low validity of reference checks. In the case of personal references, it is highly unlikely that a job applicant will knowingly offer the name of someone who will provide a bad reference (Doing so might be more of a statement about the cognitive ability of the applicant!). Most applicants are fairly confident about the type of reference they will be given. Applicants should not hesitate to ask intended referees if they will provide positive comments before listing their names on an application form. It is in the applicant's best interests to do this. The result, however, is a set of uniformly positive recommendations for each applicant. The lack of variability in the references limits their use in discriminating between candidates; this is an example of range restriction discussed in Chapter 3, which leads to low validity coefficients. This is one reason why even the slightest negative information contained in a reference may be sufficient to eliminate an applicant from the job competition (Knouse, 1983). Negative information is simply not expected in a reference.

Employers seek to screen out job applicants who have poor work behaviours or who have problematic backgrounds and often they use reference checks to obtain such information. While it is understandable that applicants will use the most favourable references, why are reference checks with previous employers equally ineffective as screening measures? Consider the following two situations.

An unproductive employee whom you supervise has applied for a job with another company. You receive a call asking for your judgment on the employee. While you may wish to be honest and helpful, you do not want to say anything that will prevent the other company from taking the employee off your hands. The result is that while you truthfully answer any questions you are asked, you do not volunteer any negative information, hoping that your problem employee will be hired away. However, if you are asked specifically about problem behaviours and you intentionally mislead the reference checker or cover up the problems, you might be liable for any economic losses suffered by the new employer after hiring your problem employee (Leavitt, 1992).

You receive a call checking on a former employee who resigned rather than face dismissal over allegations of sexual harassment. No charges were brought against the employee. If you are completely honest and express your concerns over the employee's behaviour while working for you, the former employee may not receive a job offer. The former employee then learns of your remarks and sues you and your company for slander, defamation, and the lost opportunity of a new job. While you may be able to defend yourself against the lawsuit, you will have substantial legal fees. In the United States, several states have laws that make former employers liable for any statements that wrongfully prevent job applicants from receiving offers from another employer. Given these liabilities, many Canadian employers are hesitant about making any strong, negative statements about current or former employees, even though reference checking is easier to carry out in Canada than in the United States (McFarland, 1996; "Most Employers Use," 1995).

TELEPHONE REFERENCE CHECKS Many employers are also reluctant to provide references in writing, preferring instead to do so over the phone. The telephone reference is perhaps the most common way in which Canadian employers check references. Many have also resorted to using forms that obtain standardized information on all potential employees. Regrettably, most of the questions asked as part of these reference checks ask for judgments on the part of the referee rather than focusing on objective information and suffer the same problems as more general letters of reference. Typical questions asked about the job applicant in telephone checks usually include some of the following:

◆ How long have you known the applicant? In what capacity?

◆ What sort of employee is the applicant?

◆ Does the candidate show initiative?

◆ How did the applicant get along with other employees, supervisors, clients?

- ◆ Did the applicant meet deadlines? Get work done on time?
- ◆ Was the applicant punctual? Were there attendance problems?
- ◆ Were you satisfied with the applicant's performance?
- ◆ Why did the applicant leave your company?
- ◆ Is there anything you feel I should know about this candidate?
- ◆ Would you rehire the applicant?

ASKING THE RIGHT QUESTIONS In many cases, the right questions are not asked, and many that are asked may not have any relevance to the job under consideration. Also, reference checks often fail to ask for confirmation of specific information provided by job candidates in their application materials. The referee should be asked to compare the candidate to other employees; for example, "If your worst employee is given a rating of 1 and your best a rating of 10, what rating would you give to this candidate?" Referees should be probed for more information on the candidate when their answers are not forthcoming or appear to be too qualified or general. Ask for specifics and have them describe examples of the candidate's behaviour; for example, "Describe a situation in which the candidate performed exceptionally well or exceptionally poorly." Many of the techniques discussed in Chapter 9 for developing structured or behaviour-based interview questions for employment interviews can also be adapted for use in reference checking. As in the case of interviewing, asking specific, behaviour-based questions related to job performance is likely to increase the accuracy of the information obtained through the reference check.

IS THE REFEREE COMPETENT TO ASSESS? There are implicit assumptions made when a former supervisor or a personal reference is called upon for information about a job candidate; namely, that the referees, themselves, are competent to make the assessment and sufficiently knowledgeable about the candidate to provide accurate information. These are not always well-founded assumptions. A former supervisor may not have been in a position long enough to learn much about the employee's behaviour; there is also no guarantee that the supervisor is capable of discriminating poor job behaviour from excellent. When these assumptions are met, the reference information is likely to have a higher degree of accuracy. In effect, the reference checker must also know something about the referees to establish the credibility of their references. This is why greater value is placed on references from people who are known to those evaluating the reference information.

BACKGROUND CHECKS Reference checks are on safer ground when they concentrate on verifying information obtained from the applicant's biodata, résumé, or interview. *Canadian Banker* magazine reported that recent surveys indicated that about one-third of all résumés included falsehoods related to level of education, length of time in previous job, and level of responsibility. It went on to advise its readers that the best defence against such misrepresentation was a careful check of the information provided by the candidate during the hiring process ("Looking at Job Applications," 1994). Although Jock McGregor of Deloitte and Touche Consulting Group believes lying is not an extensive problem in Canada (McFarland, 1996), it is still good procedure to carry out reference checks. When the candidate knows that the information from these sources will be checked, the accuracy of that information is likely to increase. This is one reason why candidates who are interviewed using the structured interview procedure developed by Janz (1982) are advised that any information they report about their past behaviour will be checked.

FIELD INVESTIGATIONS In most cases, checking information is limited to phone calls to supervisors and personal references. However, a very extensive search of an applicant's background may take place for some occupations or positions. Applicants for sensitive government jobs, or with security services such as the RCMP undergo field investigations that involve interviews with people who know the applicant, including former employers and co-workers, credit checks, review of police files, court records, educational records, and any other available documentation. Background checks of this sort are very expensive, but in most cases they provide an accurate description of the applicant and any problem areas that might affect job performance. Field investigations are used by corporations before they make top-level managerial appointments. Most organizations are not equipped to do such costly and elaborate investigations of potential new employees. Increasingly they are turning to a growing number of firms that specialize in this activity (Fuchsberg, 1990). A major concern with such field investigations is their invasion of the applicant's privacy. There is always the possibility that the background check will uncover information that is unrelated to job performance but disqualifies the candidate because of employer disapproval for the employee's actions or beliefs.

◆ ◆ ◆
EVALUATION OF SCREENING EFFECTIVENESS

Biographical data (including both weighted and traditional application blanks), résumés, screening interviews, and reference checks are perhaps the most frequently used methods of obtaining information used in the hiring process. The psychometric properties of these procedures vary greatly across these different methods. One difficulty in making any definitive conclusions about their overall worth is the relative lack of validity data that is available on biodata, résumés, and reference checks. It is almost that these methods have been used for so long that it is taken for granted that they are valid procedures. This is not always the case.

BIODATA Available research supports the validity of biographical data in screening job applicants. Rothstein et al. (1990) place biodata second only to cognitive ability as a valid predictor of job proficiency, supporting Reilly and Chao's (1982) earlier position that the validity of biodata was on a par with that of employment tests. Asher and Sciarrino (1974) reported that the validity coefficients for biodata exceeded .50 in six of the 11 studies they reviewed. More recent quantitative meta-analysis puts the average validity coefficient at .37 (Hunter and Hunter, 1984). Well-constructed biographical inventories that are based on a job analysis provide data that can be used to make valid inferences about an applicant's future job proficiency.

RÉSUMÉS Hardly any validation studies have been done directly on the résumé itself. Rather, studies report the validity of inferences based on information typically found on a résumé. Hunter and Hunter's (1984) meta-analysis showed that information of the type included on a résumé had relatively low validity in predicting future job success. Experience had the highest validity, .18, followed by academic achievement, .11, and education, .10. Nonetheless, a résumé and its accompanying cover letter remain the primary means by which many job applicants introduce themselves to an organization and create an impression of their fit to the job and to the company.

SCREENING INTERVIEWS There is a considerable amount of research on the validity of interviews in employee selection. Meta-analyses report the validity for unstructured employment interviews, the type mostly used in screening, as ranging from .14 (Hunter and Hunter, 1984) to .20 (Wiesner and Cronshaw, 1988). Even at .20, the validity of the interview is still substantially low in comparison to other types of selection procedures. It is likely that an interview will always play a role in hiring regardless of its validity. Employers will always want to meet the prospective employee face-to-face before making a job offer. Chapter 9 presents ways of substantially improving the interview by relating it to job analysis information. The improvements to the interview discussed in Chapter 9 should be incorporated into screening interviews as well as selection interviews. Properly developed interview questions have the potential for being excellent screening devices. The reality is that, as presently carried out, most screening interviews cannot be justified in terms of their validity. Nonetheless, they will likely continue as a basis for deciding the acceptability of job applicants.

REFERENCE CHECKS In general, references are not particularly valuable as selection devices (Muchinsky, 1979). Meta-analyses place the validity for references at either .14 (Reilly and Chao, 1982) or .26 (Hunter and Hunter, 1984). This is in the same range as the unstructured employment interview. While references do have some predictive value, as do unstructured interviews, that value is low, particularly when compared to biodata and the types of employment tests discussed in Chapter 8.

UTILITY ANALYSIS One reason for the popularity of screening devices is their cost and ease of use. They are relatively inexpensive, administered quickly, and easy to interpret. With the exception of weighted application blanks and biographical inventories, there are few, if any, development costs associated with these devices. Those using the devices do not need special training to administer or to interpret the data. However, these low costs must be compared with the potential for inaccuracy built into these devices, particularly those that have poor validities. The cost of false positives screened into the organization through these devices changes the balance of the cost-benefit equation. While no reports of formal utility analysis of screening devices are available, based on known validity and cost factors, devices based on biodata would likely show a net benefit to the organization.

Without a doubt, when they are properly used as screening techniques, these procedures are highly cost-effective (Anderson and Shackleton, 1990).

LEGAL CONSIDERATIONS All of the selection devices reviewed in this chapter have the potential for running afoul of privacy and human rights legislation, leading to charges of discriminatory hiring practices. Before any of these devices are used as part of a selection system, they must be reviewed carefully to eliminate questions prohibited under legislation. Alternatively, it must be established that the protected information is related to a bona fide occupational requirement.

◆ ◆ ◆
SUMMARY

Organizations need to be staffed with people who will not only be capable of doing the work for which they were hired, but who will also do that work in a most productive manner. While the role of the recruitment function is to secure an adequate supply of job applicants, the role of selection is to identify those job applicants who are most qualified. Like recruitment, the selection process is influenced by factors such as labour market, the legal environment, and the organization's philosophy and values, which all influence the number of job applicants. If selection is to be successful, it must be embedded in organization and job analysis and have predictive validity.

Screening, which is often the first stage in recruiting, categorizes job applicants as either acceptable or unacceptable with respect to the requirements needed for the job. Selection seeks to identify the degree to which applicants will be successful. In screening candidates, organizations commonly rely on the application form or some form of biographical data, the résumé, the preliminary screening interview, and reference checks. Candidates who pass these screening tests go on for further testing and interviews. As part of the selection process, these screening devices must meet the same psychometric and legal standards required of other more extensive and expensive selection procedures.

Screening devices try to make a prediction about future job performance based on past behaviour that is reflected in their biodata or answers. As far as biodata and interview questions focus on facts or events that can be checked, the accuracy of screening devices increases. In terms of validity, information gathered through application blanks or biodata forms seems to be a good predictor of future job performance. Traditional, unstructured screening interviews are poor predictors but can be substantially improved by including structured questions derived from a job analysis. Reference checks appear to offer little value to the screening process. These screening devices all have the potential for violating human rights legislation; care must be taken with their use.

E X E R C I S E S

1. Obtain employment application blanks from five different organizations. Determine whether the organization falls under federal or provincial jurisdiction. Do the application blanks request information that is prohibited (see Table 2.1, p. 38)? Use Table 2.1 to prepare a table showing the nature of the violations.

2. Prepare your own personal résumé using the résumé presented in this chapter as a model. Exchange your résumé with one of your classmates. Critique each other's document in terms of organization, clarity of information, style, and presentation. Write a short paragraph describing the impres-

sions you formed from reading your classmate's résumé.

3. Develop an interview guide for doing a screening interview that lists the questions that *cannot* be asked because the information relates to prohibited grounds of discrimination (See Table 2.1).

4. Develop a set of questions based on the security dispatcher's job description (Box 6.6, p. 250) that can be used to screen applicants for that position.

5. Identify the people who should provide references for applicants for the security dispatcher position. Develop a set of questions to ask those references.

References

Anderson, N., and V. Shackleton. 1990. "Staff Selection Decision Making in the 1990s." *Management Decision* 28: 5–8.

Asher, J.J. 1972. "The Biographical Item: Can it be Improved?" *Personnel Psychology* 25: 251–69.

Asher, J.J., and J.A. Sciarrino. 1974. "Realistic Work Samples Tests: A Review." *Personnel Psychology* 27: 519–23.

Baxter, J.C., B. Brock, P.C. Hill, and R.M. Rozelle. 1981. "Letters of Recommendation: A Question of Value." *Journal of Applied Psychology* 66: 296–301.

Binning, J.F., and G.V. Barrett. 1989. "Validity of Personnel Decisions: A Conceptual Analysis of the Inferential and Evidential Bases." *Journal of Applied Psychology* 74: 478–94.

Carpenter, R. 1995. "Geek Logic." *Canadian Business*, 68: 57–58.

Cascio, W.F. 1975. "Accuracy of Verifiable Biographical Information Blank Response." *Journal of Applied Psychology* 60: 767–69.

Cascio, W.F. 1976. "Turnover, Biographical Data, and Fair Employment Practice." *Journal of Applied Psychology* 61: 576–80.

Cascio, W.F., and R.A. Ramos. 1986. "Development and Application of a New Method for Assessing Job Performance in Behavioral/Economic Terms." *Journal of Applied Psychology* 71: 20–28.

Dankel, R. 1991. "Employee References: Kick the Tires Before you Buy." *Nation's Restaurant News*, April 21: 22.

Dreher, G.F., and P.R. Sackett. 1983. *Perspectives on Selection and Staffing*. Homewood, IL: Irwin.

Fuchsberg, G. 1990. "More Employers Check Credit Histories of Job Seekers to Judge their Character." *The Wall Street Journal*, May 30: B1,B3.

Gati, I. 1989. "Person-Environment Fit Research: Problems and Prospects." *Journal of Vocational Behavior* 35: 181–93.

Ghiselli, E.E. 1966. *The Validity of Occupational Aptitude Tests*. New York: Wiley.

Goheen, H.W., and J.N. Mosel. 1959. "Validity of the Employment Recommendation Questionnaire. II.

Comparison with Field Investigations." *Personnel Psychology* 12: 297–302.

Goldstein, I.L. 1971. "The Application Blank: How Honest are the Responses?" *Journal of Applied Psychology* 71: 3–8.

Guion, R.M. 1967. "Personnel Selection." *Annual Review of Psychology* 18: 105–216.

Harris, M.M. 1989. "Reconstructing the Employment Interview: A Review of Recent Literature and Suggestions for Future Research." *Personnel Psychology* 42: 691–726.

Hough, L.M., N.K. Eaton, M.D. Dunnette, J.D. Kamp, and R.A McCloy. 1990. "Criterion-Related Validities of Personality Constructs and the Effect of Response Distortion on those Validities." *Journal of Applied Psychology* 75: 581–95.

Hunter, J.E., and R.F. Hunter. 1984. "Validity and Utility of Alternative Predictors of Job Performance." *Psychological Bulletin* 96: 72–98.

Janz, T. 1982. "Initial Comparisons of Patterned Behaviour Description Interviews Versus Unstructured Interviews." *Journal of Applied Psychology* 67: 577–80.

Kabay, M. 1993. "It Pays to be Paranoid when You're Hiring." *Computing Canada*, April 26: 21.

Klimoski, R.J. 1993. "Predictor Constructs and their Measurement." In

N. Schmitt and W.C. Borman, eds., *Personnel Selection in Organizations*. San Francisco: Jossey-Bass, 99–134.

Knouse, S.B. 1983. "The Letter of Recommendation: Specificity and Favorability of Information." *Personnel Psychology* 36: 331–42.

Latham, G.P. 1989. "The Reliability, Validity, and Practicality of the Situational Interview." In R.W. Eder and G.R. Ferris, eds., *The Employment Interview: Theory, Research, and Practice*. Newbury Park, CA: Sage, 169–82.

Leavitt, H. 1992. "Should Companies be Hesitant to Give Ex-Employees References?" *The Toronto Star*, July 20: C3.

Lee, R., and J.M. Booth. 1974. "A Utility Analysis of a Weighted Application Blank Designed to Predict Turnover from Clerical Employees." *Journal of Applied Psychology* 59: 516–18.

"Little Stretches." 1996. *The Halifax Daily News*, April 5: 17.

"Looking at Job Applications? Remember—it's Hirer Beware." 1994. *Canadian Banker* 101 (May/June): 10.

McFarland, J. 1996. "Firms should Spot Rigged Résumés." *The Globe and Mail*, March 1: B7.

Mitchell, T.W., and R.J. Klimoski. 1982. "Is it Rational to be Empirical? A Test of Methods for Scoring Biographical

Data." *Journal of Applied Psychology* 67: 411–18.

Mosel, J.N., and H.W. Goheen. 1958. "The Validity of the Employment Recommendation Questionnaire in Personnel Selection: I. Skilled Traders." *Personnel Psychology* 11: 481–90.

Mosel, J.N., and H.W. Goheen. 1959. "The Validity of the Employment Recommendation Questionnaire: III. Validity of Different Types of References." *Personnel Psychology* 12: 469–77.

"Most Employers Use Reference Checks, but Many Fear Defamation Liability." 1995. *Canadian HR Reporter* March 13: 5.

Muchinsky, P.M. 1979. "The Use of Reference Reports in Personnel Selection." *Journal of Occupational Psychology* 52: 287–97.

Murphy, K.M. 1986. "When your Top Choice Turns you Down: Effects of Rejected Offers on the Utility of Selection Tests." *Psychological Bulletin* 99: 133–38.

Owens, W.A. 1976. "Biographical Data." In M.D. Dunnette, ed., *Handbook of Industrial and Organizational Psychology*, 1st ed. Chicago: Rand-McNally, 609–50.

Owens, W.A., and L.F. Schoenfeldt. 1979. "Toward a Classification of Persons." *Journal of Applied Psychology* 65: 569–607.

Payne, T., N. Anderson, and T. Smith. 1992. "Assessment Centres, Selection Systems and Cost-Effectiveness: An Evaluative Case Study." *Personnel Review* 21: 48–56.

Reilly, R.R., and G.T. Chao. 1982. "Validity and Fairness of some Alternative Employee Selection Procedures." *Personnel Psychology* 35: 1–62.

Rothstein, H.R., F.L. Schmidt, F.W. Erwin, W.A. Owens, and C.P. Sparks. 1990. "Biographical Data in Employment Selection: Can Validities be Made Generalizable?" *Journal of Applied Psychology* 75: 175–84.

Rowe, P.M., M.C. Williams, and A.L. Day. 1994. "Selection Procedures in North America." *International Journal of Selection and Assessment* 2: 74–79.

Rynes, S.L. 1993. "Who's Selecting Whom? Effects of Selection Practices on Applicant Attitudes and Behaviour." In N. Schmitt, W.C. Borman et al., eds. *Personnel Selection in Organizations* San Francisco, CA: Jossey-Bass, 240–74.

Rynes, S.L., and H.E. Miller. 1983. "Recruiter and Job Influences on Candidates for Employment." *Journal of Applied Psychology* 68: 147–54.

Saks, A.M., J.D.Leck., and D.M. Saunders. 1995. "Effects of Application Blanks and Employment Equity on Applicant Reactions and Job Intentions." *Journal of Organizational Behavior* 16: 415–30.

Schwab D.P., and G.G. Henneman III. 1969. "Relationship between Interview Structure and Interviewer Reliability in an Employment Situation." *Journal of Applied Psychology* 53: 214–17.

Smither, J.W., R.R. Reilly, R.E. Millsap, K. Pearlman, and R.W. Stoffey. 1993. "Applicant Reactions to Selection Procedures." *Personnel Psychology* 46: 49–76.

Telenson, P.A., R.A. Alexander, and G.V. Barrett. 1983. "Scoring the Biographical Information Blank: A Comparison of Three Weighting Techniques." *Applied Psychological Measurement* 7: 73–80.

Webster, E.C. 1982. "The Employment Interview: A Social Judgment Process." Schomberg, Ont: S.I.P. Publications.

Wein, J. 1994. "Rifling Through Résumés." *Incentive* 168: 96–97.

Wiesner, W.H., and S.R. Cronshaw. 1988. "A Meta-Analytic Investigation of the Impact of Interview Format and Degree of Structure on the Validity of the Employment Interview." *Journal of Occupational Psychology* 61: 275–90.

8

Selection II:
Testing

♦ ♦ ♦
CHAPTER GOALS

This chapter introduces the use of testing in personnel selection. It presents background material on the technical, ethical, and legal requirements governing the use of employment tests along with a description of different testing procedures. After reading this chapter you should

- have a good understanding of psychological tests and their use in selection;

- be familiar with the professional and legal standards that govern the use of employment tests;

- know the advantages and disadvantages of using some of the more popular selection testing procedures, including personality and ability testing;

- be aware of controversial testing methods related to honesty or integrity, physical fitness, and drug use;

- appreciate the potential of work samples, simulations, and assessment centres as selection procedures; and

- understand how both test validity and test utility can be used to evaluate testing effectiveness.

♦ ♦ ♦
APPLICANT TESTING

PSYCHOLOGICAL TESTING

We have all been tested at one time or another. You will most likely be tested on your knowledge of this chapter's contents. You may be given a set of questions related to material in this chapter; based on your answers to those questions, your instructor will assign a number to you, which reflects your knowledge and understanding of the chapter material. In preparing for the test you probably read the material, attended lectures, took notes, discussed the material with classmates, went to the library to read material on reserve, and questioned your instructor on it. All these activities or behaviours should lead to increased understanding of the material. The test you are given is simply a means of obtaining a sample of these behaviours under controlled conditions. A psychological test is nothing more than a standardized procedure used to obtain a sample of a person's behaviour and to describe that behaviour with the aid of some measurement scale (Cronbach, 1990). Psychological testing is one of the oldest and most common methods used to quantify how individuals differ with respect to some variable of interest.

USE OF TESTS Psychological tests are used for many different purposes in a variety of settings. In schools, psychological tests may be used to determine levels of academic ability, achievement, or interest. In counselling centres, tests may be used to assist in identifying different strengths and weaknesses of clients and may involve assessment of personality, attitudes, or values. In clinical settings, psychological tests are used to assist a psychologist in making a diagnosis of the suspected difficulty or problem being experienced by the client. In hospital settings, neuropsychological tests are often used to assess different types of brain damage. In business or organizational settings, psychological tests are used to hire people, to classify those selected into the most appropriate positions, to assist in promotion of people, and to identify needs for training. The focus of this chapter will be limited, primarily, to the use of psychological tests in organizational settings as part of the selection process.

EMPLOYMENT TESTING In most hiring situations, there are more applicants than there are positions to be filled. The employer's goal is to select those candidates who best possess the knowledge, skills, abilities, or other attributes (KSAOs) that lead to successful job performance. As we discussed in previous chapters, these KSAOs must be related to job performance criteria that have been identified through a job analysis. The employer believes that applicants differ with respect to essential KSAOs and wishes to measure these individual differences to meet the goal of hiring the best qualified people for the job. The central requirement for any selection tests or assessment procedures is that they "accurately assess the individual's performance or capacity to perform the essential components of the job in question safely, efficiently, and reliably" (Canadian Human Rights Commission [CHRC], 1985, 11). In Chapter 3 we discussed the process of measurement and quantification of such individual characteristics. If "knowing how to get things done" is important for job success, the employer must be able to measure know-how in a reliable and valid manner that meets the requirements imposed by relevant labour legislation and wins approval from external agencies, such as the CHRC, which may have jurisdiction over hiring decisions.

TESTING STANDARDS

Occasionally in newspapers or magazines you may come across an article that asks you to test or rate your career interests, personality, compatibility with a partner, or some other topic. You may be asked to complete a series of multiple-choice questions and, based upon your score, you are placed into a particular category that defines your personality type or interest. Rarely, if ever, do these popular tests have any value. These tests are usually created for the purpose of the article, mostly entertainment. The development of a reliable and valid test takes considerable time and effort, which can be undermined by the widespread publication of the test in the popular media. The only tests with any value in terms of hiring decisions are those that meet accepted professional standards for their development and use.

In Chapter 3, we established some fundamental measurement principles. We expect tests to assign numbers to the construct that is being assessed in a *reliable* and *valid* manner. We also expect tests to be *fair and unbiased*, and to have *utility*. Psychological tests vary in the degree to which they meet these four standards. These technical or psychometric properties of a psychological test should be established before a test is used as a decision-making tool. The development and construction of a psychological test is a major undertaking, which is governed by several sets of technical guidelines.

PROFESSIONAL GUIDELINES The Canadian Psychological Association (1987) has published *Guidelines for Educational and Psychological Testing*. This document presents the professional consensus on the appropriate procedures for constructing and evaluating tests, for using and administering tests, and for interpreting test results. The *Guidelines* apply to all tests, including those used for personnel selection. There are also supplementary guidelines, which apply specifically to the use of tests as part of the personnel selection process; the most influential of these is the *Principles for the*

Validation and Use of Personnel Selection Procedures, published by the Society for Industrial and Organizational Psychology (1987). Another document, the *Uniform Guidelines on Employee Selection Procedures* (1978), was developed by the U.S. Equal Employment Opportunity Commission, the U.S. Department of Justice, and the U.S. Department of Labor for use in evaluating personnel selection programs that fall under the regulations of the U.S. federal government. The *Uniform Guidelines* have played a prominent role in court challenges that have alleged discrimination in the selection process. While the *Uniform Guidelines* have no legal standing in Canada, they are often cited as representing professional consensus and used by different provincial and federal agencies in assessing selection programs.

CODE OF ETHICS In addition to these documents, which regulate the technical aspects of test development and use, there are also ethical standards, which regulate the behaviour of psychologists using the tests. The *Canadian Code of Ethics for Psychologists* (Canadian Psychological Association, 1986) specifies four principles on which ethical behaviour is based

1. Respect for dignity of persons
2. Responsible caring
3. Integrity in relationships
4. Responsibility to society

The ethical standards related to each of these principles apply to all testing carried out by psychologists. These ethical standards cover such issues as confidentiality of test results, informed consent, and the competence of those administering and interpreting the test results. The foremost concern is to protect the welfare and dignity of those being tested. A consumer or client may bring any concerns over a psychologist's use of tests, including selection tests, to appropriate regulatory bodies.

WHO CAN TEST? The availability of standardized tests and computerized scoring and interpretation systems often tempts unqualified people to administer tests and to interpret results from them. Proficiency in psychological testing requires a considerable degree of training and experience. Reputable test publishers require purchasers to establish their expertise in using a test before purchasing it. These safeguards help protect the public against misuse of tests and information collected through testing (Simner, 1994).

CAUTIONS

Well-designed tests provide information on different aspects of an individual, including their personality, thinking or reasoning ability, and motivation, among many others. The standards described in the preceding section were developed by professional associations to protect the welfare and rights of individuals who are being tested. These rights, which must be respected, include the following:

◆ *Informed Consent*—Job applicants must be told why they are being tested; they must be informed in clear language that the test results may be provided to the prospective employer and that those results may be used in making employment decisions. Applicants should also be given general information about the types of tests that they will be asked to take.

◆ *Access to Test Results*—Job applicants are entitled to receive feedback on their test performance and on any decisions that are based on those tests. This information must be provided in non-technical language that can be understood by the job applicants. Such feedback must be put into a proper context by explaining the purpose of the test and their results on the test relative to other applicants. Care must be taken in providing this feedback as this information may have negative implications about the applicant's ability, knowledge, or personality. Care must also be taken to avoid use of labels, or terms, that may stigmatize the applicant. Providing feedback can be a very stressful situation and is best done by a qualified psychologist or another human resources specialist who is sensitive to the possible consequences of the feedback.

◆ *Privacy and Confidentiality*—Job applicants reveal information about themselves during the job selection process. There is no justification for obtaining any information that is not job-related. Applicants have a right to privacy; information that is provided by job applicants must be held in confidence. As part of gathering information, whether through application forms, interviews, or tests, job applicants must be informed about how that information will be used and who will have access to it *before* they provide the information. The limits of confidentiality must be explained to the job applicants. Care must be taken to safeguard the use of any information collected during the selection process. Failure to respect the applicant's privacy may leave the employing organization open to legal action. Workplace privacy is a significant and growing issue. Ontario's Privacy Commissioner recently recommended that the province establish provincial standards for employee testing; municipal and provincial employees in Ontario have a right of access to and protection of their own personal information, including that obtained through employment testing, under existing freedom of information and protection of privacy legislation (Ontario Commissioner's Report, 1994).

◆ *Language and Culture*—Job applicants have the right to be tested in a language in which they are fluent. In Chapter 3 we discussed how bias can influence measurements. Bias refers to systematic measurement errors that are related to aspects of group membership. Language and culture are two important ways of identifying groups. Canada is both bilingual and multicultural. There is no guarantee that a test developed in one language or in one culture will produce meaningful results when administered to people from different linguistic or cultural backgrounds. It is not sufficient simply to translate a test into another language. The reliability and validity of the test in the new language must be established. Similarly, administering the test to applicants who do not have good command of the language in which the test is written will also lead to test bias; the test results will be confounded with their language comprehension. Both the Public Service Commission of Canada's Personnel Psychology Centre and the Canadian Forces rely on various employment tests in making hiring decisions. Both of these organizations undertake extensive research to ensure that equivalent forms of all testing materials are available in both English and French.

OTHER CONSIDERATIONS: DISABILITY Chapter 2 drew attention to the legal and human rights concerns that apply to selection procedures. A disabling condition cannot be used to screen out applicants unless it can be demonstrated that the ability in question is a *bona fide* occupational requirement. Employers are expected to make reasonable accommodation to meet the needs of employees or applicants with disabilities who meet job requirements. In Canada, the employment of people with disabilities falls under either provincial or federal human rights legislation. In the United States, this situation is covered by the *Americans with Disabilities Act of 1990*. Disabling conditions must be considered as part of selection testing. For example, some paper and pencil ability tests have time limits; a person with limited mobility of their hands or arms might have difficulty completing the test in the allowed time, leading to an ability score that falls below the level set for the job. It is impossible to state whether the low score is a true reflection of the tested ability rather than a test of the disability. In this case, provision should be made for either using a test that is not time-based or allowing for verbal responses, which are recorded by machine. The guiding principle should be that the test is given to the applicant in a way that accommodates the disability even at the expense of changing standardized testing procedures.

◆ ◆ ◆

TESTING METHODS USED IN SELECTION

The first large-scale use of tests to select or classify Canadian employees occurred during World War II. Tests were constructed to screen people for military service and for entry into different training programs (e.g., airplane pilots, Prociuk, 1988). Over the years, thousands of Canadians have been tested for a variety of purposes. Unfortunately, many people remain skeptical about the benefits of testing. People often become upset over testing, particularly that done in the schools, and the decisions that are based on test results. These concerns also arise in the use of employment tests. Although it is quite easy to demonstrate the financial benefits that can be gained through the use of employment tests, only about one-third of Canadian companies use tests to select employees (Cronshaw, 1986).

RELIABILITY AND VALIDITY ISSUES The technical guidelines and professional standards described above often act to deter companies from adopting employment tests. Many companies continue to rely on the application form, résumés, letters of reference, and interviews to select employees. Organizations may falsely believe that these selection procedures are exempt from requirements to demonstrate reliability, validity, and fairness. Human resource managers often justify not using employment tests by noting that the reliability of a test may be affected by items that may be misunderstood, by lack of uniform testing conditions, by variation in instructions, by lack of rapport between a candidate and the test administrator, and improper test items. But, how does this differ from a typical selection interview where interview questions are misunderstood, where there is lack of uniformity and standardization in interviews, where there is variation in the introduction given to candidates at the start of the interview, where there is often a lack of rapport between the candidate and the interviewer, and where improper questions are often asked?

USING TESTS DEVELOPED IN THE UNITED STATES There is no need for any organization to develop its own employment tests; unless the KSAOs required for the job are so unique, one or more of the over 1000 commercially available tests are likely to be suitable for use in most situations. Usually these tests have well-known psychometric properties that are extensively documented in technical manuals. However, most of these tests have been developed and validated on workers in the United States, thereby raising the question of whether expensive validity studies must be done in Canada before those tests can be properly used to select Canadian workers. Fortunately, validity generalization procedures like those described in Chapter 3 have established that test validities from U. S. workers generalize across the border, lessening the need to re-establish their validity in Canada (Getkake, Hausdorf, and Cronshaw, 1992). Tests that are valid for an occupational category in the United States should also be valid for the same occupational category in Canada. Just as with any other selection device, the information obtained through tests should not be used in isolation. It should be compared with information obtained from other sources. Information obtained from several valid tests and measures, which are measuring the same construct, should converge.

CHOOSING A TEST Box 8.1 presents some points that should be considered in selecting commercially available employment tests. These points reflect the technical considerations discussed above. Anyone who has the responsibility for choosing employment tests should be knowledgeable about the various standards and technical documents related to the use of tests. The remainder of this chapter presents an introduction to the wide variety of employment tests used in Canadian organizations. Box 8.2 lists some of the more common tests used to select employees.

PERSONALITY TESTS

In making hiring decisions, it's not unusual to hear a manager argue in support of one applicant over another because, "She is the right type of

BOX 8.1 POINTS TO CONSIDER IN SELECTING A TEST

1. Determine the knowledge, skills, abilities, or other qualities that have been related to job success through a job analysis.

2. Consult an information resource on testing to identify tests that are relevant to your job needs. Obtain information from several sources including test publishers or developers and human resource consultants knowledgeable about testing.

3. Obtain information on several tests related to what you want to measure. Read through the materials provided by the test developers. Reject out of hand any test for which the publisher or developer presents unclear or incomplete information.

4. Read the technical documentation to become familiar with how and when the test was developed and used. Does the technical documentation provide information on the test's reliability and validity? Does it address the issue of test fairness? Does it include normative data based on sex, age, ethnicity that is comparable to your intended test takers? Does it include references for independent investigations of the test's psychometric properties? Eliminate from consideration any tests whose documentation does not allow you to answer yes to these questions.

5. Read the independent evaluations of the tests that you are considering adopting. Does the independent evidence support the claims of the test developers? Is the test valid and reliable? Eliminate those tests that are not supported by this evidence.

6. Examine a specimen set from each of the remaining tests. Most publishers will sell a package that includes a copy of the test, instructions, test manual, answer sheets, and sample score report at a reasonable cost. Is the test format and reading level appropriate for the intended test takers? Is the test available in languages other than English? Can the test accommodate test takers with special needs? Is the content of the test appropriate for the intended test takers? Eliminate those tests that you do not feel are appropriate.

7. Determine the skill level needed to purchase the test, to administer the test and to interpret test scores correctly. Do you have the appropriate level of expertise? Does someone else in your organization meet the test's requirements? If not, can you contract out for the services of a qualified psychologist or human resource professional who does?

8. Select and use only those tests that are psychometrically sound, that meet the needs of your intended test takers, and that you have the necessary skills to administer, score, and interpret correctly.

BOX 8.2 EXAMPLES OF PSYCHOLOGICAL TESTS USED TO SELECT EMPLOYEES

Personality Tests

California Psychological Inventory

Guilford-Zimmerman Temperament
  Survey

Hogan Personality Inventory

Myer-Briggs Type Indicator

NEO-PI

Sixteen Personality Factor Questionnaire
  (16PF)

Honesty/Integrity Tests

Hogan Personality Inventory

PDI Employment Inventory

Reid Report

Stanton Survey

Vocational Interest Inventories

Jackson Vocational Interest Survey

Kuder Preference and Interest Scales

Occupational Preference Inventory

Self-Directed Search

Strong Interest Inventory

Vocational Preference Inventory

Cognitive Ability Tests

Otis-Lennon Mental Ability Test

Stanford-Binet Intelligence Scale

Watson-Glaser Critical Thinking Appraisal

Wechsler Adult Intelligence Scale (WAIS)

Wonderlic Personnel Test

Aptitude Tests

Comprehensive Ability Battery (CAB)

Differential Aptitude Tests (DAT)

General Aptitude Test Battery (GATB)

Minnesota Clerical Tests

Psychomotor Tests

O'Connor Tweezer Dexterity Test

Purdue Peg Board Test

Stromberg Dexterity Test

**Physical Ability and
Sensory/Perceptual Ability Tests**

Dynamometer Grip Strength Test

Ishihara Test for Colour Blindness

Visual Skills Test

aggressive person we're looking for to sell cars," or "He is a very pleasant, outgoing person, the type that will do well as a receptionist." Generally, these sorts of comments are made following a job interview when the manager has formed an impression of what the applicant is like as a person. The manager is stating a personal opinion that the individual's characteristics or traits qualify the applicant for the job. This is the belief that some aspects of what we call personality are related to job success. Although these arguments may be very appealing, more often than not, they fail for two reasons. First, the manager may not have demonstrated through a job analysis that such personality traits or characteristics are job-related. Second, the manager's assessment of the applicant's personality may not be objective, reliable, or valid.

DEFINING PERSONALITY One of the major difficulties in using personality for selection purposes is the lack of agreement about its definition. Personality is generally defined as a set of characteristics or properties that influence, or help to explain, an individual's behaviour (Hall and Lindzey. 1970). Different personality theories may propose different ways in which people vary (e.g., aggressiveness, pleasantness). These variables are called personality *traits*. Personality traits are thought to be stable over time and measurable. Thus, if two people differ in aggressiveness or pleasantness, appropriate measurements can be developed to reflect those differences. Traits can be distinguished from personality *states*, which are more transitory or temporary characteristics. One applicant may be very nervous and anxious during a job interview but calm otherwise; another applicant may always be anxious. In the first case, anxiety is a state, but in the second it is a trait. Sets, collections, or patterns of traits and states can be used to define a personality *type*. Personality tests attempt to measure traits and/or states and from these measures derive some indication of the type of individual being assessed. A person whose behaviour reflects traits of extreme competitiveness, achievement, aggressiveness, haste, impatience, restlessness, hyperalertness, explosiveness of speech, tenseness of facial musculature, and feelings of being under the pressure of time and under the challenge of responsibility might be said to have a Type A personality (Jenkins, Zyzanski, and Rosenman, 1979).

Self-report inventories are the most frequently used technique in assessing personality for selection purposes. A self-report inventory consists of sets of short, written statements related to various traits. The individual answers by agreeing or disagreeing with each item using a rating scale much like those presented in Chapter 5. Some items included in the inventory might relate to aggressiveness, competitiveness, need for achievement, or whatever trait is of interest. Different self-report inventories may measure different traits. A score for each trait is determined by combining the ratings for those items that belong to a specific trait. These scores can be compared to normative data that already exist for the inventory. Patterns of scores across the measured traits are often used to derive statements about personality types.

Self-report inventories are also called *objective techniques* because of their scoring methodology. Box 8.3 presents some items* that could be used to assess Time Urgency, a trait related to Type A personality, as part of an objective, self-report inventory.

BOX 8.3 TIME URGENCY

Instructions: For each statement choose the response that best reflects your behaviour, feelings, or attitudes: 1. Strongly Disagree; 2. Disagree; 3. Neither Agree nor Disagree; 4. Agree; 5. Strongly Agree.

I constantly interrupt other people when they are speaking.

I always do several tasks at the same time.

I get very frustrated when people do not get to the point.

I hate standing in lines.

People waste too much time on routine daily chores.

PERSONALITY AS A PREDICTOR OF JOB PERFORMANCE Overall, personality tests have not been overly successful as predictors of job performance. Guion (1965; Guion and Gottier, 1965) reviewed the technical and ethical problems associated with personality testing and concluded that there was insufficient evidence to justify the use of personality tests in most situations as a basis for making employment decisions about people. Guion was very concerned that personality testing invaded the privacy of job applicants and asked them to provide much information about themselves that was not clearly job-related. With few exceptions, this view prevailed until the early 1990s when both meta-analytic and empirical studies suggested that personality testing could predict certain aspects of job performance (Barrick and Mount, 1991; Hough, Eaton, Dunnette, Kamp, and McCloy, 1990; McHenry, Hough, Toquam, Hanson, and Ashworth, 1990; Tett, Jackson, and Rothstein, 1991).

THE BIG FIVE These more recent studies have been heavily influenced by the argument that the many hundreds of different personality traits could be

---

*These items, and other examples presented throughout the chapter, have been created for illustrative purposes; they are not actual inventory items.

summarized under five categories or dimensions (Digman, 1990). These "Big Five" dimensions are Extroversion, Conscientiousness, Emotional Stability, Agreeableness, and Openness to Experience. Box 8.4 presents definitions for

BOX 8.4 THE BIG FIVE PERSONALITY DIMENSIONS

Conscientiousness is a general tendency to work hard and to be loyal; to give a full day's work each day and to do one's best to perform well—following instructions and accepting organization goals, policies and rules—even with little or no supervision. It is an approach to work characterized by industriousness, purposiveness, persistence, consistency, and punctuality. It also includes paying attention to every aspect of a task, including attention to details that might be easily overlooked.

Emotional stability reflects a calm, relaxed approach to situations, events, or people. It includes an emotionally controlled response to changes in the work environment or to emergency situations. It is an emotionally mature approach to potentially stressful situations reflecting tolerance, optimism, and a general sense of challenge rather than of crisis, and maturity in considering advice or criticism from others.

Openness to experience reflects a preference for situations in which one can develop new things, ideas, or solutions to problems through creativity or insight. It includes trying new or innovative approaches to tasks or situations. It is a preference for original or unique ways of

thinking about things. It is concerned with newness, originality, or creativity.

Agreeableness reflects a desire or willingness to work with others to achieve a common purpose and to be part of a group. It also includes a tendency to be a caring person in relation to other people, to be considerate, understanding, and to have genuine concern for the well-being of others; it is an awareness of the feelings and interests of others. It is the ability to work co-operatively and collaboratively either as part of a group or in the service of others. It is involved in assisting clients and customers as a regular function of one's work, or assisting co-workers to meet deadlines or to achieve work goals.

Extroversion reflects a tendency to be outgoing in association with other people, to seek and enjoy the company of others; to be gregarious, to interact easily and well with others, to be likable and warmly approachable. It involves enjoying the company of others and a concern for their interests; it implies sociableness whether work is involved or not. Extroversion refers to being comfortable and friendly in virtually any sort of situation involving others.

each of these dimensions and examples of the traits associated with them. Barrick and Mount found that each of the Big Five dimensions could predict at least one aspect of job performance with some degree of accuracy, while Conscientiousness predicted several different aspects of job or training performance at moderate levels. Recall that Campbell (1990) believed that Demonstrating Effort and Maintaining Personal Discipline were major performance components of every job (see Chapter 5). It is quite easy to see, from the definition given in Box 8.4, how Conscientiousness could predict each of these two job dimensions. A case can also be made for other Big Five personality dimensions predicting other job performance components such as Leadership and Facilitating Team Performance and the major contextual factors identified by Borman and Motowidlo (1993). Not everyone agrees on the Big Five method of categorizing the vast array of personality traits; some argue the need for a few dimensions in addition to the Big Five (e.g., Hough, et al., 1990). The important point is not whether there are five, six, or more dimensions, but that Big Five type personality models reduce the problem of terminological confusion and make personality testing more useful in industrial and organizational contexts, particularly personnel selection (Hogan, Hogan, and Roberts, 1996).

POLYGRAPH AND HONESTY TESTING As discussed in Chapter 5, contextual performance involves activities that have not been identified through job analysis as belonging to a worker's job; nevertheless, those activities are still considered to be important for organizational effectiveness. In many cases, organizational effectiveness may be limited by employee theft or misuse of the organization's property or proprietary information, or other forms of dishonesty. The costs associated with such counterproductive behaviour have been estimated at hundreds of millions of dollars annually in Canada and Great Britain and as high as $50 billion in the United States (Temple, 1992). In response to this problem, many organizations wish to select people who are not only capable of doing the job but are also honest, reliable, or of high integrity. Honesty or integrity are personality traits and can be measured. Over the years, a number of techniques have been used in an attempt to identify these traits.

Polygraph testing, otherwise known as a lie detector, was once used extensively to check on employee honesty and to screen job applicants. The polygraph test is based on the assumption that measurable, physiological changes occur when people lie, and that no matter how hard they try to control their responses, changes take place in heart rate, breathing, blood pressure, and so on. Although lie detectors enjoy a reputation among the public for actually being able to detect lies, the empirical evidence shows that there are many unresolved issues about their reliability and validity. Polygraph results are mostly related to the skill of the polygraph operator, many of whom are poorly trained. Relatively few jurisdictions in either the United States or Canada have any licensing requirements for polygraph operators. Polygraph results are not accepted as evidence in any North American courtroom. Many legislatures, including the U.S. Congress, have also banned the use of polygraph testing as part of most pre-employment screening procedures (Jones, 1991). In Canada, Ontario has taken the lead in prohibiting the use of mandatory polygraph tests under its *Employment Standards Act*.

The restrictions placed on polygraph testing have led to an increase in the use of paper and pencil *Honesty* or *Integrity tests*. These tests are personality based measures (Sackett, Burris, and Callahan, 1989). Some types of these tests resemble personality inventories and may be included as part of a general personality inventory; for example, the *Hogan Personality Inventory* (Hogan and Hogan, 1989) contains scales that have been used to assess honesty. Other types of honesty tests ask very direct questions about the individual's attitude toward theft and other forms of dishonesty, as well as the person's prior involvement in theft or other illegal activities. Honesty tests are an increasingly popular method of screening out potentially dishonest employees. They can easily be incorporated into a selection system; they are inexpensive and typically inoffensive to most applicants. There are no legislative restrictions on their use; however, they must meet the same professional and scientific standards as any other type of employment test.

Dishonest applicants may be discouraged from applying for jobs when they know they will be tested for honesty. In the case of white-collar crime, personality-based integrity tests may be the best measure of psychological differences between white-collar criminals and honest employees (Collins and Schmidt, 1993). The limited data available on honesty or integrity tests suggests that they can be very effective. After a chain of home improvement centres in Great Britain started using an honesty test as part of its selection procedures, inventory shrinkage dropped from 4 percent to less than

2.5 percent (Temple, 1992). Nonetheless, honesty tests do have major disadvantages. Test scores from honesty tests, like those from any other personality measure, are open to misinterpretation and may constitute an invasion of the applicant's privacy; additionally, the validity of many honesty tests has yet to be established (Sackett, Burris, and Callahan, 1989). Existing data also suggest that honesty tests may have a high number of false positives; that is, they may tend to screen out a large number of applicants who are truly honest but do poorly on the test.

GRAPHOLOGY There are several indirect methods for assessing personality. These methods require an individual to respond in some fashion to an ambiguous stimulus such as a drawing or picture. The Ink Blot, or Rorschach Test, is an example of a *projective technique* that has been popularized through movies and television. The premise of such tests is that individuals project something about their personality into their responses. In the case of handwriting, the assumption is that the unique characteristics of the handwriting indirectly reflect something about personality traits, which a graphologist or graphoanalyst can interpret. While several projective techniques are useful diagnostic tools in clinical psychology; graphology does not fall into this category. There is little, if any, scientific evidence that supports the use of graphology in personnel selection. Whatever success graphologists appear to have had seems to be based on inferences drawn from information contained in the content of the writing and not in the handwriting itself (Ben-Shukhar, Bar-Hillel, Bilu, Ben-Abba, and Flug, 1986).

Nonetheless, the lack of scientific support has not deterred companies from using graphology to select employees, particularly at the executive level. Graphology is most popular in Western Europe, with reports estimating its use as a selection tool in over 50 percent of companies in France and Germany. Despite its apparent widespread use, potential French job applicants ranked it ninth out of ten selection procedures in terms of effectiveness and fairness; the only procedure to receive lower ratings was honesty testing (Steiner and Gilliland, 1996). Although there are no firm figures, a few Canadian companies and consultants are beginning to use graphology either by itself or in conjunction with other selection devices, although they are often ashamed to admit it, partly because of human rights issues that might be involved ("A New Slant," 1994). The shame is understandable; any company making hiring or placement decisions with the aid of graphology should be aware that there is no scientific evidence to support its use. They should also consider the negative impact that such a procedure may have on potential applicants.

SUMMARY Perhaps the best that can be said about the role of personality testing in selection now is that the jury is still out. With a better understanding of both the job performance domain and the nature of personality, it should not be surprising that some aspects of personality will predict some aspects of job performance. However, the relationships are unlikely to be so straightforward or simple as to allow a manager to use a gut feeling about the type of applicant that is needed for a job. The personality measure must be shown to be a valid predictor of job performance and must meet all the requirements of any selection instrument. Additionally, the concerns about privacy still remain and may prove troublesome to the point that they limit the use of personality tests. It is essential that any personality testing be carried out by trained professionals under relevant legal and ethical standards.

ABILITY AND APTITUDE TESTS

As we've seen in earlier chapters, job-related knowledge, skills, abilities, and other attributes (KSAOs) play an important role in successful job performance. Applicants for a position of electronic repair technician might be expected to have a high degree of finger dexterity (to perform repairs on circuit boards), colour vision (to tell the difference between different wires), and a potential for acquiring knowledge related to electronics (to achieve an understanding of basic circuit theory). Selection programs seek to predict the degree to which job applicants possess the KSAOs related to the job. Many different tests have been developed to measure specific human abilities and aptitudes. In the case of hiring electronic repair technicians, we would seek to employ those applicants with the highest levels of finger dexterity and colour vision, and the most aptitude for learning electronics.

ABILITY TESTS Abilities are attributes that an applicant brings to the employment situation. Abilities are general traits or characteristics on which people differ. It is of no importance whether an ability has been acquired through experience or inheritance. *Abilities* are simply general traits that a person brings with them to the new work situation. Finger dexterity is the ability to carry out quick, coordinated movements of fingers on one or both hands and to grasp, place, or move very small objects (Fleishman and Reilly, 1992). An ability can underlie performance on a number of specific tasks; finger dexterity might be required to operate a computer keyboard and to assemble electronic components. One keyboard operator may have taken several months of practice to develop the finger dexterity needed to type 100 words per minute; another may have come by that ability naturally. Both have the same ability, regardless of how it was acquired. *Skill*, on the other hand, refers to the degree of proficiency on a given task, based on both ability and practices that have developed while performing the task. Two keyboard operators may have the same level of finger dexterity; however, one may have learned to type with hands raised at an inappropriate angle in relation to the keyboard. As a result, the two have different skill levels, or proficiencies, in using a keyboard despite having the same ability. Similarly, a keyboard operator and an electronics assembler might have the same level of finger dexterity but the keyboard operator might be more skilled at word processing than the assembler is at wiring circuit boards. *Aptitude* is simply a prediction, based on a measure of ability or skill, that an individual will do well in future performance. Based on a test of finger dexterity, a human resources manager might predict that a job applicant has an aptitude for operating a keyboard, or for assembling electronic components. Over the years, Fleishman and his associates (e.g., Fleishman and Quaintance, 1984) have identified 52 distinct human abilities, which can be grouped into four broad categories: Cognitive, Psychomotor, Physical, and Sensory/Perceptual abilities. Over time, many psychometrically sound tests have been developed to assess these different abilities.

COGNITIVE ABILITY TESTS Cognitive abilities are related to intelligence or intellectual ability. These abilities include verbal and numerical ability, reasoning, memory, problem solving, and processing information, among others. The first wide-scale, systematic use of cognitive ability testing took place during World War I when a group of industrial psychologists developed the U.S. Army Alpha test. This was a paper and pencil test, which could be efficiently administered to groups of army recruits to determine how those recruits could best be employed. The Army Alpha test sought to measure intellectual or basic mental abilities that were thought to be essential to performing military duties. Today, an extensive array of paper and pencil tests are available to measure specific cognitive abilities. Most likely you have taken one or more of these during your student career. Box 8.5 presents examples of types of items that could be used to assess verbal and quantitative cognitive abilities.

More recently, there has been a move away from assessing many individual, specific abilities to a more general cognitive ability. General cognitive ability is thought to be the primary ability among those that make up

---

BOX 8.5 EXAMPLES OF ITEMS USED TO MEASURE COGNITIVE ABILITIES

Verbal Reasoning

Dog is to house as bird is to _____.
    a) song   b) nest   c) bath   d) people

Which one of the following items does not belong in the group?
    a) magazine   b) newspaper   c) book   d) radio

The word "comfort" means the same as which of the following?
    a) relief   b) support   c) relaxation   d) ease

Which word best completes the following sentence?

We will start the demonstration _____ the guests have arrived.
    a) when   b) unless   c) but   d) until

Quantitative Reasoning

Which number, when multiplied by 5, is equal to 2/5 of 100?
    a) 2   b) 4   c) 6   d) 8

Which of the following is correct?
    a) $6 + 4 = 15$ b) $5 + 21 = 25$ c) $3 - 9 = -6$ d) $8 - 4 = -4$

If fabric costs $3.00 per square metre, what will it cost to buy a piece that is 9 metres long and 12 metres wide?
    a) $36.00   b) $256.00   c) $324.00   d) $515.00

What is the next number in the series 3, 6, 12, _ ?
    a) 15   b) 18   c) 21   d) 24

---

intellectual capacity. General cognitive ability is believed to promote effective learning, efficient and accurate problem solving, and clear communications. General cognitive ability can be thought of as a manager of other, specific cognitive abilities, similar to a computer's operating system managing other software programs. General cognitive ability has been related to successful job performance in many occupations. It is related to how easily people may be trained to perform job tasks, how well they can adjust and solve problems on the job, and how well satisfied they are likely to be with the demands of the job (Gottfredson, 1986). Nonetheless, a great deal of empirical support still exists for the use of specific cognitive ability tests, rather than a measure of general cognitive ability.

Most likely, a test of general cognitive ability could provide a quick and efficient basis for selecting applicants for more extensive, and costly, testing. The National Football League (NFL) has given the Wonderlic Personnel Test, a test of general cognitive ability, to potential recruits since 1968. According to Charles Wonderlic, president of the testing company, "The test measures a person's ability to learn, solve problems and adapt to new situations" (Bell, 1996, 3C). Wonderlic test scores, along with information on the candidate's physical prowess and ability, are available to each NFL team for use in drafting players (i.e., making selection decisions.) The Wonderlic has a maximum possible score of 50. The average score for factory workers is 17, for lawyers, 30, and for NFL prospects, 21, which is the overall average for the test. A low score on the test does not eliminate an NFL prospect but red flags him as someone who may not be able to meet the demands of a game that is becoming ever more cognitively complex. The Wonderlic is used as part of a battery of tests to develop a psychological profile on each candidate.

The Canadian Forces use cognitive testing in a similar fashion. Potential recruits into the Forces complete a test of general cognitive ability as part of the application process. Applicants who meet the minimum required score, along with other criteria, are given a conditional offer of acceptance. Following this offer, they complete a medical examination and the more extensive Canadian Forces Classification Battery (CFCB). This latter test assesses several different types of cognitive abilities and knowledge related to performance of specific military job assignments within the Canadian Forces. The CFCB takes over two hours to administer, a considerable investment for both the applicant and the organization.

MULTIPLE APTITUDE TEST BATTERIES The CFCB is an example of a Multiple Aptitude Test Battery. Such tests take several hours to complete and include subtests related to various aspects of cognitive ability or intellectual functioning; they may also include tests of non-cognitive abilities. The CFCB includes subtests of word knowledge, arithmetic knowledge, mechanical comprehension, electronic information, automotive information, science knowledge, and pattern analysis. Similarly, the U.S. military administers a test battery primarily based on cognitive abilities, the Armed Services Vocational Aptitude Battery (ASVAB), to over one million high school students each year as well as to all applicants. The ASVAB is very similar to the General Aptitude Test battery (GATB), which is used as part of the selection process for jobs throughout the U.S. federal government. A version of the GATB has been developed for use at Canada Employment Centres.

PRACTICAL INTELLIGENCE Sternberg and his associates (Sternberg, Wagner, Williams, and Horvath, 1995) distinguish practical intelligence from intellectual or academic ability and argue that while tests of cognitive ability predict intellectual performance, those tests are not as successful as they should be in predicting job success. To obtain that success, measures of cognitive ability need to be supplemented by measures of practical intelligence. The distinction between academic intelligence and practical intelligence is very similar to the difference between declarative knowledge and procedural knowledge described in Chapter 5. Procedural knowledge, or tacit knowledge, is related to knowing how to get things done without the help of others. Consider two department managers competing to increase their respective budgets. Both have the intellectual ability to put together a very rational proposal based on facts and figures to support their positions. The successful manager knows that the proposal alone will not succeed; the successful manager will know how to craft the report to demonstrate that the budget increase will also accomplish the goals of the decision-makers and will know whom to lobby in the organization for support of the proposal. The successful manager knows how to get things done. Currently, tests of practical knowledge are in the development stage. It remains to be seen if they will be the best method of measuring this construct. As we will see later, a behaviour-based, structured interview may provide a good measure of practical knowledge.

PSYCHOMOTOR ABILITY TESTS Psychomotor abilities involve controlled muscle movements that are necessary to complete a task. Examples of psychomotor abilities include finger dexterity, multi-limb coordination, reaction time, arm-hand steadiness, and manual dexterity. Many tasks, from simple to complex, require coordinated movements for their success. Psychomotor abilities are often overlooked in selecting people for jobs. Consider a drummer who must independently move all four limbs and exercise hand-wrist coordination, all in a controlled and coordinated fashion; imagine an orchestra whose drummer had an extensive knowledge of music theory but very little psychomotor ability. While a test of cognitive ability might predict ability to learn to read and understand music, it would not predict the level of motor coordination.

Tests of psychomotor ability tend to be very different from cognitive ability tests. They generally require the applicant to perform some standardized task on a testing apparatus that involves the psychomotor ability in question. Cognitive ability tests, on the other hand, are generally paper and pencil tests. For example, the Purdue Pegboard Test, which is a measure of finger dexterity, requires applicants to insert as many pegs as possible into a pegboard in a given time. This test has good predictive validity for many industrial jobs including watchmaking and electronics assembly. Dental schools also use tests of finger dexterity as part of their selection process. Although psychomotor tests can be quite successful in predicting performance, they are not as popular as cognitive tests. Psychomotor tests involve individual testing on a specialized piece of equipment, and require more time and expense to administer than paper and pencil cognitive tests.

PHYSICAL AND SENSORY/PERCEPTUAL ABILITY TESTS Physical abilities are those characteristics involved in the physical performance of a job or task. These abilities generally involve the use or application of muscle force over varying periods of time either alone or in conjunction with an ability to maintain balance or gross body coordination. Physical abilities include both static and dynamic strength, body flexibility, balance, and stamina. Sensory/perceptual abilities involve different aspects of vision and audition. These abilities include near and far vision, colour discrimination, sound localization, and speech recognition, among others. Although they focus on different sets of abilities, physical abilities and sensory/perceptual abilities are very similar in their relation to job performance and in how they are assessed.

The performance of many jobs or tasks may require the worker to possess one or more physical or sensory/perceptual ability. A firefighter may need the strength to carry a body out of a burning building; a pilot may need adequate near and far vision to fly a plane; a soldier may need the strength and stamina to carry 100 kg of equipment for a long period of time and still be ready for combat; a construction worker may need strength to lift material and balance to keep from falling off a roof. These ability tests predict performance in jobs that are physically demanding or require sensory or perceptual skills. People who possess greater amounts of these abilities perform better in jobs where such abilities play an important role (Campion, 1983). As part of its comprehensive selection procedures, the Royal Canadian Mounted Police tests all applicants for physical ability.

In addition to considering its impact on performance, Canadian employers such as the Liquor Control Board of Alberta have looked at the use of physical ability testing as one way of preventing injury to workers. Statistics from the National Institute of Occupational Safety and Health in the United States indicate that workers are three times more likely to be injured while performing jobs for which they have not demonstrated the required strength capabilities. Although medical and physical fitness exams (which are discussed later in this chapter) provide a measure of wellness, they do not give sufficient indication whether the candidate can perform the task requirements safely. Thus, physical ability testing can aid employers in selecting workers who are capable of performing strenuous tasks, with such selections leading to a reduction in accidents, injuries, and associated costs, as well as potential increases in productivity (Dunn and Dawson, 1994).

Tests of physical ability are quite varied but involve physical activity on the part of the applicant. Only a few physical ability tests require equipment. For example, a hand dynamometer is used to measure static strength. The hand dynamometer resembles the hand grips used in most gyms. The applicant squeezes the grips with full strength and the resultant force is measured by an attached scale. Pull-ups or push-ups are used to measure dynamic strength, sit-ups are used to assess body trunk strength, while 1500-metre runs, step tests, and treadmill tests are used to measure stamina and endurance. The performance of the applicants on these measures must be related to normative data, which compares the physical performance on the test to that obtained from actual job occupants. It is reasonable to expect applicants to run 1500 metres in under six minutes if 90 percent of all army recruits meet that performance standard; it would be unreasonable to select only those applicants for the army who could run the 1500 metres in under four minutes. The selection would be based on performance standards higher than those in force. Establishing cutoff scores on physical tests often leads to litigation, with unsuccessful applicants challenging the appropriateness of the scores that were chosen.

Tests of sensory/perceptual abilities generally require the use of a specialized test or equipment that has been designed to assess each specific sensory or perceptual ability. Almost everyone has had their vision examined through the use of a Snellen Chart, which contains letters of various sizes. This test assesses an individual's far vision ability. Similarly, many people have experienced a test of their hearing sensitivity where they are asked to recognize a series of tones, which are presented at different levels of intensity and pitches to either or both ears through a headset.

In some cases, *physical standards*, rather than physical ability or sensory/perceptual ability tests, are used for selection purposes. A police department may require all applicants to be within certain height and weight requirements and to have uncorrected 20/20 vision. The physical standards are being used as a substitute for actual physical testing. It is assumed that people who fall within the specified range should have the physical abilities required for successful job performance. It is often very difficult to justify that the physical standards in use meet legitimate job requirements. Indeed, many physical standards were set in the past to exclude members of certain groups, particularly women. When physical standards are set in such an arbitrary fashion, they are open to challenge before human rights tribunals with the employer subject to severe penalties. It is reasonable to set physical requirements for jobs as long as those standards can be shown to be job-related and non-discriminatory. That is, the physical requirements for the job must have been established through an acceptable job analysis procedure.

PHYSICAL FITNESS AND MEDICAL EXAMINATIONS

Many employers routinely administer physical fitness tests as part of the hiring process. The intent of these physical fitness tests is not to identify job-related physical abilities, but rather to screen out unhealthy or unfit employees who may pose a liability to the employer. The employer is concerned that placing physically unfit employees in jobs that require some degree of physical effort may lead to injury or illness, or that the work will be carried out in an unsafe manner. From the employer's view, hiring physically unfit workers means lost productivity, replacement costs, and legal damages from fellow workers and customers who have been injured through their actions. The intent of physical fitness tests is to ensure that an applicant meets minimum standards of health to cope with the physical demands of the job. Canadian federal regulations also require physical or medical testing of applicants for certain dangerous occupations (e.g., deep sea diver), or for jobs that may bring them in contact with dangerous chemical substances such as lead or asbestos. In addition to identifying any health problems, the examinations provide baseline data for comparison of any job-related changes in the applicant's health that may be covered through workers' compensation or other insurance programs.

WHEN SHOULD PHYSICAL/MEDICAL EXAMS BE GIVEN? Fitness testing or physical or medical examinations should be administered only after the applicant has been given an offer of employment, which is made conditional on the applicant passing the test or exam. The physical or medical exam is generally the last step in the selection process. The employer must demonstrate that the health or fitness requirement is related to carrying out the job in question "safely, reliably and efficiently." Physical fitness testing is no different from any other assessment procedure and must meet the same technical standards. In Canada, various human rights acts require that medical or physical examinations of job candidates must be job-related.

PEOPLE WITH DISABILITIES Requiring physical examinations before any offer of employment is made raises issues of privacy and also leaves the prospective employer open to charges of discrimination. This last concern is a major issue in hiring people who may have a disability. In the United States, the Americans with Disabilities Act of 1990 prevents employers from excluding applicants who have disabilities that are not job-related, solely on the grounds of that disability. The Act further requires employers to make accommodations in the workplace for people with disabilities. An employer could not refuse to hire an applicant who was the best computer programmer simply because the programmer used a wheelchair and the employer had no provision for such disabilities in the workplace. The employer would be required to make suitable accommodations. While there is no equivalent act in Canada at present, the many decisions rendered by human rights tribunals and the judiciary have produced the same effects as the Americans with Disabilities Act.

HIV AND AIDS TESTING Employers are becoming increasingly sensitive to hiring individuals who have Acquired Immune Deficiency Syndrome (AIDS) or the human immunodeficiency virus (HIV). However, Canadian organizations are prohibited from testing job applicants for the presence of either (Belcourt, Sherman, Bohlander, and Snell, 1996). The Canadian Human Rights Commission has accepted only three narrow grounds to justify treating employees or job applicants with AIDS differently from other employees:

1. The individual carries out invasive procedures such as surgery;

2. The individual is required to travel to countries where AIDS carriers are denied entry; or

3. A sudden deterioration of the brain or central nervous system would compromise public safety.

Following these guidelines the commission ruled that the Canadian Forces was wrong in dismissing a seaman after he tested HIV-positive, and ordered the payment of compensation. Employers are required to accommodate the needs of people with AIDS, which is a disability, by redefining work duties and implementing temporary reassignments (Belcourt et al., 1996).

GENETIC SCREENING A recent study coordinated by the Health Law Institute at the University of Alberta found that 24 percent of genetic specialists felt that employers should have access to an employee's confidential medical records to determine if the employee is likely to develop a genetic disease that may be costly to the employer ("Specialists," 1995). Undoubtedly, many employers would agree. Genetic screening is a controversial issue that proposes that job applicants be screened for genetic propensity or susceptibility to illness resulting from various workplace chemicals or substances. For example, applicants who have an inherited sensitivity to lead would not be hired for work in a lead battery plant. Genetic screening raises many ethical and legal considerations (Yanchinski, 1990).

DRUG TESTING

Inevitably, societal changes find their way into the workplace. One of the most profound changes in North American society has been the increased use of drugs. Although many people justify drug use as harmless and as a recreational activity; there are serious effects in the workplace. Based on U.S. estimates, the cost of drug use to Canadian employers is likely to range from $5 to $10 billion per year. These are costs associated with employee accidents, absenteeism, turnover, and tardiness. Additionally there are costs associated with reduced product quality and productivity on the part of employees who use drugs in the workplace. In some cases, drug or alcohol use by employees while working may result in threats to the safety of the public and co-workers. In the United States, where many workers receive health insurance through their employer, there is another major concern that employers face, namely the escalating costs of health care. The presence of a significant number of drug users in an organization will likely lead to increased health insurance premiums for the employer. For these reasons, many employers, with support from the public, believe that they are justified in screening job applicants for drug and alcohol use.

DRUG TESTING IN CANADIAN ORGANIZATIONS Random or mandatory drug testing by Canadian companies is not as common as in the United States. Only 2 percent of Canadian companies had a drug testing program in place, compared to 75 percent of U.S. companies that participated in an American Management Association survey ("Storm over Drug Testing," 1992). In 1990, the Toronto Dominion Bank became one of the first Canadian organizations to require employees to undergo drug testing. It requires all new employees to take a drug test within 24 hours of receiving a job offer. If they test positive for heroin, cocaine, or marijuana on two different tests, the employees are required to undergo counselling. Refusal to take the test or failure of the test for a third time after counselling leads to dismissal. The drug testing policy was challenged by the Canadian Civil Liberties Association and submitted to a tribunal under the Human Rights Act. In 1994, the tribunal ruled that Toronto Dominion's policy was not discriminatory because it applied to all employees. Subsequently, the tribunal's ruling was challenged before the Federal Court of Canada where it was set aside. Madame Justice Sandra Simpson referred the matter back to the tribunal with instructions that if it could not link the drug testing to job performance it must find that the policy contravenes the Canadian Human Rights Act. The Federal Court's ruling is likely to be appealed. Until the issue is settled, Toronto Dominion has the right to continue drug testing and intends to do so (Gibb-Clark, 1996).

The Toronto Dominion case illustrates a number of issues that must be considered as part of implementing a drug testing program. The first question that employers must answer concerns the scope of the testing program that they wish to put in place. Do they wish to look for the presence or history of certain drugs or for all types of drug use? Are they concerned with the use of illicit drugs or the use of legal substances as well? The answers to these questions may determine both the type of testing done and its cost. In Canada, both the Department of National Defence and Transport Canada do not limit the scope of their drug testing. Transport Canada sets policy for the testing of airline and railroad personnel, among others. There is no doubt that drug testing is invasive and that it violates an individual's right to privacy. However, when drug testing takes place, the collective rights of society (and the employing organization) are deemed by Canadians to have a higher priority than the individual's right to privacy, particularly where certain physical standards are a bona fide occupational requirement (Oscapella, 1994). Obviously, the broader the scope of the drug testing, the more invasive it becomes, and the greater likelihood that it will contravene human rights legislation. In 1995, the Ontario Human Rights Commission ruled that an Imperial Oil substance abuse policy was unreasonable because it required employees to report past drinking problems or be fired (Gibb-Clark, 1996).

DRUG TESTING METHODS Methods for drug testing include analysis of samples of urine, blood, or hair obtained from the applicant. In the case of alcohol, breath samples may also be taken. Urinalysis is the most common means of testing; it is also the cheapest and the most inaccurate in terms of producing positive results in the absence of drug use. Using urinalysis to test for the presence of three drugs may cost about $20; using highly accurate but labour intensive chromatography increases the cost to over $100. Large-scale drug testing may only be cost-effective in industries such as transportation where accidents result in severe injury, or damage to equipment. Efforts to develop paper and pencil psychological tests to identify drug users are ongoing. To date such psychological tests have performed poorly in identifying drug and alcohol use (Breyer, Martines, and Dignan, 1990).

DRUG TESTING STANDARDS Drug tests must meet the same standards of reliability and validity that we expect of psychological tests. Reliability of drug tests is obtained through splitting the sample and testing both halves.

However, if the initial sample is contaminated or the laboratory procedures are inadequate, both halves may produce results that, while consistent, are erroneous. As part of the reliability and validity checks, laboratory personnel, testing protocols, and procedures are subject to standards and outside scrutiny as a means of ensuring quality control.

POSITIVE DRUG TEST RESULTS Positive results pose a dilemma for an employer. The positive results on a drug test only indicate that a person may have used the drug in the past; they do not indicate that the person is currently using the drug, or how far in the past the drug use took place. Neither can the testing identify the extent of past use. Additionally, certain foods or legitimate non-prescription drugs may produce positive results; for example, eating poppy seeds, which are used in many baked goods, will produce test results similar to those from banned substances. Therefore, a positive result may mean that the applicant is a casual user, an addict, or not a user at all. Casual drug users cannot be denied employment solely on the grounds that they have used drugs in the past. The employer must establish that the drug use interferes with performance of a particular job; this is the point of the recent Federal Court ruling with respect to the Toronto Dominion Bank's policy. The employer must also consider when the drug-testing takes place. A drug test is another aspect of a medical or physical exam. Drug tests cannot be administered indiscriminately to all applicants; they can only be required of applicants after they have been given a conditional offer of employment in writing, and where it has been established that the medical condition or drug use interferes with essential job performance. Box 8.6, adapted from rulings made by the Ontario Human Rights Commission, presents this position in the form of guidelines.

INVASION OF PRIVACY The gravest concern with both medical examinations and drug testing is the invasion of the applicant's privacy. Once an applicant submits a sample of blood, urine or other genetic material, the employer can obtain a complete profile on the applicant's health, including aspects that may not be job-related such as the presence of AIDS or HIV. Once such information is available, it is tempting to use it even if the health condition does not pose a threat to safety or job performance. Employees and potential employees are likely to support medical and drug testing only when the procedures on which those programs are based are seen to be just and

BOX 8.6 GUIDELINES FOR PRE-EMPLOYMENT MEDICAL EXAMINATIONS AND DRUG TESTING

1. Employers may not include medical examinations or drug testing as part of the pre-employment selection procedures.

2. Employment related medical examinations and drug tests are considered to be reasonable and bona fide if they are conducted under the following conditions:
   - the applicant has been given a written offer of employment; the offer may be made conditional on passing the medical or drug tests;
   - where specific abilities are required to perform essential job duties;
   - where the medical examination or drug test is limited solely to determining those medical or physical conditions that may affect performance of the essential job duties; and
   - reasonable accommodation must be made for those who do not pass the medical or drug tests (i.e., provision must be made for retesting as part of the process).

only when the testing is limited to positions or occupations that are health or safety sensitive, essentially the conditions outlined in Box 8.6 (Konovsky and Cropanzano, 1991; Tepper, 1994).

WORK SAMPLES AND SIMULATION TESTS

In Chapter 5 we discussed two types of testing that were used to develop criterion measures of work performance, work samples and simulations. Both of these procedures are more commonly used as part of the selection process. Both require the job candidate to produce behaviours related to job performance under controlled conditions, which approximate those found in the real job. The candidate is not asked to perform the real job for several reasons. Actual job performance may be affected by many factors other than the applicant's proficiency or aptitude for the job; these factors could affect candidates differentially so that two applicants with the same proficiency might perform differently. Placing the applicant in the job may also be extremely disruptive, costly, and time-consuming, if not outright dangerous in some situations. The major difference between work samples and simulations is the degree of their approximation of the real work situation.

Work samples tests include major tasks taken from the job under consideration; these tasks are organized into an assignment, which the applicant is asked to complete. The work sample and the scoring of an applicant's performance are standardized, allowing for comparisons of skill or aptitude across candidates. Work samples include both motor and verbal behaviours (Asher and Sciarrino, 1974). Motor work samples require the applicant to physically manipulate some machinery or tools; verbal work samples require the applicant to solve problems that involve communication or interpersonal skills. For example, a secretary's job might include using a computer and related software to type letters and reports, to manage the office budget, to track purchases, to send data files electronically to other people, together with operating the phone and voice mail systems, scheduling appointments, and receiving people into the office. A work sample test given to applicants for this position might include both a motor work sample, using a computer to type and to electronically transmit a standardized letter, and a verbal work sample, dealing with a message from the boss, which asks the secretary to reschedule several important appointments to allow the boss to keep a dental appointment.

The work sample test would not seek to include every aspect of the job but only those deemed to be the most important. The work sample test could be given to the candidate in the actual place of employment or in an off-work setting. Regardless of where the testing took place, it would be carried out using standardized instructions, conditions, and equipment. The results of the work sample test tell how well the applicant performed on the work sample tasks. Work sample performance is only an estimate, or prediction, of actual job performance. Recall our discussion of typical versus maximum performance in Chapter 5; work sample performance is clearly a case of maximum performance where the applicant's motivation may be quite different from that exhibited through typical, day-to-day job performance. Like any test, the validity of a work sample test must be established as part of the selection procedure; however, work sample tests, if developed properly, will predict job performance in a reliable and valid manner (Asher and Sciarrino, 1974). Because they incorporate aspects of the job into selection, work samples have the potential to attain relatively high levels of validity. At the same time, however, work samples may require expenditures on expensive equipment and personnel to administer the test to each applicant individually. As is the case with simulations, these costs may be more than offset by the increased benefits of improved selection.

Simulations, like work sample tests, attempt to duplicate salient features of the job under consideration. Candidates perform the set of designated tasks and are given an objective score based on their performance. The score is used to predict aptitude or proficiency for job performance. Unlike work samples, the tasks and the setting in which they are carried out represent less of an approximation of the actual job. That is, the simulation asks the candidate to carry out critical job tasks in a more artificial environment than work sample testing.

The most distinguishing feature of a simulation is its fidelity, the degree to which it represents the real environment. Simulations can range from those with low fidelity (e.g., using a computer game as an indicator of managerial decision-making) to those with high fidelity (e.g., using performance in a flight simulator, which highly resembles a cockpit, to predict pilot behaviour). High fidelity simulations can be quite expensive, but in some cases there may be no alternative. The simulation allows a type of hands-on performance in an environment that provides substantial safety and cost benefits compared to allowing the applicant to perform in the actual job. While a computer controlled flight simulator may cost several million dollars to develop and to construct, it is far preferable to having prospective pilots demonstrate their flying proficiency in an actual aircraft where a mistake can be deadly, as well as much more costly.

High fidelity computer-assisted flight simulators are normally used as part of training programs and are used by Air Canada and Canadian Airlines International in that capacity. The Canadian Forces, however, is one of the few organizations to use a simulator in selecting candidates for flight school; performance on the high fidelity simulator is a much better predictor of flying success on the part of future pilots than a battery of cognitive and psychomotor tests (Spinner, 1990). Generally, the savings from reductions in training failures and training time more than offset the initial cost of the simulator.

Situational exercises are a form of work sample testing used in selecting managers or professionals. Situational exercises attempt to assess aptitude or proficiency in performing important job tasks, but do so by using tasks that are more abstract and less realistic than those performed on the job. To a large extent, situational exercises are really a form of low-fidelity simulation. The situational exercise involves the types of skills that a manager or professional may be called upon to use in the actual job. Situational exercises have been designed to assess problem-solving ability, leadership potential, and communication skills.

The two most prominent situational exercises are the *Leaderless Group Discussion* and the *In-Basket Test*. In a *leaderless group discussion*, a group of candidates for a managerial position might be asked to talk about or to develop a position or statement on a job-related topic. In the leaderless group discussion used by IBM, candidates must advocate the promotion of a staff member. In a leaderless group discussion, the group is not provided with any rules to conduct the discussion; neither is any structure imposed on the group. The primary purpose of the exercise is to see which of the candidates emerge as a leader by influencing other members of the group. Each candidate is assessed on a number of factors by a panel of judges; these factors might include communication and organizational skills, interpersonal skills, and leadership behaviour.

The *in-basket test* seeks to assess the applicant's organizational and problem-solving skills. The Public Service Commission of Canada uses an in-basket test in selecting applicants for certain managerial and professional positions in the federal civil service. As part of an in-basket, each candidate is given a standardized set of short reports, notes, telephone messages, and memos of the type that most managers would have to deal with on a daily basis. The applicants must set priorities for the various tasks, determine which can be deferred or delegated, and which must be dealt with immediately. They must also indicate how they would approach the different problems the material suggests they will encounter as a manager. Each candidate's performance on the in-basket is scored by a panel of judges. The in-basket has a great intuitive appeal as a selection test for managers because it resembles what managers actually do; unfortunately, empirical evidence suggests that it does not have high validity as a selection instrument (Schippman, Prien, and Katz, 1990). In part, this may be due to the lack of agreed-upon scoring procedures for the in-basket test; successful managers who complete the in-basket do not always arrive at the same conclusions. Although situational exercises can be used as stand-alone selection tests, they generally play a prominent role in testing carried out as part of an Assessment Centre.

ASSESSMENT CENTRES

The term "Assessment Centre" is somewhat misleading. It does not refer to a physical place but rather to a standardized assessment procedure that involves the use of multiple measurement techniques to evaluate candidates for selection, classification, and promotion purposes. Mostly, the procedure is used to assess applicants for managerial or administrative positions. While some assessment procedures (e.g, an interview) may involve only one candidate, the vast majority of assessment centre procedures involve group activity. The candidates are evaluated in groups by a panel of trained assessors. The assessment centre is also unique by including managers along with psychologists and other human resource professionals in the assessment team. The managers are trained in the use of the assessment techniques and scoring procedures. The managers selected to be assessors are those who are familiar with the job for which the candidates are being selected (Finkle, 1976).

ASSESSMENT CENTRE TESTING While the specific testing procedures may vary from one assessment centre to another, depending on the purpose of the assessment, assessment centres generally include tests or procedures from each of the following categories:

◆ Ability and aptitude tests,

◆ Personality tests, both objective and projective,

◆ Situational exercises, and

◆ Interviews.

Following completion of all the assessment centre components, the team of assessors reviews each individual's performance on a number of variables. The variables represent different dimensions including administrative skills, cognitive skills, human relations skills, decision-making ability, problem-solving, leadership potential, motivation, resistance to stress, and degree of flexibility, among several others (Bray, Campbell, and Grant, 1974). Based on the ratings and observations made over the period of the assessment, the team prepares a report summarizing the information obtained through the various techniques. Candidates are provided with feedback on their performance at the assessment centre.

SCORING PERFORMANCE AT THE ASSESSMENT CENTRE When the assessment is conducted for selection purposes, the various ratings are combined into an overall assessment centre score, which can be used to rank the applicants. Generally, some score is established as the minimum needed for consideration, with employment offers made to the highest ranking appli-cant and proceeding downward until all the positions have been filled. When the assessments are made for other purposes, the assessment centre score and report may be used to predict the candidate's long-range managerial poten-tial and likelihood of promotion. Some organizations, like AT&T, require all managers at a particular level to attend an assessment centre as a means of identifying those with potential for advancement in the company. Also, the assessment centre information can be used to develop training programs for individuals within the organization, to increase their chances of future advancement.

LOCATION OF THE ASSESSMENT CENTRE The assessment procedure can be quite extensive and usually takes place over two or three days. The assess-ment centre may be located in the company but is generally held at an off-site location. Given the length of time and the number of personnel involved in the procedure, it should not be surprising that assessment centres are an expensive proposition. They require a substantial investment on the part of an organization both to develop and to operate. This cost factor generally limits their use to larger organizations, which have ongoing selection and promotion programs.

USE OF ASSESSMENT CENTRES IN CANADA In Canada, assessment centre procedures are used by the Public Service Commission of Canada to select candidates for senior managerial positions in the federal civil service and as part of its executive development and education program. They are also used extensively by Ford Motor Company, General Motors, Ontario Hydro, Northern Telecom, and Weyerhauser Canada, among many others. Assessment centres are also used by the Canadian Forces to select applicants for training as naval officers. The Naval Officer Assessment Board (NOAB) is somewhat unique in Canada because it integrates a recruiting component, orientation, into the assessment centre procedure. Following an initial screening review based on ability and aptitude tests carried out at a recruit-ing station and a review of information obtained from the candidate's appli-cation, successful applicants are invited to attend one of the several NOABs conducted each year. To provide orientation, the assessment centre is located on a naval base in Halifax with the applicants housed on board ship and all meals taken in the galley. Applicants are organized into platoons and required to wear coveralls throughout the four-day procedure, except when taking part in formal interviews. The purpose of the orientation is to provide a realistic job preview, to provide information about life in the navy, to motivate the candidates through operational demonstrations, and to begin socialization into the navy environment. The orientation also includes briefings from senior officers on the purpose and role of the navy; informal, off-the-record sessions where junior officers "tell it like it is"; physical training, including early morning runs to emphasize the importance of physical fitness; and various tours and videos to motivate and to initiate the socialization process (Rodgers, 1985).

The assessment component of the NOAB includes a cognitive/perceptual test related to navigation and three situational exercises: in-basket, leaderless group discussion, and a leadership task where each candidate must lead a group of applicants over an obstacle course. Candidates are rated on their overall interest and suitability for enrolment by their platoon leaders. They are also interviewed by a panel of senior naval and personnel officers who rate the applicants on a number of dimensions. The assessment panel also develops a score based on a review of each applicant's file including biographical data and scores from tests taken at the recruitment centre. All of this information is then assembled into a merit score with candidates selected in a top-down fashion; rarely do any candidates who fall in the bottom half of the list receive offers to enrol in the Canadian Forces as a naval officer (Rodgers, 1985).

Given the costs associated with an assessment procedure, it is important to consider whether it improves upon other selection techniques. Although both organizations and candidates who have gone through an assessment centre attest to their satisfaction with the procedure, the objective data supporting its effectiveness are equivocal. While many research studies have confirmed the validity of the procedure, a troubling number have not shown any improvement in validity that can be attributed to the assessment centre. Evaluation results for the NOAB demonstrate both these points. The NOAB predicts early training performance much better than any of the measures taken at a recruiting centre; however, it is less effective in predicting later occupational training but still better than recruitment centre measures (Bradley, 1990). Nonetheless, even small increases in validity may produce substantial savings to more than offset the costs associated with the procedure; these cost savings have been illustrated both for the NOAB (Catano, 1989) and assessment centres at AT&T (Cascio and Ramos, 1986).

Considerable research has investigated how assessors rate candidates. There is some indication that assessors may base their ratings on a candidate's past job experience or performance rather than on how the candidate performs at the assessment centre (Klimoski and Brickner, 1987). The NOAB data tend to support this position in that the *file review* component, which reflects past experience and performance, is the best individual predictor of future performance (Bradley, 1990). It may also be the case that the firsthand experience with candidates through the extensive interaction at the assessment centre allows the assessors to identify and to weight important information from the candidate's previous experience.

EFFECTIVENESS OF ASSESSMENT CENTRES Assessment centres are likely to increase in popularity as a procedure for assessing potential for managerial or professional careers. The procedure produces a wealth of information, which is useful throughout the candidate's career within the organization. It provides a comprehensive assessment of an individual and identifies strengths and weaknesses that form the basis of future development programs. Cautions are in order; assessment procedures may not be the best selection procedure in all cases. The worth of an assessment centre, like any selection device, rests on an evaluation of its psychometric properties and its utility.

◆ ◆ ◆

EVALUATING TESTING EFFECTIVENESS

Throughout this chapter we have emphasized that tests used as part of selection procedures must exhibit sound psychometric properties, particularly reliability and validity. The tests must be constructed and used in accordance with accepted professional standards and must meet any legal requirements that govern their use. These selection procedures involve the expenditure of time and money; in the case of assessment centres these can be considerable. Therefore, it is not sufficient to simply demonstrate that a selection test or procedure has acceptable psychometric properties. A more important question is whether the new selection tests improve upon the outcomes that are expected from the existing selection system. Also at issue is whether the new selection system will produce benefits or advantages that exceed the cost of operating the selection system. Utility analysis, as we discussed in Chapter 3, is a method that can be used to evaluate the performance of different selection systems by comparing the net gains that accrue to the organization through their use.

AN ILLUSTRATION OF UTILITY ANALYSIS

In Canada, the federal government offers second language training to selected employees. Suppose that 50 percent of all applicants for second language training are accepted and that of those accepted only 20 percent become fully bilingual. That is, the program has a selection ratio of .50 and a base rate of .20. In an attempt to improve the outcome, a second language aptitude test (SLAT) is developed to select applicants for training. The validity of the SLAT turns out to be .35. From the tables developed by Taylor and Russell (1939), for these values of validity, selection ratio, and base rate, the success rate will be .36, or an increase of 16 percent in utility. That is, for every 100 applicants, 18 out of the 50 candidates (.36 × 50) selected for language training with the SLAT should succeed at becoming bilingual. This change represents an increase of 8 over the 10 (.20 × 50) that would be successful under the old system. If some effort were put into improving the SLAT so that its validity reached .50, the success rate would increase to .44, representing a gain of 8 percent over the older version of the SLAT and a 24 percent increase over the base rate. Both versions of the SLAT could be considered successful in that they increased the number of successful candidates selected in every group of 50 applicants.

While the improved SLAT produced an 8 percent gain over the older version, it is difficult to say whether that increase offsets the costs of the improvement. The Taylor-Russell utility model does not provide an easy means of integrating costs and benefits. The Brogden-Cronbach-Gleser model that was presented in Chapter 3 allows such cost-benefit comparisons. We would need to assemble some additional information before we could use this model. First we would need to calculate the cost of improving the SLAT validity; let's set this cost at $100 000. Next, we need to determine the average score, in standardized form, of all those selected with the improved SLAT; let Z_x = 1.25. The value of both these variables would be obtained from data associated with the test development and with the testing. Finally, we need to estimate SD_y the standard deviation of performance in dollars. There are several ways of doing this; one procedure, which seems to produce conservative estimates, is simply to let this value equal 40 percent of the salary and benefits of the position. For our example, let salary and benefits total \$40,000; we would then use \$16 000 as an estimate of SD_y. The utility of selecting 50 employees with the improved SLAT would be:

$$U_{New} = (50) \, [(.50)(1.25) \, (\$16 \, 000)] - \$100 \, 000 = \$500 \, 00 - \$100 \, 00$$
$$= \$400 \, 000.$$

However, this figure assumes that the utility of the old selection system is zero. We know that this is not the case as the validity of the old SLAT was .35. If we assume that the old SLAT had long since paid for itself and that the only costs were the cost of purchasing and administering the test, let's say \$10 per selected applicant, then its utility was:

$$U_{Old} = (50)[(.35)(1.25)(\$16 \, 0000] - \$500 = \$350 \, 000 - \$500 = \$349 \, 500$$

The net gain would be the difference between the two utility values:

$$U_{Net} = U_{New} - U_{Old} = \$400 \, 000 - \$349 \, 500 = \$50 \, 500.$$

Of course, if we had decided to amortize the cost of development over the lifespan of the test, the utility would appear to be much greater. For example, having "paid" the development costs up front, the next 50 candidates selected, and every other group of 50 selected applicants, would return a net benefit of \$150 000 compared to using the old SLAT, assuming the same administration costs of \$10 per selected applicant. Over time the return on the investment to improve the test could be quite substantial. The net utility represents the benefits associated with the improved productivity that is obtained from hiring better qualified applicants through use of the selection system, minus the costs of that system.

Evaluating testing programs through utility analysis is more complicated than the simple illustrations presented here. Often, many assumptions have to be made about the appropriate way to calculate costs and to estimate the other parameters needed by the models. Also, as noted in Chapter 3, critics have asked whether utility provides the kind of information that managers want when making human resource decisions. Nonetheless, utility analysis does provide a means of comparing different selection systems and can provide quite useful information for the human resources specialist. Utility models can demonstrate, in quite convincing fashion, whether the implementation of personnel testing programs will produce productivity gains for the organization.

COMPARING SELECTION PREDICTORS

With the exception of the employment interview, which will be discussed in the next chapter, we have reviewed the most commonly used predictors that are used in personnel selection. Which, if any of these, are the better predictors? Which should be considered for adoption as part of a selection system? In large part the answers to these questions depend on the specific information that is being sought. Each of these predictors has different strengths and weaknesses and may be more suited to specific uses. Most of all, the selection measure must provide information that is related to the specific job, or class of jobs, that are being staffed. Consideration must also be given to the type of criterion measure that will be used. The validity of predictors may vary among criteria such as training performance, job tenure, performance ratings, and promotion.

Selection measures must meet prevailing psychometric and professional standards. They must also be reviewed in the context of fairness and legal and organizational policies. Table 8.1 has been compiled from meta-analytic studies that have reviewed the validity of different selection measures. The validities reported here are averaged across all types of criteria and are presented in descending order based on the mean validity coefficient. While these validities may be influential, the difference in utility provided by different predictors may also influence choice of a measure. The potential net gains from using different predictors in the hiring situation should be compared before making any final decision on which predictor to use.

Table 8.1 also presents data on the percentage of Canadian companies that report using some of these predictors. Data is not available for all of the selection instruments that we've discussed; nonetheless, it appears that Canadian firms, particularly small and medium sized ones, are more likely to use traditional selection instruments, which have lower validity. Larger companies are more open to using employment testing and benefiting from the higher returns from improved selection procedures. Given the advances in selection technology, there is no economic reason why small and medium firms cannot make use of newer selection procedures. Their economic survival may depend on their ability to do so.

Recall in Chapter 3 that test fairness includes the reaction of applicants to selection procedures. Adverse reactions to selection tests and procedures may impair the ability of an organization to recruit and hire the best applicants. It may also lead to costly litigation. Table 8.2 on p. 366 presents reac-

TABLE 8.1 MEAN VALIDITIES FOR PREDICTORS USED IN SELECTION

Predictor	Mean Validity	Used by Canadian Companies[#] Small/Medium	Large
Work samples *	.54	——	——
Ability Tests *	.53	39%	57%
Assessment Centre *	.43	——	——
Biographical Data *	.37	24%	26%
Psychomotor Ability *	.35	——	——
Perceptual Ability *	.34	——	——
Physical Ability **	.32	——	——
Reference Checks *	.26	72%	63%
Personality **	.15	18%	28%
Screening Interview *	.14	——	——
Résumé Components *		94%	100%
Experience	.18		
Academic Achievement	.11		
Education	.10		

Sources:
* Hunter and Hunter (1984)
** Schmitt, Gooding, Noe, and Kirsch (1984)
# Thacker and Cattaneo (1987)

tions of potential job applicants to different personnel selection techniques. The data are based on a study that had potential job applicants in the United States and France rate both the effectiveness and fairness of these methods (Steiner and Gilliland, 1996). Despite differences in language and culture, both groups gave favourable ratings to interviews, résumés, work samples, biographical data, ability tests, and references. The French group also rated personality tests favourably while the U.S. group rated it slightly lower. Both groups gave the lowest ratings to personal contacts (selection based on the influence of a connection in the company), honesty testing, and graphology. While data for Canadian applicants are not available, there is no reason to believe that they would be substantially different from those presented in Table 8.2. Canadian organizations that are considering using honesty tests, graphology, and the use of personal contacts in their hiring process should

TABLE 8.2 EFFECTIVENESS AND FAIRNESS OF SELECTION TECHNIQUES AS PERCEIVED BY APPLICANTS

Degree of Favourability*	United States	France
Above Average	Interviews Résumés Work Samples	Work Samples
Average	Biographical Data Ability Tests References	Interviews Résumés Ability Tests References Personality Tests Biographical Data
Below Average	Personality Tests Honesty Tests Personal Contacts	Graphology Personal Contacts Honesty Tests
Well Below Average	Graphology	

* Selection techniques are arranged in order of favourability within each degree of favourability.

Source: Steiner and Gilliland (1996).

consider the possible negative consequences on their ability to recruit and hire the best available people.

◆ ◆ ◆
SUMMARY

Psychological testing can be carried out for many purposes, including selection of personnel. Employment testing must meet acceptable professional and legal standards and should be carried out by professionals who are knowledgeable about tests and testing procedures. Only those tests that are psychometrically sound should be used for employment purposes. The rights of job applicants asked to take employment tests must be respected at all times. A fundamental issue is whether the test provides information that is related to those dimensions identified through job analysis.

There are a variety of tests that can be used for selection purposes. Personality tests have not had a good reputation as selection predictors, although more recent studies suggest a Big Five construction of personality may improve prediction of certain job performance dimensions. Personality tests are also increasingly being used to assess honesty or integrity with a considerable degree of predictive accuracy. Ability tests, both general cognitive ability and more specialized tests, consistently provide highly valid information about future job performance for a broad class of occupations. Employers are increasingly seeking information on applicant physical fitness and drug use. Collection of this type of information poses a threat to the applicant's privacy and must conform to human rights guidelines.

Work samples and simulations attempt to base selection on the ability of job applicants to perform actual job components either directly or in some abstract form. Assessment centres appear to be well-suited for the selection of managers and professionals and provide a wealth of information. All of these approaches are alternatives to more traditional selection procedures. Some of these new selection tools are expensive, and their costs of selection may offset the benefits they provide. Utility analysis can be used to evaluate testing effectiveness and to make comparisons between different selection systems. Before adopting specific selection techniques, consideration must be given to their perceived fairness.

E X E R C I S E S

1. Consult the government agency responsible for monitoring the use of selection tests, including physical fitness and drug testing, in your locality. This may be a human rights agency or other government body. Determine if that agency has a policy on use of selection tests. Compare that policy to the principles and standards identified in this chapter.

2. Survey 10 companies or organizations in your community to determine if they use selection tests as part of their hiring procedure. List the tests that are used. Did any organization report using honesty, fitness, or drug tests? If the company did not use any type of testing, report the procedures they used and its reasons, if any, for not using selection tests.

3. Use the information you developed as part of completing Chapter 5's exercises to develop a work sample test, including scoring procedure, that could be used to select teachers or some other profession (although your instructor may be more knowledgeable about the former occupation).

4. Design an assessment centre that could be used to select teachers. Describe the rationale for selecting the various procedures that would be included in the centre.

5. Illustrate how utility analysis could be used to evaluate the assessment centre you designed to select teachers; you may estimate information that is needed for the analysis but difficult to obtain (Hint: You may want to read the article by Cascio and Ramos, 1986).

References

Americans with Disabilities Act of 1990, 1993. West, 42 USCA § 12101 et seq.

"A New Slant on Job Applicants: How Grapho-Analysis, the Study of Handwriting, can Play a Role in the Management Hiring Process." 1994. *This Week in Business*, August 1: F3–F4.

Asher, J.J, and J.A. Sciarrino 1974. "Realistic Work Sample Tests." *Personnel Psychology* 27: 519–33.

Barrick, M.R., and M.K. Mount. 1991. "The Big Five Personality Dimensions and Job Performance: A Meta-Analysis." *Personnel Psychology* 44: 1–26.

Belcourt, M., A.W. Sherman, Jr., G.W. Bohlander, and S.A. Snell. 1996. *Managing Human Resources*. Toronto: Nelson Canada.

Bell, J. 1996. "Brain Power Counts, Too, When Evaluating Prospects." *USA Today*, April 10: 3C.

Ben-Shukhar, G., M. Bar-Hillel, Y. Bilu, E. Ben-Abba, and A. Flug. 1986. "Can Graphology Predict Occupational Success? Two Empirical Studies and Some Methological Ruminations." *Journal of Applied Psychology* 71: 645–53.

Borman, W.C., and S.J. Motowidlo. 1993. "Expanding the Performance Domain to Include Elements of Contextual Performance." In N. Schmitt, W.C. Borman, and Associates, *Personnel Selection in Organizations*. San Francisco, CA: Jossey-Bass, 71–98.

Bradley, J.P. 1990. *A Validation Study on the Naval Officer Assessment Board's*

Ability to Predict MARS Officer Training Success (Working Paper 90–7). Willowdale, Ontario: Canadian Forces Personnel Applied Research Unit.

Bray, D.W., R.J. Campbell, and D.L. Grant. 1974. *Formative Years in Business: A Long-Term AT&T Study of Managerial Lives*. New York: Wiley.

Breyer, J.B., K.A. Martines, and M.A. Dignan. 1990. "Millon Clinical Multiaxial Inventory Alcohol and Drug Abuse Scales and the Identification of Substance-Abuse Patients." *Psychological Assessment: A Journal of Consulting & Clinical Psychology* 2: 438–41.

Campbell, J.P. 1990. "Modelling the Performance Prediction Problem in Industrial and Organizational Psychology." In M.D. Dunnette and L.M. Hough eds., *The Handbook of Industrial and Organizational Psychology*, Vol. 1, 2nd ed. San Diego: Consulting Psychologists Press, 687–32.

Campion, M.A. 1983. "Personnel Selection for Physically Demanding Jobs: Review and Recommendation." *Personnel Psychology* 36: 527–50.

Canadian Human Rights Commission. 1985. *Bona Fide Occupational Requirement and Bona Fide Justification: Interim Policies and Explanatory Notes*. Ottawa.

Canadian Psychological Association. 1986. *Canadian Code of Ethics for Psychologists*. Ottawa.

Canadian Psychological Association. 1987. *Guidelines for Educational and Psychological Testing*. Ottawa.

Cascio, W.F., and R.A. Ramos. 1986. "Development and Application of a New Method for Assessing Job Performance in Behavioral/Economic Terms. *Journal of Applied Psychology* 71: 20–28.

Catano, V.M. 1989. *Naval Officer Selection Board: Methods for Assessing Utility* (Working Paper 89–9). Willowdale, Ontario: Canadian Forces Personnel Applied Research Unit.

Collins, J.D., and F.L. Schmidt. 1993. "Personality, Integrity, and White Collar Crime: A Construct Validity Study." *Personnel Psychology* 46: 295–311.

Cronbach, L.J. 1990. *Essentials of Psychological Testing*, 5th ed. New York: Harper & Row.

Cronshaw, S.F. 1986. "The Status of Employment Testing in Canada: A Review and Evaluation of Theory and Professional Practice." *Canadian Psychology* 27: 183–95.

Digman, J.M. 1990. "Personality Structure: Emergence of the Five Factor Model." In M. Rosenzweig and L. W. Porter, eds., *Annual Review of Psychology*. Palo Alto, CA: Annual Reviews.

Dunn, K., and E. Dawson. 1994. "The Right Person for the Right Job." *Occupational Health and Safety Canada* 10: 28–31.

Finkle, R.B. 1976. "Managerial Assessment Centers." In M.D. Dunnette, ed., *Handbook of Industrial and Organizational Psychology*. Chicago: Rand McNally.

Fleishman, E.A., and M.E. Reilly. 1992. *Handbook of Human Abilities*. Palo Alto, CA: Consulting Psychologists Press.

Fleishman, E.A., and M.K. Quaintance. 1984. *Taxonomies of Human Performance: The Description of Human Tasks*. Orlando, FL: Academic Press.

Getkake, M., P. Hausdorf, and S.F. Cronshaw. 1992. "Transnational Validity Generalization of Employment Tests from the United States to Canada." *Canadian Journal of Administrative Sciences* 9: 324–35.

Gibb-Clark, M. 1996. "Drug-Testing Ruling Set Aside." *The Globe and Mail*, April 24: B1, B4.

Gottfredson, L. 1986. "Societal Consequences of the G Factor in Employment." *Journal of Vocational Behavior* 29: 379–411.

Guion, R.M. 1965. *Personnel Testing*. New York: McGraw Hill.

Guion, R.M., and R.F. Gottier. 1965. "Validity of Personality Measures in Personnel Selection." *Personnel Psychology* 18: 135–64.

Hall, C.S. , and G. Lindzey. 1970. *Theories of Personality*. New York: Wiley.

Hogan, J., and R. Hogan. 1989. "How to Measure Employee Reliability." *Journal of Applied Psychology* 74: 273–79.

Hogan, R., J. Hogan, and B.W. Roberts. 1996. "Personality Measurement and Employment Decisions: Questions and Answers." *American Psychologist* 51: 469–77.

Hough, L.M., N.K. Eaton, M.D. Dunnette, J.D. Kamp, and R.A. McCloy. 1990. "Criterion-Related Validities of Personality Constructs and the Effect of Response Distortion on Those Validities" [Monograph]. *Journal of Applied Psychology* 75: 581–95.

Hunter, J.E. and R.F. Hunter. 1984. "Validity and Utility of Alternative Predictors of Job Performance." *Psychological Bulletin* 96: 72–98.

Jenkins, C.D., S.J. Zyzanski, and R.H. Rosenman. 1979. *Jenkins Activity Survey Manual*. New York: Psychological Corporation.

Jones, J., ed. 1991. *Pre-Employment Honesty Testing: Current Research and Future Directions*. New York: Quorum Books.

Klimoski, R.J., and M. Brickner. 1987. "Why do Assessment Centers Work? The Puzzle of Assessment Center Validity." *Personnel Psychology* 40: 243–60.

Konovsky, M., and R. Cropanzano. 1991. "Perceived Fairness of Employee Drug Testing as a Predictor of Employee

Attitudes and Job Performance." *Journal of Applied Psychology* 76: 698–707.

McHenry, J.J., L.M. Hough, J.L. Toquam, M.A. Hanson, and S. Ashworth. 1990. "Project A Validity Results: The Relationship Between Predictor and Criterion Domains." *Personnel Psychology* 43: 335–54.

Ontario Commissioner's Report. 1994. "Workplace Privacy." *Worklife Report* 9: 8–9.

Oscapella, E. 1994. "Drug Testing and Privacy." *Canadian Labour Law Journal* 2: 325–43.

Prociuk, T.J. 1988. "Applied Psychology in the Canadian Forces: An Overview of Current Research." *Canadian Psychology* 29: 94–102.

Rodgers, M.N. 1985. *Assessment Centre Approach to Officer Selection in the Canadian Forces.* Paper presented at the 21st International Applied Military Psychology Symposium, Paris, France. (June).

Sackett, P.R., L.R. Burris, and C. Callahan. 1989. "Integrity Testing for Personnel Selection: An Update." *Personnel Psychology* 42: 491–529.

Schippman, J.S., E.P. Prien, and J.A. Katz. 1990. "Reliability and Validity of In-Basket Performance." *Personnel Psychology* 43: 837–59.

Schmitt, N., R.Z. Gooding, R.D. Noe, and M. Kirsch. 1984. "Meta-analyses of Validity Studies Published between 1964 and 1982 and Investigation of Study Characteristics." *Personnel Psychology* 37: 407–22.

Simner, M.L. 1994. *Recommendations by the Canadian Psychological Association for Improving the Safeguards that Help Protect the Public against Test Misuse.* Ottawa: Canadian Psychological Association.

Society for Industrial and Organizational Psychology, Inc. 1987. *Principles for the Validation and Use of Personnel Selection Procedures*, 3rd ed. College Park, MD.

"Specialists Back Genetic Testing—Study." 1995. *Halifax Daily News*, December 23: 10.

Spinner, B. 1990. *Predicting Success in Basic Flying Training from the Canadian Automated Pilot Selection System* (Working Paper 90-6). Willowdale, Ontario: Canadian Forces Personnel Applied Research Unit.

Steiner, D.D., and S.W. Gilliland. 1996. "Fairness Reactions to Personnel Selection Techniques in France and the United States." *Journal of Applied Psychology* 81: 131–41.

Sternberg, R.J., R.K. Wagner, W.M. Williams, and J.A. Horvath. 1995. "Testing Common Sense." *American Psychologist* 50: 912–27.

"Storm Over Drug Testing: U.S.-Style Mandatory Programs face Heavy

Weather in Canada." 1992. *The Financial Post*, April 21: 19.

Taylor, H. C., and J.F. Russell. 1939. "The Relationship of Validity Coefficients to the Practical Effectiveness of Tests in Selection: Discussion and Tables." *Journal of Applied Psychology* 23: 565–78.

Temple, W. 1992. "Counterproductive Behaviour Costs Millions." *British Journal of Administrative Management*, April/May: 20–21.

Tepper, B. 1994. "Investigation of General and Program-Specific Attitudes toward Corporate Drug-Testing Policies." *Journal of Applied Psychology* 79: 392–401.

Tett, R.P, D.N Jackson, and M. Rothstein. 1991. "Personality Measures as Predictors of Job Performance: A Meta-Analytic Review." *Personnel Psychology* 44: 703–42.

Thacker, J.W., and R.J. Cattaneo. 1987. "The Canadian Personnel Function: Status and Practices." *Proceedings of the Administrative Sciences Association of Canada Annual Meeting* 56–66.

"Uniform Guidelines on Employee Selection Procedures." 1978. *Federal Register*, 43, 38290–315.

Yanchinski, S. 1990. "Employees Under a Microscope." *The Globe and Mail*, January 3: D3.

9

Selection III:
Interviewing

◆ ◆ ◆

CHAPTER GOALS

This chapter presents new and more effective alternatives to the traditional approaches to employment interviewing. After reading this chapter you should

- understand the purposes and uses of employment interviews;

- appreciate the selection errors associated with traditional approaches to employment interviewing;

- appreciate the legal and predictive advantages of structured employment interviewing methods;

- understand different approaches to structured interviewing and their relative advantages and disadvantages;

- begin developing competence in the design of effective interview questions and scoring guides; and

- appreciate the role of employment interviews in the changing organizational environment.

The employment interview is one of the oldest and most widely used of all selection procedures (Guion, 1976). In fact, surveys reveal that more than 99 percent of organizations use the interview as part of the selection process (Bureau of National Affairs, 1988; Kane, 1988; Karren and Nkomo, 1988; Robertson and Makin, 1986). Moreover, when making selection decisions, recruiters tend to have more confidence in the interview than in information provided from application forms, references, test results, or any other source of information about the applicant (Kane, 1988). Given its importance to the employee selection process, it is worth devoting close attention to this selection technique.

375

◆ ◆ ◆
PURPOSES AND USES OF THE INTERVIEW

Although interviews are sometimes used as preliminary screens (e.g., in armed forces recruitment centres), they are most frequently one of the last stages of the selection process. Leaving the interview until the end allows the other selection instruments (e.g., tests) to screen out unqualified applicants and thus reduces the number of people who must be interviewed. It is usually desirable to reduce the number of interviewees because interviews are relatively expensive, compared with other selection instruments such as tests or the screening of résumés.

The interview is often used to collect information that has not been provided in the résumé or application form. Interviewers are typically supervisors or line managers who have little interview training. They tend to have little time available for preparing interview questions and often use standard questions, which they hear others using or which they remember having been asked when they were interviewees. In the majority of organizations, applicants are interviewed by several interviewers, either simultaneously (panel or board interviews) or in sequence (sequential interviews) (Kane, 1988; Cox, Schlueter, Moore, and Sullivan, 1989).

Although interviews can be and have been used to assess job knowledge and cognitive ability (e.g., Campion, Pursell, and Brown, 1988), they are probably best suited to the assessment of non-cognitive attributes such as interpersonal relations or social skills, initiative, conscientiousness, dependability, perseverance, teamwork, leadership skills, adaptability or flexibility, and organizational citizenship behaviour (Arvey, Miller, Gould, and Burch, 1987; Campion, Campion, and Hudson, 1994; Latham and Saari, 1984; Latham and Skarlicki, 1995; Mosher, 1991; Motowidlo et al., 1992; Robertson, Gratton, and Rout, 1990).

Interviews are also used to sell the job to the applicant. They provide the applicant with an opportunity to ask questions about the job or the organization and to make a decision as to whether the job and the organization are appropriate for him or her. However, research evidence suggests that interviewers' effects on applicant job choice are minimal (Rynes, 1991). Factors such as pay, the job itself, or promotion opportunities tend to be much more important.

Sometimes, especially in recent years, interviews are used in the termination of employees. As organizations downsize or "rightsize," jobs are eliminated and employees must compete for a smaller number of redesigned jobs. The interview serves to assist in the identification of employees who have the necessary knowledge, skills, abilities, and other attributes (KSAOs) to perform well in the redesigned jobs and thus to remain employed by the organization. Although there is considerable debate about the merits of downsizing as a cure for ailing organizations (e.g., Cascio, 1993), such interviews are becoming commonplace (Cameron, Freeman, and Mishra, 1991).

◆ ◆ ◆
TRADITIONAL APPROACHES TO INTERVIEWING

The traditional, and still most common, approach to employment interviewing is one that has become known as an *unstructured* interview. In such interviews, the interviewer typically engages in a *free-wheeling* conversation with the interviewee. There are no constraints on the kinds of questions that may be asked and, furthermore, many of the questions used in the interview may not occur to the interviewer until part way through the interview. However, most interviewers appear to rely on a common set of questions that they have heard others use. Box 9.1 presents a list of questions often used by interviewers. An examination of the list reveals that the questions invite applicants to evaluate themselves or to describe the evaluations of others. Naturally, egotistic or boastful applicants will evaluate themselves in much more favourable terms than modest applicants when such questions are asked. Moreover, many interviewees have learned to respond to such questions with standard answers. For example, common responses to the question, "What are your weaknesses?" include "I get too involved in my work" and "I'm too much of a perfectionist." Answers to such questions reveal very little useful information about the applicant. The interviewer is forced to take on the role of an amateur psychologist trying to read meaning into vague self-evaluations, verbal expressiveness, or body language.

Some interviewees are particularly skilled at picking up cues from the interviewer concerning what answers the interviewer wishes to hear in response to interview questions. They are able to monitor and change their own responses and behaviours in order to align them with those they perceive to be desired by the interviewer. By artfully guiding the conversation

---

BOX 9.1 COMMONLY USED INTERVIEW QUESTIONS

1. Why did you leave your last job? (or, Why do you want to leave your current job?)

2. What do you consider to be your strengths? What are your weaknesses?

3. What were your strongest subjects at school? What were your weakest subjects?

4. What do you do in your spare time? What are your hobbies?

5. How would other people describe you as an individual?

6. What is your greatest accomplishment?

7. What were the most enjoyable aspects of your last job? What were the least enjoyable aspects?

8. Why do you want this job? What are you looking for from this job (or from us)?

9. Why should we hire you? What can you do for us?

10. What are your long range plans or goals? (or, Where do you plan to be five years from now?)

---

and making effective use of non-verbal behaviours, the polished interviewee is able to impress the interviewer and obfuscate the true purpose of the interview (Stevens and Kristof, 1995; Webster, 1982). Thus, instead of hiring the best *candidate*, the interviewer is likely to hire the most skilful *interviewees*. In fact, skilful interviewees can divert the conversation from relevant and important interview topics to topics that result in pleasant but uninformative conversations that cast themselves in a more favourable light. For example, upon noticing the golf trophy in an interviewer's office, such an interviewee may engage the interviewer in an amiable conversation about the game of golf, which lasts most of the interview. The interviewer, left with a good feeling about the applicant, is likely to hire him or her without actually having obtained any job-relevant information from the applicant during the interview.

Another characteristic typical of unstructured interviews is that no systematic rating procedure is used. Interviewers are free to interpret interviewee responses in any manner they choose as there are no guidelines for evaluating the responses. In fact, rather than evaluating responses or answers to interview questions, the interviewer uses the interview to get a "feeling" or a "hunch" about the applicant (Keenan, 1977; Fear, 1978). The interviewer emerges from the interview with a global, subjective evaluation of the applicant, which is biased by personal views and preferences and, therefore, is likely to be inaccurate. In fact, many interviewers report that they rely on such "gut feelings" in making their hiring decisions.

Webster (1964, 1982) and his colleagues at McGill University, as well as Arvey and Campion (1982), Schmitt (1976), and others have documented the numerous biases and perceptual and information processing errors that plague the unstructured employment interview (see Box 9.2). For example, interviewers tend to make a decision to hire or not hire the applicant within the first four to nine minutes of the interview (Springbett, 1958; Tucker and Rowe, 1977). In other words, first impressions have a very strong impact on interviewers. This is particularly troubling given that the first few minutes of the interview are often devoted to chit-chat about the weather and other non-job-related topics (unless the job is meteorologist) intended to put the applicant at ease. Interviewers also rate applicants more favourably if the applicants are perceived as being similar to themselves (e.g., Campion, 1978; Hakel, Dobmeyer, and Dunnette, 1970). Moreover, interview ratings are susceptible to halo effects (Tucker and Rowe, 1979). That is, an interviewer's initial impression of an applicant, such as might be formed upon reading the résumé, affects his or her evaluation of the candidate's answers and, thus, the rating of the candidate. Box 9.2 summarizes some of the research findings pertaining to the unstructured employment interview. These biases and errors have contributed to the poor reliability and validity of unstructured interviews.

◆ ◆ ◆
ATTEMPTS TO IMPROVE INTERVIEW EFFECTIVENESS

Given the research on the biases and errors inherent in the unstructured interview, reviews of employment interview research have, understandably, been rather pessimistic concerning the reliability and validity of the interview as a selection instrument (e.g., Schmitt, 1976). Nevertheless, as noted above, the interview has remained popular among employers. It appears the two opinions have been at odds. However, in the last few years, there have been some exciting developments in interview research, which have changed the picture. A number of researchers have been working on new approaches to employment interviewing, which have become known as *structured* interviews (e.g., Janz, 1982; Latham, Saari, Pursell, and Campion, 1980). Recent

BOX 9.2 RESEARCH FINDINGS ON THE UNSTRUCTURED INTERVIEW

Interview Decisions
- Interviewers tend to make a hire/not hire decision within the first few minutes of the interview.
- Once a "not hire" decision is made it is unlikely to be changed (however, tentative "hire" decisions can be reversed if negative information comes to light).

Interviewer Set
- Unfavourable information provided by the applicant has greater impact on interview ratings than favourable information.
- Once interviewers have formed an impression of an applicant they tend to look for information that will confirm their impression.

Temporal Placement of Information
- Interviewers remember information provided at the beginning of the interview better than information provided in the middle (primacy effect).
- Information provided at the end of the interview is also remembered better than information provided in the middle (recency effect).

Order of Interviewees
- Interviewers seeing a series of applicants tend to remember best the first and the last applicants (they tend to confuse applicants in the middle with each other).
- An applicant's interview rating is affected by the preceding applicant (contrast effects)—they benefit if the preceding applicant was relatively poor but suffer if the preceding applicant was relatively good.

Effects of Information
- Impressions formed by the interviewer as a result of information obtained about the applicant prior to the interview (e.g., by reading the résumé) affect how the applicant is rated in the interview (halo effect).
- Interviewers who have more information about the job tend to have a more accurate perception (template) of what the "ideal" applicant should look like.

Stereotypes
- Interviewers tend to see female applicants as more suitable for certain jobs whereas male applicants are seen as more appropriate for other jobs.
- Interviewers tend to give higher ratings to applicants who are most like them (similar-to-me effect).

Verbal/Non-verbal Behaviour
- An applicant's verbal skills and expressiveness affect interview ratings.
- An applicant's appearance (e.g., physical attractiveness, posture, age, clothing) and mannerisms (e.g., eye contact, handshake) affect interview ratings.

Reliability and Validity
- Agreement on ratings among interviewers interviewing the same applicants tends to be quite low (low reliability).
- Correlations between interview scores and job performance ratings (for those hired) tends to be fairly low (low criterion validity).

reviews of the employment interview literature indicate that structuring an interview appears to contribute to increased interview reliability and validity (Arvey and Campion, 1982; Harris, 1989; Webster, 1982). In fact, meta-analytic investigations of interview validity reveal that structured selection interviews have significantly greater predictive validity than traditional, unstructured interviews (Huffcutt and Arthur, 1994; McDaniel, Whetzel, Schmidt, and Maurer, 1994; Wiesner and Cronshaw, 1988). Moreover, among the variables investigated, interview structure was found to be, by far, the strongest moderator of interview validity. The effects of structure are displayed in Table 9.1, which summarizes the results of Wiesner and Cronshaw's (1988) and Huffcutt and Arthur's (1994) meta-analyses. Note the similarity of the findings in these two meta-analyses.

References to interview structure in selection interview literature tend to give the impression that structure is a dichotomous variable (i.e., that interviews are either structured or unstructured). However, interview structure can vary along a continuum, ranging from very unstructured to highly structured. In fact, Huffcutt and Arthur (1994) found that interview validity increases as the degree of interview structure increases. It is therefore useful to first consider one of the polar extremes, the very unstructured interview, and then to examine how attempts to address the interview's poor reliability and validity led to the development of highly structured interviews.

Although there has been an apparently sudden discovery of structured employment interview techniques in recent years, their development is actually due to the contributions of numerous researchers over more than half a century. These researchers sought to address what were perceived as the shortcomings of the traditional, unstructured interview by applying psychometric principles to employment interview design. However, the development of modern structured interview techniques should not be viewed as a *fait accompli*. While researchers continue making improvements in interview technology in order to meet organizational needs, organizations are undergoing changes at an increasing rate (Daft, 1992). The escalating rate of technological innovation, the globalization of the marketplace, increasing government regulation, and the changing demographics of the labour force require organizations to continually adapt and innovate if they are to survive (Porter, 1991). These organizational changes have important implications for employment interviewing practices and the development of interview technology in the future.

TABLE 9.1 CRITERION-RELATED VALIDITY OF SELECTION INTERVIEWS

Interview Source	Sample Size[1]	Number of Coefficients	Uncorrected Validity	Corrected Validity[2]
	Wiesner and Cronshaw (1988)			
All Studies	51 459	150	.26	.47
All Unstructured Interviews	5 518	39	.17	.31
Unstructured Individual	2 303	19	.11	.20
Unstructured Board	3 134	19	.21	.37
All Structured Interviews	10 080	48	.34	.62
Structured Individual	7 873	32	.35	.63
Structured Board	2 104	15	.33	.60
	Huffcutt and Arthur (1994)			
All Studies	18 652	114	.22	.37
Structure Level 1[3]	7 308	15	.11	.20
Structure Level 2	4 621	39	.20	.35
Structure Level 3	4 358	27	.34	.56
Structure Level 4	2 365	33	.34	.57

Source: The above table is adapted from Wiesner and Cronshaw (1988) and Huffcutt and Arthur (1994).

[1] Not all studies used in the Wiesner and Cronshaw meta-analysis provided sufficient information to classify interviews as structured or unstructured.

[2] Validity coefficients are corrected for restriction of range and unreliability of the criterion measure.

[3] Structure level 1 represents very unstructured interviews and is directly comparable to Wiesner and Cronshaw's unstructured classification. Levels 2, 3, and 4 represent increasing structure, with level 4 representing the most highly structured interviews. Levels 3 and 4 are comparable to Wiesner and Cronshaw's structured classification.

In order to have a meaningful perspective on possible future directions for interview research and practice it is informative to first review the historical and theoretical development of the present-day structured interview. The theoretical and historical foundations of current practice in structured interviewing have not been examined previously in a systematic way. Such a review will also provide a better understanding of the distinction between structured and unstructured interviews. It is worth noting that Canadians have been major contributors to employment interview research and literature. Webster (1964, 1982) and his students at McGill University (including Rowe and Springbett), Rowe and her students (including Tucker and Wiesner), as well as Cronshaw, Janz, Latham, and Yonge number among the Canadian contributors to employment interview research.

The following section provides a review of the development of structured interviews and how the changes in interview design were intended to address the shortcomings of unstructured interviews. The next section consists of an evaluation of the current state of structured interview research and practice. An outline of the directions interview research and practice might take in order to meet the changing needs of organizations in the future is presented in the final section of the chapter.

◆ ◆ ◆

STRUCTURED EMPLOYMENT INTERVIEWS

The inadequacies of the traditional unstructured interview led to the development of what has become known as the structured employment interview. Initial versions of the modern structured interview were simply standardized interviews. They were initially referred to as *patterned, guided,* or *structured* interviews but, most recently, have become known as *semi-structured* interviews. In these interviews, the same questions were asked of all interviewees for a particular position. These questions were to be read from a list, which had been prepared in advance, but minor deviations from or additions to the list were permitted. In addition, the use of rating scales to rate the applicant on a number of dimensions during or shortly after the interview was advocated (e.g., Fear, 1978; McMurry, 1947; Yonge, 1956).

Typically, interviewers using standardized interviews did not rate the applicant's answers to individual questions. Rather, they rated a number of dimensions or traits such as appearance, work history, or motivation. Moreover, ratings were usually made using adjective anchors (e.g., *below average, average, above average*), simple graphic or Likert scales (e.g., a scale from 1 to 5 with 1 representing *poor* and 5 representing *excellent*), or even simpler dichotomous scales (e.g., a (+) for *good* or *yes* and a (–) for *poor* or *no*). Generally, these ratings were then summed across the dimensions to arrive at an overall interview score. An example of this format was presented in Table 7.1, p. 306. The standardization of interview questions was intended to increase interview reliability and, therefore, validity.

A major disadvantage of the graphic or adjective rating scales is that raters using such scales often disagree on the meanings of different rating levels. One person's rating of 4 might be equivalent to another rater's 2 or 3 on the same trait or dimension. Maas (1965) contributed to the development of the present-day structured interview by introducing the notion of using Smith and Kendall's (1963) Behaviour Expectation Scales, rather than numerical or adjective rating scales, to rate interviews. Behaviour expectation scales consist of benchmark answers for each scale value, which are derived by using the critical incident technique (Flanagan, 1954). What is meant by a 1 or a 3 is defined for the interviewer in terms of differentially effective work behaviours, one of which applicants would be expected to engage in if they were hired. These expectations are inferred from the applicant's answers to interview questions. Maas found significantly higher interrater reliability when the behaviour expectation rating method was used. However, Maas' interviewers still rated applicants in terms of trait dimensions rather than rating the answers that interviewees gave to interview questions.

Another important characteristic of the present-day structured interview is that attempts are made to make the interview questions as job-relevant as possible (Janz, 1982; Latham, Saari, Pursell, and Campion, 1980; Latham and Saari, 1984). Fifty years ago, McMurry (1947) suggested that interviewers should be knowledgeable about the jobs for which they are interviewing. Osburn, Timmreck, and Bigby (1981) tested the effects of job information on interviewers' ratings and found that the ratings of interviewers possessing more job-relevant information were more reliable and accurate and less influenced by irrelevant information and by their own biases and stereotypes.

Rather than leaving the level of acquisition and utilization of job knowledge to the interviewer, Heneman, Schwab, Huett, and Ford (1975) and Landy (1976) developed structured interviews in which the questions themselves were based on a formal job analysis. That is, the questions were designed to tap constructs or dimensions that had been determined, in the job analysis, to be important to job performance. Although the results of either study were not particularly impressive, Landy did find that averaged interview factor or dimension scores predicted job performance ratings reasonably well whereas interviewers' overall recommendations did not. It is worth noting that the interviewers in both studies made relatively subjective dimension or trait ratings rather than rating the answers to the individual interview questions, which were based on the job analysis. The latter procedure would have resulted in more objective and, presumably, more valid interview ratings. Moreover, it appears that interviewers in both studies used graphic scales rather than behaviourally anchored scales to rate the interviewees. Relatively lower reliability and, therefore, validity should have been expected when this approach was used (Maas, 1965).

Although it has been common practice for interviewers to wait until the end of the interview before making notes (Webster, 1982), a number of researchers who have been concerned with improving the employment interview have suggested that interview ratings should be made or interview notes should be taken during the interview (e.g., Maas, 1965; Mayfield, Brown, and Hamstra, 1980; Schuh, 1978). They found that interviewers who made ratings or took notes during the interview were more accurate in their recall of what had transpired and that their ratings had greater reliability than interviewers who waited until the end of the interview to take notes.

In the last decade some of the researchers concerned with the structured interview have combined psychometric theory and previous research results to construct the most recent versions of the structured employment interview (e.g., Campion et al., 1988; Janz, 1982; Janz, 1989; Janz, Hellervik, and Gilmore, 1986; Latham, 1989; Latham and Saari, 1984; Latham et al., 1980). Although these researchers have differed in their approaches to the construction of structured interviews, they share a common conception of the structured interview as a series of job-related questions, which are consistently applied for all interviews for a particular job. Moreover, they all take a content validation approach to interview design in that attempts are made to keep job content as intact as possible when translating it into interview questions. In other words, the interviews serve as verbal work samples (Asher and Sciarrino, 1974). Whatever differences might exist among the approaches used to structure interviews, it is clear that structured interviews are superior to traditional, unstructured interviews when it comes to predicting job performance.

◆ ◆ ◆
STRUCTURED EMPLOYMENT INTERVIEW TECHNIQUES

THE SITUATIONAL INTERVIEW

One of the recent approaches to structured interviewing is the Situational Interview (SI) used by Latham et al. (1980). The interviewer describes to the applicant hypothetical situations that are likely to be encountered on the job and asks the applicant what he or she would do in the situations. The interviewer then uses a scoring guide consisting of sample answers to each question to evaluate and score the applicant's answers. The scoring guide is designed using the Critical Incidents Technique (Flanagan, 1954) in which examples of actual job-related behaviours that varied in effectiveness in particular situations are collected and refined to serve as sample answers. Thus, numerical values on the scale are illustrated with examples of answers that would be worth a 1 or a 3 or a 5. An example of an SI question is provided in Table 9.2. Please note that the scoring guide is only visible to the interviewer(s), not to the interviewee. Cover up the scoring guide in Table 9.2 with your hand and try answering the question. Once you have answered the question, compare your answer with the scoring guide.

The scoring guide for an SI question should be based on behaviours that have been shown to be either effective or ineffective in that situation in the past. However, because organizations differ, what is an effective response in one organization may not be effective in another. Thus, the scoring guide might differ from one company to another. In the example in Table 9.2, applicants who indicate that they would ignore the supervisor's remarks and insist on following through on the initial decision would be ignoring potentially important information. The result might be a serious mistake, which could cost the company considerable money. Such a response would not score well. Doing what the supervisor suggests or openly discussing the merits of the supervisor's suggestion might result in a good decision being made. However, this course of action would likely undermine the new manager's authority. The ideal answer does not have to be given exactly as written in the scoring guide. However, the interviewer would be looking for evidence that the applicant recognizes the dynamics at play in the situation and understands basic principles of human behaviour. First, it is important to recognize that there is the potential for a serious mistake if the manager

TABLE 9.2 EXAMPLE OF A SITUATIONAL INTERVIEW QUESTION

You have just been hired as the manager of our purchasing department and it's your first day on the job. After carefully reviewing product and price information you make a decision to purchase parts from a particular supplier. Your immediate subordinate, an experienced supervisor who is considerably older than you, questions your judgment in front of other employees and seems quite convinced that you are making a mistake. The employees look to you for a response, some of them smirking. What would you do?

Scoring Guide

1—I would tell the supervisor that I'm in charge and I am going with my initial decision.

3—I would do what the supervisor suggests as he knows the suppliers and materials better than I do *or* I would openly discuss the merits of his suggestion vs. my own judgment.

5—Take the supervisor to a private place, thank him for the information but instruct him never to question you in front of the employees again. Then, after asking him for information on the best supplier and dismissing him, I would think about the options again and after a brief period announce *my* decision to go with the supplier suggested in our private conversation.

persists in the original course of action. Secondly, the applicant should recognize that the manager's authority is being undermined, whether intentionally or not. The fact that the supervisor raises the issue in front of the employees and some of them are smirking suggest that there might be a test of leadership going on. Thus, the manager needs to determine the truthfulness of the supervisor's remarks and to assert authority. Recognizing that these objectives would best be accomplished in a private conversation reveals an understanding of human nature. Confronting the supervisor in public might make the supervisor defensive and evoke a need for him to "save face" in front of the employees. As much as possible, the manager needs to claim the final decision as his or her own.

The interviewer's task is to compare the applicant's answers to the examples on the scoring guides and to score the answers accordingly. There may be instances where an answer falls somewhere between two scoring guide examples (e.g., better than a 3 answer but not as good as a 5 answer). Under such circumstances the interviewer has the discretion of assigning an intermediate score (e.g., a 4 or even a 4.5).

The assumption underlying the SI approach is that intentions are related to subsequent behaviours (Fishbein and Ajzen, 1975). Critics of this approach have argued that what applicants say they would do in a given situation and what they actually do may be quite different. However, a convincing counter-argument is that just *knowing* what the appropriate response should be can differentiate effective from ineffective performers. A number of researchers (Campion et al., 1994; Latham and Saari, 1984; Latham et al., 1980; Robertson et al., 1990; Weekley and Gier, 1987) have obtained significant criterion-related validity coefficients using the situational interview (Mean r across studies = .38 [uncorrected]; interrater reliability estimates are between .76 and .87).

THE COMPREHENSIVE STRUCTURED INTERVIEW

Campion et al. (1988), in what has become known as the Comprehensive Structured Interview (CSI) (Harris, 1989), combine Situational Interview questions with questions assessing job knowledge, job simulation questions, and worker characteristic or willingness questions. The job knowledge questions assess the degree to which the applicant possesses relevant job knowledge (e.g., "When putting a piece of machinery back together after repairing it, why would you clean all the parts first?"). The job simulation questions assess job-relevant verbal skills (e.g., "Many jobs require the operation of a fork-lift. Please read this [ninety-word] fork-lift procedure aloud."). Finally, the worker willingness questions assess the applicant's willingness to engage in particular activities (e.g., "Some jobs require climbing ladders to a height of a five-storey building and going out on a catwalk to work. Give us your feeling about performing a task such as this."). Campion et al. (1988) were able to predict job performance as well using this approach (r = .34 [uncorrected]; reliability is estimated at .88).

THE PATTERNED BEHAVIOUR DESCRIPTION INTERVIEW

Finally, Janz (1982), following up on a suggestion made by Latham et al. (1980) and based on Ghiselli's (1966) findings, used another approach, which he refers to as the Patterned Behaviour Description Interview (PBDI). The interviewer is asked to predict the interviewee's behaviours in a given job situation based on the interviewee's descriptions of his or her behaviours in similar situations in the past. Table 9.3 provides an example of a PBDI question based on the same critical incidents, and thus the same dynamics, as were used in the development of the SI question in Table 9.2. However, because PBDI questions are concerned with past behaviours in a potentially wide variety of settings, their inquiry must be more general. Therefore, the goal in designing PBDI questions is to make the questions apply to as wide a variety of previous experiences or situations as possible. A comparison of the questions in Tables 9.2 and 9.3 reveals that the PBDI question is likely to generate responses with considerably broader scope than the SI question. Whereas the SI question relates to a very specific situation, the PBDI could elicit descriptions of a wide variety of situations, depending on the applicants' experiences. One applicant might relate an experience as the chair on the board of directors of an organization whereas another applicant might

---

TABLE 9.3 EXAMPLE OF A PATTERNED BEHAVIOUR DESCRIPTION INTERVIEW QUESTION

We all encounter situations when our judgment is challenged. Tell me about a time when you were not certain you had made the right decision and then someone openly challenged your decision. What did you do?

Probes: What aspect of your decision were you uncertain about?

Did the person who challenged you have essential information, which you did not possess?

Could anyone overhear the person's challenge?

What issues and possible consequences did you consider in responding to this person's challenge?

What was your final decision and what was the outcome?

Scoring Guide

1—I told the person that I was in charge and I was sticking with my decision.

3—I changed my mind and did what the person suggested *or* I openly discussed the merits of his/her suggestion (in front of others).

5—I took the person to a private place and thanked him or her for the advice but asked not to be questioned in front of other people. Then, after asking the person for suggestions, I took some time to reconsider the options and consequences. I made the decision that had the greatest probability of success, regardless of where the ideas came from, but made it clear it was *my* decision.

discuss his or her experience as a member of a group working on an assignment at school.

The broad nature of PBDI questions and probable responses makes it likely that the interviewer will need to clarify the applicant's answers in order to allow them to be scored accurately. Follow-up questions or probes are used to guide the applicant's descriptions of situations or events until sufficient information is obtained to permit scoring. Some probes are written in advance, as in the example in Table 9.3, in anticipation of probable responses and with consideration to the information that will be required for scoring. However, the interviewer is permitted to supplement the list of probes with additional probes during the interview if the information obtained is insufficient to make a rating. Probing to obtain required information without giving away the content of the ideal answer requires considerable skill on the part of the interviewer.

The example in Table 9.3 contains a scoring guide similar to the one used for the SI question. Initial approaches to PBDI did not include the use of scoring guides but, rather, had interviewers rate applicants on various dimensions or traits (e.g., motivation) based on their responses to interview questions. The process of translating answers to dimension ratings was a rather subjective one, for scores would be derived on the basis of impressions gained by interviewers listening to answers to various questions. There was not a direct correspondence between any one question and any one dimension. Such an approach would be expected to compromise interview reliability and validity (see the next section below). Recent approaches to the PBDI have incorporated scoring guides (e.g., Mosher, 1991; Motowidlo et al., 1992).

Note that the PBDI question in Table 9.3 requests information that the applicant might construe as negative and might thus be reluctant to provide. When asking questions that might be viewed as requesting negative information, it is helpful to begin the question with what is called a *disarming statement*. In the example, the disarming statement communicates to the applicant that it is normal and perfectly acceptable to have had one's judgment challenged. The disarming statement is intended to reduce the likelihood that the applicant will deny having experienced this situation and to set the applicant at ease about discussing it freely.

Like the SI and CSI, the PBDI is an attempt to apply Wernimont and Campbell's (1968) suggestion that the predictor should sample behaviours that are representative of criterion behaviours (i.e., a work sample). However, in contrast to the SI, the PBDI approach is based on the premise that the best predictor of future behaviour is past behaviour. Critics of this approach have argued that people learn from past mistakes and that situational factors (e.g., relations with supervisors, tasks, organizational norms) constrain behaviour. Therefore, past behaviours will not necessarily be repeated in the future, particularly if the situation is somewhat different or if learning has taken place. However, after describing negative experiences applicants can be asked to indicate if they would repeat the behaviour next time or to relate an experience where they were successful in a similar situation. Campion et al. (1994), Janz (1982), Latham et al. (1984), Motowidlo et al. (1992), and Orpen (1985) obtained significant criterion-related validity coefficients using the PBDI (Mean r across studies = .45 [uncorrected]).

◆ ◆ ◆
INTERVIEW PRACTICE AND THE LAW

As noted above, one of the first hallmarks of structured interviews was the standardization of interview questions. When interviews are standardized, applicants can be compared on the basis of the same criteria and the interviewer obtains a better picture of the merits of each applicant relative to other applicants. In fact, a number of researchers have suggested that standardization may contribute to increased interview reliability and validity (e.g., Fear, 1978; McMurry, 1947; Yonge, 1956).

Equally, if not more important, the standardized treatment of applicants is perceived as being fairer than non-standardized treatment in today's society. The likelihood of organizations that use standardized interview questions becoming embroiled in selection-related litigation is therefore reduced. Moreover, when such organizations do go to court, the courts tend to rule in their favour (Cronshaw, 1989; Gatewood and Feild, 1994). Standardization therefore gives the interviewer and organization some measure of protection from discrimination suits.

Another aspect of structured interviews that appears to have a strong impact on the organization's ability to defend itself against litigation is the exclusive use of job-related questions (i.e., questions based on a formal job analysis). Questions that probe areas not directly relevant to the job run the risk of being interpreted as having discriminatory intent by the applicant and by the courts (Campion and Arvey, 1989; Cronshaw, 1989; Gatewood and Feild, 1994). A question such as, "Do you plan to have children?" which is frequently posed to female but not to male applicants, is not only unrelated to job requirements but treats male and female applicants differently (i.e., is unstandardized). Such questions are particularly troublesome from a human rights perspective.

The job relevance of interview questions has a significant impact on interview validity as well (Wiesner, 1989). Structured interviews may have greater predictive validity, in part, because structuring an interview increases its reliability and accuracy in differentiating between applicant strengths and weaknesses on job-relevant dimensions (Mayfield, 1964). Moreover, the greater job-relevance of structured interview questions may direct the interviewer's attention away from irrelevant information and focus it on job-relevant information. This focusing of interviewer attention may reduce the potential effects of the biases and processing errors inherent in the unstructured interview. Therefore, the degree to which structured interview questions are job-relevant and interview ratings are reliable appears to determine the validity of the interview.

The job-relevance of interview questions does not, by itself, guarantee the reliability of interview ratings, however. Interviewers often disagree in their ratings of the same dimensions or characteristics for a given applicant and even give different ratings for the same answer to an interview question (Latham et al., 1980; Maas, 1965; Wiesner, 1989). Therefore, some kind of job-relevant rating or scoring guide is essential if high reliability among raters is to be achieved and if the interview ratings are to be based on job-relevant criteria. In fact such scoring guides appear to increase interview reliability, and therefore validity, particularly when they are used to assess the answers given by interviewees rather than trait dimensions (Latham et al., 1980; Latham and Saari, 1984; Wiesner, 1989).

The use of a standardized, job-relevant scoring system for assessing and comparing candidates also appears to contribute to an effective defense against litigation (Campion and Arvey, 1989; Cronshaw, 1989; Gatewood and Feild, 1994). The courts have been particularly concerned when there is evidence that applicants giving the same responses are treated differently on the basis of gender or race or any other grounds on which discrimination is forbidden. To build on a previous example, it is insufficient for an employer to standardize the interview by asking both male and female applicants whether they intend to have children if a male's response to the question is irrelevant to the selection decision whereas a female's response might determine whether or not she is offered the job (i.e., the *scoring* of responses is not standardized).

Latham et al.'s (1980) approach requires interviewers to sum the scores given for each individual question to give an overall interview score, rather than permitting interviewers to make global judgments. The final score can then be used to make the selection decision by ranking candidates or by determining cutoff scores, which must be exceeded by candidates if they are to qualify for the job. In essence, this approach relieves the interviewer of much of the decision-making function and isolates the selection decision from the interviewer's biases and stereotypes (Webster, 1982). The selection decision, then, is a statistical or actuarial process (Meehl, 1954), which has greater criterion-related validity than the faulty cognitive information processing or affective decision-making processes typically engaged in by interviewers when they make overall ratings or recommendations (e.g., Dougherty, Ebert, and Callender, 1986; Meehl, 1954; Sawyer, 1966). This advantage for the statistical combination of scores does not appear to hold, however, when low job-relevance interview questions are used. Rather than evaluating behaviours, interviewers using such questions make clinical judgments with respect to each answer given (Wiesner, 1989). The total interview score for such questions therefore represents the sum of several clinical judgments, which do not differ significantly from a single overall clinical rating.

It should be emphasized, with respect to the discussion above, that interview validity and reliability issues are very much related in that reliability can place an upper limit on validity (e.g., Nunnally, 1978). In fact, Wiesner and Cronshaw (1988) found that interview validity and reliability were correlated at .48 in the studies they examined. Conditions that serve to make interviews more reliable should therefore be the same as those that make them more valid.

In summary, the results of previous research concerned with aspects of interview structure suggest that interview validity can be optimized if four basic elements are included in the construction of the interview. First, interview questions should be job-relevant. As interview questions become more job-relevant, the impact of irrelevant information on the interview decision is reduced and the interview has greater reliability and validity. Job relevance can be optimized by basing the interview questions on a formal analysis of the task components of a job (i.e., a job analysis).

Secondly, interviewees' answers should be scored or recorded as soon as they are given. Delay in scoring or recording of the answers allows the scoring to be influenced by errors in the interviewer's retrieval of information from memory. Moreover, information retrieved from memory is more likely to be affected by stereotyping and the biases the interviewer holds with respect to the interviewee than information coded and scored immediately after it is provided.

Thirdly, scoring guides comprised of behavioural anchors or benchmark answers should be used to score the applicant. Behavioural anchors cue the interviewer as to the most appropriate score for a particular answer so that the interviewer encodes the information obtained in a predetermined manner rather than using his or her own encoding scheme. The use of scoring guides with behavioural anchors appears to increase reliability among interviewers as well as the validity of the interview.

Fourthly, the scores for answers to individual interview questions should be summed or averaged to provide a total score for the interview. Differential weights can be assigned to questions if particular questions are considered to be more important than others or, alternatively, more than one question can be asked to assess a particular job requirement if it is considered more important than other requirements (Pursell, Campion, and Gaylord, 1980). The summing or averaging of individual scores to yield a total score results in greater accuracy and higher predictive validity than when an overall rating of the candidate is made by interviewers at the end of the interview.

Although unstructured interviews are vulnerable targets of potential litigation, several researchers have recently examined and found little or no evidence of bias in structured interviews. Arvey et al. (1987) found no evidence of age or gender bias in their semi-structured interviews. Similarly, in their investigation of over 27 000 structured interviews for 18 different jobs, Blankenship and Cesare (1993) found no evidence of bias on the basis of age. Although Lin, Dobbins, and Farh (1992) also found no evidence of age bias in their structured interview, they found a very small effect for race. That is, interview panels or boards comprised of all black interviewers gave slightly higher scores to black applicants than did panels or boards comprised of all white interviewers (ratings did not differ for white or Hispanic applicants). However, Lin et al. (1992) found less evidence of race bias when

BOX 9.3 STRUCTURED INTERVIEWING PROCESS

1. Base interview questions on a job analysis such as the Critical Incidents Technique to ensure their job relevance.

2. Standardize the interview so that all applicants are asked the same questions. Situational, Patterned Behaviour Description, Job Knowledge or Work Simulation questions may be asked.

3. Use a scoring guide with benchmark or sample answers determined in advance. A five-point scale can be used to rate responses.

4. Take notes of the applicant's responses in as much detail as possible.

5. Score the answers to interview questions as soon as possible—either during the interview or immediately after.

6. Sum the scores across interview questions to arrive at a total score for the interview.

7. Follow the same procedures for each applicant and retain interview documentation for future reference.

structured interviews were used than when unstructured interviews were used. Moreover, they note that the true performance levels of the applicants are unknown. Nevertheless, they recommended the use of mixed-race interview boards to reduce the potential for bias. Finally, Paullin (1993) reviews seven studies, including four conducted by Motowidlo et al. (1992), and finds no consistent trends for bias with respect to gender or race or ethnic group. Any differences that do exist tend to be less than half a standard deviation and do not consistently favour any group. The studies represent a variety of jobs including marketing, entry-level management, non-managerial telecommunications jobs, and firefighting. Not only are structured interviews less vulnerable to bias than unstructured interviews, but applicants perceive them as more job-related and, thus, fairer (Harris, 1993). Therefore, applicants are less likely to contest decisions made on the basis of structured interviews.

◆ ◆ ◆
DESIGNING INTERVIEW QUESTIONS

The job analysis technique that lends itself most readily to the development of interview questions is the Critical Incidents Technique (Flanagan, 1954). The Critical Incidents Technique has been the basis of both the SI and the PBDI. Examples of effective and ineffective as well as typical behaviours that contributed to the success or failure of employees in particular situations or tasks on the job should be collected. Each important task or situation should thus be linked with several examples of typical, effective, and ineffective behaviours. This information can be obtained from incumbents and their supervisors through interviews, focus group sessions, and questionnaires.

Once the critical incidents have been collected, the situations on which they are based can be turned into CSI, PBDI, or SI questions. For SI questions, the situation should be described in sufficient detail to allow an applicant to visualize it accurately and should be followed by a "what would you do?" question. For each situation, the best critical incidents (i.e., most representative and most likely to be used as answers by interviewees) demonstrating effective, typical, and ineffective behaviours serve as behavioural anchors for the scoring guide (i.e., poor, average, and good answer, respectively). Scores are assigned so that 1 represents the *poor* answer, 3 an average answer, and 5 a *good* answer.

Care should be taken to select situations and phrase questions in a way that does not make the best answer readily apparent to the applicant. Situations where there is tension between competing demands or options are ideal if the options appear equally aversive or attractive to inexperienced individuals. Questions and scoring guides should be pretested on a group of applicants or recently hired employees to ensure that the questions are clear and elicit a range of responses. For example, if the *poor* answer is never given, the answers that are given should be examined to determine whether some of them reflect an alternative critical incident representing ineffective performance. Alternatively, the question should be reworked to create more tension.

PBDI questions are designed by examining each task or situation in order to identify the behavioural dimension underlying the situation (e.g., meeting deadlines). The dimensions are turned into PBDI questions, which retain the essence rather than the details of the original situation. In other words, the PBDI question applies to a variety of situations that share the underlying behavioural dimension (e.g., meeting deadlines in a job, at school, when sending birthday cards, etc.). As with the SI, critical incidents are used to develop a scoring guide. However, the scoring guide anchors also need to be rephrased to make them more generally applicable to a variety of situations. The underlying behavioural dimensions rather than the actual incidents serve as anchors (e.g., planning ahead, setting up contingency plans, monitoring progress v. working long hours at the last minute, asking for extensions, missing the deadline).

Probes are developed by anticipating the kinds of responses that applicants from different backgrounds or with different levels of experience are likely to give to a PBDI question. For example, applicants with limited work experience might never have been in a situation where they disagreed with a superior. A probe might then focus on responses to a disagreement with parents or friends in a situation similar to the one of relevance to the job. The probes should provide a clear understanding of the situation, the behaviour, and the outcome so that the applicant's response can be accurately scored. General probes like "What led up to the situation?" "What did you do?" "What happened?" "What was your reason for...?" or "Can you tell me more about...?" seem to apply in most circumstances.

Job knowledge or job simulation questions can be derived directly from critical incidents. The situations that lead to ineffective or effective behaviours can be simulated during the interview. For example, if problems have occurred on the job because solvents have been mixed or used inappropriately and if a contributing factor is functional illiteracy, applicants could be asked to read the directions on a solvent container aloud and then to explain in their own words what the directions mean. Similarly, an applicant could be asked to "sell" a product to interviewers playing the roles of the kinds of customers who have been challenging for salespeople in the past.

◆ ◆ ◆
COMPARISON OF RECENT APPROACHES TO INTERVIEWING

The Situational Interview, Comprehensive Structured Interview, and recent versions of the Patterned Behaviour Description Interview approaches incorporate all four of the suggestions for interview design outlined above. Although the PBDI did not initially incorporate all four of the recommendations outlined above, whereas the SI and the CSI did, research results suggest that the PBDI might have greater predictive validity than the SI and CSI (mean $r = .45$ for the PBDI v. mean $r = .38$ for the SI and $r = .34$ for the CSI). However, the sample sizes from which these data are drawn are still fairly small so it is not possible at this time to say definitively that any of these approaches is better than the others.

Predictive validity issues notwithstanding, the PBDI appears to be more appropriate in some selection situations whereas the SI and CSI appear to be more appropriate in others. In particular, the PBDI seems best suited to the selection of candidates who have had prior work experience (especially in related areas of work) or have been engaged in relevant volunteer activity or hobbies. The job knowledge questions, and possibly the job simulation and worker characteristics questions, of the CSI also appear better suited to applicants with related experience. However, the situational questions of the CSI and the SI are useful with both experienced and inexperienced applicants. Experienced applicants may still have some advantage over inexperienced applicants competing for the same job when situational questions are asked, but the difference would likely be reduced.

As noted above, interviewers appear to require a fair degree of skill in order to conduct the PBDI effectively. The SI or CSI might therefore be more foolproof in the hands of supervisors and line managers when they do the interviewing. The SI and CSI seem to require less skill or training because the interviewer simply reads the questions and compares the answers given with the scoring guide examples. Probing is not permitted. If the PBDI is to be used, a thorough training program is highly recommended.

Although a few competitive tests of the PBDI and SI approaches have been conducted, the results are conflicting and inconclusive (Campion et al., 1994; Latham et al, 1984; Latham and Skarlicki, 1995; Mosher, 1991). As a result, the above discussion of the relative merits of the two approaches is somewhat speculative. More research is needed to investigate the relative merits of the PBDI and the SI in various situations and with varying degrees of interviewer training and experience. In addition to addressing the theoretical questions surrounding the relationships of past behaviour and behavioural intentions with subsequent behaviour, such a study would provide highly useful information for improving the design of structured interviews. It may well be that both SI and PBDI approaches could be used effectively in tandem within one interview session. Applicants who have difficulty answering a PBDI question because of a lack of relevant work experience could be asked a corresponding SI question. Alternatively, SI questions could be followed by corresponding PBDI questions in order to determine whether the behavioural intentions are consistent with past behaviours.

◆ ◆ ◆
INTERVIEWER TRAINING

Interviewer training has tended to focus on reducing common sources of bias and inaccuracy such as halo error, similar-to-me effects, contrast effects, and leniency and severity errors. Interviewers are also taught to put the applicant at ease, ask open-ended questions, develop good listening skills, maintain control of the interview, take appropriate notes, and ignore or interpret correctly the non-verbal behaviours occurring in the interview. Unfortunately, most studies report that interviewer training has minimal effect on interviewer behaviour and interview outcomes, particularly when shorter training programs are examined (Campion and Campion, 1987; Maurer and Fay, 1988; Orpen, 1985). However, the University of Houston Interview Institute's five-day training program appears to produce significant changes in interview behaviours (Howard and Dailey, 1979). The institute's training program combines presentations and demonstrations with hands-on exercises and active practice using videotapes.

Training interviewers to administer a structured interview is a considerably different endeavour than training them to avoid errors and biases or develop good listening skills. Interviewers using structured interviews should need to become sufficiently familiar with the scoring guides that they do not need to be reading the behavioural anchors while the applicant is answering the question. Their attention should be focused solely on listening to the applicant's answer. Interviewers do require training on how to score an answer when it does not match the examples in the scoring guide. The training provides interviewers with decision rules to use in such circumstances. Interviewers using PBDI questions require more extensive training. They need to learn how to use probes effectively without giving away the five-point answer. Demonstrations and opportunities for active practice are likely to be essential components of a PBDI training program. The assessment of role plays is also likely to benefit from the use of behavioural role modelling techniques. Unfortunately, research on the effectiveness of training for structured interviewing methods is virtually nonexistent.

◆ ◆ ◆
FUTURE DIRECTIONS FOR INTERVIEW RESEARCH AND PRACTICE

THE BEHAVIOURAL SAMPLE INTERVIEW

A relatively new concept in selection interviewing is what might be referred to as the Behavioural Sample or Work Sample Interview (BSI). Whereas the SI focuses on future behaviours (behavioural intentions) and the PBDI focuses on past behaviours, the BSI is concerned with behaviour in the present. It could be argued that a sampling of an applicant's current behaviour should be a better predictor of job performance than either behavioural intentions or past behaviours. What applicants say or even believe they will do and what they actually do in a given situation can be quite different. Similarly, because applicants can learn from mistakes and change over time, a past behaviour may not be repeated in the future.

Several approaches have been taken to behavioural sample interviewing but they are all concerned with current behaviour. Campion et al. (1988) used Job Knowledge questions as well as Work Sample questions in their Comprehensive Structured Interview, and Wright et al. (1989) describe the use of similar questions by themselves and by Kennedy (1985). Examples of these Job Knowledge and Work Sample questions are provided in the section on Comprehensive Structured Interviews.

A related approach to Work Sample Interviewing involves role playing. One of the interviewers or an assistant plays a foil to the role played by the applicant while the interviewer or others observe and evaluate. The Edmonton Police Service uses such a role play to assess assertiveness in candidates. The applicant is to assume he or she has just set up a chair to watch a parade. The chair happens to be similar to ones set up by the city for public use. The applicant is told to assume that he or she has left the chair unattended in order to get a drink and returns to find the chair occupied (by the foil). The applicant's task is to convince the foil to vacate the chair without resorting to aggressive behaviour (physical or verbal).

Another approach to the BSI is the Walk-Through Interview used by Hedge and Teachout (1992) and Ree, Earles, and Teachout (1994) to select U.S. Air Force enlistees. The Walk-Through Interview involves asking the interviewee to describe in detail how he or she would perform a job-related task.

Like the SI and PBDI, the behavioural sample interview should be derived from the critical incidents through focused group sessions. Scoring

400

guides should also be developed using the procedures described for the SI and PBDI. However, in some respects, the BSI may be a little more difficult to construct than either the SI or PBDI. Care must be taken when simulating situations in the interview setting to ensure fidelity to the actual situation. Due to the length of time required to administer some of the BSI questions, fewer of them are likely usable in one session. They should therefore be selected judiciously to assess the most important performance domains. Nevertheless, the behavioural sample interview offers yet unexplored potential for predicting job performance.

THE CHANGING WORKPLACE

As noted at the beginning of this chapter, organizations are undergoing change at an accelerating rate (Daft, 1992). They must adapt to unanticipated innovations in technology, global competition, changing labour force demographics, and increasing government regulation and societal pressures for conformity to ethical, environmental, and human rights standards if they are to survive (Porter, 1991). The need for organizations to be responsive to such pressures for change will have a profound impact on the way jobs are defined. Until recently, job descriptions remained relatively static or evolved gradually over time as the need arose. In many occupations (e.g., secretary-typist) the kind of work employees did at the beginning of their career was not substantially different from the work done prior to retirement. Job requirements are becoming much more dynamic, however, because of the increased need for organizations to change in order to remain competitive. In secretarial occupations, for example, typewriters have been replaced by word processors and word processors, in turn, are undergoing rapid evolution. It is not at all inconceivable that in the very near future the requirements for a given job may be very different from one year to the next.

The increasingly dynamic nature of most job requirements will have a number of important implications for future developments in the field of employee selection in general and for the employment interview in particular. The currently accepted approach to employee selection involves conducting a job analysis, determining employee specifications (knowledge, skills, abilities, and other qualifications required to do the job as defined by the job analysis) using a panel of job experts, and developing or specifying selection instruments which are most appropriate for assessing the KSAOs (Gatewood and Feild, 1994). The job analysis typically involves using one or more methods to gather detailed information about worker activities or behaviours, what is produced or accomplished, the equipment used, the context and other factors of the work environment, and the personal characteristics that incumbents need to do the job. The most basic level of analysis is the individual tasks that are performed.

The current approach provides a fairly accurate view of the job at the time the job analysis is conducted. However, given the increasing pressure for organizational change and innovation outlined above, the job might be substantially changed several months (or even weeks) later. Under such conditions the job analysis provides accurate and useful information for only a limited time. In fact, by the time the job analysis information has been used to develop selection instruments and these instruments are being used to select applicants, the job information, and therefore the selection instrument, may no longer be valid. Even if an applicant is appropriately selected, a year or two later the job may have changed sufficiently to require a different set of abilities or skills, which the employee may not possess.

In addition, many organizations are beginning to rotate employees through a number of positions in order to maintain flexibility. The tasks such employees are asked to perform are determined by need and such needs are often difficult to predict. These employees must therefore be flexible as well as multi-skilled. The prospect of rapidly evolving jobs and the creation of new jobs obviously calls for a more effective approach to employee selection.

Basic knowledge or skills pertinent to the occupation will continue to be important. A secretary, for example, will generally need to know how to type (although there are indications that in the near future keyboards, as we know them, will disappear). However, specific knowledge or skills, such as knowledge of a particular word-processing software package, will diminish in importance. Specific or specialized skills and knowledge are the most susceptible to change. For example, word-processing software is constantly being revised and may well be replaced by different software from another company if that software better meets the needs of the organization. Rather than trying to keep pace with the specific skill requirements for a job, employers would be well advised to focus on more enduring abilities. Given the continual changes to be faced by employees in innovative organizations, some applicant characteristics that are likely to become vital are adaptability or flexibility, ability to handle ambiguity and stress, ability to learn (and relearn), creativity and problem-solving abilities, ability to work cooperatively with peers, ability to manage subordinates effectively, responsiveness to superiors' and customers' or clients' needs, and a high level of motivation to improve a product or service and to maintain high standards of performance. Structured employment interviews are well suited to assessing most of the abilities or constructs listed above and have been successfully used for this purpose in the past.

In conclusion, job requirements in competitive organizations are likely to be increasingly dynamic and many jobs will disappear altogether and be replaced by new kinds of jobs. In such an environment, organizations will need to hire adaptable, creative, and highly motivated employees with good interpersonal skills. Structured employment interviews, and particularly innovative approaches to interviewing exemplified by the CSI, the SI, and the PBDI, are ideally suited for assessing such applicant characteristics. Future research on structured interviews like the CSI, SI, and PBDI should therefore focus on developing questions to better assess these characteristics. Campion et al. (1994) have already begun such research. Recruiters will undoubtedly find such interviews invaluable in trying to meet the needs of innovative organizations.

◆ ◆ ◆
SUMMARY

Employment interviews are still a popular selection procedure among employers. However, most employers continue to use traditional, unstructured approaches to interviewing. These unstructured interviews have poor validity and place the employer in a legally vulnerable position. Structured approaches to employment interviewing, such as situational interviews, comprehensive structured interviews, patterned behaviour description interviews, and recent innovations such as behavioural sample interviews, provide improved predictive validity and are more legally defensible. Such interviews need to be based on a job analysis so that they assess only job-relevant attributes. Interview questions should be non-transparent and tend to be most effective when they centre on situations involving tension between competing demands. Appropriate scoring guides and rater training are essential to maintaining high rating accuracy. As job requirements change in response to the ever changing workplace, organizations are beginning to shift the focus of selection from specific job skills to organizational fit, transferable skills, and personality attributes. Structured employment interviews are well suited to assessing such attributes and will continue to play an important role in selection for the workplace of tomorrow.

EXERCISES

Interview Question Writing

1. Is the following a good interview question? If not, how would you change it?

"How did you get along with your supervisor?"

2. Is the following a good interview question? If not, how would you change it?

"Do you follow policies, rules and procedures carefully?"

3. "Are you an organized worker?" is obviously not a good interview question because it is transparent and requests a self-evaluation. Is the following wording satisfactory? If not, why not and how would you change it?

"Can you give me an example of how organized you are?"

4. Rewrite the following questions to make them more effective.
   1. Are you able to handle stress?
   2. How are you at meeting deadlines?
   3. Do you have problems working closely with others?
   4. When you make a mistake, what do you do to fix it?
   5. How are you at solving problems?
   6. Do have any problems communicating with people?
   7. How do you feel about staying late to finish a project?
   8. Are you a good leader? Can you motivate others?
   9. What do you do when you encounter obstacles to meeting your goals?
   10. Are you a good planner?

Discussion Question

Organizations exist in an increasingly dynamic environment. As a result, jobs change and employees are required to move around the organization, to do a variety of tasks, to develop multiple skills, and to "retool" or upgrade themselves on an ongoing basis. Employees are being hired less for specific job skills and more for their abilities to fit themselves to the needs of the organization. Organizations are looking for employees who are innovative, flexible, willing to learn, conscientious, and fit into the organizational culture (i.e., are good organizational citizens).

1. Can the employment interview be used to assess such personality characteristics effectively? How?
2. Are there better selection tools than the interview for assessing these

characteristics? If so, what are they and why are they superior? If not, why not?

3. Does the assessment of organizational fit and relevant personality attributes pose a danger to human rights? If so, how? If not, why not? How might you reduce the dangers of human rights violations while still pursuing employees who fit into the organizational culture?

Interview Construction

1. Select a job you have done or know well. Identify the *five* most important tasks for this job.

2. For each of the five tasks think of examples of both effective and ineffective performance, which you have observed or have been a part of (i.e., critical incidents).

3. For each task, write an SI or a PBDI question. Use the critical incidents to develop a three-point scoring guide (example of a poor answer, a typical answer, and a good answer).

This exercise can be completed individually or in small groups of three to five. The product of the exercise is used in the role play that follows. An alternative to selecting a job with which participants are familiar is to have participants develop an interview for the job of "Course Instructor."

Interview Role Play

1. Form small groups of between three and five. Assign the role of applicant to one group member and the role of interviewer to another. The remaining members of the group serve as observers. The applicant is to be interviewed for one of the jobs selected for the interview construction exercise.

2. As a group, select *five* self-evaluation questions from the list in Box 9.1, p. 378. The interviewer is to use these questions to begin interviewing the applicant for the job.

3. Next the interviewer is to continue, using the five job-relevant questions developed in the interview construction exercise.

4. While the interviewer is conducting the interview, the observers should record their answers to the following questions.

   a) How do the answers to the first five questions differ from the answers to the second five questions?

   b) Does one set of questions provide better information on which to base a selection decision? Which?

   c) Is there a difference between the two question sets in terms of how much time the applicant spends talking? If so, which takes more time and why?

   d) Of the second set of questions, are there any questions that don't seem to work as well as they should? If so, why? How would you improve these questions?

   e) How useful is the scoring guide? Would you recommend any modifications to the scoring guide? If so, how would you change it?

5. After the interview, the observers are to debrief the interviewer and applicant. How did they perceive the relative effectiveness of the two sets of

◆

questions? Where did they experience difficulties? The observers should also provide feedback to both the interviewer and applicant as to how they might improve their interview performance.

This role play can be conducted as a class demonstration with one interviewer and one applicant as role players and the remainder of the class as observers. A discussion of the relative effectiveness of the two question sets and the effectiveness of the interviewer and applicant can be held with the entire class.

References

Arvey, R.D., and J.E. Campion. 1982. "The Employment Interview: A Summary and Review of Recent Research." *Personnel Psychology* 35:281–322.

Arvey, R.D., H.E. Miller, R. Gould, and P. Burch. 1987. "Interview Validity for Selecting Sales Clerks." *Personnel Psychology* 40:1–12.

Asher, J.J., and J.A. Sciarrino. 1974. "Realistic Work Sample Tests: A Review." *Personnel Psychology* 27:519–33.

Blankenship, M.H., and S.J. Cesare. 1993. "Age Fairness in the Employment Interview: A Field Study." In R.D. Arvey, chair, *Perceptions, Theories, and Issues of Fairness in the Employment Interview.* Symposium Presented at the 101st Annual Convention of the Psychological Association, Toronto, Ontario.

Bureau of National Affairs. 1988. *Recruiting and Selection Procedures* (PFF Survey No. 146). Washington, DC: Bureau of National Affairs, Inc.

Cameron, K., S.J. Freeman, and A.K. Mishra. 1991. "Best Practices in White-Collar Downsizing: Managing Contradictions." *Academy of Management Executive* 5:57–73.

Campion, J.E., and R.D. Arvey. 1989. "Unfair Discrimination in the Employment Interview." In R.W. Eder and G.R. Ferris, eds., *The Employment Interview: Theory, Research, and Practice.* Newbury Park, CA: Sage Publications, Inc.

Campion, M.A. 1978. "Identification of Variables Most Influential in Determining Interviewers' Evaluations in a College Placement Center." *Psychological Reports* 42:947–52.

Campion, M.A., and J.E. Campion. 1987. "Evaluation of an Interviewee Skills Training Program in a Natural

Field Experiment." *Personnel Psychology* 40: 675–91.

Campion, M.A., J.E. Campion, and P.J. Hudson. 1994. "Structured Interviewing: A Note on Incremental Validity and Alternative Question Types." *Journal of Applied Psychology* 79:998–1002.

Campion, M.A., E.D. Pursell., and B.K. Brown. 1988. "Structured Interviewing: Raising the Psychometric Properties of the Employment Interview." *Personnel Psychology* 41:25–42.

Cascio, W.F. 1993. "Downsizing: What Do We Know? What Have We Learned?" *Academy of Management Executive* 7:95–104.

Cox, J.A., D.W. Schlueter, K.K. Moore, and D. Sullivan. 1989. "A Look Behind Corporate Doors." *Personnel Administrator* (March) 56–59.

Cronshaw, S.F. 1989. "Legal Implications for the Employment Interview in Canada." In S.F. Cronshaw, chair, *Improving Interview Validity and Legal Defensibility through Structuring.* Symposium conducted at the 50th Annual Convention of the Canadian Psychological Association (June).

Daft, R.L. 1992. *Organization Theory and Design.* St. Paul, MN: West Publishing Company.

Dougherty, T.W., R.J. Ebert, and J.C. Callender. 1986. "Policy Capturing in the Employment Interview." *Journal of Applied Psychology* 71:9–15.

Fear, R.A. 1978. *The Evaluation Interview*, rev. 2nd ed. New York: McGraw-Hill.

Fishbein, M., and I. Ajzen. 1975. *Belief, Attitude, Intention, and Behavior: An Introduction to Theory and Research.* Reading, Mass.: Addison-Wesley.

Flanagan, J.C 1954. "The Critical Incident Technique." *Psychological Bulletin* 51:327–58.

Gatewood, R.D., and H.S. Feild. 1994. *Human Resource Selection*, 3rd ed. Fort Worth, TX: The Dryden Press.

Ghiselli, E.E. 1966. "The Validity of the Personnel Interview." *Personnel Psychology* 19:389–94.

Guion, R.M. 1976. "Recruiting, Selection, and Job Replacement." In M.D. Dunnette, ed., *Handbook of Industrial and Organizational Psychology.* Chicago: Rand McNally, 777–828.

Hakel, M.D., T.W. Dobmeyer, and M.D. Dunnette. 1970. "Relative Importance of Three Content Dimensions in Overall Suitability Ratings of Job Applicants' Resumes." *Journal of Applied Psychology* 54: 65–71.

Harris, M.M. 1989. "Reconsidering the Employment Interview: A Review of Recent Literature and Suggestions for Future Research." *Personnel Psychology* 42: 691–726.

Harris, M.M. 1993. "Fair or Foul: How Interview Questions are Perceived." In

R.D. Arvey, chair, *Perceptions, Theories, and Issues of Fairness in the Employment Interview*. Symposium presented at the 101st Annual Convention of the American Psychological Association, Toronto, Ontario.

Hedge, J.W., and M.S. Teachout. 1992. "An Interview Approach to Work Sample Criterion Measurement." *Journal of Applied Psychology* 77: 453–61.

Heneman H.G. III, D.P. Schwab, D.L. Huett, and J.J. Ford. 1975. "Interviewer Validity as a Function of Interview Structure, Biographical Data, and Interviewer Order." *Journal of Applied Psychology* 60: 748–53.

Howard, G.S., and P.R. Dailey. 1979. "Response-Shift Bias: A Source of Contamination of Self Report Measures." *Journal of Applied Psychology* 64: 144–150.

Huffcutt, A.I., and W. Arthur, Jr. 1994. "Hunter and Hunter (1984) Revisited: Interview Validity for Entry-Level Jobs." *Journal of Applied Psychology* 79 184–90.

Janz, T. 1982. "Initial Comparisons of Patterned Behavior Description Interviews Versus Unstructured Interviews." *Journal of Applied Psychology* 67: 577–80.

Janz, T. 1989. "The Patterned Behavior Description Interview: The Best Prophet of the Future is the Past." In R.W. Eder and G.R. Ferris, eds., *The Employment Interview: Theory, Research, and Practice*.

Newbury Park, CA: Sage Publications, Inc.

Janz, T., L. Hellervik, and D.C. Gilmore. 1986. *Behavior Description Interviewing: New, Accurate, Cost Effective*. Boston, MA.: Allyn and Bacon, Inc.

Kane, J.R. 1988. *Selection Procedures: Research vs. Reality*. Paper presented at the 49th Annual Convention of the Canadian Psychological Association, Montréal, Québec (June).

Karren, R.J., and S.M. Nkomo. 1988. "So You Want to Work for Us." *Personnel Administrator* 38: 88–92.

Keenan, A. 1977. "Some Relationships Between Interviewers' Personal Feelings about Candidates and Their General Evaluation of Them." *Journal of Occupational Psychology* 50: 275–83.

Kennedy, R. 1985. "Validation of Five Structured Interviews." Unpublished master's thesis. East Carolina University.

Landy, F.J. 1976. "The Validity of the Interview in Police Officer Selection." *Journal of Applied Psychology* 61: 193–98.

Latham, G.P. 1989. "The Reliability, Validity, and Practicality of the Situational Interview." In R.W. Eder and G.R. Ferris, eds., *The Employment Interview: Theory, Research, and Practice*. Newbury Park, CA: Sage Publications, Inc.

Latham, G.P., and L.M. Saari. 1984. "Do People Do What They Say? Further Studies on the Situational Interview." *Journal of Applied Psychology* 69: 569–73.

Latham, G.P., L.M. Saari, E.D. Pursell, and M.A. Campion. 1980. "The Situational Interview." *Journal of Applied Psychology* 65: 422–27.

Latham, G.P., and D.P. Skarlicki. 1995. "Criterion-Related Validity of the Situational and Patterned Behavior Description Interviews with Organizational Citizenship Behavior." *Human Performance* 8: 67–80.

Lin, T.R., G.H. Dobbins, and J.L. Farh. 1992. "A Field Study of Age and Race Similarity Effects on Interview Ratings in Conventional and Situational Interviews." *Journal of Applied Psychology* 77: 363–71.

Maas, J.B. 1965. "Patterned Scaled Expectation Interview: Reliability Studies on a New Technique." *Journal of Applied Psychology* 49: 431–33.

Maurer, S.D., and C. Fay. 1988. "Effect of Situational Interviews, Conventional Structured Interviews, and Training on Interview Rating Agreement: An Experimental Analysis." *Personnel Psychology* 41: 329–44.

Mayfield, E.C. 1964. "The Selection Interview—a Re-Evaluation of Published Research." *Personnel Psychology* 17: 239–60.

Mayfield, E.C., S.H. Brown, and B.W. Hamstra. 1980. "Selection Interviewing in the Life Insurance Industry: An Update of Research and Practice." *Personnel Psychology* 33: 725–39.

McDaniel, M.A., D.L. Whetzel, F.L. Schmidt, and S.D. Maurer. 1994. "The Validity of Employment Interviews: A Comprehensive Review and Meta-Analysis." *Journal of Applied Psychology* 79: 599–616.

McMurry, R.N. 1947. "Validating the Patterned Interview." *Personnel* 23: 263–72.

Meehl, P.E. 1954. *Clinical Versus Statistical Prediction: A Theoretical Analysis and a Review of the Evidence.* Minneapolis, Minn.: University of Minnesota Press.

Mosher, M.R. 1991. *Development of a Behaviorally Consistent Structured Interview.* Paper presented at the 27th International Applied Military Psychology Symposium, Stockholm, Sweden (June).

Motowidlo, S.J., G.W. Carter, M.D. Dunnette, N. Tippins, S. Werner, J.R. Burnett, and M.J. Vaughan. 1992. "Studies of the Structured Behavioral Interview." *Journal of Applied Psychology* 77: 571–87.

Nunnally, J.C. 1978. *Psychometric Theory*, 2nd ed. New York: McGraw-Hill.

Orpen, C. 1985. "Patterned Behavior Description Interviews versus

Unstructured Interviews: A Comparative Validity Study." *Journal of Applied Psychology* 70: 774–76.

Osburn, H.G., C. Timmreck, and D. Bigby. 1981. "Effect of Dimensional Relevance on Accuracy of Simulated Hiring Decisions by Employment Interviewers." *Journal of Applied Psychology* 66: 159–65.

Paullin, C. 1993. "Features of Structured Interviews which Enhance Perceptions of Fairness." In R.D. Arvey, chair, *Perceptions, Theories, and Issues of Fairness in the Employment Interview.* Symposium presented at the 101st Annual Convention of the American Psychological Association, Toronto, Ontario.

Porter, M.E. 1991. *Canada at the Crossroads: The Reality of a New Competitive Environment.* Ottawa, ON: The Business Council on National Issues.

Pursell, E.D., M.A. Campion, and S.R. Gaylord. 1980. "Structured Interviewing: Avoiding Selection Problems." *Personnel Journal* 59: 907–12.

Ree, M.J., J.A. Earles, and M.S. Teachout. 1994. "Predicting Job Performance: Not Much More than *g*." *Journal of Applied Psychology* 79: 518–24.

Robertson, I.T., L. Gratton, and U. Rout. 1990. "The Validity of Situational Interviews for Administrative Jobs." *Journal of Organizational Behavior* 11: 69–76.

Robertson, I.T., and P.J. Makin. 1986. "Management Selection in Britain: A Survey and Critique." *Journal of Occupational Psychology* 59: 45–57.

Rynes, S. 1991. "Recruitment, Job-Choice, and Post-Hire Consequences: A Call for New Research Directions." In M.D. Dunnette and L.M. Hough, eds., *Handbook of Industrial and Organizational Psychology*, Vol. 2. Palo Alto, CA: Consulting Psychologists Press.

Sawyer, J. 1966. "Measurement and Prediction, Clinical and Statistical." *Psychological Bulletin* 66: 178–200.

Schmitt, N. 1976. "Social and Situational Determinants of Interview Decisions: Implications for the Employment Interview." *Personnel Psychology* 29: 79–101.

Schuh, A.J. 1978. "Effects of Early Interruption and Note Taking on Listening Accuracy and Decision Making in the Interview." *Bulletin of the Psychonomic Society* 12: 242–44.

Smith, P.C., and L.M. Kendall. 1963. "Retranslation of Expectations: An Approach to the Construction of Unambiguous Anchors for Rating Scales." *Journal of Applied Psychology* 47: 149–55.

Springbett, B.M. 1958. "Factors Affecting the Final Decision in the Employment Interview." *Canadian Journal of Psychology* 12: 13–22.

Stevens, C.K., and A.L. Kristof. 1995. "Making the Right Impression: A Field Study of Applicant Impression Management during Job Interviews." *Journal of Applied Psychology* 80: 587–606.

Tucker, D.H., and P.M. Rowe. 1977. "Consulting the Application Form Prior to the Interview: An Essential Step in the Selection Process." *Journal of Applied Psychology* 62: 283–87.

Tucker, D.H., and P.M. Rowe. 1979. "Relationship Between Expectancy, Causal Attribution and Final Hiring Decisions in the Employment Interview." *Journal of Applied Psychology* 64: 27–34.

Webster, E.C. 1964. *Decision Making in the Employment Interview*. Montréal: Industrial Relations Centre, McGill University.

Webster, E.C. 1982. *The Employment Interview: A Social Judgement Process*. Schomberg, Ont.: S.I.P. Publications.

Weekley, J.A., and J.A. Gier. 1987. "Reliability and Validity of the Situational Interview for a Sales Position." *Journal of Applied Psychology* 72: 484–87.

Wernimont, P.F., and J.P. Campbell. 1968. "Signs, Samples, and Criteria." *Journal of Applied Psychology* 52: 372–76.

Wiesner, W.H. 1989. "The Contributions of Job Relevance, Timing, and Rating Scale to the Validity of the Employment Interview." In S.F. Cronshaw, chair, *Improving Interview Validity and Legal Defensibility through Structuring*. Symposium conducted at the 50th Annual Convention of the Canadian Psychological Association.

Wiesner, W.H., and S.F. Cronshaw. 1988. "A Meta-Analytic Investigation of the Impact of Interview Format and Degree of Structure on the Validity of the Employment Interview." *Journal of Occupational Psychology* 61: 275–90.

Wright, P.M., P.A. Lichtenfels, and E.D. Pursell. 1989. "The Structured Interview: Additional Studies and a Meta-Analysis." *Journal of Occupational Psychology* 62: 191–99.

Yonge, K.A. 1956. "The Value of the Interview: An Orientation and a Pilot Study." *Journal of Applied Psychology* 40: 25–31.

10

Decision
Making

◆ ◆ ◆
CHAPTER GOALS

This chapter considers ways of reducing subjectivity and error in making selection decisions by using scientific methods that maximize selection effectiveness and efficiency. After reading this chapter you should

- appreciate the complexity of decision making in the employee selection context;

- be familiar with the sources of common decision making errors in employee selection;

- understand the distinction between judgmental and statistical *collection* of applicant information;

- understand the distinction between judgmental and statistical *combination* of applicant information; and

- understand the advantages and disadvantages of various decision making models.

"The purpose of selection is to discriminate." The preceding statement may sound strange in the context of our discussion of employment equity in Chapter 2. Unfortunately, the term *discrimination* has acquired a negative connotation because of its frequent association with the word "unfair." In fact, we do not want to discriminate unfairly, but we do want to discriminate on the basis of applicants' abilities to do the work. Just as we discriminate in the grocery store between the good fruit or vegetables and those we do not want, our task in selection is to discriminate between those applicants we believe will become effective employees and those who will not. Thus, selection involves making decisions about which applicants to hire and which not to hire, based on the information available.

Unfortunately, humans are imperfect decision makers (Simon, 1957). The use of phrases such as "I'm only human," as justification for having made mistakes, reflects our common understanding of this principle. Factors other than logic typically enter into our decisions. Decisions are influenced by emotional reactions to applicants, by political motives, as well as by a variety of constraints (Bazerman, 1986; Janis and Mann, 1977). Decision makers often make decisions based on inadequate or erroneous information. As a result, employers frequently make poor hiring decisions. The purpose of this chapter is to provide information and tools that can assist employers in making better selection decisions.

◆ ◆ ◆
THE CONTEXT OF SELECTION DECISIONS

Employers typically have to contend with a number of constraints and competing demands when making selection decisions. Often, time pressures prevent them from making logical or objective choices. If they need to fill vacant positions quickly they will tend to "satisfice" (Simon, 1957). That is, rather than searching for the best candidates, they will select the first applicants they encounter who meet minimum levels of acceptability. Similarly, if an insufficient number of suitable applicants is available or if the level of applicant qualifications is quite low, employers' standards of acceptability tend to drop (Ross and Ellard, 1986). They will accept less qualified applicants rather than continuing their recruitment efforts in order to generate applications from better qualified candidates.

Sometimes, rather than selecting for a specific job, employers select applicants for the organization. Their selection decisions are based on perceptions of applicants' overall suitability for the organization and they do not concern themselves with which job a candidate should be placed in until after the hiring decision has been made. Such organizations tend to have changeable jobs, flexible job descriptions, or to practice job rotation or rapid promotion. They tend to be small or rapidly growing companies such as Liburdi Engineering in Hamilton, Ontario. Liburdi is a very successful, innovative company that specializes in remanufacturing jet engine components for airlines around the world. Liburdi's success is highly dependent on finding high quality employees who are flexible and fit in well with the organization's culture. That culture requires employees to be flexible and innovative, always looking for ways of improving any product or process in the company.

Another form of selection involves promotion or transfer. Although promotions or transfers are often made on the basis of seniority or merit, they are most effective if treated as selection decisions. The candidates selected should be those most qualified for the vacant positions. When candidates are selected on the basis of merit or good job performance, the selection decision is based on the assumption that good performance in one job is indicative of good performance in another. However, the best salesperson or machinist will not necessarily make the best sales manager or shop supervisor. In fact, he or she might be quite incompetent in the new job (Peter and Hull, 1969). On the other hand, promotions based on seniority are based on the assumption that the most experienced employee would be most effective. But the most experienced salesperson might not even be the best salesperson, let alone the best sales manager. Therefore, just as in other selection decisions, candidates for promotion or transfer should be assessed in terms of the knowledge, skills, abilities, and other attributes they possess relevant to the positions for which they are being considered.

◆ ◆ ◆
SELECTION ERRORS

Many employers believe they have a knack for making good selection decisions. Some look for a firm handshake, unswerving eye contact, or upright posture in the applicant. Others look for confidence, enthusiasm, or personality. Most employers hold *implicit theories* about how certain behaviours, mannerisms, or personality characteristics go together. *Implicit theories* are personal beliefs that are held about how people or things function, without objective evidence and often without conscious awareness. For example, an employer might believe that unswerving eye contact reveals honesty, directness, and confidence. However, such an assumption is not necessarily warranted. Maintaining eye contact could be an interview tactic learned by the applicant or it could even reflect hostility. Moreover, in some cultures maintaining direct eye contact is considered rude and inappropriate behaviour. Applicants from these cultures would be disadvantaged if eye contact becomes a factor in the selection decision.

One employer asked applicants to lunch in order to observe them eating. The employer believed that those who eat quickly are energetic workers, that they eat quickly in order to be able to get on with their work. Before we dismiss this implicit theory as total nonsense it might be worth considering it in the light of the Type A v. Type B personality dimensions. Type A individuals are seen as energetic, driven, hard working and—yes—they tend to eat quickly. Type B individuals are seen as more relaxed and easygoing and, though they might produce quality work, tend to work more slowly. They also tend to eat more slowly. It is therefore possible that, in this case, the implicit theory could have some validity. However, although a few implicit theories might be useful in predicting job performance, most are not.

Many other employers make subjective decisions based on gut feelings about the applicant. They hire applicants simply because they like them or seem to get along well with them, at least based on the few minutes they spend together in the interview. An employer may hire applicants he or she feels sorry for, only to regret it later. Invariably, such gut feelings, as well as the implicit theories, lead to poor selection decisions.

Although employers assess a considerable amount of (often complex) information about each candidate, they must simplify this information to produce a dichotomous decision. Candidates are classified as either acceptable or unacceptable and hired or not hired on the basis of this assessment. Sometimes these decisions turn out to be correct. The applicant who is hired becomes a productive and valued employee. Other times (more often than many employers care to admit) employers make mistakes by hiring individuals who turn out to be unsuitable. The four possible outcomes of a selection decision are presented in Table 10.1. (Recall the Taylor/Russell Utility Model discussed in Chapter 3.)

TABLE 10.1 OUTCOMES OF THE SELECTION PROCESS

		Not Hired	Hired
Criterion Measures of Job Performance	Success	False Negative (Miss)	True Positive (Hit)
	Failure	True Negative (Hit)	False Positive (Miss)
		Not Hired	Hired

Selection Decision

Two of the outcomes in Table 10.1, the true positive and the true negative, are correct decisions or "hits." In the *true positive* outcome, the employer has hired an applicant who turns out to be a successful employee. In the *true negative* outcome, the employer did not hire an applicant who would have been considered a failure as an employee if hired. Obviously, an employer would wish to maximize both these "hits" or correct predictions but, as we will demonstrate later in this chapter, that can be quite difficult to accomplish. The two other outcomes represent selection errors or "misses."

A *false positive error* occurs when an applicant is assessed favourably and is hired but proves to be unsuccessful on the job. This is a costly error and may even be disastrous in some jobs. Productivity, profits, and the company's reputation may suffer when such errors are made. It may be difficult to terminate the employees once hired, termination can be costly, and grievance proceedings could result from the termination. Moreover, replacements for the unsuccessful employee must be recruited, selected, and trained, all at additional cost. Some organizations use probationary periods (e.g., between one and six months) for new employees in order to reduce the costs of false positive errors. In fact, tenure for professors is really a probation system—in this case the probationary period is five or six years.

A *false negative error* is one in which the applicant is assessed unfavourably and is not hired but would have been successful if hired. Such errors tend to go unnoticed because there are usually no obvious negative consequences for the employer as there are with false positive errors. The employer rarely finds out about the quality of the applicant that was not hired. Only in high profile occupations such as professional sports does a false negative error become readily apparent. When an athlete who is turned down by one team becomes a star pitcher, goalie, or fullback with a competing team, the first team is constantly faced with its mistake.

However, even though false negative errors are rarely that obvious in most organizations, they can be costly. Applicants for key jobs (e.g., a software designer) might develop highly successful products for a competing organization that did hire them. Furthermore, when an organization turns down a number of good candidates who are then hired by a competitor, even for non-key jobs, the competitor could gain a significant advantage in productivity. Moreover, false negative errors might adversely affect minority applicants and could result in human rights litigation.

Although it is not possible to entirely avoid or even recognize all errors when making selection decisions, they can be minimized. Valid selection methods and systematic procedures will serve to improve the probability of making correct selection decisions. One particular challenge faced by employers is how to make sense of the various, and sometimes conflicting, sources of information about applicants in order to make an informed decision. The next section considers different ways of combining complex information and suggests some systematic procedures for making selection decisions.

◆ ◆ ◆
COLLECTION AND COMBINATION OF INFORMATION

Before a selection decision can be made, information about the applicants must be collected from various sources and combined in some way. Typically, employers collect this information on application forms or from résumés, in employment interviews, and through reference checks. Many employers also administer ability, personality, and/or other tests, collect and score biographical information, or make use of assessment centres. These methods of collecting applicant information are discussed in detail in Chapters 7, 8, and 9. Sometimes all the information is in agreement and the decision can be straightforward. Other times the information is contradictory and the decision is more difficult. For example, if one applicant looks very good "on paper" (i.e., in the résumé), has a high score on a mental ability test, and receives glowing recommendations from the references, but does poorly in the interview, while another applicant does well on everything except the mental ability test, what is the appropriate decision? The employer must find some way of making sense of this information so that the best possible selection decision can be made.

Information collected from some sources, such as test scores, tends to be more objective. A good test provides a reliable and valid measure of some attribute, which can be readily used to compare applicants on a numerical or statistical basis. That is, no (or very little) human judgment is involved in collecting this score. We shall refer to these methods of collecting applicant information or data as *statistical*. Information collected from more subjective sources, such as unstructured interviews, rely much more, or even exclusively, on human judgment. We shall refer to these methods of collecting applicant information or data as *judgmental* (some authors refer to these as "clinical" methods).

Just as applicant data can be collected statistically or judgmentally, the data can be *combined* using statistical and judgmental methods. Data combined mathematically, using a formula, has been synthesized in a more objective fashion, which we shall call *statistical* combination. Combining data through human judgment or an overall impression is a more subjective process, which we shall refer to as *judgmental* combination. Thus, a number of permutations are possible. Judgmentally collected data can be combined in either a judgmental or statistical manner and statistically collected data can be combined in either a judgmental or statistical manner. Moreover, it is possible that some of the data are collected judgmentally (e.g., unstructured interview) whereas other data are collected statistically (e.g., test scores). This composite of judgmental and statistical data can also be combined in either a judgmental or statistical manner. The possible permutations of methods of data collection and combination are presented in Table 10.2.

In the *pure judgment* approach, judgmental data are collected and combined in a judgmental manner. The decision maker forms an overall impression of the applicant based on gut feeling or implicit theories rather than explicit, objective criteria. In this approach, the decision maker both collects information and makes a decision about the applicant. An employer making a selection decision based on an unstructured interview is representative of this approach. The employer who hires applicants because he feels sorry for them is using intuition or pure judgment to make his decisions.

TABLE 10.2 METHODS OF COLLECTING AND COMBINING APPLICANT INFORMATION		
Method of Collecting Data	**Method of Combining Data**	
	Judgmental	**Statistical**
Judgmental	Pure Judgment	Trait Ratings
Statistical	Profile Interpretation	Pure Statistical
Both	Judgmental Composite	Statistical Composite
Sources: Adapted from Sawyer (1966).		

The *trait rating* approach is one in which judgmental data are combined statistically. A number of judgmental ratings are made (e.g., based on interviews, application forms or résumés, or reference checks). The ratings are combined using an arithmetic formula, which produces an overall score for each applicant. Although the decision makers collect the information and make ratings on each of the components, the decision is based on the overall score generated by the mathematical formula.

Profile interpretation strategy involves combining statistical data in a judgmental manner. Data are collected from objective sources such as tests or biographical inventories. The decision maker examines these data to form an overall, subjective impression of the applicant's suitability for the job. The selection decision is based on this overall impression or gut feeling.

In the *pure statistical* approach, statistically collected data are combined statistically. Test scores or scores from other objective sources such as biographical inventories or Weighted Application Blanks are fed into a formula or regression equation, which produces an overall combined score. Applicants are then selected in order of their scores (i.e., the top scorer, then the second highest, and so on until the desired number of applicants has been selected).

The *judgmental composite* involves collecting both judgmental and statistical data and then combining them judgmentally. A decision maker might conduct interviews and reference checks (judgmental data) and have access to test scores (statistical data). The decision maker then examines the test scores and considers the impressions of the applicants gained from the interviews and reference checks in order to form an overall impression and make a decision concerning who should be hired. This is probably the most common method used by employers to make selection decisions.

The *statistical composite* also involves collecting both judgmental and statistical data but the data are combined statistically. Ratings or scores are given or obtained from each component, such as an interview, a reference check, a personality test, and a mental ability test. The ratings or scores are combined in a formula or regression equation to produce an overall score for each applicant. Selection decisions are thus based on the applicants' scores.

Although all six of the basic decision making approaches described above have been used in employee selection, they are not equally effective. A considerable body of research indicates that the pure statistical and the statistical composite approaches are generally superior to the other methods in predicting performance (Meehl, 1954; Sawyer, 1966). Both of these approaches involve combining information in a statistical manner. There are several possible explanations for the superiority of statistical methods over judgmental methods of combining information (Kleinmuntz, 1990). First, as noted previously, implicit theories are more likely to bias evaluations and contribute to error when judgmental methods are used. Irrelevant factors such as the applicant's appearance or mannerisms are likely to unduly influence the decision. Second, it is difficult for decision makers to take into account the complexity of all the information available to them when they use judgmental processes to make decisions. Because the ability to remember and process information is easily overloaded, decision makers tend to oversimplify or inappropriately simplify information to create applicant summaries that are inaccurate. Third, it is virtually impossible to assign appropriate weights to all the selection instruments when judgmental procedures are used. How important should reference checks be in comparison to ability tests or interviews? It is difficult to give even equal weighting to all selection information in a subjective manner. Sometimes particular applicant data, such as test scores, are ignored altogether in favour of impressions based on other sources, such as the interview. Statistical approaches are likely to provide better decisions, even when scores from all the selection instruments are weighted equally, because all applicant information is taken into consideration in a systematic manner.

It is worth noting that statistical approaches are compromised when poor quality information goes into the selection equation. The maxim "garbage in, garbage out" applies just as well to employee selection methods as it does to computer programming. Erroneous or irrelevant information, such as might be obtained from unstructured interviews, non-valid tests, or inaccurate references, will contribute error variance to the equation and reduce the likelihood of making good selection decisions. It is therefore important to ensure that only data coming from reliable and valid selection measures are combined to yield an overall score for each applicant.

◆ ◆ ◆

WHY DO EMPLOYERS RESIST USING STATISTICAL APPROACHES?

Although statistical approaches to decision making are clearly superior to judgmental approaches, employers tend to resist them (Gatewood and Feild,

1994). They prefer relying on gut feelings or instinct. There are probably several reasons for employers clinging to judgmental approaches. Employers might find it difficult to give up the personal control that judgmental approaches give them. They can choose to ignore or discount information that is at odds with gut feelings and they can emphasize or rely solely on information that is in accord with their feelings. When they use statistical approaches, their role becomes simply that of information collectors rather than judgmental decision makers. Employers also tend to be overconfident in their decision making abilities (Bazerman, 1986; Kleinmuntz, 1990). They generally believe that they are quite successful in selecting good job candidates. Unfortunately, few employers bother to keep track of their success or "hit" rates by reviewing the job performance of those they hired. If they did, they would become much more concerned about their abilities to judge applicant competence. Granted, there is a very small minority of employers who are able to assess job applicants with reasonable accuracy (e.g., Zedek, Tziner, and Middlestadt, 1983), but even they are outperformed by statistical models based on their own decision rules (known as *Bootstrapping*, see Kleinmuntz, 1990). Most employers are not very good judges of job applicant potential.

One method we have used quite effectively in workshops to demonstrate to managers the inaccuracy of their judgments is to show them videotapes of actual employment interviews. In fact, the applicants appearing on the videotapes had been hired and we had obtained job performance ratings from their supervisors after they had been working at least half a year. We asked the managers to rate the applicants and predict their job performance. We were then able to compare the managers' ratings and predictions with the applicants' actual job performance ratings. It was quite shocking for most of the managers to discover how badly they had misjudged the applicants.

◆ ◆ ◆
GROUP DECISION MAKING

Although most employee selection research has explored individual models of decision making, several surveys indicate that, in most organizations, selection decisions are made by groups (Cox, Schlueter, Moore, and Sullivan, 1989; Kane, 1988; Robertson and Makin, 1986). Some researchers suggest that groups can be poor decision makers (Brandstatter, Davis, and Stocker-

Kreichgauer, 1983; Janis and Mann, 1977; Steiner, 1972). Power motives, politics, conformity to the group, and other factors serve to reduce the objectivity of group decisions. However, in spite of all the potential problems encountered in group decision making, many researchers conclude that groups are generally better at problem-solving and decision making than the average individual (Hill, 1982; Michaelson, Watson, and Black, 1989; Shaw, 1981). As indicated in Chapter 9, Wiesner and Cronshaw (1988) found that selection interview boards or panels are better at predicting job performance than individual interviewers when the interview is unstructured and as good as individual interviewers when the interview is structured.

In most organizations there appears to be an intuitive understanding that groups might make better selection decisions than individuals; thus, selection teams or panels are commonplace. Having two or more individuals make the selection decision can reduce the effects of the biases that any one individual might have. Selection team or panel members are more likely to be careful in their assessments when they have to justify their ratings to other team members. The fact that differences of opinion concerning an applicant must be resolved to everyone's satisfaction will tend to reduce the impact of biases. Also, with more individuals examining applicant information it is less likely that particular information will be overlooked or distorted. A less commendable reason for organizations using selection teams or panels is that such teams make it easier to share the blame for poor decisions. Individual members could be somewhat less conscientious than they should be because they can evade personal responsibility and consequences for their decisions. Nevertheless, based on the research evidence, it is advisable that any judgmental information be collected by a selection team or panel. In fact, numerous Canadian human rights tribunals have cited the use of selection panels as an important factor in defending against discrimination suits (Gardiner and Hackett, 1996).

One recent development in the Canadian workplace is the increasing use of teams to do work. Selecting appropriate team members has thus become an important challenge and the focus of some recent research (e.g., Kichuk and Wiesner, 1996; Stevens and Campion, 1994). Not only job-related ability but also personality and interpersonal factors must be taken into consideration when selecting for a team. Some companies like Toyota, Westinghouse Canada and Dofasco, a steel manufacturer in Hamilton, Ontario, have the workteams interview and select new team members. The existing team members intimately know the work that has to be done and have a good sense of the personal qualities that will contribute effective team membership. The assumption behind allowing workteams to select their own members is that they are likely to make better decisions than a manager who has relatively limited knowledge of the work and the team. More research is needed to determine whether workteams do make better selection decisions than their supervisors or managers. In any case, it is just as important for such workteams to use objective, validated selection methods as it is for managers to use such methods.

When teams make selection decisions, there are often disagreements among team members as to appropriate ratings or who should be hired. It is important that such differences be resolved as objectively as possible. The easiest way to resolve differences is to average the team members' individual scores to arrive at a combined score for each applicant (this is analogous to statistical combination). However, as noted in the section on the collection and combination of information, such combinations can be misleading if some of the team members submit erroneous or biased ratings. As a general rule, when there is close agreement among team members' ratings, the individual ratings can be safely averaged. But when there is disagreement (e.g., a range of two or more points), team members should discuss the reasons for their ratings until they arrive at a consensus. By discussing their rationales for the ratings, team members are likely to uncover some of the misperceptions, biases, and errors in recollection that can contribute to differences in scores.

◆ ◆ ◆
SETTING CUTOFF SCORES

In the next section we will consider different models of decision making. Several of these models make use of something called a cutoff score, so it will be necessary to gain an understanding of cutoff scores before we discuss the models. *Cutoff scores* serve as criteria or thresholds in selection decisions. Applicants who score below the cutoff on a given predictor (e.g., test, interview) are rejected. Thus, cutoff scores ensure that applicants meet some minimum level of ability or qualification to be considered for a job. In college or university, a grade of 50 percent often serves as a cutoff. Students whose grade is lower than 50 percent fail the course. This cutoff has been established by convention. In most organizations, cutoffs are established based on the predictor scores of individuals who are successful on the job being selected for, or based on expert judgments concerning the difficulty of the predictor items (Schmitt and Klimoski, 1991).

One method of establishing cutoff scores involves identifying the proportion of applicants who are to be hired and determining how stringent the cutoff score should be to select only the desired number of applicants. First, the expected *selection ratio* is calculated (number of individuals to be hired divided by the expected number of applicants). Next, the distribution of the applicants' scores on the predictor is estimated by examining the predictor score distributions of past groups of applicants or of current employees (i.e., predictive or concurrent validation data). Finally, the cutoff score is established by applying the selection ratio to the predictor score distribution in order to determine the score that only the top applicants (the proportion to be hired) would attain. For example, if a fire department seeks to hire five firefighters and 150 people are expected to apply, the selection ratio will be .03 (5/150). About 3 percent of expected applicants will be accepted or, conversely, about 97 percent of expected applicants will have to be rejected. The cutoff score should therefore be set at the 97th percentile of the distribution of predictor scores (plus or minus one standard error of measurement). That is, the cutoff score is set so that only 3 percent of applicants would be expected to meet or exceed the score (or 97 percent would fall below it). This approach is limited to setting cutoffs for a single predictor. When more than one predictor is to be used, it is common to use expert judges.

There are several ways in which expert judges can be used to establish cutoffs, but they differ only slightly in their methods. We will consider the general approach and readers are encouraged to consult Cascio (1991) or Gatewood and Feild (1994) for more detailed treatments of the various methods. Experienced employees, supervisors, or managers who know the job well or industrial psychologists typically serve as expert judges. Essentially, the expert judges are asked to rate the difficulty of test items (or interview questions) and to indicate what score on each item should be attained by a minimally competent applicant. These ratings are summed for all items to yield a pass threshold or cutoff score. Cutoff scores can be established in this manner for each of the predictors used in the selection process.

♦ ♦ ♦
DECISION MAKING MODELS

There are several different decision making models that involve combining applicant information statistically (regardless of how that information was collected). These models are *multiple regression, multiple cutoffs, multiple hurdle, combination,* and *profile matching* (Gatewood and Feild, 1994). We will now consider the models in terms of their usefulness for different purposes and under different conditions.

MULTIPLE REGRESSION MODEL

In the multiple regression model, the applicant's scores on each predictor (e.g., tests, interviews, reference checks) are weighted and summed to yield a total score (e.g., predicted job performance). The appropriate regression weights or b values are determined through prior research, where the unique contributions of each predictor (X) to predicting job performance (Y) are investigated.

Table 10.3 provides some hypothetical data for purposes of illustration. The scores of four applicants on each of four predictors, the maximum scores, regression weights, cutoff scores, and mean or average scores for each predictor are presented in the table. Applicants for a retail sales position wrote a cognitive ability test, completed an extraversion scale, were inter-

TABLE 10.3 EXAMPLES OF SALES APPLICANT DATA				
	Predictor Scores			
Applicant	Cognitive Ability Test	Extraversion Scale	Structured Interview	Reference Check
Mr. A	36	30	27	11
Ms. B	32	37	16	10
Mr. C	44	22	24	13
Ms. D	37	27	28	14
Maximum Possible Scores	50	40	30	15
Regression Weights	1.0	.5	.7	.6
Cutoff Scores	30	24	18	10
Mean Scores	35	27	23	11

viewed, and provided references, which were scored. The maximum score on the cognitive ability test (X_1) is 50 and the regression weight (b_1) is 1. The maximum score on the extraversion scale (X_2) is 40 and the regression weight (b_2) is 0.5 (i.e., the extraversion score contributes only half as much as the cognitive ability score to the prediction of job performance). The maximum interview score (X_3) is 30 and the weighting for the interview score (b_3) is 0.7, while the maximum reference check score (X_4) is 15 and the score for the reference check is given a weight (b_4) of 0.6. The regression equation for predicting job performance in this case is

$$Y = b_1X_1 + b_2X_2 + b_3X_3 + b_4X_4$$

Predicted job performance = Cognitive Ability Score + 0.5 Extraversion Score + 0.7 Interview Score + 0.6 Reference Check Score. A predicted job performance score can thus be calculated for each applicant.

Applying the regression equation to the data in Table 10.3 yields a total predicted score of 76.5 for Mr. A, 67.7 for Ms. B, 79.6 for Mr. C, and 78.5 for Ms. D. The applicants can now be ranked based on their total predicted scores: (1) Mr. C, (2) Ms. D, (3) Mr. A, and (4) Ms. B. They can be selected on a top-down basis until the desired number of candidates has been obtained. If two candidates are needed, Mr. C and Ms. D would be selected.

The multiple regression model assumes that the predictors are linearly related to the criterion and that a low score on one predictor can be compensated for by a high score on another predictor. An applicant could do very poorly in the interview (e.g., receive a score of zero) and still do well if he or she receives high scores on the tests and the reference check. However, the assumptions made by the multiple regression model are not necessarily warranted. First, very high scores on some predictors might be as undesirable as very low scores. For example, while an extreme introvert might have difficulty relating to customers in a retail sales position, an extreme extrovert might annoy them and drive them away. Second, there might be a minimum level of competence required on each of the predictors for the individual to perform acceptably in the job. For example, a very low interview score might indicate that the applicant has such poor interpersonal and communication skills that he or she cannot function acceptably in retail sales, regardless of high cognitive ability and extraversion scores. The multiple regression approach also has the disadvantage of being expensive, particularly for large applicant pools, because all applicants must be assessed on all predictors.

Nevertheless, the multiple regression approach does have several advantages. It is an efficient method of combining multiple predictors in an optimal manner and it minimizes errors in prediction. Moreover, different regression equations can be produced for different jobs even if the same predictors are used for all jobs. Thus, if applicants are being selected for more than one job, they can be placed in the job for which their total score is the highest or they can be placed in the job where their total score is the farthest above the minimum score necessary for acceptable job performance. The multiple regression approach is probably the most efficient decision-making approach if the assumptions underlying the model are not violated (Cascio, 1991).

MULTIPLE CUTOFF MODEL

In the multiple cutoff model, scores on all predictors are obtained for all applicants, just as in the multiple regression model. Using the data in Table 10.3 to illustrate, all applicants would write the cognitive ability and extraversion tests, all would be interviewed, and reference check information would be scored for all. However, in this model, applicants are rejected if their scores on any of the predictors fall below the cutoff scores. In our example, both Mr. A and Ms. D score above the cutoffs on all four predictors. Ms. B's score falls below the cutoff on the structured interview and Mr. C's score falls below the cutoff on the extraversion scale. Ms. B and Mr. C would thus be rejected. Note that this is quite a different result from the multiple regression approach, where Mr. C obtained the highest score and would have been selected.

The multiple cutoff model assumes that a minimum level is required on each of the attributes measured by the predictors for successful job performance (i.e., there is a non-linear relationship among the predictors and job performance). The model also assumes that the predictors are not compensatory (i.e., it is not possible to compensate for a low score on one predictor with a high score on another predictor).

A disadvantage of the multiple cutoff model is that, just like the multiple regression approach, it requires that all applicants be assessed on all procedures. This requirement makes it expensive to administer. Another disadvantage is that the model only identifies those applicants who have minimum qualifications for the job. There is no way of distinguishing among those who have passed the minimum cutoffs. If 10 applicants have passed the cutoffs but the employer only wants to select five candidates, how is the employer to decide which ones to select?

In spite of its disadvantages, the multiple cutoff model does serve to narrow the pool of applicants to a smaller set of minimally qualified candidates and it is an easy model for managers to understand. It is probably most useful when minimum levels of certain physical abilities are required for job performance (Gatewood and Feild, 1994). For example, some occupations such as law enforcement, firefighting, or heavy manufacturing have minimum specifications for eyesight, colour vision, or strength.

MULTIPLE HURDLE MODEL

In the multiple hurdle model, applicants must pass the minimum cutoff for each predictor, in turn, before being assessed on the next predictor. As soon as an applicant has failed to meet the cutoff on a given predictor, he or she ceases to be a candidate for the job and is not assessed on any of the remaining predictors. In our example in Table 10.3, all four applicants pass the cognitive ability test and go on to write the extraversion scale. Mr. C fails to meet the cutoff on the extraversion scale and is dropped from further consideration. Only Mr. A, Ms. B, and Ms. D go on to the structured interview, where Ms. B fails to meet the cutoff and is rejected. Reference checks are performed only for Mr. A and Ms. D, who both pass and become candidates for the job.

The result is identical to the one for the multiple cutoff model but the approach is less expensive because fewer applicants need to be assessed at each stage of the selection process. Both models make the same assumptions but differ in the procedure used for collecting predictor information. The multiple cutoff approach uses a non-sequential procedure whereas the multiple hurdle procedure is sequential (i.e., applicants must pass each predictor cutoff, in sequence, before going on to the next predictor). Like the multiple cutoff approach, the multiple hurdle model narrows the pool of applicants to a smaller set of candidates meeting minimum qualifications and is also an easy model to understand.

The multiple hurdle approach has the disadvantage of being more time-consuming than the multiple regression or multiple cutoff approaches. Applicants need to be assessed and scored on each predictor before a decision can be made on whether to assess them on the next predictor. It also makes it difficult to estimate the validity of each procedure, particularly in later stages of the selection process. There are relatively fewer applicants being assessed on predictors toward the end of the sequence (e.g., interview and reference check, in our example), so restriction of range becomes a problem for estimating the validity of these predictors. One other disadvantage is that, like the multiple cutoff model, this model only identifies those applicants who have minimum qualifications for the job and does not distinguish among those who have passed all the cutoffs.

Like the multiple cutoff approach, the multiple hurdle approach is most appropriate when minimum levels of particular knowledge, skills, abilities, and other attributes (KSAOs) are necessary for job performance and cannot be compensated for by higher levels on other KSAOs. Moreover, the multiple hurdle approach is most useful when the applicant pool is large and some of the selection procedures are expensive (Gatewood and Feild, 1994). In such circumstances, the less expensive procedures (e.g., tests) can be used as hurdles at the beginning in order to screen out inappropriate applicants and reduce the applicant pool. Thus, the more expensive procedures (e.g., interviews) are used on a smaller pool of select applicants.

COMBINATION MODEL

In the combination model, all applicants are measured on all predictors and those falling below the cutoff on any of the predictors are rejected, just as in the multiple cutoff model. Then, multiple regression is used to calculate the total scores of those applicants who pass the cutoffs. The applicants are ranked by total score and selected on a top-down basis, as in the multiple regression method. The combination model is therefore a mixture of the multiple cutoff and multiple regression approaches. If we apply this model to the data in Table 10.3, Ms. B and Mr. C would be rejected because they do not pass all the cutoffs. So far, this result is identical to the result for the multiple cutoff model. Now the regression equation is applied to the remaining applicants, Mr. A and Ms. D. Recall from the section on the multiple regression model that Mr. A's total score is 76.5 and Ms. D's total score is 78.5. Ms. D is therefore ranked first and Mr. A second. If we were hiring only one candidate, Ms. D would be selected.

Like the multiple cutoff model, the combination model assumes that a minimum level of each of the KSAOs is required for effective job performance. A further assumption is that, once minimum levels have been reached, high scores on one predictor can compensate for low scores on another predictor. As might be expected, the combination model has the same advantages as the multiple cutoff model but has the additional advantage of providing a means of selecting from among those candidates who pass all the cutoffs. However, the combination approach is just as expensive as the multiple cutoff approach because all applicants are assessed on all predictors.

Obviously, the combination model is useful as long as the assumptions underlying the approach hold. It is an appropriate model when selection instruments do not vary greatly in cost and is particularly useful when a considerable number of applicants tend to pass all the cutoffs. When more applicants than can be hired pass the cutoffs, the combination model facilitates selection among those applicants.

PROFILE MATCHING

In the profile matching model, current employees who are considered successful on the job are assessed on several predictors. Their average scores on each predictor are used to form an *ideal* profile of scores required for successful job performance. One should also try to obtain average predictor scores for current employees who are considered poor or marginal performers. Obtaining scores for poor or marginal employees is not always easy because such employees are often dismissed or leave of their own accord soon after being hired or, if a valid selection system is used, tend not to be hired in the first place. If it is possible to obtain scores for poor performers, their average predictor scores should be compared with the average predictor scores of good performers to ensure that the predictors differentiate between good and poor performers. Those predictors that do not differentiate should not be included in the ideal profile of scores.

Once an ideal profile of scores has been established, applicants' predictor scores can be compared to the ideal profile. Those applicants whose profiles are most similar to the ideal profile can then be selected. One of two methods can be used to determine the degree of similarity between applicant profiles and the ideal profile: the correlation method or the D^2 method. The correlation method involves correlating an applicant's scores on the predictors with the predictor scores of the ideal profile. The higher the correlation, the greater the similarity between the applicant's profile and the ideal profile. The D^2 method involves calculating differences between an applicant's scores and ideal profile scores on each predictor, squaring the differences, and summing the squared differences to yield D^2. The larger D^2 is, the poorer is the match between the applicant's profile and the ideal profile. The D^2 method is preferred because it considers the magnitude of applicants' mean scores across the predictors, the degree to which applicant scores differ from the ideal scores, and the pattern or shape of applicant scores relative to the ideal profile. The correlation method only considers the pattern or shape of the scores (Nunnally, 1978).

In our example in Table 10.3, the mean scores across the predictors (i.e., the ideal profile) can be correlated with the applicants' scores across the predictors to produce a correlation coefficient for each of the applicants. The resulting correlation coefficients are as follows: Mr. A ($r = .987$), Ms. B ($r = .825$), Mr. C ($r = .910$), and Ms. D ($r = .979$). Using the D^2 method requires the subtraction of the mean score for each predictor from each applicant's score on that predictor to obtain a difference. The resulting differences are squared and the squares summed across predictors for each applicant to obtain a D^2 score. Our applicants in Table 10.3 obtained the following D^2 scores: Mr. A ($D^2 = 26$), Ms. B ($D^2 = 159$), Mr. C ($D^2 = 111$), and Ms. D ($D^2 = 38$). Recall that the smaller the D^2 score is, the better the match. Thus, in this example, the rank order for both the correlation and D^2 method are the same: (1) Mr. A, (2) Ms. D, (3) Mr. C, and (4) Ms. B.

Although the two methods produced identical rank orders in this example, the resulting rank orders are not always the same. Moreover, the correlation method often yields very high correlation coefficients, which barely differentiate applicants from each other. The D^2 method can also produce misleading results. An applicant whose scores substantially *exceed* the mean scores will have a high D^2 score and rank below an applicant whose scores fall close to the mean scores (whether slightly above or even below the means). Thus, this model is based on the assumption that scores that are higher than the ideal are as undesirable as scores that are lower than the ideal. In fact, the model assumes that there is one best profile when there may be several profiles that predict success just as well.

As noted previously, the profile matching model cannot be implemented if the predictors do not differentiate between employees who are poor performers and those who are good performers. Moreover, restriction of range can be a problem because truly poor performers are often difficult to find (i.e., they are asked to leave or are not hired in the first place). Also, because the profiles of successful employees could change over time, ideal profiles need to be checked periodically.

Profile matching does have the advantage of permitting the ranking of applicants based on their similarities to the ideal profile. It is an appropriate method to use when there is clearly a best type of employee for the job and when it can be demonstrated that poor employees tend to score higher as well as lower on the predictors than good employees (i.e., there is a curvilinear relationship between predictor scores and job performance). As these conditions rarely apply, multiple regression remains a more appropriate approach in virtually all circumstances (Gatewood and Feild, 1994).

◆ ◆ ◆
MAKING SELECTION DECISIONS

Regardless of which decision making model is used, the eventual aim of the selection process is to decide which applicants to hire. The models described in the previous sections lend themselves to one of two basic approaches, *top-down selection* and *banding*. Each method is based on particular assumptions and has certain advantages and disadvantages.

TOP-DOWN SELECTION

Top-down selection involves ranking applicants on the basis of their total scores and selecting from the top down until the desired number of candidates has been selected. This approach is based on the assumption that individuals scoring higher on the predictors will be better performers on the job than individuals scoring lower on the predictors (i.e., there is a linear relationship between predictor scores and job performance). As long as this assumption is not violated, top-down selection is considered the best approach for maximizing organizational performance (Gatewood and Feild, 1994). Only the top performers are hired.

One difficulty with using top-down selection is that it can have adverse impact against certain minority groups. For example, blacks tend to have slightly lower average scores than whites on certain tests. Selecting from the top down could therefore result in disproportionately more whites than blacks being hired. *Race norming* or *within-group scoring* has been suggested as a method of preventing such adverse impact. Applicants can be ranked on their predictor scores within their relevant minority groups. For example, whites could be ranked on their predictor scores relative to other whites and blacks could be rank-ordered on their predictor scores relative to other blacks. Then the top ranking black candidate and the top ranking white candidate could be selected, followed by the black and white candidates ranking second, and so on until the desired number of candidates is selected. Although top-down selection across all groups would result in the best quality candidates being hired, on average, ranking within groups permits the achievement of employment equity goals while still hiring high quality applicants (Gatewood and Feild, 1994).

Although the American Civil Rights Act of 1991 prohibits race norming, the adjustment of scores, or the use of different cutoff scores for different minority groups in the United States, there is no such legislation in Canada. Nevertheless, employment equity initiatives can be difficult to implement, as one Canadian fire department discovered. The Kitchener Fire Department attempted to increase minority representation in the department by reducing the cutoff score for women. Whereas male applicants needed a score of 85 to pass, the cutoff score for females was set at 70. The public outcry was so great that the department had to abandon this approach. Many individuals perceived this attempt as an example of reverse discrimination (i.e, discrimination against the white male applicants). An alternative approach to accomplishing employment equity is *banding*. Banding has been used successfully in the United States and should also be workable in Canada.

BANDING

Banding involves grouping applicants based on ranges of scores. The grouping process takes into account the concept of *standard error of measurement* (from classical test theory). Essentially, the standard error of measurement (SEM) reflects the fact that almost any measurement contains an error as well as a true score component. For example, if you obtain a score of 83 percent on an exam, part of that score reflects your true knowledge of the material tested but part of it reflects other factors such as your level of alertness during testing, level of stress, distractions, and luck. Not sleeping well the night before the test, experiencing personal problems, or spending considerable time studying material that turns out to be a very small component of the exam can reduce your test score so it under-represents your true knowledge. On the other hand, if you study only some of the course material but, as luck would have it, that very material constitutes virtually all of the test, if you obtain some advance knowledge of test content, or if you simply make some lucky guesses, your test score over-represents your true knowledge. Such errors of measurement are taken into account by the SEM, a statistic that reflects the reliability of an individual's score.

Bands around a given score are calculated as plus or minus two times the SEM (i.e., the score ± 2SEM). Assuming that the error is randomly distributed, we would be correct 95 percent of the time in asserting that an individual's true score lies within the band defined by plus or minus 2SEM. If the SEM in our example above is 2.53, we can establish a band of 5.06 points (2.53×2) around your score of 83. That is, there is a 95 percent probability that your true score is somewhere between 77.94 and 88.06 (83 ± 5.06). Now, let's assume you have a friend who wrote the same exam and scored 79 percent. Before you belittle your friend's lower grade, consider the effects of measurement error. If we construct a band around your friend's score of 79, we discover that his or her true score is somewhere between 73.94 and 84.06 (with a 95 percent probability). It is therefore possible that your friend's true score is higher than yours! In fact, because there is an overlap in the bands around your scores, we can assert that your scores are not statistically different from each other. From a measurement perspective, both of you can be viewed as being at the same level of proficiency with respect to the course material.

Banding is applied to selection decisions by calculating a band from the top score downwards. If the top score on a test is 96 and the SEM is 2.5, then the band extends from 96 down to 91 (96 – 5). There is no need to extend the band above 96 as 96 is the top score. Any scores falling within the band from 91 to 96 are considered equal because the differences among them are not statistically significant. We are therefore free to select any applicants we wish within the band. In fact, as long as their scores fall within the same band, we are free to select minority applicants ahead of non-minority applicants in order to accomplish employment equity objectives (Cascio, Outtz, Zedek, and Goldstein, 1991). Charges of reverse discrimination on the part of non-minority applicants scoring slightly higher than the minority applicants would be difficult to substantiate because their scores are not significantly different.

Bands can be constructed in one of two ways, fixed or sliding. *Fixed bands* are calculated starting at the top score, as described above. All the applicants within the band must be selected before a new band can be calculated. A new band is calculated starting from the highest score among those applicants who were not included in the first band. This process continues until the desired number of applicants has been hired. Table 10.4 illustrates both fixed and sliding bands with hypothetical data. The scores of 19 applicants have been ranked and some of them have been identified as minority applicants. If we assume that the SEM is 2.5, then the first band ranges from 91 to 96 (as described above). Using the fixed bands approach, we would select the applicants scoring 93 and 96 and then construct a second fixed band from 89 (the new highest score) down to 84. Within the second fixed band, we would select the minority applicants first and then the remainder of the applicants until all the required applicants scoring within the band

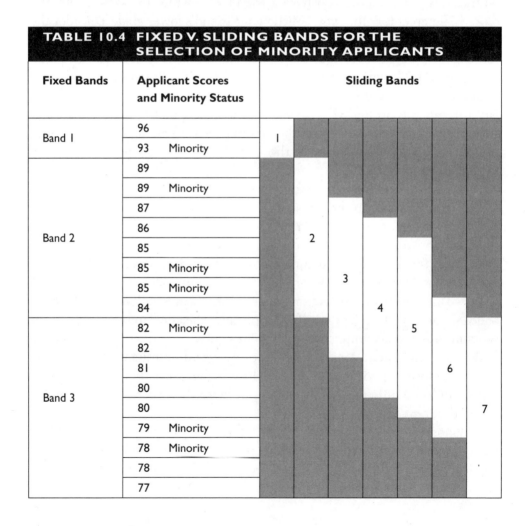

TABLE 10.4 FIXED V. SLIDING BANDS FOR THE SELECTION OF MINORITY APPLICANTS

Fixed Bands	Applicant Scores and Minority Status		Sliding Bands
Band 1	96		1
	93	Minority	
Band 2	89		
	89	Minority	
	87		
	86		2
	85		
	85	Minority	3
	85	Minority	
	84		4
Band 3	82	Minority	5
	82		
	81		6
	80		
	80		7
	79	Minority	
	78	Minority	
	78		
	77		

have been selected. If we required additional candidates, we would construct a third fixed band from 82 down to 77.

With *sliding bands*, not every applicant in the band needs to be selected before the next band is constructed. Once the top scorer in the band has been selected, a new band is constructed from the next highest score. In this manner, the band slides down each time the top scorer within the band is selected. Applying the sliding band approach to the data in Table 10.4, we would select the applicant scoring 93 and then the applicant scoring 96. Once we've selected the top scorer (96), we would construct the second sliding band from 84 to 89. Within this band we would select the three minority applicants and then the highest remaining scorer (89). Once the highest scorer has been selected, we would construct the third sliding band from 82 to 87 and so on.

The sliding band approach provides a larger number of applicants to select from than does the fixed band approach and therefore provides greater likelihood of selecting minority applicants. To illustrate, assume we wish to select seven candidates from among the applicants represented in Table 10.4. Using the traditional top-down approach, we would select as few as two and at the most three minority applicants. The fixed bands approach would result in the selection of four minority candidates whereas the sliding bands approach would result in the selection of five minority applicants. Of course, the number of minority applicants selected in any particular situation depends on a number of factors such as the proportion of applicants who are minority group members, the distribution of minority scores, and selection ratios (Murphy, Osten, and Myors, 1995). Nevertheless, on average, banding should contribute to the hiring of a greater proportion of minority applicants.

Some writers suggest that the likelihood of withstanding a court challenge to banding might be increased if applicants were *randomly* selected within bands rather than on the basis of minority status (Gatewood and Feild, 1994). However, the City of Toronto ran into trouble for using such a procedure in the hiring of 24 firefighters in 1996. Applicants were split into three bands based on test and interview scores. The 13 candidates in the top band (all white males) were hired and then the city implemented what was believed to be a fair system by holding a random draw of the 83 applicants in the second band. Not surprisingly, given the small number of minority applicants, no minority applicants were drawn. A complaint was lodged against the city by the Ontario Human Rights Commission because all 24 of the applicants hired were white males. Had the city used a preferential selection procedure (i.e., based on minority status), some minority applicants would likely have been selected and the city might have averted the complaint. In fact, Murphy et al. (1995) found that preferential selection within bands is significantly more likely to lead to the hiring of minority applicants than random selection within bands, all things considered. Of course, the City of Toronto might still have experienced some problems because of its banding procedure. The rather large second band suggests that the bands were set somewhat arbitrarily rather than being based on the SEM.

PRACTICAL CONSIDERATIONS

A variety of decision making models and methods are available for making selection decisions. Which model or method is best in a given situation depends on a number of factors. The number of applicants expected, the amount of time available before selection decisions have to be made, and the costs associated with the selection instruments all have to be considered in making a choice. However, whenever they are feasible, linear models appear to outperform other approaches to decision making.

Many of the models discussed in this chapter assume large applicant pools or frequent and regular selection activity. Yet small businesses, which constitute a growing proportion of the Canadian economy, often hire small numbers of applicants on an infrequent basis. How can selection decisions in such small businesses be made more effectively?

Most of the rating procedures described in this chapter can be simplified to serve the needs of a small business owner or manager (Schneider and Schmitt, 1986). He or she can conduct an "armchair" job analysis by considering what tasks the employee would be expected to perform and how job performance would be assessed. Next the owner or manager should determine what behaviours related to these tasks could best be assessed in an interview and/or in simulations. Subjective weights could be attached, in advance, to each of the behaviours assessed and the owner or manager should ensure that all applicants are evaluated systematically and fairly on the same criteria. Thus, although applicant information may be collected in a judgmental fashion or in a judgmental and statistical fashion, the information is combined statistically (i.e., trait rating or statistical composite) to yield a total score for each applicant. This total score can then be used to make the selection decisions.

◆ ◆ ◆
CONCLUSIONS

Although valid selection instruments are necessary for making good selection decisions, they are not sufficient. Good selection procedures must be used as well. Selection systems can be made more effective if some of the following recommendations are followed (Gatewood and Feild, 1994):

1. Use valid selection instruments;
2. Dissuade managers from making selection decisions based on gut feelings or intuition;
3. Encourage managers to keep track of their own selection "hits" and "misses";
4. Train managers to make systematic selection decisions using one of the approaches described in this chapter; and
5. Periodically evaluate or audit selection decisions in order to identify areas needing improvement.

◆ ◆ ◆
SUMMARY

Employers face a difficult task in trying to combine and make sense of complex applicant information in order to make selection decisions. They are vulnerable to numerous biases and errors and they often oversimplify information because their information processing abilities are overloaded. Although several approaches to making selection decisions can be used, methods that involve combining applicant information in a statistical manner are generally superior to other methods in reducing errors and predicting job performance. Methods such as multiple regression, multiple cutoff, multiple hurdle, combination, and profile matching can be used to make effective selection decisions when used under appropriate conditions. Selection teams or panels can also assist in improving selection decisions. Finally, banding is suggested as an alternative to conventional top-down selection because banding satisfies affirmative action objectives, while still enabling the hiring of top quality applicants.

E X E R C I S E S

Selection Decision

Assume you occasionally hire cashiers for a small store. You generally do not hire more than two or three at a time. Using the information presented in the table below, determine which of the applicants would be selected and/or, where appropriate, what their rank would be under the following decision making models:

(a) multiple regression
(b) multiple cutoff
(c) combination
(d) profile matching (D^2 only)

Applicant	Predictor Scores				
	Cognitive Test	Conscientious-ness Scale	Biodata Form	Structured Interview	Reference Check
Ms. Z	47	26	18	47	6
Mr. Y	36	36	15	45	8
Ms. W	46	36	16	32	9
Ms. V	44	30	10	36	7
Mr. U	39	38	14	41	10
Maximum Possible Scores	50	40	20	50	10
Regression Weights	1.4	.4	.5	.9	.4
Cutoff Scores	36	27	12	35	7
Mean Scores	40	35	16	39	8

Which of the selection models discussed do you believe is best suited to this situation? Why?

Discussion Question

You are human resources specialists trying to improve selection procedures in your organization. Under the current system, application forms are screened by relevant department managers to determine who should be interviewed. References are also collected. The managers do their own interviewing using individual, unstructured interviews and base their selection decisions almost exclusively on these interviews. They tend to have a lot of confidence in their gut feelings about candidates and believe they've been doing a pretty good job of selecting the right applicants. How would you go about trying to convince them that they should adopt a more structured, objective (i.e., statistical) decision-making system? What objections to your suggestion do you anticipate would be raised by the managers? How would you address these objections?

Applied Project

Conduct an interview with a knowledgeable individual in a local company concerning the selection system used in the organization. During the interview ask the following questions.

1. How many positions are filled annually? How many applications are received for each vacant position?
2. What selection devices or methods (e.g., tests, interviews, references) are used?
3. Have these selection devices been validated? If so, how?
4. What role does each of these selection devices play in selection decisions?
5. What kind of selection system is used by the organization (i.e., do they use statistical or judgmental combination)?
6. Are selection decisions made on the basis of a total score? If not, how are they made?
7. Are weightings applied to applicant data? If so, how are the weightings determined?
8. Does the organization attempt to evaluate the effectiveness of its selection system? If so, how? If not, why not?

Assess the information you obtain from the organization in light of the material presented in this chapter. Write a report detailing the strengths of the organization's selection system and making recommendations for improvements, where needed.

References

Bazerman, M.H. 1986. *Judgment in Managerial Decision Making*. New York: Wiley.

Brandstatter, M., J.H. Davis, and G. Stocker-Kreichgauer, eds. 1983. *Group Decision Processes*. London: Academic Press.

Cascio, W.F. 1991. *Applied Psychology in Personnel Management*. 4th ed. Engelwood Cliffs, NJ: Prentice-Hall.

Cascio, W.F., J. Outtz, S. Zedeck, and I.L. Goldstein. 1991. "Statistical Implications of Six Methods of Test Score Use in Personnel Selection. *Human Performance* 4: 233–64.

Cox, J.A., D.W. Schlueter, K.K. Moore, and D. Sullivan. 1989. "A Look behind Corporate Doors." *Personnel Administrator* (March): 56–59.

Gardiner, H.P., and R.D. Hackett. 1996. *The Employment Interview in Canadian Law: An Analysis of Human Rights Cases*. Unpublished manuscript, McMaster University.

Gatewood, R.D., and H.S. Feild. 1994. *Human Resource Selection*. Toronto: The Dryden Press.

Hill, G.W. 1982. "Group versus Individual Performance: Are N + 1 Heads Better than One?" *Psychological Bulletin* 91: 517–39.

Janis, I.L., and L. Mann. 1977. *Decision Making: A Psychological Analysis of Conflict, Choice, and Commitment*. New York: The Free Press.

Kane, J.R. 1988. *Selection Procedures: Research vs. Reality*. Paper presented at the 49th Annual Convention of the Canadian Psychological Association, Montreal, Quebec (June).

Kichuk, S.L., and W.H. Wiesner. 1996. *The Effects of the Big 5 Personality Factors on Team Performance: Implications for Selecting Optimal Teams*. Advanced Concepts Conference of the Interdisciplinary Centre for the Study of Work Teams. Dallas, TX. (May).

Kleinmuntz, B. 1990. "Why We Still Use Our Heads Instead of Formulas: Toward an Integrative Approach." *Psychological Bulletin* 107: 296–310.

Meehl, P.E. 1954. *Clinical Versus Statistical Prediction: A Theoretical Analysis and a Review of the Evidence*. Minneapolis, MN: University of Minnesota Press.

Michaelson, L.K., W.E. Watson, and R.H. Black. 1989. "A Realistic Test of Individual Versus Group Consensus Decision Making." *Journal of Applied Psychology* 74: 834–39.

Murphy, K.R., K. Osten, and B. Myors. 1995. "Modeling the Effects of Banding in Personnel Selection." *Personnel Psychology* 48: 61–84.

Peter, L.J., and R. Hull. 1969. *The Peter Principle.* New York: William Morrow.

Nunnally, J.C. 1978. *Psychometric Theory,* 2nd ed. New York: McGraw-Hill.

Robertson, I.T., and P.J. Makin. 1986. "Management Selection in Britain: A Survey and Critique." *Journal of Occupational Psychology* 59: 45–57.

Ross, M., and J.H. Ellard. 1986. "On Winnowing: The Impact of Scarcity on Allocators' Evaluations of Candidates for a Resource." *Journal of Experimental Social Psychology* 22: 374–88.

Sawyer, J. 1966. "Measurement and Prediction, Clinical and Statistical." *Psychological Bulletin* 66: 178–200.

Schmitt, N.W., and R.J. Klimoski. 1991. *Research Methods in Human Resources Management.* Cincinnati, OH: South-Western.

Schneider, B., and N.W. Schmitt. 1986. *Staffing Organizations.* Glenview, IL: Scott Foresmann.

Shaw, M.E. 1981. *Group Dynamics: The Psychology of Small Group Behavior.* 3rd ed. New York: McGraw-Hill.

Simon, H.A. 1957. *Administrative Behavior,* 2nd ed. New York: Free Press.

Steiner, I.D. 1972. *Group Process and Productivity.* New York: Academic Press.

Stevens, M.J., and M.A. Campion. 1994. "The Knowledge, Skill, and Ability Requirements for Teamwork: Implications for Human Resource Management." *Journal of Management* 20: 503–30.

Wiesner, W.H. and S.F. Cronshaw. 1988. "A Meta-Analytic Investigation of the Impact of Interview Format and Degree of Structure on the Validity of the Employment Interview." *Journal of Occupational Psychology* 61: 275–90.

Zedeck, S., A. Tziner, and S.E. Middlestadt. 1983. "Interviewer Validity and Reliability: An Individual Analysis Approach." *Personnel Psychology* 36: 355–70.

II

Trends in Human Resources Recruitment and Selection

♦ ♦ ♦

CHAPTER GOALS

This chapter briefly describes recent socio-economic changes and their impact on the Canadian workplace. Particular attention is given to the implications of these changes for recruiting and selecting human resources. After reading this chapter, you should be able to

♦ describe the major social and economic changes we face;

♦ describe the *impact* of these socio-economic changes on the workplace; and

♦ explain *how* recruitment and selection practices must change to accommodate emerging workplace requirements.

♦ ♦ ♦

MAJOR SOCIO-ECONOMIC CHANGES AFFECTING THE CANADIAN WORKPLACE

The workplace of today is in the midst of unprecedented change as it struggles to adapt to the new socio-economic order. This change is compelled by increasing global competition, rapid advances in information technology, and changing workforce demographics. Emerging from this turbulence are worker requirements unlike any we have seen in the past.

Let us first turn our attention to these broader socio-economic changes. Subsequently, we will consider the impact of these changes on the workplace. Finally, we will discuss the implications of these workplace changes for human resources recruitment and selection.

GLOBAL COMPETITION

Foreign trade has always been vital to the Canadian economy, dating as far back as the trading of beaver pelts in this country. As more than half of what is now produced in Canada is exported, we are extremely vulnerable to these foreign markets. Selling our products globally creates jobs for us, brings money into the country, helps sustain the purchasing power of the Canadian dollar, and contributes directly to the growth of our country. Our standard of living is at stake here, including the quality and size of our homes, the newness of the vehicles we drive, as well as our ability to purchase stereo and computer equipment—things that effect US directly.

What has changed is the *level of competition* as new players enter international markets, and trade barriers between countries are softened. Companies relying mostly on domestic markets are no less vulnerable as foreign-owned businesses set up shop in Canada. In the retail sector, for example, large U.S.-owned non-unionized discount chains such as the Price Club (Costco) and Wal-Mart are very serious threats to the survival of smaller unionized Canadian-owned retailers who must scramble to increase efficiencies and lower costs of goods and labour (Williamson, 1996).

As trade tariffs are removed between countries, foreign-owned manufacturers with branch plants in Canada will move these facilities back home, or to other countries where efficiencies and the availability of lower-cost labour provides greater return on investment. Opponents of the North American Free Trade Agreement (NAFTA), which provides for a free-trade zone between Canada, the United States, and Mexico, are concerned that Canadian jobs will be lost to Mexico, where labour costs are significantly lower. Others have argued that freer access to U.S. and Mexican markets provided by NAFTA will be a boon to the Canadian economy, resulting in far more jobs being created than are lost. Regardless of which side economic indicators support in the years ahead, let there be no mistake that Canadians must continually work on improving their competitiveness in providing goods and services domestically and internationally.

RAPID ADVANCES IN INFORMATION TECHNOLOGY

Technology refers to the tools, equipment, and machinery used in the process of performing one's work. Advances in technology over the past decade have been incredible, spurred on by the arrival of, and ongoing improvements to, the computer. Computers are increasingly evident in the design and manufacture of products (e.g., cars, movies), in provision of services (e.g., automated teller machines), in the manipulation and transfer of data (e.g., the national census, human resource information systems), and in telecommunications (e.g., Internet, electronic conferencing). Uses of advanced technology by Canadian employers are numerous. Here are a few examples drawn from across Canada.

The New Brunswick Department of Natural Resources and Energy, in partnership with NB-Tel Phoneworks Canada, introduced a user-pay automated telephone application process for moose-hunting licenses. This system vastly speeded up the processing of applications and produced $380 000 of gross revenue for the participating partners in just one season (MacIssac, 1994).

Ajax Transit in Ontario has introduced the reusable plastic smart card that passengers insert into a slot beside the driver as they board buses. The on-board computer checks whether the card is valid while recording the route, the time, the bus stop, and transfers from other buses. The computer also displays expiry dates, reminding passengers when to renew their cards. This technology has slashed petty fraud and cut fare evasion to less than 1 percent, compared to a 15 percent evasion rate for manual transit systems (McGugan, 1994).

Bus operators at Ajax Transit carry their own smart card, which they insert into a wallet-size pad at the beginning of each shift. In seconds the central database downloads their work schedule to a microprocessor embedded in the card. When boarding the bus the operator inserts the card into a similar pad, which transfers the data from the microprocessor to the on-board computer. The computer then displays routes and stop times, and beeps shortly before each stop to keep the operator on schedule. Statistical information is automatically made available on the operation of the buses, identifying which routes can be merged or pared down. The system is expected to pay for itself in savings accrued over its first three years of use (McGugan, 1994).

Avcorp Industries, an aircraft parts manufacturer based in Laval, Quebec, tracks progress on work orders with a computerized information system that provides on-line access to customers and up-to-the minute progress reports. This system has significantly reduced the number of required meetings with clients, enhanced customer satisfaction, and kept production schedules on target (Melnbardis, 1994).

Selba Industries Inc., a small Canadian kitchen cabinet design and manufacturing business, customized a computer system that automated every step of a customer order. Their system allows the cabinets to be drawn in "virtual space" according to customer specifications *before* construction, saving time and money in a business where errors are typically noticed only after the installation (Onstad, 1996).

The final example comes from British Columbia, where geographic information systems technology (GIS) has been used in determining which areas of the Cariboo-Chilcotin region should be designated for logging restrictions. This computerized mapping technology incorporates 640 maps covering eight million hectares with varying typography, vegetation, wildlife, transportation, minerals industries, and forest types. The output is detailed and graphics are of high resolution, enabling the users to simulate the effects of various cuts concentrated in different areas of the region. This technology replaced a manual mapping process that typically took several weeks of intense labour (Twigg, 1994).

CHANGING WORKFORCE DEMOGRAPHICS

The demographic makeup of the Canadian labour force is also undergoing significant transformations. The workforce is older, more gender-balanced, more culturally diverse, and more highly educated than at any other time in Canadian history. Consider the following:

◆ From 1993 to 2015 the ratio of Canadians aged 15–24 to those aged 55–64 will flip from 2:1 to 1:2 (Dumas, 1995).

◆ Women now represent close to half of the paid workforce and many of them are mothers of preschool-age children ("The Progress of Women," 1995).

◆ Dual-earner couples and single parent families have become commonplace ("Where Women Stand Now," 1995; Crompton and Geran, 1995).

◆ Multiculturalism in this country flourishes, with fully 49 percent of the increase in employment among 25–34 year olds from 1986–1991 attributable to recent immigrants (Chui and Devereaux, 1995).

◆ The majority of new entrants into Canada are from Asia, Central/South America, the Caribbean, and Africa, providing a truly multicultural mosaic (Chiu and Devereaux, 1995).

Educational trends are somewhat diverse. While formal educational attainment among workforce entrants is at an all-time high, the skills of these individuals are not well matched to the skills sought by employers (Evers, 1993). It is also ironic that during these times of unprecedented educational attainment among Canadian youth, we are in the midst of an illiteracy crisis, with one-fifth of Canadian adults unable to complete a cheque or fill out a job application (Montigny and Jones, 1990). Not surprisingly, the end result is that many individuals enter the labour force with formal educational qualifications, accompanied by high expectations of their workplace, but often lacking the basic skills required to fulfil their jobs

◆ ◆ ◆
WORKPLACE ADJUSTMENTS

There are multiple workplace adjustments resulting from the interactive forces of intense global competition, advanced technology, and demographic population shifts. As we turn our attention to some of the more notable of these adjustments, consider the implications each of these changes will have for human resources recruitment and selection.

JOB DISPLACEMENT

Labour saving technology, coupled with disappearing tariffs and intense global competition, have led to the elimination of thousands of jobs in the manufacturing sector in Canada. Clothing, tools, appliances, and countless other items once made by Canadians for Canadians are now imported from countries that can make them cheaper. Canadian employers wanting to survive in this world of global trade must trim costs wherever possible to be competitive. Whereas in the 1980s it was cheaper to add workers than to add machines, now the cost of labour in Canada is twice the cost of machines (Foot and Stoffman, 1996). Today's organizations are adding machines to replace labour for low-skilled, high-routine jobs. The unskilled low entry jobs previously available to people between the ages of 15 and 24 with less than high-school education are fast disappearing.

Labour saving technology is having a similar impact on the service sector. Recall Ajax Transit's smart card, the automated telephone system introduced in New Brunswick to process applications for moose-hunting licenses, and the geographic information system used in B.C. that now does in minutes what once took several topographers weeks to do. The common denominator throughout manufacturing and service sectors, and across worker and management functions, is that the routine aspects of jobs requiring little skill (i.e., the drudgery) are increasingly being done by technology. Peter Drucker, management guru, describes this transformation of the workplace "liberating" (Greenspon, 1996), while others have despaired over the jobs that technology has displaced.

ORGANIZATIONAL RESTRUCTURING

At the same time that technology is reducing the need for labour, organizations must cope with the aging of a large segment of their workforce, in particular, the "baby boomers" (those born from 1947 to 1966 who comprise one-third of the Canadian population). To cope, employers have been implementing layoffs, early retirement incentive packages, and restructuring. Most notably, the traditional corporate pyramid in which there is a broad base of employees at entry level positions, and fewer employees at each of several levels ascending from the bottom to top of the organization, is being flattened.

A pryamidal organizational structure works when there is a large and continuous flow of new workers into entry level positions—the 60-year-olds at the top direct the 40-year-olds in the middle and they manage the 20-year-olds at the bottom (Foot and Stoffmann, 1996). At the peak of the baby boom (1960) the fertility rate was four children per family. When these boomers grew up and went to work, labour force growth shot up to 3 percent per year in Canada, and our economy created jobs faster than any other industrialized country. But fertility rates dropped significantly from 1967 to 1979, resulting in a much smaller cohort entering the workforce 20 years later, and an annual labour growth rate of half of what it was for the boomers. This in turn has lead to too many people in their 40s looking for management positions and too few teens and 20s to fill out the lower level positions vacated by the boomers (Crompton, 1995). Companies have responded by downsizing and flattening their structures. IBM Canada, for example, has gone from 10 levels on the corporate hierarchy to four or five. Now, rather than facing a linear career path of moving up successive layers of a triangular corporate ladder, individuals move laterally to broaden their skills (e.g., stints in marketing, sales, and human resources) before being promoted to the next level. Over time, these individuals become generalists, with the flexibility to adapt quickly to rapid changes in the demand for their services. The shop floor equivalent to this is job rotation and multi-skilling.

REDEFINING JOBS

With much of the routine aspects of work now done by machines, jobs have been redefined, with a greater emphasis given to the management of technology to maximum advantage. In this post-industrial information era characterized by lateral career moves, job rotation and multi-skilling, workers are required to apply a wider range of skills to an ever-changing series of tasks. Individuals just entering the workforce will face at least three to four career changes in their lifetime; thus, the need for skill retraining and flexibility is critical. The new breed of workers will be expected to possess the skills and knowledge of two or three traditional employees (Greenbaum, 1996). On the factory floor, jobs are moving targets as they change rapidly. Yet workers are themselves constantly moving, rotating among positions, and acquiring multiple and generic skills. This poses special challenges when trying to match people to jobs. Indeed, the very concept of "job" must be reconsidered, perhaps to be replaced by "work role."

HARNESSING WORKTEAMS

To survive in today's highly turbulent environment, organizations must be nimble, able to respond quickly to frequent and rapidly changing demands of clients, suppliers, interest groups, and governmental regulatory bodies. Where previously the job description delineated the tasks to be performed, work activities are increasingly project-based, fluid, and guided by the principles of continuous quality improvement. In this new work context, teams rather than individuals are assuming responsibilities, especially where cross-functional problem solving and collaboration are critical. For example, 3M Canada's tape manufacturing plant in Brockville, Ontario, has organized its workforce into teams of six to eight people and instituted a culture to promote innovation and creativity (Zeidenberg, 1996). Unlike traditional factories that employ functional specialists to handle quality control, logistics, scheduling, and shipping and receiving, the 3M Brockville plant has assigned these responsibilities to the workteams. At the corporate level, 3M has teams of engineers and scientists working on new product development, where they develop the concepts, plan the project steps, champion the project for internal funding, and share in the profits of successful launches.

EMPOWERING EMPLOYEES

Clearly, self-directing teams require workers to think, interact, use their judgment, and make decisions. Quality improvement initiatives use employee involvement as a way of taking advantage of the knowledge that exists within an organization (Davis, 1995). Information technology brings data instantaneously to frontline workers, enabling them to make informed timely decisions (Howard, 1995). As organizations flatten and become more nimble, and information technology becomes widely available throughout the workplace, employees are being empowered to take ownership of their work, exercise discretion, and assume greater decision-making authority. For example, several Canadian banks now allow their frontline customer service representatives some discretion to negotiate rates paid on guaranteed income certificates, particularly during the registered retirement savings plans season. These negotiations are often guided by such factors as the client's overall investment and loan portfolio with the bank—information readily accessible at the tap of a keyboard. The result is more rapid processing of accounts and heightened customer satisfaction (i.e., less bureaucracy). As competition places a premium on speed, organizations benefit directly if employees at the point of contact can make needed decisions and take appropriate actions.

ALTERNATIVE WORK ARRANGEMENTS

Alternative work arrangements offer additional flexibility to organizations in their efforts to control costs and respond quickly to changes in demand for their products and services. For example, part-time work, temporary work, contract work, and self-employment in Canada increased from 1989 to1994 (Krahn, 1995). Since 1990, full-time jobs (30 or more hours per week) accounted for only one of every four new jobs created—the rest were part time (Greenspon, 1996).

Part-time employment is more heavily concentrated among females than males, and among those between the ages of 15 and 24. It is also higher in the services sector, which grew by 55 percent between 1976 and 1995, compared with only a 2 percent growth rate in goods-producing industries. The services share of total employment rose from 64 percent to 73 percent over the same period (Krahn, 1995). Interestingly, approximately one-third of the part-time workforce is part time by choice, perhaps to allow for greater balancing of home and work responsibilities.

Self-employment has grown rapidly, rising from 10.9 percent of the workforce in 1976 to 15.4 percent in 1995 (Little, 1996). This increase has been attributed, in part, to business opportunities arising from large employers downsizing and restructuring, coupled with the adoption of policies promoting contracting out and privatization by government. Long-term specific contracts with companies are replacing permanent jobs. In these cases, the company pays a flat fee for the contract and is freed from paying costly benefits.

Other innovative work arrangements being considered by Canadian employers and, in many cases, requested by the employees, are telecommuting, worksharing, and flexible work hours. *Telecommuting* is work carried out in a location remote from central offices or production facilities, with the teleworkers communicating with their supervisor and co-workers electronically. IBM Canada has instituted telecommuting arrangements, with more than 20 percent of their sales and service employees working away from the corporate offices. The employees of this program work on-site at the premises of their client or from their own home (Alaton, 1996). More recently, IBM Canada has established neighbourhood telecommuting centres where employees can share equipment, escape the isolation of home offices, or use a boardroom for meetings (Wilson, 1996). *Flextime* requires employees to work a set number of hours weekly, but provides the employee with the opportunity to choose start and finish times within time bands (e.g., any eight-hour period between 6:00 a.m. and 6:00 p.m.). *Job sharing* allows two part-time employees together to perform the equivalent of a full-time job. In addition to providing flexibility and reducing costs for organizations, these alternative work arrangements provide some accommodation for the growing number of dual career couples, single parent families, and working parents with preschool-age children struggling to balance home and work responsibilities.

SMALL BUSINESS

More than 90 percent of businesses in Canada are now classified as small businesses, with revenues of less than $10 million and employing fewer than 100 employees (Greenbaum, 1996). During the 1980s small business created 2.3 million new jobs, or 87 percent of the total growth in employment, and is expected to account for an even greater proportion of job growth in the decade of the 1990s. Accordingly, it will be the smaller businesses that will carry the weight of hiring well into the end of this century. Most of these jobs will come from innovative and daring companies, particularly in the high technology fields. Small businesses will require adaptable individuals willing to assume a variety of positions in largely unstructured and highly competitive work environments.

MANAGING WORKPLACE DIVERSITY

By the year 2000, 70 to 80 percent of new arrivals into Canada's labour market will be women and non-whites. Accordingly, diversity management will become a necessity imposed by market laws, by competition, and by the need to survive. Ethnic groups in Canada possess expertise, skills, knowledge of foreign cultures and business practices, and natural trade links with overseas markets that can be harnessed to great advantage in emerging domestic and foreign markets. Special challenges, but tremendous opportunity, will emerge from managing workplace teams that are increasingly diverse in functional expertise, gender, and culture. Additionally, advances in technology should facilitate greater integration of physically and mentally challenged individuals into the workplace through job redesign, thereby enabling a better use of their skills.

INCREASING INTERNATIONAL SCOPE

With the growth and importance of the international marketplace, and the loosening of tariffs on goods entering our country, Canadian organizations will need to aggressively compete abroad. The rise in cultural sensitivity training aimed at promoting understanding and acceptance of workplace diversity is one manifestation of this. Another is the premium paid by Canadian organizations for people with M.B.A.'s in international business, or with experience abroad, often acquired through international exchange programs or overseas assignments. These organizations are recognizing more than ever before the importance of identifying, selecting, and developing foreign ambassadors.

◆ ◆ ◆
IMPLICATIONS OF WORKPLACE ADJUSTMENTS FOR RECRUITMENT AND SELECTION

This section addresses the implications of the noted workplace changes for human resources recruitment and selection. Recruitment and selection are guided by the knowledge, skills, abilities, and other characteristics considered important for the work to be performed, which are traditionally determined by a job analysis. But traditional methods of job analysis may no longer be adequate, and there has been much discussion and some research on the importance of generic skills for today's work. Let's look at these two developments, and then turn our attention to the implications of the transformed workplace for recruiting and selecting people.

JOB ANALYSIS

Traditionally job analysis gives detailed information about the tasks and activities performed in a specific job. The job descriptions and job specifications are written from the job analysis and used to inform recruitment and selection activities. However, traditional job analysis captures the content of jobs as described at one point in time, and may be inadequate when jobs change frequently.

The more frequently jobs change, the less value there is to taking a snapshot of the job, as it will have to be soon repeated. Furthermore, given the decreased specialization and shifting of shared work assignments typical of today's work, traditional methods of job analysis are inappropriate (Morgan and Smith, 1996). That is, they are simply inconsistent with the new management practices of cross-training assignments, job and task rotation, self-managed teams, and increased responsibility at all organizational levels (May, 1996).

Sanchez (1994) recommends changing the term *job* analysis to *work* analysis, to capture a shifting emphasis from describing the content of a specific job to describing the activities performed across a variety of organizational positions (e.g., to better capture *workflow*). Recall the discussion in Chapter 4 of job and organizational analysis.

It has also been suggested that job analyses focus on the attributes required by both the tasks and the organization rather than on the tasks alone (May, 1996). For example, Morgan and Smith (1996) recommend using work analysis or the critical incident method to identify attributes cutting across specific job assignments and required by the broader organizational culture. Alternatively, one might focus on clusters of tasks or work functions, which are likely to remain stable even as some of the narrow tasks making up the cluster change. For example, Shankster, Cawley, Olivero-Wolf, and Landy (1995) suggest starting with a traditional work analysis questionnaire, and then identifying clusters of concurrent tasks (through factor analysis). These work functions could then be grouped together to form "jobs" or to depict the flow of work through the department or organization (May, 1996). Sanchez (1994) recommends the use of flowcharting, allowing one to connect the work performed by multiple people rather than limiting the scope to within the boundaries of a single job.

It has also been recommended that anticipated changes in work be captured by consulting individuals most involved in work planning and design. Once the expected changes in work activities are identified, jobs in other settings having similar activities can be analyzed to determine requisite knowledge, skills, and abilities. For example, with the health-care sector downsizing, nursing assistants will be expected to assume many of the activities currently performed by registered nurses. A future-oriented job analysis for "nursing assistant" would involve analyzing those activities performed by nurses that will transfer to nursing assistants. The knowledge, skill, and ability requirements used in recruiting and selecting nursing assistants would then reflect both the current and planned activities for this position.

Often, in restructuring, entirely new positions are created. For example, recently AFG Glass Industries Ltd. (Canada) needed to recruit and select for a newly created position of Corporate Communications Advisor. No job description existed for this position, nor was there a similar position within the organization to turn to for information. Accordingly a job analysis session was conducted with the director of human resources and the chief executive officer to whom the communications advisor would directly report. They were asked to list the expected outcomes for the position and then to identify the specific behaviours necessary to achieve each outcome. Next, the personal characteristics considered relevant to performing the job were inferred from these behaviours. A job description listing job specifications was prepared. This job description could then be cross-referenced to job descriptions of similarly titled positions within other organizations to ensure that important common activities had not been overlooked.

EMERGING IMPORTANCE OF GENERIC SKILLS

Within the transformed world of work, a premium will be placed on several generic personal attributes. Several such attributes are listed by Howard (1995) and include (a) *smart*—sufficiently intelligent to capitalize on new technology, to solve multidimensional problems, and to acquire and apply new knowledge continuously; (b) *adaptable*—capable of initiating and embracing ongoing workplace improvements; (c) *responsible*—desiring ownership of and accountability for one's work; (d) *relational*—capable of working well with others; and (e) *growing*—desiring new opportunities for self-growth, experimentation, and risk taking.

In recent years there has been considerable concern over the mismatch between the skills sought by employers and the skills of students graduating from our high schools, colleges, and universities. For example, in a recent national forum of Canada's business, labour, and academic leaders, agreement was reached on there being a "critical need for faster and better workplace training and for much closer linkages between the education system and the private sector" (National Forum of Science and Technology Advisory Councils, 1993). A chief goal arising from this forum was "to integrate a platform of *generic* skills into all levels of education and training in Canada with full industry involvement." Pierre Ducros, Chairman and CEO, DMR Group Inc., commented that the enormity of the mismatching problem is evidenced in the several thousand jobs that go unfilled during times of high unemployment in this country.

The Corporate–Higher Education Forum is a non-profit group of Canadian educators and business leaders working cooperatively to promote smooth school-to-work transitions for post-secondary students. This forum sponsored research into identifying the competencies required to meet current and future job demands in the context of changing organizations (Rush and Evers, 1985; 1986). This research served as the basis for a larger project undertaken by Rush and Evers in which they identified the following 18 skills as highly desired by employers:

- ◆ problem solving
- ◆ decision making

- ◆ managing conflict
- ◆ leadership/influence

461

- planning/organizing
- time management
- risk taking
- oral communication
- written communication
- listening
- interpersonal skills

- coordinating
- creativity/innovation
- visioning
- ability to conceptualize
- learning
- personal strengths
- technical skills

Evers contends that these 18 skills represent the skill areas widely perceived to be prerequisites for effective job performance across industry, function, and level. The 18 skills formed the focus of questionnaires completed by students, graduates, and managers (Evers, Rush, Krmpotic, and Duncan-Robinson, 1993). Students and graduates rated themselves, and managers (nominated by respondents) rated the university graduates working under them, on each skill. Data analytic techniques (factor analysis) showed that these 18 skills fall into four primary groupings, called "base competencies" (Evers and Rush, 1996).

Mobilizing Innovation and Change: Conceptualizing as well as setting in motion ways of initiating and managing change that involve significant departures from the current mode.

Managing People and Tasks: Accomplishing the tasks at hand by planning, organizing, coordinating, and controlling both resources and people.

Communicating: Interacting effectively with a variety of individuals and groups to facilitate the gathering, integrating, and conveying of information in many forms (e.g., verbal, written).

Managing Self: Constantly developing practices and internalizing routines for maximizing one's ability to deal with the uncertainty of an ever changing environment.

Communicating and *managing self* were consistently rated higher than were *mobilizing innovation and change* and *managing people and tasks*. This suggests, according to the authors, that while recent graduates appear confident in their competency in communicating and managing self, they are humbled by the realities of the workplace with regard to mobilizing innovation and change and managing people and tasks.

These findings suggest that educators should be encouraged to take risks and try non-conventional teaching formats involving teams, problem-based learning, and other such techniques, while not neglecting the development of basic communication and self management skills. Moreover, the authors recommend that these basic competencies be taken into consideration by recruiters.

RECRUITMENT

Economic performance is determined largely by the interaction of four variables: financial capital, technology, people, and how effectively management uses these resources. In the long run, all successful firms will raise capital at roughly the same cost. There is no sustainable advantage there. Technology transfers today occur at a dizzying speed, so, on its own, technology cannot give a competitive advantage for long. It is innovation and service or product quality that are crucial to staying ahead. Innovation and service or product quality depend heavily on people and how well they are managed, as noted by the Conference Board of Canada (Benimadhu, 1995). Consensus is growing that sustainable competitive advantage increasingly will be achieved through people, starting with *recruiting* the best.

LINKING HR RECRUITMENT TO ORGANIZATIONAL STRATEGY The role of human resources departments is changing fundamentally to become a key part of business strategy, according to the Conference Board of Canada (Benimadhu, 1995). The report issued by the Conference Board entitled "Adding Value: The Role of the Human Resource Function," is based on interviews with a dozen chief executives, case studies, and surveys of about 100 line managers and 200 human resources professionals. In this study, linking human resources planning to the strategic business plan was ranked second among the top five issues facing Canadian organizations in the next five years. Linking human resources *recruitment* to organizational strategy involves expanding standardized and formalized job descriptions to reflect the broader and more changeable strategic requirements of the organization (Snow and Snell, 1993). The knowledge, skills, abilities, and other requirements for the work to be performed must be derived from both the technological and cultural requirements of the company's strategy. They must take into consideration the synergy sought within and between teams and the role of each team within the organization's overall structure. Recruitment can then be directed accordingly.

For example, recently the Guelph, Ontario, plant of Asea Brown Bovari (ABB), manufacturer of transformers, adopted a participative team-oriented workplace. They recruited individuals to serve as "team leaders" (replacing the role of "foremen"). The position requirements called for individuals who, in addition to having the expertise to provide technical support, had good interpersonal skills and were comfortable working in a participatory team-oriented culture. These qualities were assessed largely through behaviour-based interviews and personality inventories. In moving to this team-based structure, considerable effort went into explicitly linking individual and team performance to the overall mission of the plant. This was done to help employees attain a better sense of where they fit in within the organization (consistent with efforts to empower the workforce).

As an alternative to recruiting and offering full-time employment to individuals with a specific set of skills to match any one organizational strategy, companies may seek employment relationships that enhance their ability to quickly change strategy as circumstances require. Specifically, they may recruit individuals with the skills and abilities to complement a particular strategy, but hire them under a short-term contract. Should organization strategy change, calling for a different mix of human resources, the organization could then recruit individuals with the attributes to complement this new strategy. The short-term contracts earlier entered into could then be allowed to lapse (Snow and Snell, 1993). The success of this approach will depend on the organization developing a network from which it can quickly and effectively recruit. For example, establishing close ties (i.e., co-op arrangements, partnerships) with colleges and universities.

LINKING HR RECRUITMENT TO THE BOTTOM LINE The Conference Board of Canada (Benimadhu, 1995) has reported that human resources professionals are increasingly going to be called upon to explicitly link their activities to the bottom line. Sixty-one percent of the chief executive officers consulted said that they require some form of measurement of the effectiveness of human resources activities. However, in only 15 percent of these cases were effectiveness measures required for recruitment programs. With the growing emphasis on recruiting, selecting, and developing human capital for competitive advantage, these activities become much more visible to the top executives. Without doubt, recruiters will be increasingly required to demonstrate the effectiveness of their programs. They will have to either develop these skills (i.e., providing cost-benefit analyses) within the organization or contract for them.

OUTSOURCING Outsourcing refers to the practice of contracting with outside vendors to take over specified human resource functions (e.g., recruitment). The Conference Board reports that 55 percent of the human resources executives they surveyed would be outsourcing more of their activities over "the next five years" (Benimadhu, 1995). Outsourcing may take many forms. An organization may contract with an executive recruitment agency for a specific position. Alternatively, organizations may contract with outside firms to recruit and hire people for various positions. In this arrangement, the employee is actually "leased" from the outside firm. The individual recruited is employed by the outside agency but assigned to a position with the client organization. The outside firm assumes all payroll responsibilities (pay and benefits), but charges the client administration and placement costs, usually prorated to salary. If the client chooses to hire the individual to a full-time permanent position, then additional fees are paid to the personnel agency. Some Canadian banks now meet part of their staffing needs through these arrangements. Client organizations benefit from increased workforce flexibility and savings in administrative costs. They also get to see the worker on the job over a period of time before any decisions to hire directly are made. Demands for such services are likely to grow over the next decade. However, it is not yet clear how individuals with highly marketable skills will respond to these indirect hire arrangements. They may be more receptive to those employers who do direct hiring, and offer more permanent positions with full benefits.

REALISTIC JOB PREVIEWS Traditionally, recruiters have tried to sell their best candidates on the organization, often neglecting to inform them of some of the less desirable aspects of the work (e.g., weekend work, limited promotional opportunities). With an increasingly educated workforce come heightened expectations of the workplace, including opportunities for heightened skill development, and input into decision making (i.e., empowerment). Realistic job previews (discussed in detail in Chapter 6) are associated with higher job satisfaction and lower rates of voluntary turnover. With the education level of the workforce at an all-time high, accompanied by heightened workplace expectations, the use of realistic job previews is likely to become more widespread. A move in this direction is also consistent with recent attempts by organizations to improve communications and strengthen bonds of trust with their members.

HARNESSING TECHNOLOGY To enable quick movement of people with required competencies into projects as needed, organizations are embracing the latest technology. For an extensive discussion, consult *Human Resources Management Systems* (Rampton et al., 1996), a companion text in this series. For example, skills databases are becoming more comprehensive, including information on individuals internal and external to the organization. *Restrac Incorporated* offers software that allows jobs to be posted on the World Wide Web (WWW), and enables corporate clients like American Express, Fidelity, Dow Chemical, and Johnson and Johnson to search for key words or skills, and immediately receive e-mailed or faxed résumés that are stored electronically (Velie, 1996). The *Monster Board*, a WWW job database (http://www.monster.com/home.html) boasts 55 000 job openings and 26 000 "hits" a day from 1500 companies. This process makes unnecessary the need to post on the company home page, provides broader exposure for the job opening, and eliminates the need to scan résumés individually into company computers. Other web sites from which employers can access résumés include "*Job Web*—http://www.jobweb.org/; *Career Mosaic*—http://www.careermosaic.com/; *The Online Career Center*—http://www.occ.com/; and *Career Magazine*—http://careermag.com/careermag/.

Human Resources Development Canada has signed Victoria-based JCI Technologies Inc. to create an on-line employee pool that electronically matches Canadian job hunters with employers via the Internet (Rowan, 1995). In the trial phase of this project, job seekers entering Canada Employment Centres hand their résumé to a JCI employee who then scans it into the JCI system. This information is then accessible via the Internet to employers who can search for people with highly specific skills and qualifications. As of November 1995, JCI had 23 616 electronic résumés on file and 4400 Canadian companies dipping into its labour pool.

There are also several newsgroups devoted to job matching, often organized by geographical region. These newsgroups are similar to electronic bulletin boards and contain specific job information. Most are set up by employment agencies. Canadian examples include can.jobs (jobs across Canada), tor.jobs (Toronto), ont.jobs (Ontario), ott.jobs (Ottawa), bc.jobs (British Columbia), ab.jobs (Alberta), kw.jobs (Kitchener-Waterloo, Ont.), and nb.jobs (New Brunswick) (Rowan, 1995). Additionally, search engines such as Yahoo (http://www.yahoo.com) can be used with search criteria such as "Canada, Employment, Jobs".

Soon all professional and college entry positions will involve some use of this latest recruitment technology. Remote on-line application to companies will become commonplace. However, many corporations embracing these technologies do so quietly in their continuous efforts to acquire a competitive edge (Crispin, 1996).

PARTNERING WITH LINE MANAGERS As a result of decentralization, line managers will participate more directly in recruitment activities. Peter Arnold, Occidental Petroleum Ltd., explains "HR will no longer think of line managers simply as customers, but increasingly as business partners" (Benimadhu, 1995, 10). Direct involvement in recruitment by line managers is made easier by their ready access to electronic skills databases.

ATTRACTING THE BEST The likelihood of job candidates accepting an offer of employment is closely associated with the perceived attributes of the position and the work environment. Given the increasing educational level of the workforce, jobs providing autonomy, decision making authority, and opportunities for self-development will win out over those that lack these attributes. Moreover, with the increase in dual career couples, single parent families, and female representation in the workforce, organizations that offer special accommodations and flexible work arrangements gain competitive advantages in recruiting. Flextime, worksharing, on-site or subsidized daycare, and telework fall into this category. For positions requiring geographical relocation of candidates, employers that assist working spouses to secure local employment will gain further advantage. Finally, organizations perceived as hostile to workplace diversity will see the effectiveness of their recruitment efforts significantly compromised, and the quality of their overall applicant pool adversely affected. Women, visible minorities, aboriginal people, and the physically challenged should participate as front-line recruiters to help send a clear message of equal employment opportunities.

INTERNATIONAL ASSIGNMENTS Canadian organizations are going global and need competencies that may be quite different from those required in domestic operations. Recruiting someone competent to head a project in another country, where risk of opportunity costs is very high (i.e., loss of key markets, write-off of investments), has become critically important to organizations expanding their businesses into foreign markets. Typically, Canadian organizations have gone the route of recruiting domestically for foreign assignments, often drawing from their own people and paying them up to three times their normal salaries to get them to accept the post (Ondrack, 1996). Use of expatriates by North American firms, however, has had a high rate of failure. Such failure has been linked with problems of family adjustment to the new culture and the manager's lack of personal adjustment to the foreign business environment (Ondrack, 1996).

Canadian firms will have to do a much better job of identifying, recruiting, and selecting for those competencies related to success abroad. As an alternative to expatriates, organizations may recruit a host-country national, someone native to the foreign country who is well versed in its laws and culture. Recently, Motorola offered free technology training in China. In addition to making inroads in the Chinese markets, Motorola used such training sessions as an opportunity to identify and recruit Chinese people to hire as local representatives of the company ("Training for the Next Millennium," 1994). Alternatively still, organizations may elect to recruit a third-country national—someone from another country who possesses a wealth of knowledge and experience in the foreign market in which the organization is doing business.

With the development of the international electronic résumé databanks, and accumulated experience in international staffing, recruitment for assignments abroad should become easier in the years ahead.

SELECTION

This section considers the impact of workplace adjustments on current practices and future directions in human resources selection. Emphasis will be given to issues surrounding the practice of selection within the Canadian context.

GENERAL COGNITIVE ABILITY Measures of general cognitive ability remain among the most powerful predictors of success in training and job performance for a variety of occupational groups (see Gottfredson, 1986). The growing demands on workers to learn new tasks quickly as they move among assignments and encounter ever changing technology will not diminish.

Accordingly, the power of general cognitive ability measures to predict job success is likely to strengthen. Cognitive ability testing is extremely cost-effective and has withstood court challenges both in Canada (*Persad* v. *Sudbury Regional Police Force*, CHRR, 1994) and the United States (Gottfredson, 1986). With very few exceptions then, a measure of general cognitive ability should be used in selection.

PERSONALITY TESTING Workers are expected to assume higher levels of responsibility, exercise initiative, embrace lifelong learning, and work well in teams. Accordingly, personality assessment is bound to become more widely used in selection. Recent quantitative reviews of the personality literature have shown that measures of "conscientiousness" predict job performance across a variety of occupational groups, and measures of extroversion predict success in jobs requiring frequent interaction with others, such as sales (Barrick and Mount, 1991). Not surprisingly, personality assessment provides for improved prediction of job performance over and above the use of cognitive ability tests alone. Administering a personality assessment along with a measure of general cognitive ability is also likely to lower any adverse impact to minorities that may be associated with administering a cognitive ability test alone (Day and Silverman, 1989). Interestingly, administering a cognitive ability test along with a personality inventory reduces the perceived intrusiveness of assessment associated with administering personality inventories alone (Rosse, Miller, and Stecher, 1994).

Clearly, the two types of assessment complement each other well and should be a part of most selection programs. Be cautioned, however, that there are many personality instruments currently on the market for which there are no credible supporting empirical data. Unfortunately, purchasers of these tests do not know where to begin in evaluating the merits of a personality test. This is unfortunate, as in many cases employers end up paying large sums of money for no return. It is highly recommended that someone trained in industrial psychology be contracted to review the technical manual accompanying any commercially available test. If the commercial provider cannot supply a technical manual, then an industrial psychologist is not required—as this in itself tells you that there are no supporting data. Incidentally, it is not good enough to accept on faith testimonials that the supporting research has been done and is available. It is essential to ask for the technical manual.

INTEGRITY TESTING As more responsibility is entrusted to employees, integrity testing is likely to become more common. With the increasing attention given to integrity tests by practitioners, the American Psychological Association issued a position paper on the topic (Goldberg, Grenier, Guion, Sechrest, and Wing, 1991). It was favourable to integrity testing. Since then, a large quantitative review of validity studies found integrity tests successfully predict a wide range of job behaviours, including absenteeism, tardiness, violence, and substance abuse (Ones, Viswesvaran, and Schmidt, 1993). This review covered 665 validity coefficients, over 180 studies, 25 different measures of integrity, and a wide range of performance measures. The mean predictive validity coefficient (correlation) between integrity tests and supervisory ratings was a very respectable .41. This relationship generalizes across work sites. This study also showed that using an integrity test in addition to a cognitive ability test improves prediction of performance over using cognitive ability testing alone. Combining the two reduces any adverse impact to minorities that may be associated with cognitive ability testing when used on its own.

WORK SAMPLE AND SIMULATION TESTS Many of the generic skills and competencies of the sort identified by Evers (1993) as prerequisites for effective job performance across industry, function, and level require assessments beyond what is provided by traditional cognitive ability and personality testing. For example, written communication skills are best assessed by obtaining a sample of the candidate's writing; oral communication skills are best assessed by watching the candidate giving an oral presentation; leadership and influence within teams is best assessed by observing the candidate participate in a simulated unstructured group situation. The Kitchener, Ontario, Prison for Women, for example, hired a professional actor to play the part of an inmate to assess a candidate's handling of difficult interpersonal situations (Thompson, 1995). While these assessments are labour intensive and costly to develop and administer, the importance of making the right selection decision increases with organizations expecting so much more from fewer employees. For small businesses, selecting the right individual can be fundamentally critical. Additionally, because the relationship of these assessments to the job is so transparent to candidates, they are perceived by candidates as fair by gender and ethnic groups. This is most desirable given the growing minority segment of the workforce. For these reasons, we are likely to see an increase in the use of work samples and simulation tests in coming years. It will be incumbent upon assessors, however, to ensure that scoring of candidates is done systematically and objectively.

Variations of the work sample approach are co-op arrangements, temporary placements, and contract employment, where employers get to see how the individual performs in the position over several months before deciding whether to extend an offer of more permanent employment. This approach will be limited, however, by the degree to which work performance is not objectively appraised, and the incumbent does not get the opportunity to demonstrate the generic skills that will be important over longer term employment with the organization.

INTERVIEWING Another effective way to assess attributes such as leadership, decision making, conflict management, and adaptability is through structured interviews. These come in essentially two types, situational interviews (SIs) and patterned behaviour description interviews (PBDIs). As described in Chapter 9, SIs present to candidates a scenario (situation) similar to one they are likely to encounter in the position to which they have applied. Candidates are then asked to describe what they would do in that specific situation (i.e., you are leading a team on a project that has stalled—what would you do?). The PBDI asks candidates to recall a specific situation similar to one they are likely to encounter on the job, and then to describe what they actually did in that situation (i.e., think of a time in the recent past when a team project that you were leading stalled? What did you do?). Several such questions can be crafted from an analysis of the position and organizational requirements to elicit desired candidate attributes. Typically, scoring keys are then developed for each question.

Structured interviews can be readily tailored to assess many competencies. They have a solid foundation of empirical studies testifying to their usefulness in predicting job performance, and they hold up very well under legal challenge (Gardiner and Hackett, 1996). Moreover, they can easily incorporate questions to assess attributes that are likely to emerge as important over time (i.e., future oriented). That is, they are very pliable. For these reasons, we can look forward to continued growth in the use of structured interviewing.

SELECTING FOR TEAMS As the workteam concept sweeps over Canadian organizations, we need to know how best to select individuals into teams to maximize team performance. In many cases team selection will be continual for multi-skilled (multi-functional) teams that are assembled and disassembled as projects come and go. Group-based situational tests, wherein candidates are observed and rated for their behaviours in a simulated group situation, are likely to become more common. Unfortunately, quicker and less labour intensive technology for making team selections (e.g., a paper and pencil test) is not yet available, regardless of claims to the contrary. There is simply no strong empirical foundation for team selection.

Often management will defer to the workteam to make their own selection decisions. For example, teams at 3M Canada's Brockville, Ontario, plant select their own recruits when hiring externally (Zeidenberg, 1996). However, team member selection becomes very salient in a highly diverse workforce. Several issues arise. Will allowing teams to select their own members promote team heterogeneity (i.e., diversity) or team homogeneity (i.e., sameness) in abilities, skills, and personal attributes (i.e., gender, ethnicity)? Which most promotes team performance—within-team diversity or within-team sameness—and under what conditions? Unfortunately, research addressing these questions is in its infancy (Landy, Shankster-Cawley, and Moran, 1995).

DECENTRALIZING HR SELECTION The Conference Board of Canada reports that many of the human resource activities within Canadian organizations are being decentralized (Benimadhu, 1995). Human resources departments are downsizing, management layers are being flattened, and employees are being empowered to take on more responsibility for their work, and to choose with whom they work. The Conference Board found that 61 percent of the 106 line managers they surveyed now "participate fully" in recruitment and selection. More notably, 68 percent of this same group indicated that they should play the *lead role* in these activities. Consider once again the 3M Canada tape manufacturing plant in Brockville, Ontario. There, workers on the shop floor are responsible for administering the entire selection process. They interview candidates, administer tests of problem solving ability, assess whether the values of the candidate are compatible with those of the company, and place candidates in a group situation to assess how well they are likely to work in a team (Zeidenberg, 1996). The workers at 3M were trained to carry out these assessments—activities once done by human resources staff. This example is representative of a trend.

Many companies are delegating selection decisions to line managers and workteams. Employers choosing to go this route will need to ensure that these people are well trained in the basics of assessment. That is, their assessments must be objective, fair, job related, and legally defensible. As the first wave of this trend, several organizations are now seeking interview skills training for their general managers and line supervisors. This training is also being sought by start-up businesses that have no human resources department to call upon.

"NEW LOOK" MANAGERS The criteria for selecting managers are changing. Organizations in today's world of work seek managers who will enthusiastically embrace, not be threatened by, participatory teamwork environments. International experience, and experience with managing a diverse workforce will be assets. Dynamic entrepreneurial organizations are replacing those with static bureaucratic structures. Employers will want managers who are self-starting, innovative, adaptive, creative, comfortable with new technologies, and capable of working well within loosely structured, highly uncertain environments. Communication and interpersonal skills will need to be first rate. Compare these qualities to the skills assessed in the more traditional managerial assessment centre: planning, organizing, delegation, follow-up, decision making, and sensitivity to the chains of command. As organizational hierarchies flatten, administrators and supervisors will give way to leaders and facilitators.

HARNESSING TECHNOLOGY Technology will no doubt offer new possibilities for selection, as it has for recruitment. Employers are now able to download résumés from the Internet, select their choice applicants, and conduct interviews through video teleconferencing. For example, in a recent bid on a project with the Royal Canadian Mounted Police (RCMP), several consulting teams from across the country were finalists. To reduce this short list further, the RCMP had the competing teams go to their local video teleconferencing centre for the first interview. Travel and accommodation costs for the interview panel and members of each consulting team were never incurred. The few who successfully made it over this first hurdle were then invited for a second interview, which was conducted in person.

Other possibilities present themselves. For example, computerized testing allows applicants at a terminal to complete a personality inventory, a cognitive ability test, and perhaps even respond to structured interview questions. Scoring is automatic and a complete profile of the candidate becomes immediately accessible from the applicant database, to which the profile has been electronically transferred. Likewise, with the technology of *virtual reality*, some very "real" situational exercises and work samples can be created and modified as necessary. Not only does this technology allow the creation of performance samples and measurement of individual attributes not possible with paper and pencil testing, it is also completely transportable to remote locations by means of notebook or desktop computer. Moreover, the ability of computers to accept multiple forms of responses (i.e., mouse, keyboard, voice commands) should allow better accommodation of the physically challenged in assessment and in job design (Burke, 1993).

With electronic databases, statistical computations are made easy. These databases can be accessed for immediate psychometric analyses (e.g., reliabilities, adverse impact). Where performance measures on new employees are electronically stored and can be merged with the applicant database containing their pre-selection test scores, validation studies are done quickly and cost-effectively. Clearly this is not an exhaustive list of possibilities.

SELECTION FOR INTERNATIONAL ASSIGNMENTS With rapid expansion of Canadian business into international markets, and the high rate of failure of expatriates in recent years, better use must be made of the available assessment technology in selecting for these assignments. As previously stated, failure with such assignments is due largely to difficulties experienced by the expatriate's family in adjusting to the foreign culture, and the expatriate's own difficulties adjusting to the foreign business environment. We are accordingly challenged to go beyond individual assessment (traditional model) to assessing the suitability of the expatriate's family for these assignments. Moreover, we must extend beyond the job and organizational analyses recommended in Chapter 4 and do a cultural analysis of the foreign country as well. That is, an understanding of the cultural adjustments required of expatriates and their families is necessary.

Successful assignments will clearly necessitate systematic thorough selection and intense training. However, if the analyses are done in advance, and position requirements (technical, social, and cultural) of expatriate and family are identified, then a profile of the ideal expatriate and "supporting cast" can be drawn up. The task would then be to select and mold (through training) to achieve the best match possible. Structured interviews, personality assessment (e.g., openness to experience), work samples, and international experience are likely to prove most useful for this task. Given the enormity of the challenge, Canadian organizations are likely to make more use of host-country nationals or third-country nationals for these assignments. This would be likely to lessen the importance of the family adjustment factor, but give added weight to technical and managerial competencies.

BOX 11.1 HARNESSING THE LATEST HR SELECTION TECHNOLOGY AT TOYOTA CANADA

Recruitment and selection at the Toyota (Cambridge, Ontario) plant in 1996 exemplifies nicely the changing workplace requirements described in this chapter and their impact on human resources practices. After receiving thousands of applications for 1200 blue-collar positions, Toyota took prospective employees through a rigorous comprehensive multistage assessment process. According to Sandie Halyk, Assistant General Manager for human resources, Toyota "wants people who take pride in their work and are able to work well with others .... If you're not comfortable working for a team, you won't be comfortable working here." Their selection process involves realistic job previews, paper and pencil cognitive ability and personality assessment, tests of fine and gross motor coordination, work samples, and structured employment interviewing. The work sample alone entails a six-hour manufacturing assembly exercise that involves individual and group problem solving. Group leaders and first-line supervisors are active participants in the panel selection interview. For those "making the grade," references are checked, and health and fitness tests are undertaken. Ms. Halyk says the process is designed to "find out if you're able to identify problems and do something about them ... and to ensure a good fit between the company and the new employee."

Source: Keenan, 1996.

WHOLE-PERSON ASSESSMENT In the new world of work, traditional distinctions blur between white-collar and blue-collar jobs. Evers (1993) has argued that the generic skills identified in his study are important regardless of level, function, or organization. Many of the same generic skills were identified as "core proficiencies" required for entry-level positions in a large U.S. national study commissioned by the U.S. Department of Labor in 1990. Included among them were ability to use resources such as time and money effectively (self-management), good interpersonal skills, ability to work well in teams, ability to work well with culturally diverse individuals (managing others), and the ability to use technological systems (Camara, 1994: Offerman and Gowling, 1993). But which of these would not also be important for positions beyond entry level? Whether or not a definitive list of generic skills or attributes important to all jobs is ever agreed upon, clearly individual assessments for positions at all levels and functions will need to be broadened to include a larger array of competencies than has been the case in the past.

BROADENING THE PERFORMANCE DOMAIN The usefulness of our selection measures is assessed by how well they predict performance. Typically, performance ratings from the person's manager or supervisor are obtained for this purpose. Less frequently, hard measures of performance are available, such as dollar sales, units produced, and absenteeism data. With the work of today and tomorrow, our concept and measurement of performance will have to be broadened. Our measures will need to capture the contributions workers make as they move from one assignment to another, and from team to team. Frequently, they will have to come from multiple sources (e.g., peers, customers, supervisors). For validating our selection measures, we will need to decide whether we wish to predict a few of these multiple performance indicators or some composite of them. If the former, then we must establish a procedure for determining which aspects of performance most contribute to the success of the organization. If the latter, we are challenged to derive a formula for aggregating the multiple performance indicators from multiple sources. For guidance, we may wish to turn to the recent research on "360 degree performance feedback systems" (see "Special Issue," 1993).

PROBLEM OF SMALL SAMPLES Securing samples large enough for empirical validation studies has always been a challenge for Canadian organizations. This problem is going to intensify with organizational downsizing, and the rapid growth in small businesses. In many cases, traditional approaches to test validation will simply not be possible. There are several *small sample* approaches to validation to which we can turn (Sackett and Arvey, 1993):

◆ Build a database by combining *similar* jobs *across* organizations, with special care taken to ensure comparability of performance measures.

◆ Accumulate selection scores and performance measures *over time*, as workers leave and are replaced.

◆ Generalize to your particular case the mean (average) predictive validity for a test as found for jobs similar to the one to which you wish to generalize (i.e., *validity generalization*).

◆ Generalize to your case the *specific* validity of the test as previously established for a similar job in another setting (i.e., *validity transportability*).

Frequently, however, a *content sampling* strategy may be necessary. The steps for this process are

1. Tasks (or activities) of the target position are identified by job experts.

2. Job experts infer, on a task-by-task basis, the required knowledge, skills, abilities, and other attributes (KSAOs).

3. Job experts independently rate the relevance of each KSAO for each task.

4. Assessment items (i.e., test questions, situational exercises, interview questions) are developed to measure the most relevant KSAOs.

5. Job experts provide independent ratings of the degree to which each assessment item links to the KSAOs.

6. Job experts evaluate the relationship between performance on each of the selection assessments and job success.

7. A scoring scheme is developed for the selection assessments.

The case for the validity of the selection system is then argued on the basis of an explicit systematic linking of the selection assessments (interview questions, test items, situational exercises) to the position requirements (KSAOs), as established by job experts.

◆ ◆ ◆
SUMMARY

This chapter has highlighted some of the key socio-economic changes related to the transformation of the world of work today. It has also provided some insights into how human resources recruitment and selection are being affected by these changes. These are exciting times, presenting new possibilities and plentiful opportunities for Canadian workers and their organizations. Are *you* up to the challenge?

EXERCISES

1. Labour saving technologies have displaced thousands of jobs in recent years. Argue the pros and cons of these labour saving technologies and discuss their likely impact on human resources recruitment and selection.

2. It has been suggested that with the fundamental changes in the nature of work now occurring, our concept of "job" should be expanded to that of "work role." Explain. In your opinion, is this a good thing for the average worker?

3. Workplace change is requiring us to rethink traditional job analysis methods. Explain. Illustrate by example.

4. What are the primary clusters of generic skills considered essential to today's workplace? What might employers do to ensure their needs for individuals with such skill sets are met?

5. What changes in human resources assessment and selection can be antici-pated given changing workplace requirements?

6. Provide examples of how technology can be harnessed to facilitate and improve human resources recruitment, assessment and selection.

7. What special challenges are presented in recruiting and selecting for international assignments? How can organizations best meet these challenges?

8. Workplace changes necessitate a rethinking of the way we do performance assessments. How is performance appraisal likely to change and why is this an important issue from a human resources selection perspective?

9. Identify the primary socio-economic, demographic, and technological changes affecting the workplace, and provide examples of how each type of change is having an impact on human resources recruitment and selection.

References

Alaton, S. 1996. "The Key Issue in Telecommuting: Personal Fit." *The Globe and Mail*, June 11, C1.

Barrick, M.R., and M.K. Mount. 1991. "The Big Five Personality Dimensions and Job Performance: A Meta Analysis." *Personnel Psychology* 44:1–26.

Benimadhu, P. 1995. *Adding Value: The Role of the Human Resource Function*. The Conference Board of Canada, 157–95.

Burke, M.J. 1993. "Computerized Psychological Testing: Impacts on Measuring Predictor Constructs and Future Job Behavior." In N. Schmitt, W.C. Borman, and Associates, *Personnel Selection in Organizations*. San Francisco: Jossey-Bass.

Camara, W.J. 1994. "Skill Standards, Assessment and Certification: One-stop Shopping for Employers?" *The Industrial-Organizational Psychologist* 32, No. 1: 41–49.

Chui, T., and M.S. Devereaux. 1995. "Canada's Newest Workers." *Perspectives on Labour and Income* 7, No. 1: 17–23, Statistics Canada, 75-001E.

Crispin, G.T. 1996. *Personal communication*. (June 27).

Crompton, S. 1995. "Employment Prospects for High School Graduates." *Perspectives on Labour and Income* 7, No. 3: 8–13, Statistics Canada, 75-001E.

Crompton, S. and S.L. Geran. 1995. "Women as Main Wage Earners." *Perspectives on Labour and Income* 7, No. 4: 26–29, Statistics Canada, 75-001E.

Davis, D. (1995). "Form, Function, and Strategy in Boundaryless Organizations." In Ann Howard, ed., *The Changing Nature of Work*. Jossey Bass, San Francisco, 112–138.

Day, D.V., and S.B. Silverman. 1989. "Personality and Job Performance: Evidence of Incremental Validity." *Personnel Psychology* 42: 42–36.

Dumas, J. 1995. "Greying of the Workforce: Report on a Symposium." *Perspectives on Labour and Income* 7, No.1: 34, Statistics Canada, 75-001E.

Evers, F.T. 1993. "Making the Match: How Ontario's Employers can Help Graduates Develop Exactly the Right Skills Portfolios They'll Need as Tomorrow's Corporate Managers." *Challenges* (Fall): 8–9.

Evers, F.T., and J.C. Rush. 1996. "The Bases of Competence: Skill Development During the Transition from University to Work." *Management Learning* 27 (3): 275–99.

Evers, F.T., J. Rush, J.A. Krmpotic, and J. Duncan-Robinson. 1993. *Executive Summary: Making the Match, Phase II, Final Technical Report*. (March).

Foot, D.K., and D.K. Stoffman. 1996. *Boom, Bust and Echo: How to Profit From the Coming Demographic Shift*. Macfarlane Walter and Ross, Toronto, Ontario.

Gardiner, H.P., and R.D. Hackett. 1996. *The Employment Interview in Canadian Law: An Analysis of Human Rights Cases*. Working paper. MGD School of Business, McMaster University. (June).

Goldberg, L.R., J.R. Grenier, R.M. Guion, L.B. Sechrest, and H. Wing. 1991. *Questionnaires Used in the Prediction of Trustworthiness in Pre-Employment Selection Decisions*. Washington, DC: American Psychological Association.

Gottfredson, L.S. 1986. "The *g* Factor in Employment." *Journal of Vocational Behaviour* 29: 293–450.

Greenbaum, P.J. 1996. "Canada's Hiring Trends: Where Will Canadian Jobs Come From in the Next Millennium?" *HR Today*, July. Canadian Institute of Professional Management, Ottawa, Ontario.

Greenspon, E. 1996. "Economy Changing Far Faster than People." *The Globe and Mail* (April 20): A1.

Howard, A. 1995. *The Changing Nature of Work*. Jossey-Bass, San Francisco.

Keenan, G. 1996. "Toyota's Hunt for 1,200 Team Players." *The Globe and Mail* (January 5): B7.

Krahn, H. 1995. Non-Standard Work on the Rise. *Perspectives: On Labour and Income*. Vol. 7, No. 4: 35–42. Statistics Canada, 75-001E.

Landy, F.J., L. Sankster-Cawley, and S.K. Moran. 1995. In Ann Howard, ed., *The Changing Nature of Work*. San Francisco: Jossey-Bass, 252–82.

Little, B. 1996. "Lone Wolves Who are Turning Grey." *The Globe and Mail* (April 22): A8.

MacIssac, R. 1994. "The Red Tape Revolution." *Canadian Business*, November: 45.

May, K.E. 1996. "Work in the 21st Century: Implications for Job Analysis."

The Industrial Organizational Psychologist 33, No. 4: 98–100.

McGugan, M. 1994. "Road Warrior." *Canadian Business*, November: 28.

Melnbardis, R. 1994. "A Factory Takes Off." *Canadian Business*, November: 45.

Montigny, G., and S. Jones. 1990. "Overview of Literacy Skills in Canada." *Perspectives on Labour and Income* 2: 32–39 (Winter).

Morgan, R.B., and J.E. Smith. 1996. *Staffing the New Workplace: Selecting and Promoting for Quality Improvement*. Milwaukee, WI: ASQC Quality Press.

National Forum of Science and Technology Advisory Councils: Final Report 1993. McMaster University, Ontario (April 14, 15, 16).

Offermann, L.R., and M.K. Gowling. 1993. "Personnel Selection in the Future: The Impact of Changing Demographics and the Nature of Work." In N. Schmitt and W.C. Borman, and Associates, *Personnel Selection in Organizations*. San Francisco: Jossey-Bass, 385–417.

Ondrack, D. 1996. "Global Warning." *Human Resources Professional* May: 27–29.

Ones, D.S., C. Viswesvaran, and F.L. Schmidt, 1993. "Comprehensive Meta-Analysis of Integrity Test Validities: Findings and Implications for Personnel Selection and Theories of Job Performance." *Journal of Applied Psychology* 78, No. 4: 679–703.

Onstad, K. 1996. 1995 Canadian Information Productivity Awards. *Canadian Business*, February: 39.

Rampton, G., I. Turnbull, and A. Doran. 1996. *Human Resources Management Systems*. Scarborough, Ontario: Nelson Canada.

Rosse, J.G., J.L. Miller, and M.D. Stecher. 1994. "A Field Study of Job Applicants' Reactions to Personality and Cognitive Ability Testing." *Journal of Applied Psychology* 79, No. 6: 987–92.

Rowan, G. 1995. "Ottawa Sets Up Internet Job Line." *The Globe and Mail*, Nov. 17: B3.

Rush, J.C., and F.T. Evers. 1985. "Making the Match: Canada's University Graduates and Corporate Employers." *Business Quarterly* 50 (Winter): 41–47.

Rush, J.C., and F.T. Evers. 1986. *Making the Match: Canada's University Graduates and Corporate Employers*. Montreal: Corporate-Higher Education Forum.

Sackett, P.R., and R.D. Arvey. 1993. "Selection in Small N Settings." In N. Schmitt, W.C. Borman, and Associates, eds. *Personnel Selection in Organizations*. San Francisco: Jossey-Bass, 418–447.

Sanchez, J.I. 1994. "From Documentation to Innovation: Reshaping Job Analysis to Meet Emerging Business Needs." *Human Resource Management Review* 4, No. 1: 51–74.

Shankster, L., B. Cawley, M. Olivero-Wolf, and F.J. Landy. 1995. *US West Learning Systems: Organizational Re-Design Final Report*.

Snow, C.C., and S.A. Snell. 1993. "Staffing as Strategy." In N. Schmitt, and W.C. Borman, and Associates, *Personnel Selection in Organizations*. San Francisco: Jossey-Bass, 448–80.

"Special Issue." 1993. *Human Resource Management*. Vol. 32.

"The Progress of Women." 1995. *The Globe and Mail*, August 11: A10.

Thompson, C.T. 1995. "Actress to Help Test Applicants for Jobs at Prison." *Kitchener Record*, July 13: B1.

"Training for the Next Millennium." 1994. *Business Week*, March: 158.

Twigg, J. 1994. "Treasure Maps." *Canadian Business*, November: 39.

Velie, E. 1996. *Human Resource Management on the World Wide Web*. Thesis. Hawaii Pacific University.

"Where Women Stand Now." (1995). *The Globe and Mail*, August 12: A6.

Williamson, R. 1996. "Food Fights put Squeeze on Workers." *The Globe and Mail*, June 7: B4.

Wilson, D. 1996. "Telework Centres the Place to Be." *The Globe and Mail*, June 11: C4.

Zeidenberg, J. 1996. "HR and the Innovative Company." *Human Resources Professional* 13, No. 4: 12–15.

Index

To the owner of this book

We hope that you have enjoyed *Recruitment and Selection in Canada,* and we would like to know as much about your experiences with this text as you would care to offer. Only through your comments and those of others can we learn how to make this a better text for future readers.

School _____ Your instructor's name _____

Course _____ Was the text required? _____ Recommended? _____

1. What did you like the most about *Recruitment and Selection in Canada?*

_____

_____

_____

2. How useful was this text for your course?

_____

_____

_____

3. Do you have any recommendations for ways to improve the next edition of this text?

_____

_____

_____

4. In the space below or in a separate letter, please write any other comments you have about the book. (For example, please feel free to comment on reading level, writing style, terminology, design features, and learning aids.)

_____

_____

_____

Optional

Your name _____ Date _____

May ITP Nelson quote you, either in promotion for *Recruitment and Selection in Canada* or in future publishing ventures?

Yes _____ No _____

Thanks!

 **I⊤P**® **Nelson**

an International Thomson Publishing company

 MAIL ➤ POSTE

Canada Post Corporation
Société canadienne des postes

Postage paid	Port payé
if mailed in Canada	si posté au Canada
Business Reply	Réponse d'affairess

0066102399   01

0066102399-M1K5G4-BR01

ITP NELSON
MARKET AND PRODUCT DEVELOPMENT
P.O. BOX 60223 STN BRN 8
TORONTO ON M7Y 2H1